Critics and Criticism

(ABRIDGED EDITION)

Essays in Method

By

R. S. CRANE

W. R. KEAST

RICHARD McKEON

NORMAN MACLEAN

ELDER OLSON

BERNARD WEINBERG

Edited and with a New Preface by

R. S. CRANE

Phoenix Books

THE UNIVERSITY OF CHICAGO PRESS
CHICAGO & LONDON

*The unabridged edition of this book is available in a
clothbound edition from*

THE UNIVERSITY OF CHICAGO PRESS

Standard Book Number: 226-11793-6 (paperbound)
Library of Congress Catalog Card Number: 57-7903

THE UNIVERSITY OF CHICAGO PRESS, CHICAGO 60637
The University of Chicago Press, Ltd., London

PREFACE

THE eight essays in this volume were first assembled, along with a dozen others, in *Critics and Criticism: Ancient and Modern* in 1952. Since then that book has been frequently and even vigorously discussed by prominent critics here and abroad. The discussion has often been conscientious; it has shown how lively is the concern nowadays with questions of critical method; and it has brought out many interesting points. Perhaps it would be ungrateful to insist too strongly that not all of these are relevant to what the Chicago writers were doing: yet a few matters ought to be set straight if the essays now reprinted are to be read in the spirit in which they were written.

They were written at a time when controversy among literary theorists centered chiefly on the "true" nature of poetry and the "proper" character of criticism. It was therefore natural to ascribe to their writers these same interests and to assume that they too were engaged in defending a single system of literary aesthetics and critical procedure. It was easily possible, moreover, by generalizing from one part of their writings, to discover what this alleged system was; and so these critics have come to be referred to generally as "The Chicago Neo-Aristotelians."

They have been puzzled by the term in this broad use of it, though not so much as by some of the other terms that have been applied to their supposed doctrines, such as "holism," "mimeticism," "genericism," "anti-mythicism," "anti-symbolicism," "anti-modernism," and the like. The name of "Neo-Aristotelians" was first given to them in one of the earliest discussions of the group by their friend Kenneth Burke, who was aware of their active study at that time of the *Poetics* and other treatises of Aristotle. They have never adopted it, but they can recognize that, in Burke's restricted meaning, it does point to one obvious direction of their activities. They have been greatly interested, all along, in the particular class of critical problems which Aristotle was the first, possibly the last, to discuss systematically, and for the study of which he evolved an appropriate and workable method. They have thought that these are crucial problems for practical critics, literary historians, and teachers of literature, and have deplored the neglect of them by most critics since antiquity. They have accordingly tried to begin where Aristotle left off and to pursue similar lines of study in the poetics of modern literature, using the distinctions he had suggested where these were relevant but attempting to enlarge his analysis in various ways in the light of the new things modern writers have achieved.

iii

Aristotle is thus conspicuously behind what they have sought to do in many of their essays in poetic theory and practical criticism. But their relation to Aristotle, as they see it, is not too different from the relation of modern biologists specializing in genetics to the long-neglected founder of that science; and if they are to be called "Neo-Aristotelians," it should be in the same limited sense in which it is accurate to call these biologists "Neo-Mendelians." They have never supposed, that is, that poetics in the Aristotelian tradition can dominate the whole of criticism any more than genetics in the tradition of Mendel can dominate the whole of biology. They would be bad Aristotelians, in fact, if they thought otherwise. The kind of poetics they have tried to develop (as in the essays in Section I of this collection) is one critical method among others, and they have explicitly presented it only as such. It can enable one to do certain things with literary works, and they are persuaded that these are of major importance; but it can hardly be used effectively, as an instrument of practical criticism and literary history, except in conjunction with other methods—linguistic, historical, philosophical, for instance—which rest on principles of a different order. It would make no sense to think of it as an all-embracing system of critical philosophy, and the Chicago writers have never done this: witness the many essays in *Critics and Criticism* (some of them reprinted in Sections II and III of this volume) which show that, if they are interested in Aristotle, they are also interested, strongly and sympathetically, in critics as far removed from him in method as Plato, Longinus, Johnson, and Coleridge.

These essays, indeed, are as much an essential part of the program of the Chicago group as their essays in "Aristotelian" poetics. And the only critical philosophy that underlies them all is contained in the very un-Aristotelian attitude toward criticism, including the criticism of Aristotle, which they have called "pluralism." The term may be unfortunate: what they meant it to convey was simply their conviction that there are and have been many valid critical methods, each of which exhibits the literary object in a different light, and each of which has its characteristic powers and limitations. They have stated this as a middle position between the extremes of dogmatism and skepticism: it asserts, against the dogmatists, that no one system of criticism, however broadly based, can be completely subsumptive of the truth about literature, and, against the skeptics, that nevertheless general truths about literature are possible. It does not imply that one cannot compare the results obtained in a given method (for instance, that of Plato) with the results obtained in another (for instance, that of Aristotle); or that one can never appeal beyond a critic's version of the literary facts to the facts themselves; or that one has to take all methods critics have used at face value, with no possibility of saying that some are more comprehensive than others or more appropriate to the known facts of literature and literary history. There is a great difference between "pluralism" and "relativism," and also between "pluralism" and a merely amiable tolerance of half-truths, bad reasonings, and preposterous interpretations.

The essays in this volume, then, are far from being a manifesto for any one conception of poetry or any one manner of discussing it. If they contain a manifesto at all, it is in support of something quite different from this, which these writers have thought peculiarly relevant to the times. They had come together at the University of Chicago in the middle thirties, at a moment when criticism was rapidly acquiring an importance in higher literary studies such as it had not had for more than a generation. This they considered an exceedingly happy development, and they did what they could in their teaching and writing to encourage it. However, as time went on, and the newer criticism became what Mr. John Holloway has recently called "The New 'Establishment' in Criticism," they began to have misgivings, and especially about two things. One was the fact that, despite the great flourishing of practical criticism, there were few signs that this was moving beyond the rather narrow set of ideas and interests which the critics of the thirties had derived from Eliot, Hulme, and Richards or had taken over from the psychoanalysis, analytical psychology, and cultural anthropology of the first years of the century; this criticism, indeed, appeared to be hardening into a routine, in which literary works were treated only in terms of aspects which could be fitted to the fashionable categories of "symbolism," "irony," "complexity," and "archetype." The other thing was the striking effect of unscholarly improvisation that characterized much of the literary theorizing of this period from Richards on—as if none of the essential problems of literature had ever been discussed before or any important light thrown on them in the more than a score of centuries during which literature had been an object of critical attention. And among both practical critics and theorists there seemed to reign a spirit of unexamined confidence in what they were doing.

What the times appeared to require, therefore, was an enlargement rather than a further restriction of the resources of criticism; and in publishing their essays in "Aristotelian" poetics and their studies of critics and critical developments of the past and present, the Chicago writers hoped that they might do a little to bring this about. Above all, what they thought most needed was a more ✓ critical approach to criticism itself, in something like the Kantian sense of "critical": a consideration of criticism, as a mode of inquiry, that would go behind the doctrines of different schools and try to uncover the basic assumptions about literature and literary study on which these are founded. The sort of thing they had in mind can be seen most clearly in the final essay in this volume and in the opening section of the first; but the same concern with the "grounds of criticism"—with the conditions that determine the cogency or adequacy of statements and the appropriateness or workability of methods—is implicit in all the others. In some of these, the starting point is a given aspect of literary form—the structures of different kinds of literary works, for instance, or the possibilities of poetic language—and the problem is what method of discussion, involving what assumptions, will enable one to deal with this aspect most successfully. In others, the starting point is a given method of discussion—that of Plato or Aristotle or Johnson or William Empson, for instance—and the problem is what its peculiar assumptions will and will not permit one to say intelligibly and truly about literature.

If there is, then, any "Chicago manifesto," its theme is the desirability of looking at criticism from this "critical" point of view. There is no reason why the habit of doing so should inhibit one from practicing any mode of criticism that seems interesting, important, or useful. It might well have the effect, however, of making one's practice much more a matter of reasoned conviction, based on knowledge of what one is and is not committed to and why, than of mere routine acceptance of current formulas. And it might well have the effect also, when brought to bear on the criticism we have inherited from the past, of transforming what have seemed dead doctrines into living and still significant inquiries, and so vastly enlarging the store of ideas with which criticism today can fruitfully work.

R. S. C.

CONTENTS

I

II

III

I

AN OUTLINE OF POETIC THEORY[1]

ELDER OLSON

I

WHEN, in any field of learning, discussions of the subject are based upon different principles, employ different methods, and reach different conclusions, such differences tend to be interpreted, by expert and layman alike, as real disagreement. The differences are not of themselves dangerous to the subject; the tendency to interpret them as contradictions is. The dogmatist, however sound in his own method, usually regards them as signs of the chaos that must await any who depart from his position. The syncretist regards them as signs that all positions are at least partly false, and collects "truths," which frequently lose, in his synthesis, not only their supporting arguments but their original significance as well. The skeptic, finally, interprets such differences as implying the impossibility of philosophical knowledge in the field. All these views are potentially harmful to learning in so far as, in suppressing discussion, they suppress some (and in the case of skepticism, all) of the problems and because, consequently, they retard or even arrest progress within the subject. Skepticism, indeed, is most dangerous of all, for it does not arrest progress merely in certain respects but arrests it wholly; and, once given head, it does not pause until it has also canceled whatever has been achieved in the past.

Criticism in our time is a sort of Tower of Babel. Moreover, it is not merely a linguistic but also a methodological Babel; yet, in the very pursuit of this analogy, it is well to remember that at Babel men did not begin to talk nonsense; they merely began to talk what *seemed* like nonsense to their fellows. A statement is not false merely because it is unintelligible; though it will have to be made intelligible before we can say whether it is true. The extreme diversity of contemporary criticism is no more alarming than—and, indeed, it is connected with—the similar diversity of contemporary philosophy; and the chief import of both is of the need for some critique which shall examine radically how such diversity arises, by considering what aspects of a given subject are amenable to treatment, what problems they pose, and how these may be

1. Reprinted from *Critiques and Essays in Criticism, 1920–1948*, ed. Robert Wooster Stallman (New York: Ronald Press Co., 1949). This essay represents, in a very condensed form, an argument developed much more fully in a forthcoming book to be entitled "General Criticism and the Shorter Forms of Poetry."

diversely formulated. For the diverse may be contradictory or not; theories of criticism which are not contradictory or incompatible may be translated into one another or brought to supplement one another, and a just decision may be given between those which are really contradictory, provided that we can isolate the differences of formulation from the differences of truths and falsities. True interpretation is impossible when one system is examined in terms of another, as is true refutation when the refutative arguments are systematically different from those against which they are directed. To propose such a critique is, in effect, to state the possibility of a fourth philosophic attitude: that of pluralism. Dogmatism holds the truth of a single position and the falsity, in some degree at least, of all others; syncretism holds the partial falsity of all; skepticism the total falsity of all. All these take into their consideration doctrines alone; pluralism, taking both doctrine and method into account, holds the possibility of a plurality of formulations of truth and of philosophic procedures—in short, of a purality of valid philosophies.

Such pluralism is possible both in philosophy and in criticism because criticism is a department of philosophy. A given comprehensive philosophy invariably develops a certain view of art; the critical theories of Plato, Aristotle, Hume, and Kant, for instance, are not any random views but are generated and determined by their respective philosophies. And while a given criticism or theory of art may not originate in a comprehensive philosophy and may resist reference to one already existent, it is not therefore really independent of a more comprehensive system, for the discussion of art must entail assumptions which involve more than art; it is merely part of a whole as yet undeveloped. In short, since criticism or the theory of art is part of philosophy, it has the same bases as philosophy and is determinate or variable according to the same principles.

It is impossible within the scope of this essay to discuss all the factors in the foundations of philosophies and criticisms; but perhaps a rough and partial statement may serve for illustration. I propose that the number of possible critical positions is relative to the number of possible philosophic positions and that the latter is determined by two principal considerations: (1) the number of aspects of a subject which can be brought into discussion, as constituting its *subject matter*; (2) the kinds of basic dialectic which may be exerted upon that subject matter. I draw this distinction between the subject and the subject matter: the subject is what is talked about; the subject matter is that subject in so far as it is represented or implied in the discussion. Philosophers do not discuss *subjects themselves;* they can discuss only so much as the terms or materials of the discussion permit; and that is the subject matter. We cannot discuss what we cannot, first of all, mention, or what we cannot bring to mind. In other words, any discussion of a "subject" is relative to its formulation. But, further, any discursive reasoning must employ some method of reasoning or inference; and, since there are various possible systems of inference, we may say that a given discussion is a function of its subject matter and of the dialectic, i.e., system of inference, exerted upon that subject matter.

Whatever art in itself may be, as a *subject*, it is clear that criticism has employed certain aspects of it as subject matters. Thus one aspect of an art is its product; another, the instrumentality, active or passive, which produced the product; another, the product as relative to or determined by that instrumentality, and hence as a sign of the nature of that instrumentality, whether this last be viewed as actual or potential. Another is the relation of an art to a certain subject or means, as a consequence, and hence as a sign, of these; still another aspect is its production of a certain effect, either of activity or of passivity, upon those who are its spectators or auditors; and, lastly, there is the art viewed as instrumental to that effect. We may sum up all this by saying that criticism has viewed art variously as a product; as an activity or passivity of the artist; as certain faculties or as a certain character of the artist; as a certain activity or passivity of the audience; as certain faculties or as a certain character of the audience; as an instrument; or as a sign, either of certain characteristics of the artist or his audience or of something else involved in art, e.g., its means, subject, etc.

The significances which the term "poem" assumes in critical discussions may illustrate this. In its most obvious meaning it refers to the product of the poetic art; but critics have often used it to refer to what they considered more important aspects of poetic art or have differentiated it by reference to such aspects. Thus those who think that it is characterized by its instrumentality mean by "instrumentality" either the poet or the poetic powers; those who define poetry in terms of the poet see the poet as active craftsman or as the passive instrument of his inspiration or as a mixture of the two; while those who define poetry in terms of poetic powers see the poet as possessed of faculties or qualities either of a certain kind or of a certain degree. With these differences, both consequently view the poem as a kind of behavior of the poet; and, for both, the literal poem—the product—becomes a sign of that behavior, which is, in turn, a sign of the poetic character or faculties. Others find that the poem properly exists in the audience; the audience is the true poet, for, without it, the poem could never come to life; and the audience, like the poet, can be viewed as actualizing certain active or passive potentialities or merely as possessing such potentialities—hence the theories of "audience-participation" (the active view) or "art as experience" (the passive view), etc. Finally, "poem" may mean the end to which the product is instrumental, e.g., the psychological cure or ethical or political attitude or behavior.

These seem like "conflicting views"; hence they have been treated so in the history of criticism. If "conflicting" merely means "different," there is no quarrel, for these views are different enough. But if it means "contradictory" or "inconsistent," nothing could be more absurd. For, in the first place, all these doctrines have different references, and it is impossible to have contradiction except in the same reference; and, secondly, where contradiction exists, one view must be false if the other is true, whereas all these views are perfectly true in their proper senses, for all are founded upon perfectly obvious aspects of art, poetic or otherwise. Nor, if they are not contradictory, are they inconsistent, in the sense that they proceed from, or result in, contradiction; for, asserting the existence of certain aspects of art as they do, they are all true in some sense, and it is impossible for true propositions to be inconsistent. Indeed, nothing prevents certain philosophers, like Plato and Aristotle, from investigating all these aspects of art.

Whatever aspect of art a critic may fix upon, he usually seeks to explain its nature by reference to certain causes or reasons; thus those who are concerned with the product of art, for instance, have thought to explain the nature of the product by reference to its matter or medium, to the subject represented or depicted, to the depictive method of the artist or some other productive cause, or to the end or effect of the product; and some have employed merely one of these causes or reasons, while others have used several or all. Aristotle, for instance, employs differentiations of object, means, manner, and effect to define tragedy, whereas a critic like Richard Hurd finds the nature of poetry adequately defined by its subject matter.

I have remarked that the kind of dialectic exerted upon the subject matter is the other determinant of a given mode of criticism. The variety of dialectics is an exceedingly complex question, but we may occupy ourselves here only with a single characteristic of dialectics—their concern with likeness or difference, or both. The integral or likeness-dialectic reaches solutions by combination of like with like; the differential or difference-dialectic, by the separation of dissimilars. Thus a criticism integral in its dialectic resolves its questions by referring poetry, for example, to some analogue of poetry, finding characteristics of poetry which are shared by the analogue; whereas a criticism differential in its dialectic resolves its questions by separating poetry from its analogues, finding characteristics which are peculiar to poetry.

Thus—to confine our illustrations to the various criticisms which deal with the product of art—we find criticisms differing as they center on either the subject matter of art or its medium or its productive cause or its end or several of these, and as they proceed integrally or differentially. Subject-matter criticism of the integral kind resolves the subject matter of the arts into something not peculiar to the arts, on the basis of likeness; and the principles of art, when so found, are always the principles of things other than art as well. Thus Plotinus finds the beautiful in art to consist in the imitation of the beautiful; but inquiry into that characteristic, for him, shows it to be common also to natural objects and to actions, and so upward to the Beauty which is almost indifferentiable from the Good; and the ultimate solution of artistic as well as of all other problems lies, for him, in the contemplation of God. Differential criticism of this order, on the other hand, separates the kinds of subject matter and argues on the basis of such separation, either to distinguish the arts from other faculties or activities or to distinguish them *inter se*.

In pure subject-matter criticisms, once the subject matter has been found, it determines all other questions, e.g., of artistic capacity or character or of the techniques, forms, processes, criteria, and ends of art. For example, if the subject matter in the raw, so to speak, is all-sufficient, the characteristics of the artist tend to appear as sharpness of observation and readiness of comprehension; if the subject matter requires order and selection, correlative capacities for order and selection are constituents of the artistic character; and so on. A similar determination operates throughout all other problems: criteria, for instance, are produced from some correspondence or opposition, absolute or qualified, between the subject and the medium, or the artist, or the effect. Thus many of the theories of artistic realism have as their criterion the absolute correspondence of the effects of art with those of reality itself; art is thus copyistic, and the work is a "slice of life," all formal criteria (such as order) being supplanted by attributes of the reality. Where the subject matter of art is opposed to the reality, however—whether it requires an order and selection not found in reality or differs from reality even more radically—such correspondence is qualified, or even negated, as in modern nonrepresentationalist theories.

Comparably, criticisms centering on the medium can be integral or differential, and solve their problems through reference to the medium. The integral criticism of this order is exemplified in the innumerable attempts to find general criteria for all literature, whether poetic, historical, philosophic, or personal, on the ground that all literature employs words; and the differential criticism is exemplified in the theories of men like I. A. Richards and Cleanth Brooks, who seek to differentiate poetry from prose by differentiation of the kind of diction employed in each, in order to discriminate appropriate criteria for each.[2] The character of the artist varies as the character of the medium is stated; where the medium is viewed as indifferent to form, the capacities of the artist are at the maximum, and, conversely, where the medium is viewed as tending toward form, the artist frequently appears as a kind of midwife to nature,

2. See below, pp. 25 ff.

assisting the bronze or the marble to a form which it implicitly contains. Criteria, again, can be found, by consideration of the degree to which a given work actualizes or fulfils the potentialities of the medium.

When the productive cause is central, the integral criticism establishes analogies between the artist or the artistic process and some more general cause, e.g., nature or natural process, or God and the divine creative process (Coleridge). Extreme criticisms of this order reduce the art-product almost to a by-product of the artistic character; Fracastoro and Carlyle, for example, refuse to limit the name of poet to those who actually write poems, since poetry is merely incidental to the possession of poetical character. Differential criticism of this kind, again, confines the conception of the artist to the unique maker of a certain product. When discussion centers on the natural elements of the artist, the artistic character lies outside the possibility of any deliberate achievement, as in Hazlitt; conversely, when the artistic character is defined in terms of acquired traits or disciplines (as in Reynolds), discussion of genius and inspiration is at a minimum, and the artistic character itself appears as amenable to art and, indeed, often as the *chef d'œuvre* of the artist.

When criticism turns on the ends of art, integral and differential dialectics are again possible; the ends of art can be analogized to other purposes of men or to some natural or divine teleology or, conversely, can be differentiated from all else. And, here, as above, the nature of the problems and of their solutions is determined by the choice of the ground-term.

All such criticisms may be called "partial," for each attempts to resolve all problems by consideration only of a part. All fix upon a single *cause*, in Aristotle's sense of the word, and account for everything in terms of it, as if one were to account for a chair merely in terms of its wood or merely in terms of its maker. None permits a full account, for the respects in which art is compared with, or contrasted to, other things are always only a part of its actual characteristics. This partiality remains, even if several of these causal factors are combined, unless, indeed, all are involved.

As opposed to such partial criticisms, there are comprehensive criticisms such as those of Plato and Aristotle, the former being primarily integral, the latter primarily differential, although each includes both likeness and difference. These systems permit not only the discussion of all aspects of art but a full causal account; for, whereas Aristotle makes the maximum differentiation of causes, Platonic dialectic employs only a single cause, but one subsuming all. The difference—not in truth or in cogency of argument but in *adequacy*—between comprehensive and partial systems can be readily seen by comparing, say, Aristotle with the "Aristotelian" Scaliger: Aristotle can discuss any aspect of poetry, but Scaliger, basing all merely upon the medium and viewing that only in its most general light—the universal power of language being to express fact or opinion—thereby confines himself to the treatment of poetry only as the instrument of instruction.[3]

Recognition of the methodological differences between systems of criticism, and of their consequent respective powers and limitations, quickly establishes the fact that twenty-five centuries of inquiry have not been spent in vain. On the contrary, the partial systems of criticism correct and supplement one another, the comprehensive intertranslate, to form a vast body of poetic knowledge; and contemporary theorists, instead of constantly seeking new bases for criticism, would do better to examine the bases of such criticisms as we have and so avail themselves of that knowledge. Many a modern theory of criticism would have died a-borning, had its author done a little more reading as he thought, or thinking as he read. Critical knowledge, like all knowledge, must be constantly extended; but no one is very likely to extend it who is not fully aware of what has already been accomplished or of what consequences follow from such accomplishments.

If a plurality of valid and true kinds of criticism is possible, choice must still be exercised, for it is impossible to employ all methods simultaneously, and the selection of method is by no means a matter of indifference. Choice is determined by the questions one wishes to ask and the form of answer one requires and by the relative adequacy of given systems. The discovery of properties peculiar to a given kind of poetry demands a differential method, as that of properties which poetry holds in common with other things requires an integral method. If one wishes to know the nature of a given kind of poetry, as a certain *synolon* or composite, a whole and its parts specified with the maximum differentiation possible without the destruction of the universals upon which science depends, an Aristotelian criticism is requisite; if one proposes to view poetry in terms of principles of maximum community, a Platonic criticism is demanded. Every philosophy is addressed only to certain questions and can answer them only in certain forms.

II

In the method of Aristotle, which underlies the following sketch, poetics is a science concerned with the differentiation and analysis of poetic forms or species in terms of all the causes which converge to produce their respective emotional effects. Scientific knowledge falls into three classes: theoretical, practical, and productive. The end of the first class, comprising metaphysics, mathematics, and the natural sciences, is knowledge; that of the second, com-

3. Cf. Bernard Weinberg, "Scaliger versus Aristotle on Poetics," *Modern Philology* XXXIX (1942), 337–60.

prising ethics and politics, is action; that of the third, comprising the fine and the useful arts, is some product over and above the actions which produce. Only the theoretical sciences are exact; the productive sciences, or arts, are less exact than the practical, since they involve a greater number of principles, and principles derived from many other sciences.

The poetics of a given species takes as its starting point the definition of the product, i.e., a statement of the nature of the whole composite produced by an art, and thence proceeds by hypothetical reasoning to treat of the questions specific to that whole and its parts. Such analysis does not exhaust all aspects of the art; but any which it excludes are referred to other sciences. Thus the consideration of art as a skill falls under ethics; that of art as a political and social instrument, under politics; and that of art as a mode of being, under metaphysics, in accordance with the general Aristotelian practice of assigning questions to their appropriate sciences. A given special poetics, therefore, does not treat centrally of the faculties requisite for production, or of the effects to be produced by art, but of the special product, viewed as a differentiable synthesis of differentiable parts, and, as such, having the capacity or power (*dynamis*) of producing certain peculiar effects.

Before we can consider the various special arts of poetry, however, we must discuss the significance of certain concepts of a more general nature. Unity, beauty, and imitation, for instance, relate to things other than poetry but are not therefore less important to poetic discussion. The term "imitation" is used coextensively with "artificial"; it differentiates art from nature. Natural things have an internal principle of motion and rest, whereas artificial things— a chair or a table—have, qua products of art, no such principle; they change through propensities not of their form but of their matter. Natural and artificial things alike are composites of form and matter; but art imposes a form upon a matter which is not naturally disposed to assume, of itself, such a form. The acorn of itself grows into the oak; the stone does not of itself become a statue or tend to become a statue rather than a column. Art may be said to imitate nature either in the sense that the form of the product derives from natural form (e.g., the human form in the painting resembles the natural human form) or in the sense that the artistic process resembles the natural (e.g., artificial fever in the art of medicine does what fever does naturally). The useful and the fine arts are both imitative; but the latter have as their end the imitation itself, as a form possessed of beauty. Since every imitation has some form imposed somehow upon some matter for some end, specification of all these factors results in a definition of a given species of art; e.g., by specifying *what* is imitated in tragedy (object of imitation), *in what* (means of imitation), *how* (manner of imitation), and to what effect we construct the definition of tragedy. Such definitions are the principles from which reasoning proceeds in the arts; if a certain product or whole is to be produced, it will have a certain number of parts of a certain nature ordered in a certain way, etc.[4]

A poem has unity in the sense in which anything which has continuity is unified; but, more than that, it is one in that it has a single form and is an ordered and complete whole. A piece of wire is one because it is continuous, and if you break the continuity you have two pieces; but some things are totals rather than wholes—a cord of wood, for instance, because the parts need merely be present, and not in any particular arrangement—and others are wholes proper, because they are not only complete and have all their parts but also have them in the proper arrangement, i.e., the least important ordered to its superior part, and so on until the principal part is reached. Parts of a shoe stitched together anyhow are one in the sense of continuity, but not one in the sense of assemblage into a certain single form, the shoe; a poem is similarly an ordered and complete whole.

Moreover, it is not only a whole, but one of a certain nature; it is an imitation in a certain means; hence, since a given means can imitate only certain objects (color and line cannot imitate the course of thought, or musical tones a face), poetry must imitate action, character, or thought; for a given means can be used to imitate only something having the same characteristics as it or something of whose characteristics its own characteristics are signs, and speech (the medium of poetry) is either action or the sign of action, character, and passion. (For example, painting can represent color directly, but the third dimension only by signs, such as perspective diminution, faintness, etc., of objects.) Media are not such things as certain pigments or stones but such as line, color, mass, musical tones, rhythms, and words. The object imitated, therefore, must be some form which these can take or which they can imply by signs. Hence inference plays a large role in all the arts.

Inference and perception serve to institute opinions and mental images concerning the object, and opinions and mental images produce emotion. We see or infer the object to be such and such, and, according to our opinion of what it is, we react emotionally in a certain specific way. If we have the opinion, we react, whether the thing, in fact, is so or not; and if we do not have it, we do not react, whether the thing is so or not. The opinion that a disaster is imminent produces fear; and the opinion that the victim suffers undeservedly produces pity; and so on.

Emotions are mental pains (e.g., pity), pleasures (e.g., joy), or impulses

4. It should be borne in mind that the present discussion applies strictly only to what I have elsewhere called "mimetic," as distinguished from "didactic," poetry. See below, pp. 44 ff.

(e.g., anger) instigated by opinion. The basis of our emotions toward art may be explained as follows: We feel some emotion, some form of pleasure or pain, because our desires are frustrated or satisfied; we feel the desires because we are friendly or hostile to, or favor or do not favor, the characters set before us and because we approve or disapprove the events; and we are friendly or hostile to the characters because of their ethical traits; in brief, we side with the good against the bad or, in the absence of significant differentiations of moral character, upon grounds still moral, as with the oppressed against the oppressor, with the weak against the strong, etc., our judgment now being primarily of the action rather than of the agents.

Since the object of imitation as we conceive it determines the emotions which we feel and since moral differentiation lies at the basis of our conception of the object, the possible objects of imitation in poetry, drama, and fiction may be schematized in terms of extremes, as follows: The serious, i.e., what we take seriously, comprises characters conspicuously better or worse than we are or at any rate such as are like ourselves and such as we can strongly sympathize with, in states of marked pleasure or pain or in fortunes markedly good or bad. The comic, i.e., the ridiculous, comprises characters as involved in embarrassment or discomfiture to whom we are neither friendly nor hostile, of an inferiority not painful to us. We love or hate or sympathize profoundly with the serious characters; we favor or do not favor or condescend to the comic. Serious and comic both divide into two parallel classes: the former into the tragic kind, in which the character is better than we, and the punitive, in which the character is worse; the latter into what may be called "lout-comic," in which the character, though good natured or good, is mad, eccentric, imprudent, or stupid, and the "rogue-comic," in which the character is clever but morally deficient. These kinds are illustrated in drama by *Hamlet*, *The Duchess of Malfi*, *She Stoops To Conquer*, and *The Alchemist;* the protagonists in these are, respectively, a man better than we, wicked men (the brothers of the Duchess), a good man with a ridiculous foible, and rogues. Between these extremes of the serious and the comic lie what I have called the "sympathetic" or the antipathetic; i.e., forms in which the morality of the characters does not function in the production of emotional effect so much as does our judgment of the events as, for example, just or unjust; the man is indifferent, but the suffering is greater than even a criminal should undergo, etc. The emotions produced by the contrary objects are themselves contrary; for instance, the pity and fear of tragedy are opposed by the moral vindictiveness and the confidence of retribution in the punitive kinds. Again, the emotions are contrary as the events are contrary; that is, the spectacle of a good man going from good fortune to misfortune or from a pleasant to a painful state effects emotions contrary to those evoked by the spectacle of a good man going from misfortune to fortune or from pain to pleasure. Again, comic "catastrophe" is mere embarrassment or discomfiture, and effects emotions contrary to those produced by catastrophe in the serious forms.

In short, the emotions we feel in poetry are, generally speaking, states of pleasure and pain induced by mental images of the actions, fortunes, and conditions of characters to whom we are well or ill disposed, in a greater or lesser degree, because of our opinions of their moral character or, such failing, because of our natural sympathy or antipathy; or, in other words, our emotions are determined by the object of imitation and vary with it.[5] Emotion in art results, thus, not because we believe the thing "real" but because we vividly contemplate it, i.e., are induced by the work of art to make mental images of it. Compare such expressions as "He was horrified at the mere thought of it," "The very notion filled him with ecstasy," etc.

Pleasure, in general, is a settling of the soul into its natural condition; pleasure in poetry results primarily from the imitation of the object and secondarily from such embellishments as rhythm, ornamental language, and generally any such development of the parts as is naturally pleasing. Where the object of imitation is itself pleasant and vividly depicted, pleasure is direct; when the object is unpleasant, pleasure results from the catharsis or purgation of the painful emotions aroused in us, as in tragedy. Pleasure is commensurate, in other words, with the beauty of the poetic form; and distinctive forms, as they have peculiar beauties, evoke peculiar pleasures.[6]

By "beauty" I mean the excellence of perceptible form in a composite continuum which is a whole; and by "excellence of perceptible form" I mean the possession of perceptible magnitude in accordance with a mean determined by the whole as a whole of such-and-such quality, composed of such-and-such parts. Assuming that parts of the number and quality required for the whole have been provided and ordered hierarchically to the principal part, the whole will be beautiful if that prime part is beautiful; and that part, as a continuity, must have magnitude and be composed of parts (e.g., plot, the prime part of tragedy, has magnitude and has parts); since it has magnitude, it admits of the more and the less, and hence of excess and deficiency, and consequently of a definite and proper mean between them, which constitutes its beauty. Specifically, in terms of the form itself, this mean is a proportion between whole and part and, consequently, is relative to the different wholes and parts; in reference to perception, it is a mean between such minuteness of the parts and such

5. But cf. below, p. 50.

6. For a further discussion of the relation between pleasure and poetry see *Critics and Criticism* (original ed.), pp. 588–89.

extension of the whole as would interfere with the perception of the parts, as of their proper qualities, and as in interrelation with each other and the whole. Thus in tragedy the mean of plot-magnitude lies between the length required for the necessary or probable connection of the incidents and the limit imposed by the tragic change of fortunes. The constituents of beauty are, therefore, definiteness, order, and symmetry; the last being such commensurability of the parts as renders a thing self-determined, a measure to itself, as it were; for example, plot is symmetrical when complication and denouement are commensurate. As a thing departs from its proper magnitude, it either is spoiled (i.e., retains its nature but loses its beauty) or is destroyed (i.e., loses even its nature). Compare a drawing of a beautiful head: alter its definitive magnitude to a degree, and the beauty is lost; alter it further, and it is no longer recognizable as a head.

III

These questions are not peculiarly poetic ones but rather matters belonging to metaphysics, psychology, and ethics. The problems we now approach, however, are poetic and may be divided into two kinds—general questions, common to all the poetic arts, and special questions, peculiar to a given poetic art. Biology offers a parallel; for some attributes are common to all forms of life, others are peculiar. Similarly with poetics; some questions come about merely because the imitation is of action, like Aristotle's discussion of plot prior to chapter 13, others because of something specific, like his discussion of the tragic plot, imitating a certain kind of action. I shall here deal with both kinds, though illustratively only, and take up first the question of the definition of forms.

In their scientific order, all the arts, as I have said, begin with definitions of their specific products as wholes, which they utilize as the principle or starting point of their reasoning. These definitions, far from being arbitrary resolutions, must be collected from a conspectus of the historical growth of the species to which they relate; a kind of art, to be known and defined, must first actually exist. Not every aspect of the growth of artistic species, however, is relevant to their artistic character; hence their historical development must be examined in terms of their character as imitations. No single line of differentiation suffices for the separation of species. Most broadly, the arts are distinguished in terms of their media, for, since nothing can be made actual which is not potentially in the medium, the potentialities of the medium, as matter, determine all else; yet the means, even when fully differentiated, singly and in combination, is insufficient for specific distinction, for arts which have the same means may imitate opposite objects, as do comedy and tragedy. In turn, objects may be differentiated, but even such further differentiation is not definitive, for imitations may still differ in manner, although the possibilities of manner are now broadly determined. With the distinction of modes or manners of imitation, the account of the parts of imitation qua imitation is complete, and the historical survey of the rise of the arts—the synthesis of these differentiated parts into distinct wholes—is now possible. Such history begins as the causes emerge. The poetic arts, like the other fine arts, originate in instinct, some matter being given a form not natural to it, by an external efficiency, for the sake of the pleasure produced. Yet, though imitation is natural to man, instinct is insufficient to account for the further development of art; for art ramifies rather than remains constant, as the universal cause of instinct would suggest; and its ramifications are determined by the character of the artist: the noble minded imitate the noble, the low-minded the low. Even so, the tale is not complete: for art develops further until a form is achieved and valued for its own sake. Art passes, thus, through three stages—the instinctive, the ethical or practical, and the artistic—the first two of which are determined by the nature and character of the artist, and the last by the form. The achievement of form is signalized by a revolution in the ordering and constitution of the parts: once the specifically pleasurable effect has luckily been produced, the part which is primarily effective becomes principal, develops its proper extension and qualities, and all other parts readjust to it, in their proper artistic order. A distinctive synthesis—a species of art—has now formed, and its poetics may begin, for the formulation of the distinctive means, object, manner, and effect of the synthesis gives all four of the causes which are collectively, but not singly, peculiar to it, and a definition results.

Aristotle has frequently been defended on the ground that all poetic species reduce to those which he has enumerated, and more frequently attacked on the ground that they do not. Both defense and attack are mistaken, the former because it makes poetics predictive, the latter because it assumes that, since Aristotle did not define certain species, his theory could not afford a basis for their definition. In fact, as the above account has shown, the poetics of a given species must always develop after the species has come into actual being, the definition being formed by induction; but, on the other hand, the poetic arts in their development do not leave their bases; they do not cease to have means, objects, and manners, or even the differentiations of these mentioned by Aristotle; they merely differentiate these further and produce new syntheses. The distinction between narrative and dramatic manner, for instance, has not been rendered obsolete, although it affords no significant distinction, in itself, between Homer and Henry James; yet, to distinguish them, we must begin with the different possibilities of telling, as opposed to impersonating, and discriminate the various complexities of narrative device.

Elder Olson

Once object, means, manner, and effect have been specified to the emerging species, the definition of the artistic whole which so results permits an analysis into parts; and when the principal part has been identified and the order of importance of the remaining parts established, the proper construction of the principal part must be ascertained. That part is itself a whole composed of parts, and these parts—its beginning, middle, and end—must be determined, and the character of their conjunction—necessity and probability—must be shown. But the whole is not only a whole, but a whole of some magnitude; and, since it is, moreover, to be a beautiful whole, it must be a whole of some definite magnitude. As I have remarked, this definite magnitude lies in a mean between excess of the part and excess of the whole, the former producing such vast extension that the whole cannot be comprehended, the latter such minuteness that the parts cannot be apprehended. This formula, however, is general and must be specified to the species of art involved. Relatively to perception, it must always be determined in the temporal arts by the limits of memory, since in these arts the parts are not coexistent but successive and, consequently, must be remembered if the whole is to be comprehended; but even this is relative to the species, differences of the parts and wholes of which impose different burdens upon the memory. (A given lyric might be too long to be remembered, while a given tragedy might not.) The wholeness, completeness, and unity of the principal part once established, the part can be divided into its species; hence, for example, Aristotle divides plots into simple and complex, which are different wholes, since the complex plot consists of differentiable parts (peripety and discovery) according to the efficient cause of the change of fortunes with which tragedy is concerned.

"Aristotelian" criticism has frequently centered merely upon this much, to produce mere *Formalismus;* but Aristotle himself goes farther. The principal part is only materially a whole, complete, one, etc.: formally, it has an effect or power of a certain specific order; tragic action, for instance, is not merely action, nor even serious action, but action differentiated by a certain act—the tragic deed committed in a certain way by the tragic hero—and Aristotle, investigating the possibilities of character and action, determines which of these result in the tragic effect, for that effect—the "working or power" of tragedy —is the form. Comparably, the poetics of any species must be addressed to the differentiation of its principal part, since it is this that primarily determines the emotional effect.

Once the principal part has been treated, the subordinate parts can be dealt with in the order of their importance and according to their causes, the final cause of each being to serve its superior part, the formal cause being the beauty of the part itself. The whole analysis, thus, not merely indicates the possibilities of poetic construction but discriminates among them as better or worse, to exhibit the construction of a synthesis beautiful as a whole, composed of parts of the maximum beauty consistent with that whole, and productive of its proper emotional effects to a maximum degree.

The method—one of multiple differentiation and systematic resolution of maximal composites into their least parts—may obviously be extended to poetic species which have emerged since Aristotle. Aristotle distinguishes broadly and between extremes; later theorists in his method must follow the basic lines and go farther. For example, his poetics, as we have it, deals only with such poetry as has plot, i.e., such as imitates a *system* of actions. These are maximal forms; there are, that is, no "larger" poetic forms or any which have more parts than these; smaller forms, such as the species of lyric, can be treated by carrying such systems back to their elements.

Four kinds of action or behavior can thus be distinguished, without regard to seriousness or comicality, etc.: (1) a single character acting in a single closed situation. By "closed situation" I mean here one in which the character's activity, however it may have been initiated or however it may be terminated, is *uncomplicated* by any other agency. Most of what we call lyric poetry belongs here: any poem in which the character commits some verbal act (threatening, persuading, beseeching) upon someone existing only as the object of his action (Marvell's "To His Coy Mistress"), or deliberates or muses (Keats's "Ode to a Nightingale"), or is moved by passion (Landor's "Mother, I Cannot Mind My Wheel"). (2) Two or more characters in a single closed situation. "Closed situation" here means "uncomplicated by any other agency than the characters originally present and remaining so throughout." This parallels the notion of "scene" in French classical drama; here belong all the *real* colloquies of persons acting upon and reacting to one another (e.g., Browning's "The Bishop Orders His Tomb"), although not the metaphorical colloquies, such as dialogues between Body and Soul, etc. (3) A collection of such "scenes" as I have just mentioned about some central incident, to constitute an "episode" (Arnold's *Sohrab and Rustum*). (4) A system of such episodes, constituting the grand plot of tragedy, comedy, and epic which is treated by Aristotle.

These are whole and complete "actions"; hence the first differs from a speech in a play, the second from a dramatic scene, the third from a fragment of a tragedy; nevertheless, it is clear that, *in a sense*, the combination of speeches produces a scene, that of scenes an episode, that of episodes a plot. These classifications must not be confused with species; they are not poetic species but lines of differentiation of the object of imitation which must be taken into account in defining species. Similar analysis of means and manner would extend Aristotle's system to include all poetic forms.

So much for Aristotle's general method and his apparatus for the definition of forms; I shall presently return to such questions again, in order to sketch a special poetics, but for the moment I wish to deal with three more problems of general poetics: those of unexpectedness, suspense, and representation, although we can do little more here than touch on general points.

All emotions are greater if produced from their contraries—for example, fear in one who has been confident—and the unexpected effects just this. Like suspense, it is common to all temporal arts, the parts as well as the wholes, for whatever involves temporal succession may involve anticipation, and wherever we have anticipation we may have the unexpected. Expectation is the active entertainment of the opinion that something is necessary or probable at a given time, place, in certain relations, etc. The audience must infer, and infer incorrectly; they have the premises, so to speak, for otherwise what happens would be improbable; but they cannot connect them to infer correctly, for otherwise what happens would be expected. Since they do not infer the probable, and do infer the improbable, two things must be noted: the causes of wrong inference and the causes of failure to infer rightly. Since the premises must be considered together for inference and since the audience will reason only from premises which they actively entertain and take to be true, failure to infer will be due to (1) forming no opinion or forming a contradictory one, so that one or both of the premises will not be used; (2) failure to collect the premises, although both are entertained; (3) failure to infer correctly, although both are entertained and collected. All these can be developed to show what the poet may possibly do: for instance, opinion can be prevented by the use of remote signs (i.e., such as involve many inferences), or many and apparently contradictory signs, ambiguity of words or acts; acceptance as true can be prevented by the use of unusual consequents, by contrariety to general belief, by dependence upon the words of an apparently untrustworthy character, or by contradiction of an apparently trustworthy one; and so on.

All these things lead to nonexpectation; but the truly unexpected comes about when the thing is not only not expected but contrary to expectation. This will happen if the poet provides premises which seem to prove the contrary. It is best when failure to infer the right thing and the faulty inference are brought about by the same premises. This is effected by the use of qualification. For example, if A happens, B usually follows, except in circumstance C, but if that circumstance happens, the opposite of B results; now if C is bound to happen, but people do not know that, they will expect B after A, whereas the opposite results. Surprise will vary in degree with expectation of the contrary; consequently, the audience will be most surprised when they are most convinced that B will happen. The less important, apparently, the reversing circumstance, the more surprise. Again, since the all-but-completed process makes its end most probable, expectation will be highest here; hence reversal just before the end will be most surprising. This underlies many "hair's-breadth escapes." Most surprising of all is the double unexpected, which occurs when from A comes the unexpected result B, which leads to the previously expected result C, which is now unexpected as the result of B. This is exemplified in Sophocles' *Oedipus*, where the inquiry into blood-guilt leads to the question of parentage, which seems at some remove; but the question of parentage resolves unexpectedly the question of blood-guilt.

Suspense is anxiety caused by extended anticipation—hence (1) by the uncertainty of what we wish to know and (2) by delay of what we wish to have happen, although we know it already. (Gossips are in the first state before they have been told the scandal, in the second until they impart it.) The first results whenever we want to know either the event or the circumstances of the event, whether in past, present, or future time; hence the poet must avoid the necessary, the impossible, or the completely probable, or that which is unimportant either way, for we are never in suspense about these; instead, he must choose the equally probable or else that which is probable with a chance of its not happening, and something which is of a markedly pleasant, painful, good, evil, or marvelous nature. Suspense of the second order is produced by unexpected frustration, by having the thing seem just about to happen, and then probably averting it. The anticipated thing must have importance exceeding the suspense; otherwise irritation and indifference result.

Representation—what parts of the action are told or shown, and how, and what is left to inference—is a question of manner of imitation. Obviously, poets sometimes exhibit more than the action (e.g., tragic poets exhibit events which are not part of the plot), sometimes less, leaving the rest to inference; sometimes follow the plot-order, sometimes convert it (e.g., using flashbacks); exhibit some things on a large and others on a small scale; and there are many other possibilities as well. It is impossible here to do more than suggest; in general, representation is determined by necessity and probability, emotional effect, and ornament, i.e., these are the main reasons for representing something. The poet must represent things which by their omission or their being left to inference would make the action improbable; hence, if an event is generally improbable but probable in a given circumstance, it must be represented in that circumstance (e.g., Antony's speech in *Julius Caesar*). Again, he must omit whatever would contradict the specific emotional effect (hence disgusting scenes, such as the cooking of Thyestes' children, are omitted, since disgust counteracts pity) or include what would augment the effect (hence scenes of lamentation and suffering in tragedy, since these make us poignantly aware of the anguish of the hero). Masques, pageants, progresses, etc., are ornaments. Representation, whether narrative or dramatic, always makes things more vivid, and the latter is more vivid than the former; and it affords the audience knowledge, whether directly or through inference by signs. In any poetic work the audience must at certain times know some things and not know others; generally the denouement discloses all, except in works which have wonder as their prime effect. Unless the audience knows somewhat, emotion is impossible, for emotion depends upon opinion; and unless it is ignorant of certain things, unexpectedness and some kinds of suspense are impossible. Hence in any work something is withheld until the end: either how the action began or continued or how it ends; the audience is ignorant of one or several of the following circumstances: agent, instrument, act, object, manner, purpose, result, time, place, concomitants. What must be concealed is the primary question; the next is the order in which things must be disclosed; and theory can make available to the poet a calculus of the frame of mind of the audience, of the nature of emotions, etc., to determine the order of representation which will produce the maximum emotional effect.

All these questions can be developed to afford a vast body of working suggestions for the poet and of criteria for the critic; I shall be happy if I have suggested, even faintly, the character of the problems and the method of their treatment.

IV

We have seen that in any special poetics—whether that of tragedy or epic or some kind of lyric or novel—reasoning proceeds from the distinctive whole which is the product of the art to determine what parts must be assembled if such a whole, beautiful of its kind, is to result, and that such terms as "whole," "part," "beauty," etc., must be specified to the given art, because, for example, the beauty of a tragedy is not the same as the beauty of a lyric, any more than the distinctive beauty of a horse is the same as that of a man. Indeed, lyrics and tragedies even have some different parts; for instance, a lyric does not have plot, but plot is, in fact, the principal part of tragedy.

We may illustrate the nature of a special poetics a little further by outlining briefly that of the species to which Yeats's "Sailing to Byzantium" belongs.[7] It is a species which imitates a serious action of the first order mentioned above, i.e., one involving a single character in a closed situation, and the

---

7. For a detailed "grammatical" analysis see the (University of Kansas City) *University Review*, VIII (1942), 211–15.

An Outline of Poetic Theory

character is not simply in passion, nor is he acting upon another character, but has performed an act actualizing and instancing his moral character, that is, has made a moral choice. It is dramatic in manner—the character speaks in his own person; and the medium is words embellished by rhythm and rhyme. Its effect is something that, in the absence of a comprehensive analysis of the emotions, we can only call a kind of noble joy or exaltation.

There are four parts of this poetic composite: choice, character, thought, and diction. For choice is the activity, and thought and character are the causes of the activity, and diction is the means. The choice, or deliberative activity of choosing, is the principal part, for reasons analogous to those which make plot the principal part of tragedy. Next in importance comes character; next thought; and last, diction.[8]

8. Nowadays when the nature of poetry has become so uncertain that everyone is trying to define it, definitions usually begin: "Poetry is words which, or language which, or discourse which," and so forth. As a matter of fact, it is nothing of the kind. Just as we should not define a chair as wood which has such and such characteristics—for a chair is not a kind of wood but a kind of furniture—so we ought not to define poetry as a kind of language. The chair is not wood but wooden; poetry is not words but verbal. In one sense, of course, the words are of the utmost importance; if they are not the right words or if we do not grasp them, we do not grasp the poem. In another sense, they are the least important element in the poem, for they do not determine the character of anything else in the poem; on the contrary, they are determined by everything else. They are the only things we see or hear; yet they are governed by imperceptible things which are inferred from them. And when we are moved by poetry, we are not moved by the words, except in so far as sound and rhythm move us; we are moved by the things that the words stand for.

A gifted British poet, G. S. Fraser, has objected to these remarks on diction ("Some Notes on Poetic Diction," *Penguin New Writing*, No. 37 [1949], pp. 116 ff.): "I think, on the contrary, that criticism should pay a very close attention to diction. I agree with Mr. Allen Tate: 'For, in the long run, whatever the poet's philosophy may be, however wide may be the extension of his meaning . . . by his language shall you know him.' And I do not find that Mr. Olson's sturdy-looking piece of reasoning stands up very well to my regretful probing. In what sense is it true that we are simply 'moved by the things that the words stand for,' and not by the words themselves? Certainly not in any sense in which other words would do as well: in which the fullest paraphrase, or the most intelligent exposition, would be a substitute for the original poem. And certainly not in any sense in which the situation that the poem refers to, if we were capable of imagining that *without* words—if, for instance, we could draw a picture of it—would be a substitute for the original poem, either. Not, that is, in any sense, in which 'the things the words stand for' means merely the kind of physical object, abstract concept, or emotional state at which the words point. The pointing is the least of it."

I willingly concede what I have never debated: that diction is very important to poetry; that, as Tate suggests, distinction of language is an important index of poetic power (although I cannot agree that it is the sole index or even the prime index); that criticism ought to pay the utmost attention to diction; that, as T. S. Eliot has said, the poet is likely to be extraordinarily interested in, and skilful with, language; that we are not "moved by the things that the words stand for" in any sense that would allow us to dispense with the particular words by which the "things" are constituted for us; and all similar propositions. The point is not whether diction is important, but whether it is more or less important than certain other elements *in* the poem. In one respect, I repeat, it is the most important; the reader, if he does not grasp the words, cannot grasp anything further, and the poet, if he cannot find the appropriate words and arrange them properly, has not written a poem. In another respect, however, the words are the least important, in that they are governed and determined by

The "activity" of the character is thought or deliberation producing choice determined by rational principles; it is thus, as I once remarked, a kind of argument or arguing. But there is a difference between logical proof and such poetic argument as we have here; in logical proof the conclusion is determined by the premises; here it is, of course, mediated by the character of the man arguing, just as argument in a novel or a play is not supposed to be consistent with the premises but with the character. The limits of the activity are the limits of the deliberation; the parts of the activity are the phases of that deliberation, and they are conjoined by necessity and probability.

This species of poem, then, if it is to be beautiful, must have a certain definite magnitude as determined by the specific whole and its parts; and the proper magnitude will be the fullest extension possible, not exceeding the limits mentioned above, and accomplished by phases connected necessarily or probably. This is, it will be noted, different from the magnitude proper to comedy or tragedy, and even different from the magnitude proper to a speech exhibiting choice in any of these; for example, tragedy does not aim at making its constituent speeches or actions as full and perfectly rounded as possible absolutely, but only qualifiedly, in so far as that is compatible with the plot. Hence in properly made drama there are few if any "complete" speeches, let alone speeches developed to what would be their best proportions independently of the whole; this is true even in declamatory drama, where the speeches are of more importance than in the better kinds.

The activity, however, is not merely to be complete and whole, with its parts probably interrelated; it must effect certain serious emotions in us by exhibiting the happiness or misery of certain characters whom we take seriously. Hence the character must be better than we, but not so completely noble as to be beyond all suffering; for such people are godlike and can awaken only our admiration, for they are in a sense removed from such misfortunes as can excite dolorous emotions. Moreover, the choice imitated cannot be any choice, even of a moral order, but one which makes all the difference between happiness and misery; and, since it is choice, it must be accomplished with full knowledge and in accordance with rational principle, or as the man of rational prudence

---

every other element in the poem. There is agreement on all hands that words "function" in poetry; there should be no difficulty therefore, no matter how we conceive of the structure of poetry, in seeing that words must be subordinate to their functions, for they are selected and arranged with a view to these. Mr. Fraser himself has no difficulty with this fact, although he is disturbed by my statement of the fact; for he goes on to discuss (pp. 123 ff.) "a wide-scale current use of poetic diction in a really vicious sense to disguise a failure of choice, a confusion of character, or a lack of clear thought"; and he also remarks (p. 126) that "one cannot ask people to express themselves as confusingly as possible, in the hope that their confusions will prove to have a clear underlying structure; for, as Mr. Schwartz truly says, 'if this were the only kind of poetry . . . most poetry would not be worth reading.' " On this whole question see below, pp. 50 ff.

would determine it. Again, it must be choice not contingent upon the actions or natures of others, but as determined by the agent. And there must be no mistake (*hamartia*) here, as in tragedy; for, since this is a single incident, *hamartia* is not requisite to make future consequences probable.

We could proceed indefinitely here, as on all of these points; my intention, I repeat, is the merest illustration.

V

Thus far we have proceeded on the supposition that the imitative poetic arts have as their ends certain pleasures, produced through their play upon our emotions. Certainly, these are ends of art and such as any consideration of art must embrace; but to suppose that art has no further effect and that it may have no further ends relative to these is vastly to underestimate the powers of art. It exercises, for example, a compelling influence upon human action—individual, social, or political—for among the causes of the misdirection of human action are the failure to conceive vividly and the failure to conceive apart from self-interest; and these are failures which art above all other things is potent to avert, since it vivifies, and since in art we must view man on his merits and not in relation to our private interests. It is not that art teaches by precept, as older generations thought, nor that it moves to action; but clearly it inculcates moral attitudes; it determines our feelings toward characters of a certain kind for no other reason than that they are such characters. The ethical function of art, therefore, is never in opposition to the purely artistic end; on the contrary, it is best achieved when the artistic end has been best accomplished, for it is only a further consequence of the powers of art. The same thing is true of any political or social ends of art, provided that the state be a good state or the society a moral society. To reflect on these things is to realize the importance and value of art, which, excellent in itself, becomes ever more excellent as we view it in ever more general relations.

Yet these relations can scarcely be recognized unless we first recognize the distinctive powers of each form of poetic art; these relations are possible, indeed, because art has, first of all, certain powers. And it is to these powers, in all their variety and force, that the poetic method of Aristotle is directed. Indeed, (the most distinctive characteristic of Aristotle as critic seems to be that he founds his poetic science upon the emotional effects peculiar to the various species of art and reasons thence to the works which must be constructed to achieve them.)

WILLIAM EMPSON, CONTEMPORARY CRITICISM, AND POETIC DICTION[1]

ELDER OLSON

THE last quarter of a century has seen the rise, in England and America, of a new critical movement. Its mere longevity would perhaps entitle it to some importance in the eyes of future literary historians; but that importance is guaranteed and augmented by the esteem which it has won and by the distinction and persistent fame of the persons who are regarded as its chief practitioners. The "new criticism," as this movement is called by both its friends and its foes, seems to be almost universally regarded as having at last brought literary study to a condition rivaling that of the sciences. It has, we are frequently told, established itself upon principles the scientific character of which is assured by the fact that they are drawn from such sciences as psychology, biology, anthropology, linguistics, economics, and so on, in their most modern development; it has led, according to its proponents, to an unparalleled accuracy and minuteness in the treatment of texts, and in the employment of terminology and critical techniques; it has, we are assured, an over-all, if not specific, unity of method, as well as a doctrine sufficiently established to permit a list of "heresies" and "fallacies"; finally, and best of all, it not only can discuss more and explain it better than the outworn criticisms which it supplants, but it is still, like the sciences, in a happy condition of growth.[2]

Mr. William Empson is among the principal exponents of this movement, and it might almost be said that where he is mentioned, it is mentioned, and where it is, he is. Nor is this extraordinary; in certain respects it can be said that he has produced it, and it, him. His prestige, briefly, is enormous; his theories, never too vigorously assailed, have gained wider acceptance with the years, and his particular interpretations of texts are regarded as pretty nearly exhaustive and definitive. The recent re-publication of one of his prin-

1. Reprinted from *Modern Philology*, May, 1950.

2. I do not, of course, imply that every one of these views is held by every critic, and with equal conviction and enthusiasm. But I have taken pains to construct a statement which should convey as fully as possible, and without too great inaccuracy, the general attitude which the "new critics" assume toward their criticism. See John Crowe Ransom, *The New Criticism*, Preface; William Elton, *A Glossary of the New Criticism* (Chicago, 1949), pp. 3–5; Robert W. Stallman, "The New Critics," in *Critiques and Essays in Criticism* (New York, 1949), p. 506.

cipal works, *Seven Types of Ambiguity,*[3] as a "classic of modern criticism," affords us an occasion to examine the critical method of Empson and, in that connection, of the "new criticism" as well.

I

For Empson, as for his master I. A. Richards, poetry is simply an aspect or condition of language; it is therefore definable in terms of its medium; it is language differentiated from other language by a certain attribute. Richards first proposed that this distinguishing feature was ambiguity, and occupied himself with exhibiting the complexities of response which ambiguity engenders; Empson has followed by enumerating seven kinds of ambiguity.

The term "ambiguity" here does not carry its usual meaning. Ambiguity as Empson conceives it is not the mere possession of double meaning; an obvious pun or a patent irony is not ambiguous, for instance, "because there is no room for puzzling";[4] although such expressions when less obvious are called ambiguous "even by a critic who never doubted their meaning," since they are "calculated to deceive at least a section of their readers."[5] Nor is ambiguity simply concision, nor the quality of language which produces mixed emotions; it is, rather, "any verbal nuance, however slight, which gives room for alternative reactions to the same piece of language."[6] The important point here is that of alternative reactions; Empson illustrates his meaning by remarking that a child might view the sentence "The brown cat sat on the red mat" as part of a fairy story or as an excerpt from *Reading without Tears.*[7]

The ambiguities are types of "logical disorder," arranged as stages of advancing disorder,[8] or, what is apparently the same thing, "in order of increasing distance from simple statement and logical exposition."[9] The seven types, then, are kinds in which (1) "a detail is effective in several ways at once"; (2) "two or more alternative meanings are fully resolved into one"; (3) "two apparently unconnected meanings are given simultaneously"; (4) "alternative meanings combine to make a complicated state of mind in the author"; (5) "a fortunate confusion" is present, "as when the author is discovering his idea in the act of writing or not holding it all in his mind at once"; (6) "what is said is contradictory or irrelevant and the reader is forced to invent interpretations"; and (7) "full contradiction" is present, "marking a division in the author's mind." These kinds are general and have subdivisions; the first, for example, divides into "comparisons with several points of likeness," "antith-

3. 2d ed., rev. and reset; New York: New Directions, 1947.

4. P. x.   7. P. 2.

5. *Ibid.*   8. P. 48.

6. P. 1.   9. P. 7.

eses with several points of difference," " 'comparative' adjectives," " 'sub-dued' metaphors," and ambiguities of rhythm, or, as Empson puts it, "extra meanings suggested by rhythm."[10]

One of his best-known passages is in illustration of "comparison with several points of likeness," and is a good example of his method in operation:

> There is no pun, double syntax, or dubiety of feeling, in
>
> > Bare ruined choirs where late
> > the sweet birds sang,
>
> but the comparison holds for many reasons: because ruined monastery choirs are places in which to sing, because they involve sitting in a row, because they are made of wood, are carved into knots and so forth, because they used to be surrounded by a sheltering building crystallized out of the likeness of a forest, and coloured with stained glass and painting like flowers and leaves, because they are now abandoned by all but the grey walls coloured like the skies of winter, because the cold and Narcissistic charm suggested by choir-boys suits well with Shakespeare's feeling for the object of the sonnets, and for various sociological and historical reasons (the protestant destruction of monasteries, fear of puritanism), which it would be hard now to trace out in their proportions; these reasons, and many more relating the simile to its place in the Sonnet, must all combine to give the line its beauty, and there is a sort of ambiguity in not knowing which of them to hold most clearly in mind. Clearly this is involved in all such richness and heightening of effect, and the machinations of ambiguity are among the very roots of poetry.[11]

The broad theory underlying Empson's method seems to be as follows: Poetry uses language, and language is meaningful and communicative; hence poetry is communicative. In analyzing communication, there are three possibilities: one may speak about what happened in the author's mind, about what is likely to happen in the reader's mind, or "about both parties at once," as involved in the communication itself.[12] The first two kinds of discussion, according to Empson, make the claim of knowing too much; "the rules as to what is conveyable are so much more mysterious even than the rules governing the effects of ambiguity" that the third possibility is best. Hence in the main he talks about the third, although he is by no means, he says, "puristic" about this.[13] Apparently the poet communicates ideas, like everyone else, and the reader is affected by these ideas according to their kind; the poet, however, would seem to be a poet, not in virtue of the emotional quality of his ideas, but in virtue of the devices of ambiguity which he consciously or unconsciously employs. Moreover, the effects *proper* to poetry are not the emotions evoked by the ideas; rather, since ambiguity is the essence of poetry, the process of

---

10. These quotations have been extracted from the analytical Table of Contents, pp. v–vi.

11. Pp. 2–3.

12. P. 243.　　　　　　　　13. P. 235 n.

reading is a process of "inventing reasons" why certain elements should have been selected for a poem, as in the passage just quoted, and the peculiar pleasure derived from poetry is produced by the mental activity in response to these ambiguities.[14] It is, to use Empson's own word, a pleasure of "puzzling," apparently different from the pleasure afforded by riddles, charades, and anagrams in that these latter involve matters emotionally indifferent.

The method of interpretation which rests upon this theory is, as we might expect, one reducing all poetic considerations to considerations of poetic diction, and one reducing all discussion of diction, even, to problems of ambiguities. The method might be described as the permutation and combination of all the various "meanings" of the parts of a given discourse, whether these parts be simple or complex; out of the mass of "meanings" so found, Empson selects those which "give room for alternative reactions," i.e., which satisfy the fundamental condition of ambiguity. The instrument by which he detects the possible meanings of words is the *Oxford English Dictionary;* although it is seldom mentioned by name, its presence everywhere is neither invisible nor subtle. Its lengthy lists of meanings seem to have impressed no one so much as Empson. Apparently he reasons that, since poetry is language highly charged with meaning, the poetic word must invariably stagger under the full weight of its dictionary significances. Since the mass of significances achieved by permutation and combination is often very great, and since ambiguity is so extensive a principle of selection, the discovery of the main meaning or meanings of a passage often becomes for Empson an embarrassing matter. At such points he invokes the aid of rather general and often highly dubious historical, ethical, and psychological propositions about the poet and the audience. I suspect that such propositions are mainly conveniences for him; he does not, at any rate, worry too greatly when he finds they are false.[15]

The resulting interpretation is not always so prettily fanciful as the remarks on the Shakespearean sonnet may suggest; fanciful it is always, indeed, but the method of "permutation and combination," as I have called it, is a mechanical method, and it is capable of all the mindless brutality of a machine. Witness the treatment of a famous speech of Macbeth:

> If it is an example of the first type [of ambiguity] to use a metaphor which is valid in several ways, it is an example of the second to use several different metaphors at once, as Shakespeare is doing in the following example. It is impossible to avoid Shakespeare

14. "Two statements are made as if they were connected, and the reader is forced to consider their relations for himself. The reason why these facts should have been selected for a poem is left for him to invent; he will invent a variety of reasons and order them in his own mind. This, I think, is the essential fact about the poetical use of language" (p. 25; see also p. 57).

15. See, e.g., p. 21 n.

in these matters; partly because his use of language is of unparalleled richness and partly because it has received so much attention already; so that the inquiring student has less to do, is more likely to find what he is looking for, and has evidence that he is not spinning fancies out of his own mind.

As a resounding example, then, there is Macbeth's

> If it were done, when 'tis done, then 'twere well
> It were done quickly;

(double syntax since you may stop at the end of the line)

> If th' Assassination
> Could trammel up the Consequence, and catch
> With his surcease, Success; that but . . .

words hissed in the passage where servants were passing, which must be swaddled with darkness, loaded as it were in themselves with fearful powers, and not made too naked even to his own mind. *Consequence* means causal result, and the things to follow, though not causally connected and, as in 'a person of consequence,' the divinity that doth hedge a king. *Trammel* was a technical term used about netting birds, hobbling horses in some particular way, hooking up pots, levering, and running trolleys on rails. *Surcease* means completion, stopping proceedings in the middle of a lawsuit, or the overruling of a judgment; the word reminds you of 'surfeit' and 'decease,' as does *assassination* of hissing and 'assess' and, as in 'supersession,' through *sedere*, of knocking down the mighty from their seat. . . .

He continues this at some length, concluding: "The meanings cannot all be remembered at once, however often you read it. . . ."[16]

Such a passage as this needs only attentive reading to make manifest its utter absurdity; but then that very absurdity in a fashion protects it, and gains a certain credence for it; it is so absurd that we in a measure believe it, merely because we are loath to believe that anything could be so absurd. To escape such spurious persuasion, we must, I think, forcibly remind ourselves of the facts. We are actually being asked to believe that the speech actually *means* all these various things; that Macbeth, trembling on the brink of murder, and restrained only by his fears of what may follow, is babbling of bird-nets, pothooks, levers, trolleys, assessments, lawsuits, and what not; and all this on the shadowy grounds that the *OED*, or whatever dictionary, lists alternative meanings for "trammel," "surcease," and "assassination," and that poetic language is ambiguous. This is a wrenching of a text if I ever saw one; what is worse, it is a wrenching to no rational purpose. The remark about "double syntax" is typical; there is no double syntax in

> If it were done, when 'tis done, then 'twere well
> It were done quickly . . . ;

for if you pause at the end of the line, as Empson suggests, you leave an un-accounted-for and absolutely unintelligible residue in the next line; and as a

16. Pp. 49–50.

matter of fact you make nonsense, anyway, of the first. In short, the "double syntax" here owes its existence only to the supposition that poetry is necessarily ambiguous.

There are many other marvels of interpretation: at one point Empson not only confuses Macbeth with the witches, but the play itself with *King Lear;*[17] in *Hamlet*, the line "In the dead vast and middle of the night" is made to suggest a personification of Night as one of the terrible women of destiny, on the grounds of possible puns (*vast:waste:waist, middle* of night:*middle* of body);[18] and Crashaw's translation of the *Dies Irae*, on equally compelling grounds, refers to the defecation of God—hence the poet, "to find an image for the purest love . . . falls back on sexuality in its most infantile and least creditable form."[19] But one of the most common results of Empson's procedure is that poets appear to him unintelligible, or, to use his own word, "muddled." For example, Shakespeare's Sonnet XVI, with which I imagine few readers have found difficulty, is "muddled."[20]

These things of course result, as I have said, from the theory of ambiguity; and one would suppose that a principle so ruthlessly applied would be of absolute force, especially since it is the "essence" of poetry. As a matter of fact, Empson is not quite willing to credit it with as much authority as he demands from it. An ambiguity, while it can be "beautiful,"[21] is "not satisfying in itself, nor is it, considered on its own, a thing to be attempted; it must in each case arise from, and be justified by, the peculiar requirements of the situation."[22] "On the other hand, it is a thing which the more interesting and valuable situations are more likely to justify."[23] This is an admission, I take it, that ambiguity is not even in Empson's view the *principle* of poetry, since its propriety or impropriety is determined by something else—an unanalyzed thing vaguely called "the situation." Rather, it is a sign, and by no means an infallible sign even for Empson, that an interesting and valuable situation is involved. (The statement even of that much is, by the way, left undefended and unsupported by Empson, although his whole position depends upon it.) And he seems to discuss the sign—ambiguity—rather than the "interesting and valuable situation" of which it is a sign only because the sign is "less mysterious."[24] In short, he appears to be in the position of many of the ancient theorists who sought to discuss the elevated style; the style itself evaded their formulations, but since it predominantly involved certain tropes, the tropes might be ana-

17. P. 18, par. 3.

18. Pp. 96–97.

19. Pp. 222–24.

20. P. 57. The sonnet is analyzed on pp. 54–56.

21. P. 235.

22. *Ibid.*

23. *Ibid.*

24. P. 243.

lyzed, although, it was recognized, the mere production of tropes would not constitute elevation of style.

Indeed, Empson is really a tropist *manqué*, and the seven types are really tropes, as can be seen from the fact that the regular tropes fall under his divisions; the first type, for instance, includes metaphor and antithesis, and the subclasses are clearly subclasses of tropes. But there are certain important differences between the types of ambiguity and the ancient tropes; the types are not nearly so comprehensive; they do not offer nearly such clear distinctions between figures of language; they are not organized upon nearly so clear a principle; and, what is most crucial, they are not nearly so useful. The main difficulty with the tropes, as they were generally treated, was that, in Samuel Butler's phrase, "All a rhetorician's rules/Teach nothing but to name his tools"; that is, their treatment was not sufficiently functional; but they did offer a precise and exhaustive distinction, at their best, between kinds of grammatical devices. Hence, once a trope has been identified, one is in a position to inquire how it has been used, and thereby arrive ultimately at judgments of value. Empson's types, however, do not even permit the distinction of the device; I fear that only Empson can find instances of them, and even he is sometimes unsure.[25]

But, indeed, to deal rigorously with Empson's ideas, to attempt to state them clearly, to demand precision and adequacy of proof for them, is in a sense to be very unfair to him. It is unfair, perhaps, even to inquire into his exact meaning. As a matter of fact, I am not sure that he means anything exactly. He is constantly offering statements; but there is not one—even of his cardinal doctrines—which he is willing to stand by. It would appear that he is offering a method of verbal analysis based on ambiguity; but he is not quite sure what he means by "ambiguity."[26] It requires certain conditions; but these conditions are not always satisfied by his examples.[27] His first definition of ambiguity was that it "adds some nuance to the direct statement of prose." But, he continues, "this begs a philosophical question and stretches the term ambiguity so far that it becomes almost meaningless." Even his new definition "is not meant to be decisive but to avoid confusing the reader; naturally the question of what would be the best definition of ambiguity . . . crops up all through the book."[28] Elsewhere, he remarks in a footnote: "Effects worth calling ambiguous occur when the possible alternative meanings of word or grammar are used to give alternative meanings to the sentence"[29]—but this would disallow much of his

25. E.g., "The fundamental situation, whether it deserves to be called ambiguous or not . . ." (p. 2).

26. See Preface to the 2d ed., pp. vii–xv.

27. E.g., p. 214, par. 2.

28. P. 1 n.

29. P. 70 n.

own practice, for he constantly confounds potential with actual meaning, as in the examples we have just considered. The real truth of the matter is, I suspect, in the following sentence: "Apart from trailing my coat about minor controversies, I claimed at the outset that I would use the term ambiguity to mean anything I liked, and repeatedly told the reader that the distinctions between the Seven Types which he was asked to study would not be worth the attention of a profounder thinker." And he remarks, briefly afterward: "I have tried to clear the text of the gratuitous puzzles of definition and draw attention to the real ones."[30]

After such admissions it is almost improper to remark what is nevertheless plain to behold. Empson is not sure of the types of ambiguity; for instance, he is not sure that the first type *is* ambiguous.[31] He is not sure of the principles of classification. He is not sure that his method is useful to poets—on the contrary, poets ought to avoid ambiguity[32]—nor that it is of too much use even to readers, for, he says, they need not remember or apply it.[33] In short, it would seem that his only safeguard against complete and utter refutation is his slipperiness of statement and his ability to insist that any counterargument, any refutation, does not affect his ideas, but is merely a criticism of his expression.

These traits might seem to convict him of sophistry also; but they are rather a clue to the interpretation of his work. He is pointing to a problem; whatever we may think about his statement and treatment of it, the problem itself undoubtedly exists: what kind of minute and precise discussion of poetic language is requisite in order to make manifest the subtleties of genius and art? His principal difficulty is that contemporary criticism, for reasons that we shall examine later, affords no devices by which such a problem can be handled. In fact, it cannot even be accurately stated; for the only alternatives to his theory which Empson can conceive are the theories of "Pure Sound" and of "Atmosphere," as he calls them;[34] since neither of these is tenable, he pursues his own course. He seems utterly innocent of any knowledge of the history of criticism; as a consequence, he is a victim of the collapse of the theory of art in his own day. Possessing no clear or adequate poetic principles, he nevertheless has his intuitions, and he must use language to express these. If the language permits the concept to shine through, well and good; if not, one must alter the language. Recognizing that poetic language can be enormously effective, he supposes that this is due to denseness of meaning; and since denseness of meaning implies ambiguity, one must discuss ambiguity.

It is, indeed, on this topic of meaning, so crucial to his system as well as to

30. Preface to the 2d ed., pp. vii–viii.

31. P. 2.

32. Pp. 235–36.

33. P. 256.

34. P. 8.

that of Richards, that his confusions are least manifest and most serious. Perhaps most serious of all is that between meaning and implication or inference.

The discrimination of four conditions of meaning and inference may perhaps clarify this issue. First, meaning may be present without inference, or, if inference is present, it is based wholly upon linguistic or other semantic matters —for example, if language is involved, upon the meanings of words and upon syntactical laws. Meaning here is the simple resultant of the significant powers of words and of their combinations; the meaning of what Empson calls "direct" statement or expression is of this order. Inference, if present at all, is here minimal; from what a child knows, for instance, of the elemental parts (word-meanings) and of types of construction (attribution, predication, etc.) he may infer the meaning of the primer sentence. This would be simple part-whole inference, and wholly linguistic in character; if the child fails to infer the whole, he is reminded by analysis into parts and types of construction. Sentences which have a meaning of this order may be of infinite grammatical complexity; they will still be direct or simple in meaning, since the meaning is the resultant only of verbal signs.

But, secondly, meaning may be the resultant of more than verbal signs. It may, that is, result from inferences based on the character or purpose of the speaker, the manner of delivery (e.g., facial expression, gesture, etc.), our presupposed knowledge or opinions of the subject, the situation, and many other circumstances; and—while such inferences are frequently unrelated to the meaning, or do not affect it—frequently also they serve to modify, emphasize, or even contradict the meaning of the words uttered. For instance, irony, as we now conceive it, is possible because we can infer from something over and above the verbal expression that the expression means the opposite of what it says. Sentences affected by such inferences never mean quite what they say; however simple their form, their meaning is never a simple resultant of the verbal expressions.

Thirdly, meaning, if it is produced by inference, also produces inference which is not, however, part of the meaning. Not every inference which can be drawn from a fact is *meant* by the sentence which states the fact. An axiom of geometry does not, in its statement, *mean* every theorem which can be drawn from it. Similarly, a sentence is in itself a fact, but inferences drawn from that fact are no part of its meaning. For example, if a certain sentence is possible, it is inferable that language is possible; but the sentence itself—say, Empson's "The brown cat sat on the red mat"—does not, as he thinks, *mean* "Language is possible" or "This is a statement about a cat."

Fourthly, inference is possible quite apart from meaning. If I see a bloody ax and infer that something was killed with it, no question of meaning is involved, for all arbitrary signs are absent; a fact implies a fact, even in the absence of language and meaning.

Now while Empson talks of meaning and implication, he makes no effective distinction between these four cases. All are equally "meaning" for him. The cat sentence does not have merely its obvious meaning (case 1), but it *means* that it might have come out of a fairy story or a primer (case 2) and that it is a statement about a cat (case 3). The confusion would not be so serious, perhaps, if it did not carry with it his commitment to dictionaries. As one can readily see, dictionary meanings are absolutely determinative, if anywhere, only in the first case; and they grow less and less so, until they are not involved at all in the last case.

The confusion becomes particularly important when Empson is talking of the "meaning" of poetry. For, strictly speaking, a *mimetic* poem, an imitation— and he is mainly concerned with poems of this kind—has no meaning at all. It is a certain kind of product, like a picture, a symphony, or a statue; like an ax, a bed, a chair; it has no more meaning *as a poem* than these have.[35] It is a fact; from that fact we may make inferences, to which we respond emotionally and about which we make judgments; but it means nothing; it is. In short, to speak of the "meaning" of a poem is to confuse meaning with the implication of a fact.

Presumably, however, Empson means the diction of the poem when he speaks of poetry. In that case he confuses the diction with the poem; but his question may be very readily answered. In the broadest sense, what the diction means, precisely, is the poem itself.

The importance of these distinctions, which at first sight may seem pedantic and useless, is that they lead, so far as poetics is concerned, to a distinction—a very important one for the problems in which Empson is interested—between *lexis* and *praxis*; between speech as meaningful and speech as action. What the poetic character says in the mimetic poem is speech and has meaning; his *saying it* is action, an act of persuading, confessing, commanding, informing, torturing, or what not. His diction may be accounted for in grammatical and lexicographical terms; not so his action. And the profundity and complexity in poetry which so much interests Empson is due primarily to action and character, which cannot be handled in grammatical terms, rather than to diction, which can. That profundity is only in a small degree verbal, in the sense that verbal analysis will yield the whole of it; and even then it is very seldom a

---

35. I trust that these statements will not seem to make me a member of what Empson calls the "cult of Pure Sound" and that they will give no encouragement to slovenly and irresponsible reading. I do not imply here that the attempt to discover meaning should be foregone but that more than meaning is involved in poetry. The ensuing discussion will, I hope, clarify the somewhat terse statement here.

matter of verbal ambiguity. Shakespeare's profoundest touches are a case in point. "Pray you, undo this button" and "The table's full" are profound, not as meaningful verbal expressions but as actions permitting an extraordinary number of implications, in that they are revelatory of many aspects of character and situation. We shall not explain them by jumbling the dictionary meanings of "button" and "table," but by asking, among other things, why Lear requested the unfastening of a button and why Macbeth thought the table was full. This is true even in lyric poetry: the "Once more" of "Lycidas," for instance, has no profound verbal meaning; it is affecting because it implies the repeated suffering of bereavement.

The theories of Richards and Empson illustrate a tendency, very prevalent among critics who rate diction as important, to rate it as entirely too important. In the order of our coming to know the poem, it is true, the words are all-important; without them we could not know the poem. But when we grasp the structure we see that in the poetic order they are the least important element; they are governed by everything else in the poem. We are in fact far less moved by the words as mere words than we think; we think ourselves moved mainly by them because they are the only visible or audible part of the poem. As soon as we grasp the grammatical meaning of an expression in a mimetic poem, we begin drawing inferences which we scarcely recognize as inferences, because they are just such as we habitually make in life; inferences from the speech as to the character, his situation, his thought, his passion, suddenly set the speaker vividly before us and arouse our emotions in sympathy or antipathy; our humanity is engaged, and it is engaged by humanity. But where we can draw no such inferences, where no such impression of humanity is conveyed, we remain largely indifferent in the face of the finest diction. These inferences, moreover, largely determine our interpretation of the language itself; we recognize a pun or an ambiguity when we see a human reason why the character should deal in puns and ambiguities, and not when the dictionary lists a variety of meanings.

We do indeed say the character must be so-and-so *because* his words are such-and-such, as well as that the words must be such-and-such *because* the character is so; thus, at first sight, diction and the other parts of the poem seem mutually determinative; on closer inspection, however, we see that *because* has a different sense in each case, since it refers to a cause of a different order. The words are a cause of our conjecturing the character; the character is a cause of the words being said. We can see this even if we are speaking merely of words and meaning: the words are a cause of our knowing the meaning; but the meaning is the cause of the words in their selection and ordering.

If the words, then, are not what is primarily responsible for the effect, purely verbal interpretation, however essential, will not explain poetry, any more than stringing fine diction together will constitute it. Indeed, even Empson in a manner admits this; for he tells us that ambiguity must be justified by the "situation"; but he makes the fatal error of supposing that, because the situation is not something verbal, it is therefore outside the bounds of poetic consideration. As a consequence of this, he defines the poetic pleasure itself much too loosely; that pleasure is not, as he thinks, a logical pleasure produced by puzzling over the relation between statements; it is a pleasure produced by a play of emotions aroused in us by an exhibition of the actions and fortunes of men. Inference is indeed involved, and carries a pleasure of its own; but inference is only a necessary condition, and not a sufficient cause, of the poetic pleasure.

This looseness of treatment might seem to broaden the scope of Empson's inquiry; but it tends rather to restrict. He can conceive of metaphors, for instance, only as comparisons based upon real similarity; the more real likenesses present, the better the metaphor; the better the metaphor, the better the poem. His treatment of "Bare ruined choirs" is an instance. What he misses entirely is the governance of metaphor by thought, of thought by character, or character by action. For a metaphor is not simply a figure of diction in poetry; it is also someone's thinking, significantly, that something resembles something; it is the thought, that is, of a certain character in a certain situation, and it is significant of these things. The best similitudes are not always good metaphors in a given poem, and the best metaphors are not always good similitudes.[36]

In short, something is missing in all this; and what is missing is the nature of poetry.

II

Empson's theory, then, deals only with a single part of poetry, and that part the least important one poetically; indeed, only with a single attribute of that part, and one only vaguely and suppositiously attached to poetry, for ambiguity is neither peculiar to poetry nor universal to all, or to the best, poetry. Moreover, his treatment even of that attribute is so limited as not merely to send inquiry in the wrong direction, but also to preclude proper explanation and supplementation of whatever truths it may, as a system of discussion, contain. Nor are these faults peculiarly Empson's; they abound everywhere in the "new criticism," and, for that matter, in contemporary criticism generally. Scrutinizing the "new criticism" as a whole, I do indeed find that "unity of method" which Ransom, Elton, and others have claimed for

36. Mr. Empson has replied to these criticisms (*Kenyon Review*, XII [1950], 599–601). His chief point is that by "meaning" he means everything: plot, character, thought, and all. This makes his extreme dependence upon the dictionary all the more incomprehensible to me.

it;[37] I find it also in contemporary criticism generally; and on examining that method, I find it directly responsible for all the faults I have noted.

Contemporary criticism seems, for a variety of reasons, to have broken with the past, and to have begun afresh upon a discussion of principles. Such a venture required a new determination of the subject matter of criticism and re-opened the question of the nature of poetry, thereby giving rise to an indefinite number of definitions and hypotheses. The principal reason for the rejection of preceding theories was the belief that these were incommensurate, and incapable of being made commensurate, with the growth of poetry in our time, having been, it was supposed, founded upon conceptions of poetry entirely too narrow and limited. The "new criticism" was to comprehend all that has been called "poetry," to discover its true nature and determine methods of its proper criticism and construction. A second important reason stemmed from the advances made in certain sciences which might have some bearing on poetry; psychology, for instance, was thought to have advanced considerably and to possess new techniques and hypotheses that applied immediately both to the creative process of the artist and the emotional responses of the audience.

Commendable as these motives may be, the task of establishing and developing the principles of art is a formidable one always, even for the philosopher, and in this instance it was complicated by certain difficulties. Chief among these was the absence of any clear, fruitful, and widely accepted metaphysics, epistemology, philosophy of science; a discipline—call it what you will—capable of articulating and organizing the arts and sciences, establishing and criticizing their principles and methods, and, in short, settling the broader and more general questions which the pursuit of any department of inquiry must involve. How seriously this lack has affected contemporary criticism may be seen by anyone who takes the trouble to note the frequency of metaphysical questions, as well as the infrequency of happy solutions to these, in any critical discussion which seeks, nowadays, to rise above the mere particulars of art. Definitions are made by men who know neither what a definition is, nor how it is constructed, nor what it is for, and methodology is discussed by men who would be hard put to it to say what method is. The excellent amateur of poetry has become a sadly amateurish philosopher. But the fault in this instance must be laid at the doors of the philosophers.

A second difficulty lay in the fact that the term "poetry," or its equivalents, had from antiquity been applied to a great number of things of widely different natures. The attachment of a name to something is, after all, only the reflection of an opinion of likeness; and custom had quite naturally extended the applica-

37. Ransom, *op. cit.*, Preface, p. x. While, strictly speaking, Ransom is speaking of R. P. Blackmur, he is clearly discussing him as a representative instance of a "new critic."

tion of the name of poetry, not merely to poetry itself, but to anything that involved the use of poetic devices such as verse, rhyme, ornamental diction, etc. Now it is impossible to have a single art, science, or discipline unless some homogeneity can be found in the subject matter; and criticism was thus faced with the impossible task of finding homogeneity among heterogeneous things: that is, of finding a common principle among things that had no common principles, and of finding a single definition that should state the common nature of things that had no common nature.

Criticism had to find points of likeness among an accidental accumulation of things of diverse natures, which had been called "poetry" because in accidental respects they resembled it; and likenesses it found; but these were *accidental* likenesses, as one might expect under the circumstances. Even where the characteristic selected was itself a necessary condition of poetry—as, for example, the use of language—there remained the difficulty of discerning in what special respects it was related to the nature or essence of poetry. Language functions very differently in the epigram, the didactic verse-treatise, and mimetic tragedy; if you call all of these "poetry" and inquire into the nature of poetic language, you will end up with some description which, because it must be common to all of these, will be very general and will shed little light upon the special functioning of language in, say, mimetic tragedy. Moreover, it was in the nature of the case that certain of these characteristics, being very general, should turn out to be common to things which were obviously not poetry, in any of the accepted senses, at all. For example, language is common to all the things called "poetry"; but nothing is more evident than that scientific prose, for instance, is very different from poetry, although it too is language; it must therefore be differentiated from poetry—but what is the proper differentia? You decide, at this point, that scientific prose is bare, poetic diction ornamented; or the latter is more highly charged with meaning than the former, or something of the sort; and if this does not sufficiently distinguish it, you proceed further, through differentiae of the differentia, until definition is finally achieved. Despite the fact that the definition was founded on a characteristic accidentally found in common among an accidental collocation of things, you will now, if you are a typical modern critic, consider that you have stated the nature or essence of poetry.

These "definitions" are not necessarily false, in the sense that they attribute to poetry characteristics which it does not have; but they are certainly not definitions; they certainly do not state the nature of poetry. The accidental characteristics of things, and hence the possible comparisons in terms of these, are limitless; thus an infinite number of definitions of the same thing can be generated in this fashion, all equally valid, since they are based upon and warranted by precisely the same procedure of definition. If so, they are equally "essential"; but—which of these "essences" is the *essence?* An examination of the construction of these definitions will disclose in every instance that the definition has a minimum reference to the object defined, or it touches only a certain attribute which is itself not shown to be essential to the object; all the rest is provided by the apparatus and mechanism of comparison. In short, these "definitions" are at most indications of the light in which the object "poetry" is to be viewed.

But may not these definitions even in that case have some value? Doubtless they may, as devices for permitting the discussion of a subject the nature of which is unknown, and where they function so, they are unexceptionable. It is frequently the case that, before we can state the nature of a thing, much preliminary discussion is needed: the properties, even the accidents, of the subject must be considered in order to be dismissed; and even when erroneous definition results, no great harm is done, for inquiry is still in progress; definition serves as matter for inquiry, and not as the basis of inquiry; it is itself examined and tested, it does not as yet fix and determine the whole approach to the subject. The definitions proposed by contemporary criticism do not, however, function thus heuristically; instead, they operate as a basis for proof, as principles of demonstration; and as such they are sources of misreasoning and error, and hinder rather than foster further discussion. It is one thing to suppose tentatively that poetry is language characterized by ambiguity, and then to inquire whether this characteristic is common to all poetry, whether it is peculiar to poetry, whether it accounts for all that poetry is and does; it is quite another thing to employ it to insist that any interpretation of poetry must turn upon ambiguities, and to twist the language of *Macbeth* into a meaningless and tasteless muddle, merely because, according to the definition, poetry must be ambiguous. It is the reverse, not merely of science, but also of sense, to erect a hasty guess into a principle of method, so that, far from being tested by the data, it tests the data by itself, silencing all adverse testimony, and forcing assent where it should itself yield to correction.

If the definitions of contemporary criticism are thus not strictly definitions, the hypotheses which are framed to support or supplement them are also not strictly hypotheses. In Empson's case, for instance, the definitive property of poetry, ambiguity, rests upon the hypothesis that there is a connection between ambiguity and interesting or valuable situations; that is, if poetry deals with interesting and valuable situations, and these tend to involve ambiguity, poetry must involve ambiguity. Such a hypothesis does not really give the *cause,* for it does not state why the *thing* is such-and-such; it is merely a *reason,* a ground of belief, stating why the theorist *thinks* the thing is so. It is not a poetic principle; it is the rationalization of an opinion. Even if the opinion and its ground were not false, however, both would still be inappropriate, for the terms in which they are couched are much too general: neither ambiguity nor a concern with interesting and valuable situations is peculiar to poetry. Moreover, even if they were appropriate, they would be falsely reductive; ambiguity, when it is present in poetry, is present through a variety of causes, and not simply through the fact that a certain kind of situation tends to involve it.

The hypotheses of contemporary criticism are not, as a matter of fact, hypotheses in any technical sense at all; they are rather a sort of postulate. We may distinguish, I think, three sorts of hypotheses: the heuristic, the demonstrative, and the nameless kind that serves both functions. The heuristic hypothesis is the first principle of a given science, used as a basis for inquiry into more general principles; thus dialectic, according to Plato, "uses hypotheses not as first principles, but as genuine hypotheses, that is to say, as stepping stones and impulses, whereby it may force its way up to something that is not hypothetical, and arrive at the first principle of everything."[38] The demonstrative hypothesis is a first principle in a given science, without which scientific knowledge in that particular sphere is impossible. Both of these imply completed inquiry within the given science; the third kind, which is hypothesis in the sense intended in modern science, implies no such completion; it is a tentative principle, a supposition either of "fact" or of the cause of a "fact." Obviously the hypotheses of contemporary criticism are not hypotheses in the first two senses; nor are they hypotheses in the third sense, although they have the same function as the tentative suppositions of modern science, viz., to explain facts or other hypotheses, or to render them consistent and compendent. For the true hypothesis, in this third sense, is characterized by reciprocal implication; as Descartes remarks, the facts must imply the hypothesis, and the hypothesis must imply the facts; and these are conditions which the modern critical "hypotheses" fail to satisfy. Empson's hypothesis, for instance, satisfies neither condition: it neither implies the data nor is implied by them. A canvass of interesting and valuable situations will not show that they "tend to involve ambiguity"; conversely, even if they did, this would prove nothing about individual instances, for a statistical attribute of a large class ("tend to involve ambiguity" is of this order) does not belong, affirmatively or negatively, necessarily or probably, to any subclasses of that class.

The characteristic hypotheses of contemporary criticism tend, finally, to have two salient traits which vitally affect the systems based upon them. First, they are inadequate; second, they are preclusive of supplementary hypotheses which might compensate for their inadequacies.

38. *Republic* vi. 511.

A very little discussion will, I hope, make this clear. All poetic theory is a form of causal explanation; and such explanation must comprise all the causes requisite to make a thing what it is. Unless the causal account is complete, the explanation is inadequate; if it is insisted upon as adequate, if it is claimed to account for the whole and not merely for the part, it is also preclusive. The theories of the early Greek physicists offer an example. Thales, for instance, thought to account for the phenomenal universe in terms merely of its material cause, the principle of water; but, as numerous philosophers have pointed out, this would at most account for the substrate; it does not explain the distinctive forms which water assumes as rain, cloud, ice, or snow, nor the motive forces which cause water to assume such forms, nor the functional organization of animate things; it offers only one principle of explaantion where several are required.

Modern criticism is very much in the condition of Thales.[39] It may be divided into two principal kinds: criticism based upon hypotheses concerning the medium of poetry, and hence given to the explanation of poetry as language, or language of a certain kind, and criticism based upon hypotheses concerning the subject matter of poetry, and hence given to the explanation of poetry as myth, as knowledge, as experience, or something of the kind. The first seeks to establish some distinction between poetic language and language in any other form or use. Thus Richards opposes poetry to scientific discourse, finding the latter ordered to clarity and the former to ambiguity, the latter informative and the former emotive;[40] Yvor Winters opposes poetry "to other kinds of writing," finding that poetry takes "special pains . . . with the expression of feeling";[41] John Crowe Ransom opposes poetry to unmetrical and unrhymed language, finding poetry a "compromise" between "meaning and metre";[42] but the end result is largely the same: in each case the nature of poetry is ultimately determined solely by the critic's hypotheses as to the nature or functions of language. All these statements contain a measure of truth; but they are inadequate as hypotheses. If tragedy, comedy, epic, and lyric be poetry, how shall they be described as distinctive species of language? Upon what special properties of language does each depend, so that, once these are determined, we shall have a given species of poetry? Is the difference between drama and narrative a difference of language? Are the differences between the large and complicated actions of epic and the small and simple of lyric, the differences between tragic

39. See *Critics and Criticism* (original ed.), pp. 29 and 84 ff.

40. *Principles of Literary Criticism* (New York, 1930), p. 267.

41. *The Anatomy of Nonsense* (Norfolk, Conn., 1943), p. 12.

42. *Op. cit.*, pp. 294–95. But see the whole final chapter, "Wanted: An Ontological Critic."

and comic action and character, the differences between the emotional effects of tragedy and those of comedy—are all these differences of language? Can we account for any differences of poetic language without taking into consideration such differences of poetic form as these? As a matter of fact, is there any attribute of poetic language which cannot also be found, and that abundantly, in other forms of discourse?

These positions are like arguing that ice is ice because it is water; they are attempts to derive the form from the matter. All such argument runs, obviously, in the wrong direction; it would infer the design of a house from the shape and weight of the bricks. No product is what it is simply because its matter is such-and-such; its matter is indeed a necessary, but not a sufficient, condition of its existence and nature. A saw, for instance, is not a saw because the steel determined it should be. The reverse is the case; I wish to cut the fibers of wood a certain way: I must therefore have a blade of a certain kind; it must therefore be made of a substance capable of assuming a certain shape, and hard enough to retain that shape; hence the steel. And, if I am to give a complete account, I must talk not merely about the steel but about the form given it, and how it was given it, and the function of cutting.

The hypotheses concerning subject matter take a variety of forms: poetic fiction is set against truth, or poetic truth against other truths; certain concepts or orderings of concepts are opposed to others, imaginables against credibles, and so on. The principal position is that poetry is myth, or at any rate closely related to myth; it is currently fashionable, numbering among its proponents Maud Bodkin, Robert Penn Warren, nearly all the psychological and political critics, and the critics who talk of "symbolic structure."[43] Superficially various as these hypotheses are, all are based, like those concerned with the medium, upon a simple dichotomy between what is poetic and what is not. With a little translation, the objections against the linguistic theories also apply to them.

Indeed, the subject-matter hypotheses and the linguistic hypotheses are fundamentally the same, being only separate developments from the same general hypothesis: viz., that all discourse is differentiable in terms of subject matter and style. This supposition, which may be traced at least as far back as the Ciceronian distinction between *res* and *verba*, has proved less profitable and more influential than any other single proposition in the history of criticism.[44] To apply it to poetry is to assume that poetry of whatever kind is a form of discourse, and to suppose that poetic organization is necessarily comparable to the organization of any other form of discourse. Such a supposition makes it

43. See *Critics and Criticism* (original ed.), pp. 108 ff. and 138 ff.

44. Cf. *Modern Philology*, XL (1943), 278–79, 281–82.

impossible to differentiate any form of poetry except in terms of characteristics which it has in common with other discourse; it burkes all discussion of important peculiar characteristics of poetry for which there is no analogue in other discourse. That is, it provides no distinctions whereby any kind of poetry—whatever we may mean by the term—may be isolated and discussed as a separate kind.

III

I have remarked already that the term "poetry" is ambiguously used. On the one hand, it stands for such works as *Hamlet*, the "Ode to a Nightingale," and "Sailing to Byzantium," all of which are imitations; on the other hand, it stands for any works which, although nonimitative, involve devices or characteristics especially associated with mimetic poetry. In this latter sense, philosophical treatises like Parmenides' *On Nature*, Lucretius' *De rerum natura*, Sir John Davies' *Nosce teipsum;* medical treatises like Fracastoro's *Syphilidis;* histories like the chronicles of Geoffrey Gaimar and Wace or the *Dittamondo* of Fazio; ethical works, like Pope's *Essay on Man* and his *Moral Essays* have all been called poetry. The distinction is not one of value, but of kind; witness the fact that the *Divina commedia* belongs to the second class. The works of the first class are of a quite different order and are constructed on, and hence have to be judged by, quite different principles from those of works in the second.

This distinction, simple as it is, is likely to prove difficult if not repugnant to a twentieth-century mind. Distinctions of kind are nowadays likely to be called "scholastic"[45]—an epithet which means, I presume, that they are pedantic and useless; and, even if that charge be waived, we have become so used to considering poetry a matter of quality, or even of a degree of a quality, that the distinction is likely to seem a wrong one. Surely, one may say, the *De rerum natura* has more in common with *Hamlet* than with the *Critique of Pure Reason* or the *Essay Concerning Human Understanding;* obviously it ought, therefore, to be considered as poetry rather than as philosophy, especially since the philosophic content is quite incidental, in the view of most readers, to the beauty of the poetry; hence, if kinds are to be distinguished, they must be distinguished on different principles. The proper distinction, however, is not one of kind but of quality transcending all such schoolmasterly distinctions of kinds; one finds poetry in any kind of composition if the *poetic quality* is present.

This skeleton of argument underlies, I am sure, much of modern criticism; and it is by no means pointless or baseless. The objection that no one has yet

45. The latest instance occurs in an article by Murray Krieger, "Creative Criticism . . . ," *Sewanee Review*, LVIII (1950), 41.

defined the poetic quality is scarcely a fair one, and the objection that investigation of a quality common to all literature cannot produce sound or fruitful criticism is patently absurd; great critics, Longinus, Sainte-Beuve, and Arnold among them, have done just that. The weaknesses of contemporary criticism are not due to this position but to inept treatments of this position; to the position itself perhaps only two rejoinders can be made. First, the legitimacy of inquiring into a quality common to all art, if granted, does not imply the illegitimacy of inquiring into the distinctive characteristics of each art; and, second, inquiry of the first kind cannot provide such knowledge as the second kind would provide. Inquiry into a common quality as such cannot of itself provide knowledge of distinctive qualities. Qualitative criticism can at best tell the poet how to construct, the critic how to judge, poetry generally; it can scarcely give information for the construction and judgment of a poem of a given kind. In short, in so far as the problems of constructing and judging the various kinds of poetry are the same or similar, qualitative criticism may be useful; but, in so far as these problems differ, it is useless, and may sometimes be pernicious.

It has, for instance, a dangerous tendency to bring about the discredit of principles perfectly valid within a given sphere of art, simply because they are not universally valid. The result is to make most literary theories and judgments curiously unstable, and to make the surviving principles, supposedly universal to a whole art or group of arts, few and very far removed from any particular artistic problems. Art is not composed wholly of universal and absolute principles; if we look at the whole range of art without prejudice, with absolutely open eyes, it is not difficult to see that universality and validity are not necessarily connected. Certain principles underlie all art; others apply only to the temporal, or only to the spatial arts; others apply only to certain arts below these, and so on; but a principle is not less valid in a certain art merely because it happens to be specific to that art, and is invalid in any other. Yet, if we look at the history of criticism, we can readily see that many of its revolutions and counterrevolutions have turned precisely upon this confusion of validity with universality; false universalization—the elevation of something to absolute truth and force when it had only conditional truth and force— and a false demand for universality—the insistence that a principle could not hold for anything unless it held for everything—are the offspring of this confusion; and have time and again thrown criticism into chaos.

Criticism is likely, in the course of its development, to provide many propositions of conditional truth only, and to forget, because such propositions fitted the conditions exactly, that they were only conditionally true. In this fashion many a convention became a rule, many a rule a principle. Such tyranny usually brings revolt; but those who revolt tend to forget, in turn, that if what is conditionally true is not so absolutely, the false conditionally is also not false absolutely. The Three Unities, after long tyranny, have been utterly destroyed as false; but with them was destroyed the little measure of truth which they as doctrines contained. Not every play, it is true, need confine its action within one day and one place; but it is also true that the actions of certain plays would have been much more effective if they had been so confined. The theory of genres has been demolished; but what was true and useful in it perished along with what was false and dangerous. Criticism has been either wholly general or wholly particular ever since; and its present plight, indeed, is in great part due to its lack of such *specific* principles as might have eventually developed out of the theory of genres.

A second dangerous tendency of qualitative criticism is that, in emphasizing the common poetic quality, it is likely to blind us to the great variousness of poetry. We need, I think, to consider only the two major branches of poetry mentioned above to realize that their differences of kind must be respected if they are to be properly constructed, interpreted, or judged.

Greek epic and drama are mimetic poetry; despite their origin in ritual and myth, they require no reference to these in order to be intelligible and effective. Whatever the mythical origin of an Odysseus, an Achilles, or an Orestes, these are characters simply, and must be interpreted as such; neither they nor their actions and fortunes require allegorical interpretation; whatever symbolic significance they may have possessed as myth they have lost as materials of poetry. Plato, it is true, practiced the allegorical interpretation of poetry which Theagenes and Anaxagoras are said to have initiated in Greece; but he did so clearly as a consequence of his philosophic approach, rather than as a consequence of any characteristics of Homer and the dramatists; and doubtless the case was the same with his predecessors.

Such interpretations indicate, not the inherent necessity of interpreting epic and dramatic poetry as allegory, but the tendency to interpret them so when in their literal interpretation they conflict with doctrine. When the Christian doctrine arose, pagan poetry, literally interpreted, conflicted both with its theological and its moral teachings; and those who sought to defend such poetry were forced by the nature of the case, not only to interpret it allegorically, but also to insist that allegory was the essence of poetry. Moreover, if poetry was to be brought into accord with doctrine, it had itself to become doctrinal, and hence didactic. It is not surprising, in these circumstances, that poetry came to be thought of as didactic allegory.

Didactic allegory presents many superficial resemblances to mimetic poetry; but the differences between them, while perhaps few and obscure, are fundamental. Didactic poetry, whether allegorical or not, must always either propound a doctrine or determine a moral and emotional attitude toward a doctrine in such a way as to command action in accordance with it. The didactic structure must always, therefore, involve explicitly or implicitly some pistic or argumentative element: either the poem argues the doctrine directly, or the argument is left to the reader, as in the case of parables and fables. Argument of some form, however, is always involved; and, whatever form it takes, it inculcates either knowledge or action. In this respect it resembles either the theoretical or the practical syllogism. The principle of didactic poetry, therefore, is its doctrine or thesis, in the peculiar acceptance, theoretical or practical, required for it. Everything in the work mediately or immediately exists and has its peculiar character in order to enforce the doctrine; for instance, the argument itself exists only to prove the thesis and is absolutely determined by it. Such poetry is, of course, really a kind of dialectic or of rhetoric; and it is not surprising that ages which gave themselves over to such poetry should have identified poetry with rhetoric or dialectic in their critical treatises.[46]

Didactic allegory, as a branch of this kind of literature, comes about when the argument is given a particular metaphorical turn. Like fable and parable, it depends upon the possibility of extended metaphor, which in turn depends upon the possibility of discovering multiple analogies between a thing and its analogue, not only as wholes, but as wholes corresponding part for part. The salvation of the soul, for example, can be allegorically represented as a journey because likenesses can be found not merely between salvation and a journey, but also between the stages of salvation and the stages of a journey. The metaphor or symbol may, moreover, be an action, and as such be narratively or dramatically represented. It then bears, to a superficial view, a close resemblance to a plot—particularly to the episodic plot; and readers who are unaware of, or uninterested in, its metaphorical import are quite likely to disregard the import and become interested in the action for its own sake, treating it, consequently, as if it were a plot. *The Faerie Queene* and *Pilgrim's Progress* are very commonly read in this fashion, as romances rather than as allegories. Anyone who wishes to read them so, purely for the excitement and pleasure which they produce, of course may do so; but he is reading them only in part, and for the sake of certain qualities of that part which are incidental to the primary intention; and if he proceeds to judge these works as romances, to complain that the "plot" is not as effective or that the characters are not as convincing as might be, he is being unreasonable: he is insisting that, because a work happens in part to conform to his accidental interest, it should conform to his interest wholly. For the action of an allegory is quite different from a

46. See *Critics and Criticism* (original ed.), pp. 285 ff.

plot. Its characters and incidents are determined, like those of a thesis-novel, by the doctrine to be urged; the only difference is that they are metaphorical, whereas the thesis-characters and -incidents are literal and instantial. The characters very generally represent the subjects, and the incidents the predicates, of the doctrinal proposition; such is the case, for example, in the *Divina commedia*. They exist because the doctrine exists and because it must be presented in a certain way; they are what they are because the doctrine has certain characteristics. The allegorical incident happens, not because it is necessary or probable in the light of other events, but because a certain doctrinal subject must have a certain doctrinal predicate; its order in the action is determined not by the action as action, but by the action as doctrine; and whatever emotional quality and force it may have is determined rather by the emotional attitude which the doctrine must inculcate toward a certain object than by the context of action in which it occurs. Allegorical characters are what they are because we must view virtue or vice or whatever is involved in a certain light; not because we must adopt a certain attitude toward agents and patients if the action is to affect us in a certain way. Such poetry is a mode of statement; everything in it is representative of parts of discourse.

The construction of such mimetic poetry as epic, tragedy, and comedy is very different; these are ordered, not to a doctrine, but to a plot. And the construction of a plot is very different from that of an allegorical action. A plot is not a string of interesting incidents, but a system of incidents so constructed as to give us a specific pleasure by arousing and allaying our emotions.[47] It is not, like allegorical action, complete because it completely expresses a given doctrine but because, as action, it resolves those issues out of which it has begun. It does not, like allegorical action, seek to inculcate certain moral attitudes by arousing our emotions; on the contrary, it makes use of our moral attitudes to arouse our emotions. It does not engage our interest and emotions in particulars of the action in order to instruct us generally; on the contrary, it instructs us about particulars of the characters and actions in the poem in order to engage our emotions and interest in behalf of these very characters and actions. Whereas didactic poetry assumes that if we can be made to feel a certain way in the presence of certain objects we shall be able to make certain moral distinctions, mimetic poetry assumes that if we make certain moral distinctions we shall feel a certain way in the presence of certain objects. Didactic is antecedent to the formation of moral character; mimetic, subsequent. The former assumes that the reader is imperfect and requires to be perfected; the latter, that the reader is perfect and may enjoy a virtuous pleasure.

The characters in plot are present because an action, if it is to effect emotion,

47. See below, pp. 67 ff.

must be morally determinate and hence must involve agents and patients of a determinate moral cast, or because they are convenient to the effective representation of that action. The incidents in plot occur because they are necessary or probable, or because they increase the emotional effectiveness of the work. We are not required in mimetic poetry, as we are in allegory, to ask what the characters or the incidents stand for; we are required to interpret the characters only as men and women, and the incidents only as fortunate or unfortunate, and seriously so or not. Mimetic poetry is not statement; doctrine appears, not as something urged, but as something assumed, and chiefly as what the poet assumes to be necessary or probable, or to be evocative of this or that emotion or moral attitude.

The language of didactic allegory is always many-meaninged or "polysemous," as Dante called it, because the things for which the words stand always stand for something further. The language of mimetic poetry, however, is ambiguous only when plot, character, thought, or the exigencies of representation demand that it be so. Hence these forms must differ even in the analysis of their language.

Custom has given these kinds of poetry the same general name; and perhaps courtesy requires that we should withdraw it from neither. But we need not therefore be misled by the name to suppose that these kinds are the same and to be given the same treatment. The critic who reads the *Divina commedia* as if it were mimetic poetry is likely to feel severely rebuked if he ever encounters the Epistle of Dante to Can Grande della Scala; for the poet makes clear that he is writing a scholastic treatise. The critic who, on the other hand, reads mimetic poetry as allegory commits the converse fault of Fulgentius, whose *Continentia Virgiliana* contains interpretations as far-fetched as any in our contemporary mythologists.

IV

There are no necessary differences between poetic diction, as diction, and the diction of any other kind of composition. There are no devices of language which can be pointed to as distinctively poetic; any other kind of composition may utilize metaphor, images, rhythm, meter, rhyme, or any of the "devices of poetic language," and poetry may utilize any of the devices associated with any other literary kind. We talk properly, therefore, about poetic diction as "poetic"—whatever we may mean by poetry—not when we deal with a given order of diction but when we talk about language in its poetic employment. It is true that in given poetic works the language is markedly different from language in nonpoetic functions; but in any properly constructed work these differences are brought about, not by any fixed rule of poetic language, but by the functions which the language serves. Whether we refer to didactic, mimetic, or other forms of poetry, language can never be the sole issue, it can never even be the principal issue of poetic analysis. Language is always merely a medium, a material, never a form. Even in the extreme case of Arthur Machen's hero,[48] who wrote meaningless verses purely for their sound, diction is subsidiary; in this case rhythm and melody were formal. If, therefore, we must always talk about poetic diction in terms of some principle over and above language, it follows that discussions of poetic diction must differ, to some extent at least, in accordance with the different principles on which different kinds of poetry are composed.

It might seem at first sight that any such discussion must turn on tropes and figures;[49] but, in fact, it need not, and perhaps it should not. Important as tropes and figures may be, they are devices with many possible uses, and consequently the mere fact of their employment cannot tell us much about their actual function in given works. Moreover, most, if not all, of them are capable of being used for quite different, in fact opposite, ends, especially when they are used in combination. A metaphor indicates likeness; but a metaphor coupled with irony indicates difference. Furthermore, tropes and figures have been so repeatedly arranged in impressively exhaustive classifications that we are likely to be given two false impressions: first, that they are really complete and cannot be added to, because it is "against logic" that anything should be added to an exhaustive division; secondly, that their uses or functions have also been exhaustively treated. The first impression is false because it takes no account of development and growth; the second impression is false because poets are inventive and because new uses for old devices and old uses for new devices are among the things they invent.

Discussion ought therefore to proceed, not from devices to functions, but from functions to devices. In the remaining pages of this essay I shall try to illustrate how language functions in relation to some of the most general aspects of mimetic form. In order to do so, it will be necessary first to consider what might be called the general mechanism of such form; that is, how it is constructed and how it operates.

The vicissitudes of literary criticism have made it almost impossible to convey a notion of mimetic form by the simple enumeration of such names as tragedy, comedy, epic, and lyric; for these have all been applied to nonmimetic forms. Furthermore, if the names of literary kinds have broadened in meaning, they have also narrowed in other respects; for example, the name "poetry"

48. In *The Hill of Dreams*.

49. Cf., e.g., W. K. Wimsatt, Jr., "Verbal Style: Logical and Counterlogical," *PMLA*, LXV (1950), 5–20, and the earlier articles by the same writer cited *ibid.*, p. 13, n. 13; also Maynard Mack, " 'Wit and Poetry and Pope': Some Observations on His Imagery," in *Pope and His Contemporaries: Essays Presented to George Sherburn* (Oxford, 1949), pp. 20–40.

itself is today denied to the types of narrative and dramatic prose, although these were commonly regarded as poetry, and their authors as poets, until the early nineteenth century. On the whole, therefore, it is safer to say that mimetic form includes *some* tragedies, comedies, epics, lyrics, novels, short stories, and so on. Differ as they may from each other, all these have in common the fact that they present to us some spectacle of human happiness or misery, of actualized virtue or vice, or of pleasure and pain; that is, some human action or suffering. It is to the effective emotional presentation of this action or suffering that they are ordered as to a principle; that is, the action or suffering is the part which is chief, which gives form to the work, and to which all else is ordered. By that human spectacle, if I may call it thus, they evoke emotion in us. This is not to say, with Maud Bodkin and others, that they evoke emotion by the reference of their action to one or more generalized myths; on the contrary, they affect us by their particular representation of their respective objects; we react, not to man, but to Oedipus and Hamlet, and to these as presented by Sophocles and Shakespeare, and not to these as detached from the poems in which they are found. Our basic human nature, of course, underlies our reactions; but the capacity for moral or merely sympathetic emotion is a capacity only; what we actually feel is what is actually called forth by the poet through his representation of objects capable of so affecting us. We feel, both in art and in life, what we are capable of feeling; but we feel a given emotion only when there exist the proper conditions for that emotion; otherwise we should suffer all emotions simultaneously and continually.

The emotions are states of consciousness attended by pleasure and pain; their exciting causes are our opinions; for instance, we grow angry when we think we have been offended, fearful when we think we are in danger, and we do not feel these emotions unless we have these opinions. But emotions do not result merely from the operation of an exciting cause upon our basic human nature; the same exciting cause may produce different and in fact opposite emotions in different persons, or even in the same person at different times. Emotion is also a product of the frame of mind in which we are—of, that is, our disposition as determined by what we have experienced and felt—and of our moral character. Moreover, our opinion is twofold: we opine about persons and about the occasions on which they do or suffer something. There are, therefore, three factors in any emotion: our disposition, the person, and the occasion; for instance, we feel angry when we are disposed to be angry, with persons capable of arousing our anger, when the occasion for anger arises.

We feel a given emotion precisely when these three factors have been brought to concur; the history of the emotions invoked in us by a mimetic poem is precisely, therefore, the history of such concurrences effected by the poet through his imitation. Thus the analyst who would know what the audience is feeling from time to time in the course of a poem—in so far as their emotions are controlled by the poem—must follow the line of such concurrences, taking them, of course, in their proper sequence.

Most broadly, our emotions are determined by the object which is imitated; e.g., in tragedy, by the action. But, while the object is thus the foundation of what we feel, our emotions are very much modified by the particular manner in which the incidents and characters are disclosed to us; in fact, what we feel at a given moment is much more particularly determined by the manner of representation than by the object. Finally, the words employed by the poet modify still further the emotions produced in us by object and manner, and determine even more particularly what we feel. What we feel concerning the object of imitation, in short, is dependent upon the devices of disclosure which reveal that object to us.

Language is the device of disclosure in most mimetic poetry; in theatrical productions it is, of course, supplemented by the spectacle and sometimes by music (only, however, when the music interprets what is happening or may happen). But it would be a mistake to suppose that language can be adequately analyzed as an instrument of disclosure merely by talking about its *meaning*. I have already distinguished, in the first part of this essay, between speech as action (*praxis*) and speech as meaningful (*lexis*); to neglect that distinction is, I think, to blind one's self to a great deal of the poetic mechanism. Most of what is termed "meaning" by critics and poets is not meaning at all, but implications of character, passion, and fortune derived from the interpretation of speech as action. Unless the meaning of the words is grasped, we cannot, to be sure, grasp the nature of the speech as action; but when we grasp the nature of the speech as action, we make inferences—which, as I have argued, are not *meanings*—as to the character and his situation; we perceive an object which is the principal cause of our emotions in poetry.

How far language as diction affects us can be seen if we consider that, from one point of view, the causes of emotion in mimetic poetry fall into four classes: (1) the precedent context, not of words merely, but of the action as a whole up to a given point; (2) the particular speech-action, together with its implications; (3) the speech as diction; (4) ornament. The "Pray you, undo this button" speech of Lear affects us, according to this division, (1) because the whole poem has, up to this point, excited certain emotions with respect to Lear and his fortunes, and has left us in a certain frame of mind; (2) because the plea sets before us his utter helplessness, his anguished hope to save Cordelia, the bitter repentance implied in that hope, and so on; (3) because the diction simply and starkly expresses that plea; and (4) because the ornament—

in this case, the rhythm merely—affects us as well. Of these four classes of emotional causes, only the last two depend upon the particular choice and arrangement of words. A translation good enough to permit the operation of the first two would not be greatly inferior; indeed, the principal difficulty of translations, even in lyric poetry, is not so much that the translator fails in respect to the last two, as that, in his efforts to achieve a certain literary manner or a certain rhythm, or even to give the literal meaning, he fails to preserve the significance of the speech as action; he loses the passionate anger, or the fright; he loses the characteristic marks of nobility or meanness; he translates the meaning only, or the style, or the rhythm.

It is speech as action which plays more powerfully upon our emotions; it provides us with the signs from which we infer such things as plot, character, and thought, the most powerful elements in the work; but the signs which it offers us are natural, and not arbitrary, signs. The signs by which we infer from speech that a man is, say, frightened or resolute, or of this character or that, are not fixed by any convention of language; they differ no more from one tongue to another than weeping in Africa differs from weeping in Alaska, or a groan in Italy from a groan in Spain. And much of the "richness" of poetic language is due to this aspect of it. Much of what is currently discussed as "meaning" is this implication of the speech as act.

A great deal, then, of suspense, surprise, and emotion is effected by something other than diction as diction; nevertheless, diction can enhance these, and on occasion even generate them itself. It is this aspect of poetic language—of diction as diction—that I wish particularly to examine. Its problems are problems of word-choice and word-arrangement; they can never be solved without reference to conventional signs, although they can be discussed generally apart from a given language. The problem of diction is not one of how a frightened man, say, would talk, or of how, more generally, speech serves as an indication of character, passion, or situation; it is one of how, given all such determinations of the speech, words as words may prove most effective. As I have said, this is in one sense the least important part of poetics, for the words are determined by everything else in the poem; in another sense, it is the most important, because the words are all we have to go by, they alone disclose the poem to us. The effectiveness of what they disclose must be kept distinct from their effectiveness as instruments of disclosure; the "startling statement" in drama is startling because it discloses something startling, usually, not because it is startling as a matter of words and their arrangement; but what the words disclose can be effective only if the words are effective in their disclosure of it.

But, while disclosure is the general function of the words, what is disclosed must be disclosed properly and in the proper order. Language is a temporal medium; its parts are not coexistent, like those of a spatial medium, but successively existent; when one part is existing, one has ceased or will come to exist; its effects can never have the simultaneity of the effects of color and line in a painting. Moreover, the object imitated in mimetic poetry is always an activity, however minute; even a mood which is momentary is not something static and timeless; hence the object is temporal, too. Consequently, the activity must be remembered, if it is to be seen as a whole and have its whole effect; the language must be such as to permit this. This means that certain parts of the action must be rendered vivid, to have this full and proper emotional force, while others must be dimmed; language can produce such vividness or lack of it by the direction of our attention. Again, all arts that have temporal media, since they cannot exhibit everything at once, involve anticipation, as the spatial arts do not, since they present everything to perception simultaneously; and where anticipation is present, we have also suspense and the unexpected, since our anticipation can be played upon and can be surprisingly foiled. It is clear, therefore, that language can be artfully used to conceal or half-conceal. Finally, since language can be pleasing in itself, it has an ornamental function in poetry as well.

While language, then, has, strictly speaking, the general functions of disclosure and of ornamentation, it is useful to treat it under more special heads which follow from the foregoing argument. The mimetic poet, like any other, may be said to have seven subsidiary aims, with respect to language; I call them "subsidiary" because this essay has made it obvious that they could not be principal. These aims are disclosure, partial disclosure, concealment, direction of attention, evocation of suspense, production of the unexpected, and ornament. What must be disclosed, concealed, etc., belongs to the parts of poetics which deal with plot, character, and thought, and cannot be analyzed here; our present concern is simply the functioning of language as meaningful with respect to these aims.

Disclosure is at a maximum when language is as concise and clear as possible. There are two kinds of concision in language: one is obtained by the use of as few words as possible to express the meaning, while nevertheless expressing the full meaning; the other by expressing only part of the meaning, leaving the rest to inference. Thus the use of enthymeme for syllogism is concise in the latter way; and the famous Lacedaemonian dispatch "Dionysius in Corinth" is of this order. The implication involved here is different from the implications of character, etc., by speech as action in that what is implied is *meaning*, whereas the implications of speech as action are derived from meaning. For instance, the full meaning of the dispatch is "If you attack us, you will be served like a similar aggressor, Dionysius, who was also a great king and is now living, an exile and a private citizen, in Corinth." With the meaning clear, the speech may now be interpreted as an act of defiance implying the moral qualities of Spartans. Concision is possible also apart from language, when an act is a concise sign, i.e., one which has many implications; and poetic concision is greatest when both language and action are concise. For example, the "Who's there?" of *Hamlet* is not only concise as diction; the fact that the wrong man challenges shows tension, fright, doubt whether the sentinel on duty had suffered some unknown misfortune, an expectation of some foreign and possibly hostile presence, etc. The particular devices for obtaining concision of diction when the meaning is fully expressed vary according to the linguistic structures of the various languages; in general it may be said that such languages as have the same syntactical elements (e.g., the same parts of speech) tend to permit the same abridgments; thus asyndeton is possible in all tongues having conjunctions; and similarly such languages as form their words in the same way permit of the same devices of compounding several words into one. Concision of diction where only part of the meaning is expressed varies similarly with the language; it is also based, perhaps more importantly, on expectation and on logical implication.

Clear language is not language which raises no problems—for example, a scientific fact raising numberless problems may be clearly expressed; indeed, if language when clear never raised problems, questions could never be clear. It is, rather, language which raises no problems as to its meaning for those adequately acquainted with the tongue in which it is couched, however many and however profound the problems arising when its meaning is grasped. Anyone who thinks clear language is possible thinks that it consists in using clear words clearly; and in fact, generally speaking, that is all there is to it. But it is useful to analyze further, especially since the devices of ambiguity and indirection depend upon such analysis.

Whether we think of language as evocative, as evoking concepts, or as significative, as standing for something, the possibility of language depends upon a certain condition: the condition that the powers assumed for language by the speaker in his act of speech—whatever the extent and nature of such powers—should not also simultaneously be denied by the speaker, as evinced by the mode of utterance. I do not mean that he may not decide a given expression is inappropriate or incorrect, or change his mind, or reveal his true opinion by offering us an apparent statement and then withdrawing it; I mean that, since language consists of arbitrary signs, which have only such powers as we assign them, the speaker cannot at once assign and refuse to assign them. This is different from the principle of contradiction; the principle of contradiction is not the source of this condition but a consequence of it—indeed, operates only when certain powers of language are assumed. This fundamental condition is the linguistic warrant, without which language is impossible as language, although it may produce effects in us merely as sound. When it is really violated, lack of clarity does not result because there is no language to be clear; but apparent violations of it result in lack of clarity. Such apparent violations occur when any unit of speech seems to negate itself, either openly, as in oxymoron and paradox, or covertly, as when the things stated do not constitute oxymoron, paradox, etc., but imply them. An example is Donne's analogy of a woman's virtue to a snake's venom. All of these apparent violations relate to the conditions of clarity, and not those of language.

The conditions of clarity itself can be seen if we consider that it is dependent upon three things: the words, the syntactical arrangements, and the relations of sentences. Clarity is produced by the words in so far as they are prime, immediate, commensurate, consonant, and familiar. Words are prime if their use does not suggest that they are not being used in their first literal meaning; for example, "dog" or "animal" are both prime as applied to the beast on the hearthrug. Any word is capable of ambiguity; but, conversely, any ambiguous word is capable of being made prime. Words are immediate if they do not in themselves require any special calculation before they yield their meaning; thus the "not-not-not man" of logic-books is not immediate because it requires a calculus of negations, and Eliot's "polyphiloprogenitive" requires etymological calculation. In general, no word is immediate unless it is intelligible as a synthesis. This is merely a distinction between simple and familiar compounds, on the one hand, and unfamiliar compounds, such as coined words, on the other; and it is different from the question of being prime—once we have calculated what "not-not-not man" means, nothing leads us to suppose that it is not prime. Words are commensurate when they are neither too general nor too particular for the thing they stand for; thus "animal" or "Socrates" is incommensurate with "man." Words are consonant if they belong to the same order or level of discourse, in that they contain, as words, no implication of incompatible or inconceivable predication or attribution. For example, a pejorative word used to denote something admirable is used inconsonantly, and is unclear, since we have to wonder about its use. Words are familiar when they not only are commonly employed but are used in their customary grammatical functions, i.e., qua parts of speech; for instance, if a given word is commonly used as a noun and rarely as a verb, it is not wholly familiar when it is used as a verb.

Clarity is produced by syntactical arrangement when amphibology is absent, when grammatical construction is familiar, when the order is the com-

mon order, when the material sequence is observed, when predication and attribution are immediate, when the sentence is unified and complete, when the
sentence form is primary, when the rhythm is appropriate to the emphasis, and
when the sentence is of the proper magnitude. Not all of these need explanation.
By observing the material sequence I mean such things as observing the natural
order of events; for instance, Shelley's "I die, I faint, I fail" does not observe
the material sequence. By immediate predication or attribution I mean that the
predicate or the modifier lies adjacent to the subject to which it attaches. Thus
parenthetical expressions of any length between subject and predicate produce
lack of clarity. By unified sentence I mean one which connects matter which
ought to be connected. For example, "She mourned his death and subsequently
became very proficent in athletics" is not a unified sentence. By primary sentence form I mean the posing of a question in the interrogative, a statement in
the declarative form, and so on. By proper magnitude I mean that the sentence
should not be so long that the beginning is forgotten before the end is reached.

Clarity is produced in the relations of sentences when the proper signs of
subordination, co-ordination, and transition are employed; when the material
sequence is observed; and when the whole correlation (the paragraph) is unified, complete, and of the proper magnitude. Sentences are related to each other
in four ways: additively, qualificatively, antithetically, and inferentially; they
either add fresh information, qualify what has been said, oppose each other in
some way, or are related as parts of an argument. Question and answer and
command and compliance are not separate relations, but types of additive relation. The interrogative sentence always presents a subject and demands an
attribute, or presents an attribute and demands a subject, or presents both and
demands to know their connection; the answer adds the missing point, just as
a blank is filled in a questionnaire. The compliance similarly adds information.
Clarity results from the relations of sentences when grammatical signs make
explicit, in any doubtful cases, which of the four relations is involved; this is
particularly necessary when the words or the syntactical arrangements have
not been clear.

In general, language is clear in proportion as it requires fewer mental operations to derive its meaning, however many mental operations may result from
the meaning once it is known. Hence clear language never involves any misdirection of the mind of hearer or reader, except as this is caused by the tongue
in which it is couched; hence language is clear in proportion as it follows normal expectation in all things, for we are not misdirected if what follows is what
we expected, whereas any unexpectedness necessitates readjustment; hence
familiar words in familiar arrangement are always clearest, since familiarity
determines expectation. Language which follows expectation can always be

more concise than other language, without sacrificing clarity; for we need only occasional indications that we are on the right track.

It is far from true that ambiguity is the essence of poetry; on the contrary, poetic language should always be as clear as possible, not in the absolute sense, but in the qualified one of maximum clarity consistent with the requirements of the individual poem as a whole. That is, there should be no *unnecessary* misdirection of the reader; and in this respect the greatest poetry is not "puzzling" or unclear, but amazingly clear. Indeed, it would seem that in proportion as the *implications* of the language increase in number and in importance, the language itself is clearer; compare the later poetry of Yeats.

Clarity is not, however, always consistent with the maximum effectiveness of the poem. If everything were disclosed as quickly and clearly as possible, interest, suspense, and surprise and, indeed, the poet's whole control of our emotions would be minimized, and the emotional force of poetry would be greatly lessened. In proportion as characters and situations are made vivid to us, they exert more powerfully their peculiar emotional force, and they can be disclosed too rapidly to be vivid. We are, for instance, more vividly aware of the vice of a man when we realize that we were mistaken in the supposition that he is virtuous, and we are more vividly aware of virtue which we have misjudged; our reaction in each case is proportional to our vivid awareness. Interest and suspense must diminish, once we know all; and surprise is impossible when only the expected happens. Hence, obviously, the poet must, if merely upon these grounds, conceal some aspects of his subject and misdirect us in our interpretation of it; and, although language is not the only instrument of concealment and misdirection, it is nevertheless an important one.

All the points involved in disclosure, as analyzed above, generate devices of partial disclosure and concealment. An example or two must suffice here. Partial disclosure is produced by vagueness, among other things; and vagueness is produced most generally by the incommensurateness of terms, by ambiguity either of terms, syntax, or sentence-relation, and by altering circumstances within the poem. All but the last are clear; I mean by it such phenomena as are produced when a verbal expression changes meaning as the poem advances, not because of verbal ambiguity as such, but because of changing circumstances, just as "King of England" may now mean one man, now another. This is different from ambiguous prophecies such as those in *Macbeth*. The powerful effect of vagueness in inducing suspense and otherwise augmenting attention and emotion is admirably exemplified, as Coleridge has observed, by Shakespeare's treatment of the ghost in *Hamlet*; it is first disclosed to the audience as a "thing" which "appears," has appeared before, and may momently be expected to appear again, then as something that may be fantasy, as something that might not be believed, then as a "dreaded sight" twice seen, and as an "apparition"; after such verbal preparation the ghost appears, and that unexpectedly. This is indeed, as Coleridge says, "admirable indefiniteness," and it is particularly effective, since the prior discussion has induced a certain frame of mind in the audience. Complete disclosure here, by the use of the word "ghost," would have ruined the effect. The vagueness of the incommensurate word is not necessarily a matter of generality; for instance, T. S. Eliot achieves many effects by the use of words more specific than his meaning, e.g., the proper names which turn out, after all, not to have an individual reference. In general, it may be said that the poet must disclose as much of his subject, and only so much, as is requisite to produce the opinion and frame of mind on which the desired emotion depends; and obviously language can help or hinder in this.

Since emotions are produced, not from mere opinions, but from opinions actively entertained, and since this active entertainment results from the focusing of our attention, clearly the direction of attention is of great importance. It is achieved in many ways: by the mere mention of something where other things are left unmentioned; by repetition; by the repeated omission or avoidance of the obvious word where the whole context insists upon it; by implication, especially when the premise given is dull, but the conclusion implied is shocking or startling, or vice versa when the conclusion is given; by treatment on a larger scale than that afforded other things, provided that the scale is not so large as to weary the attention; by use of suspense and surprise; by understatement, overstatement, or irony; by changes of style, as from the circumlocutory to the terse; and by images and metaphors.

Only a few of these require explanation. Omission of the obvious word can be achieved by breaking off the grammatical member short of the word, or by substituting an incommensurate or an inconsonant word; or, what is rather a matter of invention than of diction, by substituting attributes for subjects, antecedents for consequents, and so on. The chapter called "The Grindstone" in *A Tale of Two Cities*, for example, directs atttention to the bloodiness of Paris not merely by repeatedly using the word "blood," but by naming attributes of blood such as redness and imparting them to the whole scene. Attention is produced by the unexpected in various ways, and especially when the whole meaning is reversed so that, for example, a compliment becomes an insult. Thus the speech of the elder Yeats at the Abbey Theatre: "This Ireland, this land of saints—plaster saints"; and thus John Barrymore's declining of an invitation: "I have a previous engagement which I shall make as quickly as possible."

Suspense and the unexpected are based upon disclosure and concealment;

nevertheless, not everything concealed or disclosed produces these. The matter disclosed or concealed is, of course, the primary determinant, and it must be matter which engages interest and anticipation; but, this granted, suspense and surprise may nevertheless be enhanced by the diction. Broadly speaking, we are in suspense until we have found the meaning of any discourse that engages our attention, merely because of the nature of language as temporal; but suspense can be artificially produced by delaying what we wish to know; hence, by stopping the sentence short of the informing word, or by using vagueness at the point that should inform, e.g., paraphrasis, especially where the paraphrasis resolves the familiar into the unfamiliar, so that we are delayed by having to conjecture (cf. Stefan Zweig's "wooden wedge affixed to a hollow tube" for "rifle"); by interruption of predication through apposition, parenthesis, and so on; by oxymoron, paradox, and the other devices that rest on apparent contradiction (for we must pause to consider how "rash timidity" or "drunken sobriety" is possible); by extension of the grammatical parts, e.g., making an attributive adjective into a predicate or a relative clause, etc.; by giving the facts in such order that knowledge is incomplete until the last (e.g., by saying "There, in the drawer, lay a shiny cylinder . . . fitted with a needle, the tip of which was still stained dark brown" instead of "There . . . lay the hypodermic syringe which had been the instrument of murder"). In general, suspense will be produced by every device of diction which delays the discovery of meaning.

An image is a verbal expression capable of conveying a conception of the form either of some sensory presentation or of some bodily feeling. Images therefore derive from three sources: the "common sensibles," which are perceptible to all senses or more than one, such as magnitude, motion, rest, figure, and number; the external sensibles, e.g., an object of vision; and bodily feelings, such as pain, heat, cold, pressure, fatigue, tension, etc. As our perceptions are limited—we do not, for instance, see all that is presented to the eye—so images are limited; an image must not therefore be a complete depiction, but the formula of an *aperçu*. An image, moreover, must consist of parts (a subject and its attribute, as the minimum); yet the statement must be concise enough so that all details fuse and operate as one perception. Such a synthesis is impossible if the elements are too many or too indeterminately related to each other. For instance, a contemporary novelist takes several sentences to say that a man's face was composed of V's, which effects nothing despite the elaborate statement of how it was so composed, because the V's have to be imagined in various positions and because the memory cannot retain them all; a second description of the man as "a blond satan" conveys a better picture, but it is still not really an image. For an image must be distinguished from a mere description of an object; otherwise every descriptive catalogue would be full of images;

and it is also different from a word effecting a picture, or every concrete noun would be an image. What distinguishes the image from ordinary description is that it effects a mental representation such as a particular perception might, with a speed as nearly approaching simultaneity as words permit. Thus it must consist of elements readily conceivable and simultaneously conceivable as what a single perception would present; any change of point of view or other condition of perception is fatal: Coleridge was right in rejecting "the furrow followed free," because this necessitated a change of place. The novelist mentioned above speaks of a speeding car appearing to one of its passengers as "a tan streak beneath us"; this similarly refuses to synthesize into an image. From what has just been said about the content of an image, it follows that the diction of an image should be clear, concise, and "heightened." By "heightened" language I mean slightly exaggerated; the words should suggest a color clearer or brighter than would apply to the real perception, since mental images are necessarily fainter than real perceptions; this increases vividness.

"Vivid images" are commonly confused with images of vivid things; but a vivid image is so because of its depiction and not its object. Thus the imagery of Yeats's early poems is vivid, although it depicts dim things like "moth-like stars" and "glimmering moths." Obviously, images should always be vivid; whether the things they present should be made vivid is another question. Poets frequently try to gain a kind of spurious vividness of imagery by the insertion of words like "bright" and "vivid," but this is, on the whole, bad; anyone can make vivid imagery of that sort. The effect of imagery ought to be more like that of dramatic presentation than of narration; we must feel as though we are seeing or hearing, not as though someone were describing something to us. The "brightness" should be brought out by an accurate word, or implied, or suggested by metaphor. Images are made more vivid by contrast or by the inclusion of an uncommon or unexpected element, just as objects themselves are—for instance, Wallace Stevens' "rouged fruits in snow." Vividness results also from the selection of an unusual object—cf. Eliot's "jeweled unicorns draw by the gilded hearse"—or from an unusual perception of it; this is, however, a matter of content. Much more might be said; perhaps it will suffice here to say one thing further: that, while good images do not necessarily make a good poem, bad ones can damage a poem greatly.

Aristotle has distinguished four kinds of metaphor; we may supplement his remarks by observing that such metaphors as he calls "proportional" divide into the simple and the complex, according as the likeness on which the metaphor is based is in terms of a single attribute or several. For instance, "pearl-pale hand" is simple, whereas "angelic hair" is complex; the former sets only a certain pallor before us, whereas the latter suggests sheen, delicacy, length, color, etc. Complex metaphors give us either a mere conjunction of attributes or a correspondence of whole with whole and part with part. The latter is exemplified in the famous analogy, in Ecclesiastes, of the body to a citadel; in the comparison of the body to a castle in *The Faerie Queene;* and of the state to a body in *Coriolanus.*

There are three elements in every metaphor: perhaps we may call them the "referent," or thing analogized; the "analogue," or thing to which the referent is analogized; and the "continuum," or ground of likeness, whether in fact or thought, which permits the analogy. A metaphor is clearly stated as metaphor when these are explicit and when the grammatical indications of similitude are present or easily understood. But a metaphor to be clear as metaphor must be something more than the clear statement that something resembles something in a certain respect; it must be intelligible as a likeness. A metaphor can never be false; it must be true, either in that the analogy is real, or in that someone in a certain condition might think it real. Hence a metaphor can be "difficult" in three principal ways: through omission of one of its elements, through unclear statement grammatically, through apparent falsity. Difficult metaphor always produces suspense and is useful for forcing inference; that is, the difficulty produces curiosity which impels the reader to infer; the inference involves delay, and thus suspense. When one element of the metaphor is suppressed, a riddle always results: for example, "Why is a snake's venom like a woman's virtue?" Curiosity, and therefore suspense, are heightened when the things involved are seemingly disparate, and heightened even more when seeming paradox is involved, as in Donne's metaphor just mentioned; for the comparison of a snake's venom to a woman's virtue implies that good is like bad.

When the continuum is a sensible quality, the metaphor is bound to be easy; where it is not, it always involves some difficulty. Anyone knows that the sun is like a lamp in respect of light; but why a flea is like marriage, or why lovers resemble compasses, is another matter. The metaphysical metaphor takes referents and analogues with no apparent continua; or states the continua last.

When both referent and continuum are suppressed, or only vaguely intimated, the metaphor becomes a symbol; what we speak of as "symbolism" is, so far as diction is concerned, merely the employment of symbolic metaphor.[50] When even the symbol is ambiguous, either because it involves the unfamiliar use of the familiar, or because it has been vaguely or partially stated and must be clarified by the context, suspense due to metaphor is at a maximum. Eliot's "little old man" is an example; for when we have translated *gerontion* into that, the familiarity of the expression keeps us from realizing that it is a symbol.

50. But see *Critics and Criticism* (original ed.), pp. 586–87.

Many other kinds of metaphor may be distinguished; among them what might be called the "correlative metaphor." Hart Crane's "adagios of islands" is of this kind. This type makes an attribution to the correlative of one of the terms of the metaphor, rather than to the term. For example: *motion of ship: motion of adagio music;* the motion is now transferred to the correlative, i.e., to that with reference to which the ship moves; hence *adagios of islands.*

Among kinds of unexpected metaphor, there is the kind which unites terms commonly united, so that the likeness appears trite; a new continuum is involved, however, in the light of which the metaphor is suddenly vivid and startling.

Again, there is what I shall call the "subsumptive metaphor" or the "subsumptive symbol." This is a general metaphor comprising many metaphors as its parts, and uniting all; the Platonic process of "combination" must be used in order to produce such metaphor. It is particularly powerful because of the dialectic which it entails. The magical mythology of Yeats's *Vision* involves it, and Eliot's Wheel is of the same order.

Somewhat akin to metaphor is the use of words which, while not constituting metaphor, have metaphorical suggestion, either determinately suggesting some analogue, or leaving the analogue vague. For instance, "The train glided out of a hole in the mountain and slid into a dark wood" suggests a serpent determinately, although without real metaphor, for these are perfectly literal attributes. Use of more general attributes in this instance would render the analogue indeterminate, but have the effect of metaphor still. This is very useful for producing "atmosphere."

Many other developments of diction are, like these last kinds, fairly new; the study of diction, even as tropes and figures, may scarcely, therefore, be regarded as completed; and still less the investigation of its complex uses in relation to the various kinds of poetic ends.

THE CONCEPT OF PLOT AND THE PLOT
OF *TOM JONES*[1]

R. S. CRANE

O F ALL the plots constructed by English novelists that of *Tom Jones* has probably elicited the most unqualified praise. There is "no fable whatever," wrote Fielding's first biographer, that "affords, in its solution, such artful states of suspence, such beautiful turns of surprise, such unexpected incidents, and such sudden discoveries, sometimes apparently embarrassing, but always promising the catastrophe, and eventually promoting the completion of the whole."[2] Not since the days of Homer, it seemed to James Beattie, had the world seen "a more artful epick fable." "The characters and adventures are wonderfully diversified: yet the circumstances are all so natural, and rise so easily from one another, and co-operate with so much regularity in bringing on, even while they seem to retard, the catastrophe, that the curiosity of the reader . . . grows more and more impatient as the story advances, till at last it becomes downright anxiety. And when we get to the end . . . we are amazed to find, that of so many incidents there should be so few superfluous; that in such variety of fiction there should be so great probability; and that so complex a tale should be perspicuously conducted, and with perfect unity of design."[3] These are typical of the eulogies that preceded and were summed up in Coleridge's famous verdict in 1834: "What a master of composition Fielding was! Upon my word, I think the Oedipus Tyrannus, The Alchemist, and Tom Jones, the three most perfect plots ever planned."[4] More recent writers have tended to speak less hyperbolically and, like Scott, to insist that "even the high praise due to the construction and arrangement of the story is inferior to that claimed by the truth, force, and spirit of the characters,"[5] but it is hard to think of any important modern discussion of the novel that does not contain at least a few sentences on Fielding's "ever-to-be-praised skill as an architect of plot."[6]

1. Reprinted, with alterations and additions, from the *Journal of General Education*, January, 1950.

2. Arthur Murphy (1762), quoted in Frederic T. Blanchard, *Fielding the Novelist: A Study in Historical Criticism* (New Haven, 1927), p. 161.

3. *Dissertations Moral and Critical* (1783), quoted in Blanchard, pp. 222–23.

4. *Ibid.*, pp. 320–21.   5. *Ibid.*, p. 327.

6. The phrase is Oliver Elton's in *A Survey of English Literature, 1730–1780* (New York, 1928), I, 195. See also Wilbur L. Cross, *The History of Henry Fielding* (New Haven, 1918),

I

The question I wish to raise concerns not the justice of any of these estimates but rather the nature and critical adequacy of the conception of plot in general and of the plot of *Tom Jones* in particular that underlies most if not all of them. Now it is a striking fact that in all the more extended discussions of Fielding's masterpiece since 1749 the consideration of the plot has constituted merely one topic among several others, and a topic, moreover, so detached from the rest that once it is disposed of the consideration of the remaining elements of character, thought, diction, and narrative technique invariably proceeds without further reference to it. The characters are indeed agents of the story, but their values are assessed apart from this, in terms sometimes of their degrees of conformity to standards of characterization in literature generally, sometimes of the conceptions of morality they embody, sometimes of their relation to Fielding's experiences or prejudices, sometimes of their reflection, taken collectively, of the England of their time. The other elements are isolated similarly, both from the plot and from one another: what is found important in the thought, whether of the characters or of the narrator, is normally not its function as an artistic device but its doctrinal content as a sign of the "philosophy" of Fielding; the style and the ironical tone of the narrative are frequently praised, but solely as means to the general literary satisfaction of the reader; and, what is perhaps more significant, the wonderful comic force of the novel, which all have delighted to commend, is assumed to be independent of the plot and a matter exclusively of particular incidents, of the characters of some, but not all, of the persons, and of occasional passages of burlesque or witty writing.[7]

II, 160–61; Aurélien Digeon, *Les Romans de Fielding* (Paris, 1923), pp. 210–16; Elizabeth Jenkins, *Henry Fielding* (London, 1947), pp. 57–58; and George Sherburn, in *A Literary History of England*, ed. Albert C. Baugh (New York and London, 1948), pp. 957–58; cf. his interesting Introduction to the "Modern Library College Editions" reprint of *Tom Jones* (New York, 1950), pp. ix–x.

7. The explanation of this procedure lies, partly, in a still unwritten chapter in the history of criticism. When works of prose fiction became objects of increasing critical attention in the eighteenth century, it was natural that the new form should be discussed in terms of its obvious analogies, both positive and negative, to drama and epic and that critics of novels should avail themselves, consequently, of the familiar categories of "fable," "characters," "sentiments," and "language" which had been long established, in the neoclassical tradition, as standard devices for the analysis of tragedies, comedies, and heroic poems. In remote origin these distinctions derived from the four qualitative "parts" which Aristotle had shown to be common to tragedy and epic (cf. *Poetics* 5. 1449^{b}15 ff.; 24. 1459^{b}8–11). In the course of their transmission to the eighteenth century, however—as a result partly of the influence of Horace and partly of a complex of more general causes operative from the beginnings of Aristotelian commentary in the Renaissance (see *Critics and Criticism* [original ed.], pp. 319–48) —the analytical significance of the scheme had undergone a radical change. For Aristotle, concerned with the construction of poetic wholes that afford "peculiar pleasures" through their imitations of different species of human actions, the four terms had designated the essential elements upon the proper handling and combination of which, relatively to the in-

All this points to a strictly limited definition of plot as something that can be abstracted, for critical purposes, from the moral qualities of the characters and the operations of their thought. This something is merely the material continuity of the story considered in relation to the general pleasure we take in any fiction when our curiosity about the impending events is aroused, sustained, and then satisfied to a degree or in a manner we could not anticipate. A plot in this sense—the sense in which modern novelists pride themselves on having got rid of plot—can be pronounced good in terms simply of the variety of incidents it contains, the amount of suspense and surprise it evokes, and the ingenuity with which all the happenings in the beginning and middle are made to contribute to the resolution at the end. Given the definition, indeed, no other

---

tended over-all effect, the quality of a tragedy or epic necessarily depends. They are distinct parts in the sense of being variable factors in the complex problem of composing works which, when completed, will produce their effects, synthetically, as organic wholes. Hence it is that in the *Poetics* they are treated, not discretely as co-ordinate topics, but hierarchically in a causal sequence of form-matter or end-means relationships in which plot is the most inclusive or architectonic of the four, subsuming all the others as its poetic matter; in which character, while subordinated materially to plot and effect, is similarly a formal or organizing principle with respect to thought and diction; in which thought, while functioning as matter relatively to character, incident, and effect, is the form which immediately controls the choice and arrangement of language in so far as this is employed as a means to imitative rather than ornamental ends; and in which diction, though necessarily having a form of its own by virtue of its rhythmical, syntactical, and "stylistic" figuration, is the underlying matter which, as significant speech, at once makes possible all the other "parts" and is in turn, mediately or immediately, controlled by them. The nature of the four elements is such, in short, that, although a critic in his analysis of a given tragedy or epic may take any one of them as his primary object of attention, he can make no adequate judgment of the poet's success or failure with respect to it without bringing into his discussion all the others to which it is related, directly or indirectly, either as matter or as form.

Of this causal scheme only the general outlines survived in the doctrines of subsequent critics in the "Aristotelian" line. The distinction of the four parts was retained and, along with it, the substance of the rules which Aristotle had formulated for their handling; what disappeared was precisely the rationale which in the *Poetics* had justified not only the rules but the discrimination, definition, and ordering of the parts themselves. In its place various new principles and schemes of analysis were substituted by different theorists and critics, the general tendency of which was to make of poetics a practical rather than a productive art and hence to reduce tragedy and epic to modes of ethical or rhetorical discourse designed to serve, each in its specialized way, the common purposes of all such discourse, namely, the delight and instruction of mankind. The consequence was that, although critics continued to distinguish aspects of tragedies and epics that corresponded roughly with the Aristotelian "parts" and although these served to determine the framework of the discussion at least in the most systematic treatises and essays, the discussion itself no longer turned on the nature and functional interrelations of the four parts as elements in an artistic synthesis of a particular kind but on the general qualities which the poet ought to aim at in each, in order to enhance its independent power of pleasing, moving, and edifying spectators or readers. And when this apparatus was carried over from the statement of tragic or epic theory to the practical criticism of tragedies or epics (as in Addison's papers on *Paradise Lost* or Pope's Preface to the *Iliad*), the disjunction of the four elements tended to become still more marked. They were no longer functional parts in an organic whole but so many relatively discrete *loci* of critical praise and blame; and critics could write *seriatim* of the beauties or defects in the fable, characters, sentiments, and language of a given tragedy or heroic poem without assuming any synthesizing principles more specific than the decorum of the genre or the

criteria are possible, and no others have been used by any of the critics of *Tom Jones* since the eighteenth century who have declared its plot to be one of the most perfect ever planned. They have uniformly judged it as interesting story merely—and this whether, as by most of the earlier writers, "the felicitous contrivance and happy extrication of the story" is taken to be the chief "beauty" of the novel or whether, as generally nowadays, preference is given to its qualities of character and thought. It is clearly of plot in no completer sense than this that Oliver Elton is thinking when he remarks that, although some "have cared little for this particular excellence, and think only of Partridge, timorous, credulous, garrulous, faithful, and an injured man; of Squire Western, and of the night at Upton, and of wit and humour everywhere," still "the common reader, for whom Fielding wrote, cares a great deal, and cares rightly, for plot; and so did Sophocles."[8]

When plot is conceived thus narrowly, in abstraction from the peculiar characters and mental processes of the agents, it must necessarily have, for the critic, only a relatively external relation to the other aspects of the work. That is why, in most discussions of *Tom Jones*, the critical treatment of the plot (as

---

necessity (e.g.) that the sentiments expressed should be consonant with the characters of the persons who uttered them (many illustrations of the procedure may be found in H. T. Swedenberg, Jr., *The Theory of the Epic in England, 1650–1800* [Berkeley and Los Angeles, 1944]; cf. the Index under "Fable or action," "Characters," "Sentiments in the epic," and "Language of the epic").

It was at this stage in the history of the Aristotelian "parts" that they entered into the criticism, both general and applied, of modern prose fiction. See, for example, besides many notices of novels in the *Monthly Review* and the *Critical Review*, the anonymous *Critical Remarks on Sir Charles Grandison, Clarissa, and Pamela* (1754); Arthur Murphy's "Essay on the Life and Genius of Henry Fielding," in *The Works of Henry Fielding* (1762); James Beattie's "On Fable and Romance," in his *Dissertations* (1783); and John More's "View of the Commencement and Progress of Romance," in *The Works of Tobias Smollett* (1797). In spite of the general indifference of criticism since about 1750 to questions specific to the various poetic kinds (see above, pp. 14, 459), the tradition of method thus established has persisted, especially in academic circles, to the present day; its influence still lingers in the topical divisions of treatises or textbooks dealing with the technique of fiction; and it still provides the commonplaces of a good many "studies" of novelists and novels (e.g., the pages on *Tom Jones*, already referred to, in Elton's *Survey*). The undoubted deficiencies of the scheme (in its neoclassical degradation) as an instrument of critical analysis and judgment have not passed unnoticed in recent years, particularly among critics of the *Scrutiny* group, who point out, justly enough, that "plot" and "character" are treated in a fashion that abstracts them unduly from the continuum of the novelist's language through which alone they affect us. These critics, however, are usually content to offer, as a positive substitute for the traditional scheme, only a still more extreme reduction of Aristotle's principles, in which everything in the discussion of a novel is made to turn on the relations between diction, in the sense of the author's "verbal arrangements," and thought, in the sense of the "experience" which he communicates by imposing "the pattern of his own sensibility" on the reader through the medium of language. See, for example, Martin Turnell, "The Language of Fiction," *Times Literary Supplement*, August 19, 1949, pp. 529–31; reprinted in his *Novel in France* (New York, 1951).

8. *Op. cit.*, I, 195.

distinguished from mere summary of the happenings) is restricted to the kind of enthusiastic general appreciation of which I have given some examples, supplemented by more particular remarks on various episodes, notably those of the Man of the Hill and of Mrs. Fitzpatrick, which appear to do little to advance the action. The plot, in these discussions, is simply one of several sources of interest and pleasure afforded by a novel peculiarly rich in pleasurable and interesting things, and the problem of its relation to the other ingredients is evaded altogether. Occasionally, it is true, the question has been faced; but even in those critics, like W. L. Cross and Oliver Elton, who have made it most explicit, the formulas suggested never give to the plot of *Tom Jones* the status of more than an external and enveloping form in relation to which the rest of the novel is content. It is not, as they see it, an end but a means, and they describe it variously, having no language but metaphor for the purpose, as a "framework" in which character (which is Fielding's "real 'bill of fare' ") is "set"; as a device, essentially "artificial," for bringing on the stage "real men and women"; as a "mere mechanism," which, except now and then in the last two books, "does not obtrude," for keeping readers alert through six volumes.[9]

I do not believe, however, that it is necessary to remain content with this very limited and abstract definition of plot or with the miscellaneous and fragmentized criticism of works like *Tom Jones* that has always followed from it. I shall assume that any novel or drama not constructed on didactic principles[10] is a composite of three elements, which unite to determine its quality and effect —the things that are imitated (or "rendered") in it, the linguistic medium in which they are imitated, and the manner or technique of imitation; and I shall assume further that the things imitated necessarily involve human beings interacting with one another in ways determined by, and in turn affecting, their moral characters and their states of mind (i.e., their reasonings, emotions, and attitudes). If this is granted, we may say that the plot of any novel or drama is the particular temporal synthesis effected by the writer of the elements of action, character, and thought that constitute the matter of his invention. It is impossible, therefore, to state adequately what any plot is unless we include in our formula all three of the elements or causes of which the plot is the synthesis; and it follows also that plots will differ in structure according as one or another of the three causal ingredients is employed as the synthesizing principle. There are, thus, plots of action, plots of character, and plots of thought. In the first, the synthesizing principle is a completed change, gradual or sudden, in the situation of the protagonist, determined and effected by character and thought (as in *Oedipus* and *The Brothers Karamazov*); in the second, the

9. Cross, *op. cit.*, II, 159–61; Elton, *op. cit.*, I, 195–96.
10. See above, pp. 44–47, and *Critics and Criticism* (original ed.), pp. 588–92.

principle is a completed process of change in the moral character of the protagonist, precipitated or molded by action, and made manifest both in it and in thought and feeling (as in James's *The Portrait of a Lady*); in the third, the principle is a completed process of change in the thought of the protagonist and consequently in his feelings, conditioned and directed by character and action (as in Pater's *Marius the Epicurean*). All these types of construction, and not merely the first, are plots in the meaning of our definition; and it is mainly, perhaps, because most of the familiar classic plots, including that of *Tom Jones*, have been of the first kind that so many critics have tended to reduce plot to action alone.[11]

If this is granted, we may go farther. For a plot, in the enlarged sense here given to the term, is not merely a particular synthesis of particular materials of character, thought, and action, but such a synthesis endowed necessarily, because it imitates in words a sequence of human activities, with a power to affect our opinions and emotions in a certain way. We are bound, as we read or listen, to form expectations about what is coming and to feel more or less determinate desires relatively to our expectations. At the very least, if we are interested at all, we desire to know what is going to happen or how the problems faced by the characters are going to be solved. This is a necessary condition of our pleasure in all plots, and there are many good ones—in the classics of pure detective fiction, for example, or in some modern psychiatric novels—the power of which depends almost exclusively on the pleasure we take in inferring progressively, from complex or ambiguous signs, the true state of affairs. For some readers and even some critics this would seem to be the chief source of delight in many plots that have obviously been constructed on more specific principles: not only *Tom Jones*, as we have seen, but *Oedipus* has been praised as a mystery story, and it is likely that much of Henry James's popularity is due to his remarkable capacity for provoking a superior kind of inferential activity. What distinguishes all the more developed forms of imitative literature, however, is that, though they presuppose this instinctive pleasure in learning, they go beyond it and give us plots of which the effects derive in a much more immediate way from the particular ethical qualities manifested in their agents' actions and thoughts vis-à-vis the human situations in which they are engaged. When this is the case, we cannot help becoming, in a greater or less degree, emotionally involved; for some of the characters we wish good, for others ill, and, depending on our inferences as to the events, we feel hope or fear, pity or satisfaction, or some modification of these or simi-

11. This accounts in large part, I think, for the depreciation of "plot" in E. M. Forster's *Aspects of the Novel*, and for his notion of a rivalry between "plot" and "character," in which one or the other may "triumph." For a view much closer to that argued in this essay see Elizabeth Bowen, "Notes on Writing a Novel," *Orion*, II (1945), 18 ff.

lar emotions. The peculiar power of any plot of this kind, as it unfolds, is a result of our state of knowledge at any point in complex interaction with our desires for the characters as morally differentiated beings; and we may be said to have grasped the plot in the full artistic sense only when we have analyzed this interplay of desires and expectations sequentially in relation to the incidents by which it is produced.

It is, of course, an essential condition of such an effect that the writer should so have combined his elements of action, character, and thought as to have achieved a complete and ordered whole, with all the parts needed to carry the protagonist, by probable or necessary stages, from the beginning to the end of his change: we should not have, otherwise, any connected series of expectations wherewith to guide our desires. In itself, however, this structure is only the matter or content of the plot and not its form; the form of the plot—in the sense of that which makes its matter into a definite artistic thing—is rather its distinctive "working or power," as the form of the plot in tragedy, for example, is the capacity of its unified sequence of actions to effect through pity and fear a cartharsis of such emotions.

But if this is granted, then certain consequences follow for the criticism of dramas and novels. It is evident, in the first place, that no plot of this order can be judged excellent *merely* in terms of the unity of its action, the number and variety of its incidents, or the extent to which it produces suspense and surprise. These are but properties of its matter, and their achievement, even to a high degree, in any particular plot does not inevitably mean that the emotional effect of the whole will not still be diffused or weak. They are, therefore, necessary, but not sufficient, conditions of a good plot, the positive excellence of which depends upon the power of its peculiar synthesis of character, action, and thought, as inferable from the sequence of words, to move our feelings powerfully and pleasurably in a certain definite way.

But this power, which constitutes the form of the plot, is obviously, from an artistic point of view, the most important virtue any drama or novel can have; it is that, indeed, which most sharply distinguishes works of imitation from all other kinds of literary productions. It follows, consequently, that the plot, considered formally, of any imitative work is, in relation to the work as a whole, not simply a means—a "framework" or "mere mechanism"—but rather the final end which everything in the work, if that is to be felt as a whole, must be made, directly or indirectly, to serve. For the critic, therefore, the form of the plot is a first principle, which he must grasp as clearly as possible for any work he proposes to examine before he can deal adequately with the questions raised by its parts. This does not mean that we cannot derive other relevant principles of judgment from the general causes of pleasure operative in all artistic imitations, irrespective of the particular effect, serious or comic, that is aimed at in a given work. One of these is the imitative principle itself, the principle that we are in general more convinced and moved when things are "rendered" for us through probable signs than when they are given merely in "statement," without illusion, after the fashion of a scenario.[12] Critical judgments, valid enough if they are not taken absolutely, may also be drawn from considerations of the general powers of language as a literary medium, of the known potentialities or requirements of a given manner of representation (e.g., dramatic or narrative), and of the various conditions of suspense and surprise. We are not likely to feel strongly the emotional effect of a work in which the worse rather than the better alternatives among these different expedients are consistently chosen or chosen in crucial scenes. The same thing, too, can be said of works in which the thought, however clearly serving an artistic use, is generally uninteresting or stale, or in which the characters of the agents, though right enough in conception for the intended effect, are less than adequately "done" or fail to impress themselves upon our memory and imagination, or in which we perceive that the most has not been made of the possibilities implicit in the incidents. And there is also a kind of judgment, distinct from any of these, the object of which is not so much the traits of a work that follow from its general character as an imitative drama or novel as the qualities of intelligence and moral sensibility in its author which are reflected in his conception and handling of its subject and which warrant us in ascribing "greatness," "seriousness," or "maturity" to some products of art and in denying these values to others no matter how excellent, in a formal sense, the latter may be.

Such criticism of parts in the light of general principles is indispensable, but it is no substitute for—and its conclusions, affirmative as well as negative, have constantly to be checked by—the more specific kind of criticism of a work that takes the form of the plot as its starting point and then inquires how far and in what way its peculiar power is maximized by the writer's invention and development of episodes, his step-by-step rendering of the characters of his people, his use and elaboration of thought, his handling of diction and imagery, and his decisions as to the order, method, scale, and point of view of his representation.

All this is implied, I think, in the general hypothesis about plot which I have been outlining here and which I now propose to illustrate further in a re-examination of the "ever-to-be-praised" plot of *Tom Jones*.

12. The meaning and force of this will be clear to anyone who has compared in detail the text of *The Ambassadors* with James's preliminary synopsis of the novel (*The Notebooks of Henry James* [New York, 1947], pp. 372–415). See also the excellent remarks of Allen Tate, apropos of *Madame Bovary*, in his "Techniques of Fiction" (*Forms of Modern Fiction*, ed. William Van O'Connor [Minneapolis, 1948], esp. pp. 37–45).

II

It is necessary to look first at its matter and to begin by asking what is the unifying idea by which this is held together. Elementary as the question is, I have not read any answers to it that do not, in one way or another, mistake one of the parts of Fielding's novel for the whole. Doubtless the most common formula is that which locates the essence of the story in the sustained concealment and final disclosure of Tom's parentage. "It is pleasant," writes Oliver Elton, "to consider *Tom Jones* as a puzzle and to see how well the plan works out." For others the most important unifying factor is the love affair of Tom and Sophia; for still others, the conflict between Tom and Blifil; for others again, the quasi-picaresque sequence of Tom's adventures with women and on the road. The novel, it is true, would be quite different in its total effect if any of these four lines of action had been left out, but no one of them so subsumes all the rest as to justify us in considering it, even on the level of material action, as the principle of the whole. A distinctive whole there is, however, and I venture to say that it consists, not in any mere combination of these parts, but rather in the dynamic system of actions, extending throughout the novel, by which the divergent intentions and beliefs of a large number of persons of different characters and states of knowledge belonging to or somehow related to the neighboring families of the Allworthys and the Westerns are made to cooperate, with the assistance of Fortune, first to bring Tom into an incomplete and precarious union, founded on an affinity of nature in spite of a disparity of status, with Allworthy and Sophia; then to separate him as completely as possible from them through actions that impel both of them, one after the other, to reverse their opinions of his character; and then, just as he seems about to fulfil the old prophecy that "he was certainly born to be hanged," to restore them unexpectedly to him in a more entire and stable union of both affection and fortune than he has known before.

The unity of *Tom Jones* is contained in this formula, but only potentially; and before we can properly discuss the plot as an artistic principle we must examine, in some detail, the intricate scheme of probabilities, involving moral choices, mistaken judgments, and accidents of Fortune, which binds its many parts together from the time we first see Tom in Allworthy's bed until we leave him, calmly enjoying his double good luck, at the end of Book XVIII.

There are three major stages in the action, the first of which, constituting in relation to the other two stages a "beginning," is complete by chapter vii of Book V. The starting point of everything is Bridget's scheme to provide security for both herself and her illegitimate son by palming off Tom on Allworthy as a foundling, with the intention, however, of ultimately informing her brother of the truth. The first part of the plan works beautifully: the affection which "the good man" at once conceives for the child assures Tom of a proper home and upbringing, and suspicion is diverted from his mother by Allworthy's discovery of parents for him, first in Jenny Jones (who, as Bridget's agent, is in the secret) and then in Partridge (who is not), and by the consequent departure of both of these from the neighborhood. In the end, too, Bridget's second purpose is fulfilled; but meanwhile she has put both parts of her scheme for Tom in jeopardy by her marriage (facilitated, again, by Allworthy's "penetration") with Captain Blifil. As a result, no early disclosure of Tom's true parentage is possible, and in addition the boy acquires a potential rival, in the younger Blifil, for both the affection and the fortune of Allworthy. On the other hand, although the intrigue against him begins immediately after the marriage, its only result at this stage, thanks to the goodness of Allworthy and the obvious innocence of Tom, is to make him thought of henceforth as the son of Partridge. This damages him in the eyes of the "world," but his status as protégé and heir, along with young Blifil, of the benevolent Allworthy is still secure and will remain secure so long as his protector has no reason to think him unworthy of his favor.

A second phase of the "beginning" opens in Book III, with the emergence of moral character in the two half-brothers. There are now, so far as Tom is concerned, two main problems. The first has to do with his relation to Allworthy, for whom by this time he has come to feel as strong an affection as Allworthy has felt, and continues to feel, for him. There can be no change on his part no matter what Allworthy does, since his feelings are based not on any opinion of interest but on the instinctive love of one good nature for another; and there can equally be no change on Allworthy's part that will lead to a separation between them unless something happens to convince him that Tom's nature is after all bad. That under certain circumstances Allworthy should be capable of such a verdict on Tom is made probable, generally, by the excessive confidence in his ability to judge of character which has led him long before to condemn Partridge, and, particularly, by his implicit and, in the face of Bridget's favoritism for Tom, even aggressive belief in the good intentions of young Blifil, as well as in the integrity of the learned men he has chosen, in his wisdom, as tutors for the two boys.

Occasions for passing judgment on Tom present themselves increasingly from his fourteenth year; and Blifil, seconded by Thwackum and Square, misses no chance of using them to blacken his character in his guardian's eyes. The occasions are given by Tom's well-intentioned but quixotic and imprudently managed actions toward Black George and his family, before and after his seduction by Molly. In the first series of these, no harm, in spite of Blifil, is done; on the contrary, as we are told, Tom by his generosity has "rather improved than injured the affection which Mr. Allworthy was inclined to entertain for him." And it is the same at first with the actions that culminate in Tom's mistaken confession that he is the father of Molly's child; angry as Allworthy is at Tom's incontinence, he is "no less pleased with the honour and honesty of his self-accusation" and he begins "to form in his mind the same opinion of this young fellow, which, we hope, our reader may have conceived"; it is only later, after having pardoned him, that he is induced by the sophistry of Square to entertain his "first bad impression concerning Jones." But even this is not fatal to Tom: he is assured again after his injury, though with a warning for the future, that what has happened is "all forgiven and forgotten"; he remains a beneficiary, in proportion to his supposed status, in Allworthy's will; and he is thought of by Allworthy, as we learn from the latter's speech in Book V, chapter vii, as one who has "much goodness, generosity, and honour" in his temper and needs only "prudence and religion" to make him actually happy. Fortune is still, however hesitatingly, on the side of Tom.

The other problem concerns the attachment that has been developing meanwhile between Tom and Sophia. The basis of the attachment is again one of likeness of nature, and the function of the incidents in Books IV and V in which the two are thrown together (Tom's intervention on behalf of Black George, his rescue of Sophia and his convalescence at her house, the affair of the muff, etc.) is simply to make credible its rapid progress, in spite of Tom's initial indifference and his entanglement with Molly, to the stage of mutual recognition reached in Book V, chapter vi. From this point on, we need not expect any change in Tom's feelings toward Sophia, no matter what he may do in his character as gallant; and there is an equally strong probability, in terms of her character, that Sophia will never cease to love Tom. She is, for one thing, a better judge of persons than Allworthy and is in no danger of being deceived, as he is, by the formal appearances of virtue in Blifil and of vice in Tom. "To say the truth, Sophia, when very young, discerned that Tom, though an idle, thoughtless, rattling rascal, was nobody's enemy but his own; and that Master Blifil, though a prudent, discreet, sober young gentleman, was at the same time strongly attached to the interest only of one single person . . ." (IV, v). She has, moreover, been even more completely aware than Allworthy of Tom's affair with Molly, and yet, for all her hurt pride, she has not altered her opinion of his worth; Tom will have to behave, or appear to behave, much worse than this before she will decide to cast him off. In the meantime, however, their union is apparently condemned by circumstances to be one of affection only. Her father, though very fond of Tom, will not approve a marriage which offers so little prospect of fortune for his beloved daughter; she will not act counter to her father's wishes, even though she will not agree to marry against her own feelings; and as for Tom, though his life is now "a constant struggle between honour and inclination," he can do nothing that will injure Sophia, show ingratitude to Western, or violate his more than filial piety toward Allworthy. The only possible resolution of their problem, it is plain, must be some event that will alter fundamentally Tom's position as a foundling.

Such an event is indeed impending at precisely this point in the action. For Bridget, dying, has just confided her secret to her attorney Dowling and has commanded him to carry the all-important message to Allworthy in fulfilment of the second part of her original design.

Blifil, however, aided by Fortune (which now turns temporarily against Tom), here intervenes, with two important results: immediately, that a chain of happenings is set in motion, constituting the "middle" of the plot, which leads to the complete separation of Tom from both Allworthy and Sophia; and remotely, that, when Bridget's message is at last delivered in Book XVIII, the position to which Tom is then restored is made, by reason of the delay, one of even greater security and happiness than would have been possible had his relationship to Allworthy become known at the time Bridget intended to reveal it.

The action from the moment when Bridget gives Dowling her message to the moment, many weeks later, when Allworthy receives it falls into three main parts. The first begins with Allworthy's illness and ends with Tom's expulsion and Sophia's flight. The events in this stage form a single complex sequence, in which Fortune conspires with the malice and ambition of Blifil, the pride and family tyranny of the Westerns, and the easily imposed-on sense of justice of Allworthy, first to thwart the purpose of Bridget and then to turn the indiscreet manifestations of Tom's love for Allworthy and joy at his recovery and of Sophia's love for Tom into occasions for the condemnation and banishment of Tom as "an abandoned reprobate" and for the persecution of Sophia as a recalcitrant daughter. The separating action of the novel thus comes to its first major climax, with Tom now resolved, for the sake of Sophia, to renounce her and leave the country, and with Sophia, unable to endure the prospect of a marriage with Blifil, determined to seek refuge in London with her cousin Lady Bellaston, not without hopes of again seeing Tom. Blifil, now dearer than ever to Allworthy because of Tom's "ill-treatment of that good young man," has apparently triumphed, though not completely, since Sophia is still out of his grasp. In reality, he has already made his fatal mistake, the mistake that will inevitably ruin him and restore Tom if and when Allworthy discovers it; and in addition, by driving Tom out, he has made it more rather than less probable that the truth he has concealed will eventually come to light, since, besides himself, it is also known, in part or in whole, to three other persons—Partridge, Jenny Jones, and Dowling—any or all of whom it is more likely now than before that Tom will meet.

This is, in fact, what happens during the next stage of the action, all the incidents of which converge on bringing Tom into contact, first with Partridge, then with Dowling, and finally with Jenny (now Mrs. Waters). The first meeting leads to a kind of negative resolution: Tom now knows that he is not Partridge's son. From the meetings with the others, who alone, save Blifil, know the whole truth, no resolution immediately follows, being prevented in both cases by the same causes that have determined Tom's fate hitherto: in the case of Jenny by Fortune, which sees to it that there is no encounter between her and Partridge at Upton; in the case of Dowling, who is ready to sell his knowledge for a price, by Tom's quixotic disinterestedness. The crucial discovery is thus postponed, but when we consider that Tom is now known to Dowling and to Jenny (though to the latter not as Bridget's son) and that both of these now become attached to persons in the Allworthy-Western circle—Jenny to Sophia's cousin-in-law Fitzpatrick and Dowling to Blifil—it is clear that the probability of its eventually taking place, and possibly in more auspicious circumstances, is increased rather than diminished by what has occurred.

In the meantime, with the happenings at Upton, the complication has entered its last and longest and, for Tom, most distressing phase, the climax of which, at the end of Book XVI, is his receipt in prison of Sophia's letter of condemnation and dismissal. The principal villain is again Fortune, which as we have been told (V, x), "seldom doth things by halves," and which, having already robbed Tom of the good will of Allworthy, now seems bent on completing his unhappiness by using his too complaisant good nature and his capacity for indiscretion to deprive him of Sophia and perhaps even of his life. It all begins with the chapter of accidents at the inn, where, because of his gallantry to Jenny, Tom first has an angry encounter with Fitzpatrick (who is seeking his runaway wife) and then misses Sophia, who departs at once on learning of his infidelity and makes her way, in the company of Mrs. Fitzpatrick, to London and Lady Bellaston. Some harm has now been done, but not much, as Tom learns when, having pursued her to London, he finally meets her again at Lady Bellaston's and is told, in a tender scene, that what has really disturbed her has not been so much his misconduct with Jenny, which she can forgive, as Partridge's free use of her name in public.

This happy resolution, however, comes too late; for already, although with the best intentions—namely, of finding his way to Sophia—Tom has been seduced into the affair with Lady Bellaston which is his closest approach, in the novel, to a base act. The affair does indeed lead him to Sophia, but only by chance, and then under circumstances which, while they do not betray him to Sophia, turn the wrath of his new mistress against her and lead to a fresh series of efforts to separate her from Tom. The first of these, the attempted rape by Lord Fellamar, is thwarted when Western, having learned of his daughter's whereabouts, rescues her in the nick of time and carries her away to his lodgings to face another course of family persecution and threats of imminent marriage to Blifil. It is on hearing of this that Tom, his thoughts now centered wholly on Sophia in spite of his despair of ever winning her, decides to break with Lady Bellaston, and adopts the expedient for doing so without dishonor which nearly leads to his ruin. For the effect of his proposal of marriage is to draw the Lady's vengeful feelings upon himself and Sophia at once, with the result that she arranges for his kidnapping by a press gang at the same time that she makes sure Sophia will never marry him by sending her the letter of proposal as proof of his villainy. With Sophia her scheme succeeds, so incapable of any other interpretation does the evidence seem. She is foiled, however, in her design against Tom, and once more by a delayed effect of the events at Upton. But the meeting which Fortune brings about with the still angry Fitzpatrick, though it saves Tom from being pressed into the navy, spares him only for what promises to be a worse fate.

The separating action has now come to its second major climax—much the more serious of the two for Tom, since he has not only lost Sophia as well as Allworthy but lost her, he thinks, as a direct result of his own vice and folly. He can still, if Fitzpatrick dies, be separated from his life, but otherwise all the possibilities of harm to him contained in his original situation have been exhausted. Not, however, all the possibilities of good; for the very same incidents proceeding from the affair at Upton which have so far been turned by Fortune against Tom have also had consequences which Fortune, bent upon doing nothing by halves, may yet exploit in his favor.

The most important of these in the long run is the moral change produced by his recent experiences in Tom himself, as manifested by his break with Lady Bellaston and by his rejection of the honorable advances of Mrs. Hunt and the dishonorable advances of Mrs. Fitzpatrick. It is not so much what he is, however, as what he is thought to be by Allworthy and Sophia that immediately counts; and he has had the good luck, by virtue of coming to London, of acquiring in Mrs. Miller a character witness who knows the best as well as the worst of him and who will at least be listened to by her old friend and benefactor Allworthy and perhaps by Sophia. There is, moreover, as a result of what has happened, rather less danger than before that Sophia, who, in spite of her reason, still loves Tom, will be forced to marry Blifil; for, though she is again in the power of her family, the machinations of Lady Bellaston have led to

a conflict between the two Westerns over the rival merits of Blifil and Lord
Fellamar. Time has thus been gained for Tom; and meanwhile Allworthy and
Blifil have come up to town in response to Western's summons and have taken
lodgings with Mrs. Miller. Dowling has come too, and so also has Jenny, now
living with Fitzpatrick in lieu of the wife he has been seeking since Upton and
whose whereabouts he has just learned. All those, in short, who know Bridget's
secret—and Blifil's villainy in suppressing it at the time of her death—are now
assembled, for the first time, in close proximity to Allworthy. And then Blifil,
made overconfident by his success and believing Fitzpatrick about to die of his
wound, decides to use the opportunity afforded by the presence of Lord
Fellamar's press gang at the duel to strike one last blow at Tom.

But this time all the acts of Fortune work to the advantage of our hero, and
the resolution moves rapidly to its end, first by the reunion of Tom with Allworthy and then by his reunion with Sophia. The first requires a reversal of
Allworthy's judgment of Tom's character and actions at the time of his banishment. This is prepared by Mrs. Miller's insistence upon his present goodness
and the services he has rendered her family, but the decisive event is the letter
from the dying and repentant Square, which sets in a new light Tom's acts
during Allworthy's illness, although without clearly implicating Blifil. The
result is to restore Tom to his foster-father's affections more or less on the
footing which he had at the beginning of Book V, but with the added circumstance that he has since suffered unjust persecution. The new Tom is not yet
fully known, or the entire extent and cause of the injuries that have been done
him. Mrs. Miller indeed suspects, but the blindness of Allworthy prevents a
discovery; and it requires a second intervention of Fortune, aided by the rash-
ness of Blifil, to bring the revelation about. For not only does Blifil think
Fitzpatrick's wound more serious than it is, but in his zeal to gather all possible
evidence damaging to Tom he has made it inevitable that Jenny will come to
know who Tom is, that she will at once go to Allworthy with her story, that
Dowling will then be questioned, and that he, seeing where his profit now lies,
will tell the truth about the suppression of Bridget's dying message. Thus here
again Fortune has done nothing by halves, with the result that the exclusive
place which Blifil has all along sought for himself in Allworthy's fortune and
favor is now, with his unmasking and subsequent banishment, properly ac-
corded to Tom. In relation to the original conditions of the action, moreover,
the reversal is equally complete: Bridget's intended disclosure of her secret has
at last been made, and with it both of her mistakes—of concealing Tom's
parentage and then of marrying the elder Blifil—are finally canceled out.

The reunion with Sophia is likewise prepared by Mrs. Miller, who is able to
convince her that Tom's letter proposing marriage to Lady Bellaston was at

worst an indiscretion. But though Allworthy also intervenes on his nephew's behalf and though Western is now as violent an advocate for Tom as he has earlier been for Blifil, the resolution comes only when Sophia, faced with the repentant young man, finds once more (as after his previous affairs with Molly and Jenny) that her love for him is stronger than her injured pride and that it is now a pleasure to be able to obey her father's commands.

It is in nothing short of this total system of actions, moving by probable or necessary connections from beginning, through middle, to end, that the unity of the plot of *Tom Jones* is to be found. It is the unity, clearly, of a complex plot, built on two continuous but contrary lines of probability, both stemming from the double scheme of Bridget respecting Tom and from her marriage with Captain Blifil, and both reinforced, from Book III onward, by the combination in Tom's character of goodness and indiscretion: the one producing immediately, throughout the complication, ever more bad fortune and distress for Tom, the other at the same time preparing for him the good luck he finally comes to enjoy after the discovery and reversal in Book XVIII. It is no wonder that this "plot," in which so many incidents, involving so many surprising turns, are all subsumed so brilliantly under one principle of action, should have been praised by all those critics from the eighteenth century to the present who have had a taste for intricate and ingenious constructions of this kind.

If the plot of *Tom Jones* is still to be praised, however, it ought to be for reasons more relevant than these to the special artistic quality of the novel we continue to read. For what has just been outlined as the "plot" is obviously something from which, if we had never read the work itself, we could hardly predict with any assurance how Fielding's masterpiece, as composed for readers in a particularized sequence of words, paragraphs, chapters, and books, would be likely to affect our opinions and feelings. It is therefore not the plot proper of this novel but, at most, its necessary substrate of unified and probable action; and, if we are to say what the plot proper is and be able to use our account for critical purposes, we must go beyond the material system of happenings—however intrinsically admirable this may be in its ordered magnitude—and look for the formal principle which makes of this system a definitely effective whole and which actually operates, in so far as we concentrate closely on the text, to direct our emotionalized expectations for Tom and the others and our subsequent responses when the hoped-for or feared events occur.[13]

13. The distinction can also be stated in terms of the decisions Fielding had to make in writing the novel. It would obviously not have been the novel it is, had he not conceived, at some stage of the process of construction, the particular system of actions I have sketched above; but, on the other hand, the conception merely of this intricate scheme of incidents would have been insufficient to allow him to proceed securely in the writing without a further decision, or complex of decisions, as to the precise nature of the over-all effect, among

III

In stating this principle for any plot, we must consider three things: (1) the general estimate we are induced to form, by signs in the work, of the moral character and deserts of the hero, as a result of which we tend, more or less ardently, to wish for him either good or bad fortune in the end; (2) the judgments we are led similarly to make about the nature of the events that actually befall the hero or seem likely to befall him, as having either painful or pleasurable consequences for him, and this in greater or less degree and permanently or temporarily; and (3) the opinions we are made to entertain concerning the degree and kind of his responsibility for what happens to him, as being either little or great and, if the latter, the result either of his acting in full knowledge of what he is doing or of some sort of mistake. The form of a given plot is a function of the particular correlation among these three variables which the completed work is calculated to establish, consistently and progressively, in our minds; and in these terms we may say that the plot of *Tom Jones* has a pervasively comic form. The precise sense, however, in which the form is comic is a rather special one, which needs to be carefully defined.

To begin with, it is obviously a plot in which the complication generates much pain and inner suffering for the hero, as a result of misfortunes which would seem genuinely serious to any good person. He is schemed against by a villain who will not stop even at judicial murder to secure his ends, and, what is worse in his eyes, he loses the good will of the two people whom he most loves, and loses it as a consequence not simply of the machinations of his enemies but of his own mistaken acts. From near the beginning until close to the end, moreover, he is made to undergo an almost continuous series of distressing indignities: to be insulted on the score of his birth, to be forbidden the sight of Sophia, to see her being pushed into a hated marriage with Blifil and persecuted when she refuses, to be banished abruptly from home, to be reduced to poverty and forced to take money from Lady Bellaston, to be laid in wait for by a press gang, to be compelled to run a man through in self-defense, and finally, in prison, to be faced with the prospect of a disgraceful death.

The hero, furthermore, to whom all this happens is a naturally good man—

several more or less distinct possibilities, he wished his story to have on its readers. The plot proper of *Tom Jones* is thus not its system of actions alone but this system so qualified, with respect to its "working or power," as to determine specifically rather than generally the successive artistic problems which Fielding faced in putting it into words. It is only in this sense that we can speak intelligently or usefully of "plot" as a constructive first principle in *Tom Jones* or in any other imitative novel or drama.

I should add that several of my friends, while willing to accept the foregoing analysis, would prefer that I should use some other word than "plot" to designate the formal principle I have been attempting to define. I am inclined to agree with them, and only wish that they or I could think of a better term.

not notably virtuous, but, for all his faults, at least the equal of ourselves and of any other character in the novel in disinterestedness, generosity, and tender benevolent feeling. These traits are impressed upon us in the third book and are never obscured even in the worst of Tom's troubles in London; they are, in fact, revivified for us, just at the point when we might be most tempted to forget them, by the episodes of Anderson and of Mrs. Miller's daughter. We favor Tom, therefore, even if we do not admire him, and we wish for him the good fortune with Allworthy and Sophia which he properly wishes for himself and which, in terms of his basic moral character, he deserves to get. We follow him through his troubles and distresses, consequently, with a desire that he will eventually be delivered from them and reunited to his friend and mistress, and this all the more when, at the climax of his difficulties, we see him acting, for the first time, in a way we can entirely approve; in the end, when our wishes for him are unexpectedly realized, and to a fuller degree than we had anticipated, we feel some of the satisfaction which Fielding says (XVIII, xiii) was then felt by the principal characters themselves. "All were happy, but those the most who had been most unhappy before. Their former sufferings and fears gave such a relish to their felicity as even love and fortune, in their fullest flow, could not have given without the advantage of such a comparison."

Having conceived a plot in which so sympathetic a character is subjected in the complication to experiences so painful, it would have been relatively easy for Fielding to write a novel similar in form to his *Amelia*, that is to say, a tragicomedy of common life designed to arouse and then to dissipate, by a sudden happy resolution, emotions of fear and pity for his hero and of indignation toward his enemies. There is, indeed, an even greater material basis for such an effect in *Tom Jones* than in the later novel: the evils that threaten Tom and the indignities he undergoes are, in the abstract, more serious than anything Booth has to fear, and the same thing is true of the persecutions endured by Sophia as compared with those which Amelia is made to suffer. And yet nothing is more evident than that, whereas the emotions awakened in us by the distresses of Booth and Amelia are the graver emotions of anxiety and compassion that yield what Fielding calls "the pleasure of tenderness,"[14] our feelings for Tom and Sophia, as we anticipate or view in actuality the greater evils that befall them prior to the final discovery, partake only in the mildest degree of this painful quality. We do not actively fear for or pity either of them, and our indignation at the actions of their enemies—even the actions of Blifil—never develops into a sustained punitive response.

Nor is the reason for this hard to find. It is generally the case that whatever tends to minimize our fear in a plot that involves threats of undeserved misfor-

14. *Amelia*, Book III, chap. i.

tune for the sympathetic characters tends also to minimize our pity when the misfortune occurs and likewise our indignation against the doers of the evil; and fear for Tom and Sophia as they move toward the successive climaxes of their troubles is prevented from becoming a predominant emotion in the complication of *Tom Jones* chiefly by two things.[15]

The first is our perception, which in each case grows stronger as the novel proceeds, that the persons whose actions threaten serious consequences for the hero and heroine are all persons for whom, though in varying degrees, we are bound to feel a certain contempt. The most formidable of them all is of course Blifil. As a villain, however, he is no Iago but merely a clever opportunist who is likely to overreach himself (as the failure of his first schemes shows) and whose power of harm depends entirely on the blindness of Allworthy; he deceives Tom only temporarily and Sophia and Mrs. Miller not at all; and after we have seen the display of his personal ineptitude in the proposal scene with Sophia, we are prepared to wait, without too much active suspense, for his final showing-up. Blifil is too coldly selfish, perhaps, to strike us as positively ridiculous, but in the characters of the other agents of misfortune the comic strain is clear. It is most obvious, needless to say, in Squire Western and his sister: who can really fear that the persecutions directed against the determined and resourceful Sophia by such a blundering pair of tyrants can ever issue in serious harm? For Allworthy, too, in spite of his excellent principles, it is hard for us to maintain entire respect; we should certainly take more seriously his condemnation of Tom in Book VI had we not become accustomed, as a result of earlier incidents in the novel, to smile at a man who could believe in the goodness of the two Blifils and whose pride in his own judgment could make him dispose so precipitously of Jenny and Partridge. There are evident comic traits also in all the persons who cause trouble for Tom and Sophia in the later part of the action: in Dowling, the man always in a hurry; in Lady Bellaston, the great dame who pursues a plebeian with frenzied letters and nocturnal visits to his lodgings; in Lord Fellamar, the half-hearted rake; in Fitzpatrick, the unfaithful but jealous husband who will not believe the evidence of his own eyes. In respect of her relations with Tom, though not otherwise, Sophia, too, must be added to the list, as a virtuous girl with a proper amount of spirit (not to say vanity) whose good resolutions against Tom never survive for long in the presence of her lover. These are all manifestations of the ineffectual or ridiculous in a plot in which the impending events are materially painful, and

15. I confine myself here to devices in some sense implicit in the plot itself as distinguished from devices, serving the same purpose, which involve Fielding's manner of representation; on the latter, see Section IV, below. A full solution of the problem would also have to take into account, as one of my friends reminds me, such things as the choice of names for the characters and the general nonserious expectations suggested by the title of the work.

they contribute, on the principle that we fear less or not at all when the agents of harm to a hero are more or less laughable persons, to induce in us a general feeling of confidence that matters are not really as serious as they appear.

A second ground of security lies in the nature of the probabilities for future action that are made evident progressively as the novel unfolds. From the beginning until the final capitulation of Sophia, the successive incidents constantly bring forth new and unexpected complications, each seemingly fraught with more suffering for Tom than the last; but as we read we instinctively infer from past occurrences to what will probably happen next or in the end, and what steadily cumulates in this way, in spite of the gradual worsening of Tom's situation, is an opinion that, since nothing irreparable has so far happened to him, nothing ever will. In one sense—that which relates to its material events— the action becomes more and more serious as it moves to its climax, in another sense—that which relates to our expectations—less and less serious; and I think that any close reader who keeps in mind the earlier parts of the novel as he attends to the later is inevitably made aware of this, with the result that, though his interest mounts, his fear increasingly declines. We come thus to the first climax in Book VI recalling such things as Jenny's assurance to Allworthy that she will someday make known the whole truth, the sudden reversal of the elder Blifil's sinister plans, the collapse, after initial success, of young Blifil's first scheme against Tom, and Tom's return to favor with Allworthy after the incident of Molly's arrest; and all these memories inevitably operate to check the rise of any long-range apprehensions. And it is the same, too, with the second and apparently much more serious climax at the end of Book XVI, when Tom, dismissed by Sophia, lies in prison awaiting the death of Fitzpatrick, who has been given up by his surgeon: we cannot but remember how, in the affairs of Molly and then of Mrs. Waters, Sophia has more than once demonstrated her inability to inflict any great or prolonged punishment on Tom for his sins with other women and how, on the occasion of Allworthy's illness in Book V, the outcome had completely disappointed the gloomy predictions of the doctor.

The attenuation, in these ways, of fear, pity, and indignation is a necessary condition of the peculiar comic pleasure which is the form of the plot in *Tom Jones*, but it is only a negative and hence not a sufficient condition. A comic effect of any kind would be impossible if we took Tom's increasingly bad prospects with the same seriousness as he himself takes them, but what in a positive sense makes Fielding's plot comic is the combination of this feeling of security with our perception of the decisive role which Tom's own blunders are made to play, consistently, in the genesis of all the major difficulties into which he is successively brought—always, of course, with the eager assistance of Fortune and of the malice or misunderstanding of others. The importance of this becomes clear when we consider how much trouble he would have spared himself had he not mistaken his seduction by Molly for a seduction of her by him; had he not got drunk when he learned of Allworthy's recovery or fought with Blifil and Thwackum; had he not suggested to Western that he be allowed to plead Blifil's case with Sophia; had he not allowed himself to be seduced by Jenny at Upton; had he not thought that his very love for Sophia, to say nothing of his gallantry, required him "to keep well" with the lady at the masquerade; and, lastly, had he not accepted so uncritically Nightingale's scheme for compelling her to break off the affair.

The truth is that each successive stage of the plot up to the beginning of the denouement in Book XVII is precipitated by a fresh act of imprudence or indiscretion on the part of Tom, for which he is sooner or later made to suffer not only in his fortune but his feelings, until in the resolution of each sequence, he discovers that the consequences of his folly are after all not so serious as he has feared. This characteristic pattern emerges, even before the start of the complication proper, in the episode of Tom's relations with Molly and Sophia in Book IV and the first part of Book V; it dominates the prolonged suspense of his relations with Allworthy from the time of the latter's illness to the final discovery; and it determines the course of his troubles with Sophia from Upton to the meeting in London and from the ill-conceived proposal scheme to her sudden surrender at the end.

The comic pleasure all this gives us is certainly not of the same kind as that produced by such classic comic plots as (say) Ben Jonson's *The Silent Woman* or, to take a more extreme instance of the type, his *Volpone*, in which a morally despicable person is made, by reason of his own folly or lapse from cleverness, to suffer a humiliating and, to him, though not to others, painful reversal of fortune. The comedy of Blifil is indeed of this simple punitive kind,[16] but our suspense concerning Blifil is only in a secondary way determinative of the effect of Fielding's novel, and the comedy of Tom and hence of the plot as a whole is of a different sort. It is not simple comedy but mixed, the peculiar power of which depends upon the fact that the mistaken acts of the hero which principally excite our amusement are the acts of a man for whom throughout the plot we entertain sympathetic feelings because of the general goodness of his character: we do not want, therefore, to see him suffer any permanent indignity or humiliation, and we never cease to wish good fortune for him. This favorable attitude, moreover, is not contradicted by anything in the acts themselves from which his trouble springs. We perceive that in successive situations, in-

16. I borrow this term from Elder Olson's "An Outline of Poetic Theory" (see above, p. 12).

volving threats to his fortune or peace of mind, he invariably does some imprudent or foolish thing, which cannot fail, the circumstances being what, in our superior knowledge, we see them to be, to result for him in painful embarrassment and regret; but we realize that his blunders arise from no permanent weakness of character but are merely the natural errors of judgment, easily corrigible in the future, of an inexperienced and too impulsively generous and gallant young man. We look forward to the probable consequences of his indiscretions, therefore, with a certain anticipatory reluctance and apprehension—a kind of faint alarm which is the comic analogue of fear; it is some such feeling, I think, that we experience, if only momentarily, when Tom gets drunk and goes into the wood with Molly and when, much later, he sends his proposal letter to Lady Bellaston. We know that trouble, more trouble than the young man either foresees or deserves, is in store for him as a result of what he has done, and since, foolish as he is, we favor him against his enemies, the expectation of his inevitable suffering cannot be purely and simply pleasant.

And yet the expectation is never really painful in any positive degree, and it is kept from becoming so by our counter-expectation, established by the devices I have mentioned, that, however acute may be Tom's consequent sufferings, his mistakes will not issue in any permanent frustration of our wishes for his good. In this security that no genuine harm has been done, we can view his present distresses—as when he anguishes over the wrong he thinks he has done to Molly, or finds Sophia's muff in his bed at Upton, or receives her letter—as the deserved consequences of erroneous actions for which any good man would naturally feel embarrassment or shame. We do not therefore pity him in these moments, for all his self-accusations and cries of despair, but rather laugh at him as a man who has behaved ridiculously or beneath himself and is now being properly punished. And our comic pleasure continues into the subsequent resolving scenes—the discovery of Molly in bed with Square, the meeting with Sophia in London, and the final anticlimax of her agreement to marry him the next morning—when it appears that Tom has after all worried himself overmuch; for we now see that he has been doubly ridiculous, at first in not taking his situation seriously enough and then in taking it more seriously than he should. But Tom is a good man, and we expect him to get better, and so our amused reaction to his sufferings lacks entirely the punitive quality that characterizes comedy of the Jonsonian type. If the anticipatory emotion is a mild shudder of apprehension, the climactic emotion—the comic analogue of pity—is a kind of friendly mirth at his expense ("poor Tom," we say to ourselves), which easily modulates, in the happy denouement, into unsentimental rejoicing at his not entirely deserved good fortune.

This, however, is not quite all; for not only does Tom's final good fortune seem to us at least partly undeserved in terms of his own behavior, but we realize, when we look back from the end upon the long course of the action, that he has, in truth, needed all the luck that has been his. Again and again he has been on the verge of genuinely serious disaster; and, though we expect him to survive and hence do not fear for him in prospect, we perceive, at the resolution of each of his major predicaments, that there has been something of a hair's breadth quality in his escape. The cards have indeed been stacked against him; from the beginning to the ultimate discovery, he has been a young man whose lack of security and imprudence more than offset his natural goodness, living in a world in which the majority of people are ill-natured and selfish, and some of them actively malicious, and in which the few good persons are easily imposed upon by appearances. It is against this background of the potentially serious—more than ever prominent in the London scenes—that the story of Tom's repeated indiscretions is made to unfold, with the result that, though the pleasure remains consistently comic, its quality is never quite that of the merely amiable comedy, based likewise upon the blunders of sympathetic protagonists, of such works as *She Stoops To Conquer* or *The Rivals*. We are not disposed to feel, when we are done laughing at Tom, that all is right with the world or that we can count on Fortune always intervening, in the same gratifying way, on behalf of the good.

IV

This or something very close to this, I think, is the intended "working or power" of *Tom Jones*, and the primary question for the critic concerns the extent to which Fielding's handling of the constituent parts of the novel is calculated to sustain and maximize this special pleasure which is its form.

It must be said that he sometimes fails. There are no perfect works of art, and, though many of the faults that have been found in *Tom Jones* are faults only on the supposition that it should have been another kind of novel, still enough real shortcomings remain to keep one's enthusiasm for Fielding's achievement within reasonable bounds. There are not infrequent *longueurs*, notably in the Man of the Hill's story (whatever positive values this may have), in Mrs. Fitzpatrick's narrative to Sophia (useful as this is in itself), in the episode of Tom's encounter with the gypsies, and in the final complications of the Nightingale affair. With the best will in the world, too, it is impossible not to be shocked by Tom's acceptance of fifty pounds from Lady Bellaston on the night of his first meeting with her at the masquerade and his subsequent emergence as "one of the best-dressed men about town"; it is necessary, no doubt, that he should now fall lower than ever before, but surely not so low as to make it hard for us to infer his act from our previous knowledge of his character and of the rather modest limits hitherto of his financial need; for the moment at least, a different Tom is before our eyes. And there are also more general faults. The narrator, for one thing, though it is well that he should intrude, perhaps intrudes too much in a purely ornamental way; the introductory essays, thus, while we should not like to lose them from the canon of Fielding's writings, serve only occasionally the function of chorus, and the returns from them, even as embellishment, begin to diminish before the end. What chiefly strikes the modern reader, however, is the extent of Fielding's reliance, in the novel as a whole, on techniques of narrative now largely abandoned by novelists who have learned their art since the middle of the nineteenth century. It could be shown, I think, that as compared with most of his predecessors, the author of *Tom Jones* had moved a long way in the direction of the imitative and dramatic. Yet it cannot be denied that in many chapters where he might better have "rendered" he merely "states" and that even in the most successful of the scenes in which action and dialogue predominate he leaves far less to inference than we are disposed to like.[17]

Despite all this, however, there are not many novels of comparable length in which the various parts are conceived and developed with a shrewder eye to what is required for a maximum realization of the form.[18] A few examples of this will have to serve, and it is natural to start with the manner in which Fielding handles the incidents that follow directly from Tom's mistakes. The pattern of all of these is much the same. Tom first commits an indiscretion, which is then discovered, and the discovery results in his immediate or eventual embarrassment. Now it is clear that the comic pleasure will be enhanced in proportion as, in each incident, the discovery is made unexpectedly and by precisely those persons whose knowledge of what Tom has done will be most damaging to him, and by as many of these as possible so that the consequences for him are not simple but compounded. Fielding understood this well, and the effects of his understanding are repeatedly evident in *Tom Jones*, from Book IV to the end of the complication. Consider, for example, how he manages the discovery of Tom's original entanglement with Molly. It is necessary, of course, when Molly is arrested after the fight in the churchyard, that Tom should at once rush to Allworthy with his mistaken confession; but it is not necessary—only highly desirable—that he should intervene in the fight himself as Molly's champion, that Blifil and Square should be with him at the time, that the news of the arrest should reach him while he is dining with Western and Sophia, whose charm he is just beginning to perceive, and that, when he leaves in a

17. Perhaps the chief exception to this, in its relatively large use of "intimation," is the scene of Tom's conversation with Dowling in Book XII, chap. x.

18. I am indebted for several points in what follows to an unpublished essay by one of my students, Mr. Melvin Seiden.

hurry, the Squire should joke with his daughter about what he suspects. Or, again, there is the even more complicated and comically disastrous sequence that begins with Tom's drunkenness after Allworthy's recovery. This in itself is ridiculous, since we know the illness has never been serious; but observe how the succeeding embarrassments are made to pile up: Tom's hilarious joy leading to his fight with Blifil; this to his retirement to the grove, his romantic meditation on Sophia, and his surrender to Molly; this to the discovery of his new folly by Blifil and Thwackum; this to the second fight, much bloodier than the first; and this in turn, when the Westerns unexpectedly appear on the scene, to Sophia's fresh discovery of Tom's wildness and, what is much more serious, to the misconstruction of her fainting fit by her aunt, with results that lead presently to the proposal of a match with Blifil, the foolish intervention of Tom, the discovery by Western of the true state of affairs, his angry appeal to Allworthy, Blifil's distorted version of what has happened, Tom's expulsion from home, and Sophia's imprisonment. All this is probable enough, but there is something of the comically wonderful in the educing of so many appropriately extreme consequences from a cause in itself so apparently innocent and trivial. And the same art of making the most out of incidents for the sake of the comic suspense of the plot can be seen at work through the rest of the novel: in the great episode at Upton, for example, where all the happenings are contrived to produce, immediately or remotely, a maximum of pseudo-serious suffering for Tom, and also in the various later scenes in which the discovery to Sophia of Tom's intrigue with her cousin is first narrowly averted, with much embarrassment to him, and then finally made under circumstances that could hardly be worse for the young man. A less accomplished artist seeking to achieve the same general effect through his plot would certainly have missed many of these opportunities.

A less accomplished artist, again, would never have been able to invent or sustain characters so good for the form, as well as so interesting in themselves, as the two Westerns and Partridge. We need not dwell on the multiple uses to which these great humorists are put; it is more important, since the point has been less often discussed, or discussed in part to Fielding's disadvantage, to consider what merits can be found in his handling of the other characters, such as Tom himself, Allworthy, Sophia, and Blifil, who are intended to seem morally sympathetic or antipathetic to us and comically inferior only by virtue of their erroneous acts. With the exception of Sophia, who is made charming and lively enough to constitute in herself good fortune for Tom, they are not endowed with any notably particularized traits, and the question for criticism is whether, given the comic form of the novel as a whole, any more lifelike "doing" would not have entailed a departure from the mean which this imposed. I think the answer is clear for Blifil: he must be made to seem sufficiently formidable in the short run to arouse comic apprehension for Tom but not so formidable as to excite in us active or prolonged feelings of indignation; and any further individualizing of him than we get would almost certainly have upset this balance to the detriment of the whole. The answer is clear also, I think, for Tom. We must consistently favor him against his enemies and think it probable that he should suffer acute embarrassment and remorse when he discovers the consequences of his mistakes; but, on the other hand, any appreciably greater particularizing of his sympathetic traits than is attempted would inevitably have made it difficult for us not to feel his predicaments as seriously as he does himself, and that would have been an error; it is not the least happy of Fielding's inventions, for example, that he repeatedly depicts Tom, especially when he is talking to Sophia or thinking about her, in terms of the clichés of heroic romance. There remains Allworthy, and concerning him the chief doubt arises from a consideration of the important part he is given, along with Sophia, in the definition of Tom's final good fortune. For the purposes of the comic complication it is sufficient that we should see him acting in the character of a severely just magistrate who constantly administers injustice through too great trust in his knowledge of men; it is not for this, however, but for his "amiability" that Tom loves him and cherishes his company in the end; yet of Allworthy's actual possession of that quality we are given few clear signs.

A whole essay, finally, could be written on the masterly way in which Fielding exploited the various devices implicit in his third-person "historical" mode of narration in the service of his comic form. Broadly speaking, his problem was twofold: first, to establish and maintain in the reader a general frame of mind appropriate to the emotional quality of the story as a whole and, second, to make sure that the feelings aroused by his characters at particular moments or stages of the action were kept in proper alignment with the intended over-all effect.

That the first problem is adequately solved there can be little doubt; long before we come to the incidents in which Tom's happiness is put in jeopardy by his own blunders and the malice of Blifil, we have been prepared to expect much unmerited calamity and distress for him, and at the same time to view the prospect without alarm. Our security would doubtless have been less had not Fielding chosen to represent at length the events contained in Books I and II, with the vivid impressions they give of the fallibility of Allworthy on the one hand and of the impotence for permanent harm of the elder Blifil on the other: we cannot but look forward to a repetition of this pattern in the later parts of the novel. This is less important, however, as a determinant of our frame of mind than the guidance given us by the clearly evident attitude of

Fielding's narrator. He is, we perceive, a man we can trust, who knows the whole story and still is not deeply concerned; one who understands the difference between good men and bad and who can yet speak with amused indulgence of the first, knowing how prone they are to weakness of intellect, and with urbane scorn, rather than indignation, of the second, knowing that most of them, too, are fools. This combination of sympathetic moral feeling with ironical detachment is bound to influence our expectations from the first, and to the extent that it does so, we tend to anticipate the coming troubles with no more than comic fear.

It is when the troubles come, in Book V and later, that Fielding's second problem emerges; for, given the kinds of things that then happen to Tom and especially the seriousness with which, as a good man, he necessarily takes them, there is always a danger that our original comic detachment may give way, temporarily, to tragicomic feelings of fear, pity, and indignation. That this seldom happens is another sign of how successfully, in *Tom Jones*, the handling of the parts is kept consonant with the formal demands of the whole. It is a question primarily of maximizing the general comic expectations of the reader by minimizing the possible noncomic elements in his inferences about particular situations; and the devices which Fielding uses for the purpose are of several kinds. Sometimes the result is achieved by preventing our attention from concentrating long or closely on potential causes of distress for Tom; it is notable, for example, that we are given no representation of Blifil scheming Tom's ruin before his speech to Allworthy in Book VI, chapter xi, and that from this point until Book XVI Blifil and his intentions are not again brought to the fore. Sometimes the device consists in slurring over a painful scene by generalized narration and then quickly diverting us to an obviously comic sequence in another line of action: this is what Fielding does, to excellent effect, with the incident of Tom's condemnation and banishment; we should feel much more keenly for him if, in the first place, we were allowed to hear more of his talk with Allworthy and, in the second place, were not plunged so soon after into the ridiculous quarrels of the Westerns. Or, again, the expedient may take the simple form of a refusal by the narrator to describe feelings of Tom which, if they were represented directly and at length, might easily excite a non-comic response; as in the accounts of his "madness" at Upton after he finds Sophia's muff and of the torments he endures ("such that even Thwackum would almost have pitied him") when her message of dismissal comes to him in prison. And the same general minimizing function is also served by the two episodes in the middle part of the novel which have occasioned so much discussion among critics. Both the story told to Tom by the Man of the Hill and that recounted to Sophia by Mrs. Fitzpatrick, however much they owe to the convention of interpolated narratives which Fielding had inherited, along with other devices, from the earlier writers of "comic romance," are clearly designed as negative analogies to the moral state of the listeners, from which the reader is led to infer, on the eve of the most distressing part of the complication for the hero and heroine, that nothing that may happen to them will be, in comparison, very bad.

The controlling influence of the form can be seen in all these expedients, and it is no less apparent in Fielding's handling of the intrigue upon which the action of the novel ultimately depends—Bridget's affair with Summer, her scheme of temporary concealment and eventual disclosure of Tom's parentage, and the frustration of the second of these intentions, until the denouement, by Blifil. Without this series of events and the consequences they entail in the opinions and acts of the characters, the plot as we have it could not have existed; but there was nothing in the nature of the events themselves to prescribe the particular manner in which they must be brought before the reader. At least two alternative modes of procedure were open to Fielding besides the one he actually chose. He could, on the one hand, have let the reader into the secret, either from the beginning or at the point in Book V where Bridget's dying message is brought by Dowling: in the former case a brief statement by the narrator would have been sufficient (since he plainly knows the facts); in the latter case, a brief report, for which there are precedents elsewhere in the novel, of Blifil's thoughts. Or, on the other hand, he could have contrived to keep our curiosity regarding the mystery more continuously and actively awake, especially in the long stretches of the story between Book III and the final scenes in London: this need not again have required any invention of new incidents, but only manipulations of the narrative discourse, such as an explicit direction of the reader's mind to the circumstance that Dowling brought a letter from Bridget as well as the news of her death, a hint that Blifil now had some new and surprising information about Tom, and an occasional reminder thereafter that the full truth concerning Tom's birth was still to be learned and that it might, when known, have important bearings, for good or possibly for ill, upon his fortunes.

Given, however, the form which Fielding, according to our hypothesis, was attempting to impose on the materials of his plot, with its distinctive line of seriocomic expectations and desires, either of these two courses would clearly have been incorrect. The second would have injected into the middle sections of the narrative a competing principle of suspense, diverting our attention unduly from the question of what is likely to befall Tom as a result of his mistakes to the question of who he is; the novel would then have become in fact the mystery story which, on a partial and erroneous view, it has sometimes been taken to be. And the consequences of the other course would have been equally, perhaps more, disruptive. For the complication in that case would have become, in large part, the story of a completely foreseen and wished-for discovery repeatedly deferred, with the result, on the one hand, that our complacency about the eventual outcome would have been increased to such a degree as sensibly to lessen our comic fear and hence our comic mirth in the successive anticlimactic reversals and, on the other hand, that our preoccupation with the comic aspects of Tom's well-intentioned blunderings would have tended to give way excessively to a concern with the original injustice done him by Bridget and with the villainy of Blifil. A mean between emphasis on the existence of a mystery and full revelation of the secret to the reader was therefore indicated as the right technique, and it was his perception of this that guided Fielding's procedure both in Books I and II, where the question of Tom's parentage is formally inquired into by Allworthy and settled to his own satisfaction, and in Books V–XVII, where the question is reopened, in intent but not in result, first by the confession of Bridget and then by the advances of Dowling to Tom. Something close to the proper mean is achieved by concentrating the narrative in the opening books on the objective acts and declarations of Bridget, Jenny, and Partridge subsequent to the finding of Tom in Allworthy's bed and representing these by signs sufficiently ambiguous so that, although we discount the inferences drawn by Allworthy from the behavior of the two supposed parents, we are yet given no adequate premises from which to reason to any particular alternative explanation. We surmise that one will ultimately be forthcoming, but in the meantime we are easily persuaded by the narrator to suspend our curiosity, especially since we perceive that neither of Allworthy's discoveries will make any difference in his treatment of Tom. We are predisposed therefore to yield our attention to the events recounted in the middle books of the novel without active speculation concerning their remoter causes or growing impatience for further disclosures. Ambiguous disclosures do indeed continue to be made. There is the pervasive irony (in the world of this novel) of a young man assumed by nearly everyone in his circle, including himself, to be base-born who yet manifests all the signs, in appearance and sensibility, of being a gentleman and is regularly taken as one by strangers until they learn his story; and there are also the more specific clues to the real state of affairs afforded by Bridget's increasing preference for Tom as he grows up, the suddenly intensified animosity of Blifil toward the foundling after he learns the content of Bridget's message, Partridge's disavowal of the role in which he has been cast as Tom's father, and, most pointed of all, Dowling's sly reference to "your uncle" in the interview which he forces on Tom in Book XII. But though hints of the truth are thus given in the events themselves, it is only in retrospect, at the moment of the discovery scene in Book XVIII, that we grasp their cumulative import; so effectively, in the narrator's discourse up to the very eve of this scene, has the question of who Tom is been kept subordinate to the question, upon which the main comic effect depends, of what will immediately follow from his imprudent acts.

V

These are only a few of the things that can be said, in the light of our general hypothesis about plot, concerning the plot of *Tom Jones* and the relation to it of the other parts of the novel. I have given no consideration, thus, either to the functions served by the minor characters and by the many passages of extra-dramatic thought in defining the moral quality of the "world" in which the action takes place, or to the formal purposes governing Fielding's highly selective use of dialogue, or to the manner in which the diction and imagery of the narrative parts help to hold our responses to the right comic line even when the incidents themselves seem most serious.

An adequate study of the plot of *Tom Jones* considered as a first principle of artistic construction would require answers to these and possibly still other questions, all of them of a kind which the traditional ways of discussing works with "plots" have tended to leave out of account. My intention, however, has been not so much to attempt a revaluation of *Tom Jones* as to make clear the assumptions and illustrate some of the possibilities for practical criticism of a kind of whole-part analysis of narrative compositions such as has not too often, I think, been undertaken. Like all critical methods it has its limitations, and it must be judged, accordingly, in terms not only of the problems it is peculiarly fitted to deal with but of those which lie beyond its scope. Its distinctive character derives, in the first place, from the fact that it views a work of art as a dynamic whole which affects our emotions in a certain way through the functioning together of its elements in subordination to a determinate poetic form. It is better suited, therefore, to exhibit the degree of efficiency with which the parts of a work or section thereof contribute to the maximum achievement of its effect than to do full justice to the qualities over and above this which characterize, in all fine works, the development of the parts themselves: there are many strokes in the representation of Partridge, for instance, which no one would wish away, yet which are bound to seem gratuitous when considered merely in the light of his somewhat minor role in the evolution of the comic action.[19] The method, again, is specific, in the sense that it seeks to appraise

19. The kind of thing I have in mind is well illustrated by the late George Orwell's remarks on the "unnecessary detail" in Dickens (see his *Dickens, Dali & Others* [New York, 1946], pp. 59–65). Of the same order is the following sentence from the account of the fight with the captain in *Joseph Andrews*, Book III, chap. xi (italics mine): "The uplifted hanger

a writer's performance in a given work in relation to the nature and requirements of the particular task he has set himself, the assumed end being the perfection of the work as an artistic whole of the special kind he decided it should be. It is a method better adapted, consequently, to the appreciation of success or failure in individual works than it is to the making of comparative judgments based on criteria of literary "greatness" or "seriousness" that transcend differences of kind: we clearly need other terms and distinctions than those provided by a poetics of forms if we are to talk discriminatingly about the general qualities of intelligence and feeling reflected in *Tom Jones* or even be able to defend Fielding against the recent, and surely somewhat insensitive, judgment that his "attitudes and his concern with human nature, are simple, and not such as to produce an effect of anything but monotony (on a mind, that is, demanding more than external action) when exhibited at the length of an 'epic in prose.' "[20] Finally, the method is one which depends on the analytical isolation of works of art, as finished products, from the circumstances and processes of their origin. It is therefore better fitted to explain those effects in a work which would be specifically the same in any other work, of whatever date, that was constructed in accordance with the same combination of artistic principles, than those effects which must be attributed to the fact that the work was produced by a given artist, in a given period, at a given stage in the evolution of the species or tradition to which it belongs: we have obviously to go beyond formal criticism if we would assess Fielding's originality as a writer of "comic romance" or account for that peculiarly eighteenth-century flavor in *Tom Jones* which causes us to reflect that, unique and unrepresentative as Fielding's novel is when considered as a whole, it could yet have been written at no other time.

The criticism of forms needs thus to be supplemented by the criticism of qualities, in both of the senses just indicated, and also by historical inquiries of various sorts. This granted, however, two things can be said, the first of which is that, although the criticism of forms is only one among a number of valid and useful critical methods, it is still the sole method capable of dealing adequately—i.e., with a minimum of unanalyzed terms—and at the same time literally—i.e., in terms of causes and effects rather than analogies—with those characteristics and values in any literary work which derive from its construction as a self-contained whole endowed with a power of affecting us in a par-

---

dropped from his hand, and he fell prostrated on the floor with a lumpish noise, *and his half-pence rattled in his pocket. . . .*" It is difficult to conceive of any functional analysis, however refined its principles, that would afford premises for the discussion of such traits; and yet their presence or absence is obviously an important factor in our discrimination between distinguished and undistinguished writing.

20. F. R. Leavis, *The Great Tradition* (New York, [1949]), p. 4.

ticular way by virtue of the manner in which its internal parts are conceived and fitted together. It is a method, therefore, which ought to have a strong appeal to the many students of literature in our time who wish to consider their subject, in a now famous phrase, "as literature and not another thing," but who are temperamentally averse to analogical procedures and intellectually dissatisfied with those modern critical systems which, however literal, provide no analysis of any except one or two of the internal causes of literary effects. And the second point is perhaps equally clear: namely, that although the criticism of qualities and the investigation of historical origins and significances may achieve important results independently of the criticism of forms, as the past history of practical criticism and literary scholarship shows, both of these modes of judging literary productions would gain considerably in rigor and scope if they were founded on, and hence controlled by, a prior analysis of works from the point of view of their peculiar principles of construction and the special artistic problems which these presented to their writers. We should then, perhaps, have less qualitative criticism of the dogmatic sort which reproaches writers of poems, dramas, and novels perfect enough in their respective kinds for not exhibiting virtues of language or thought incompatible with the specific tasks these writers chose to undertake, and likewise fewer literary histories in which the achievements of authors are discussed exclusively in terms of materials and techniques without reference to the formal ends that helped to determine how these were used.

EPISODE, SCENE, SPEECH, AND WORD: THE MADNESS OF LEAR

NORMAN MACLEAN

I

IT WOULD, of course, be an exaggeration to say that the history of the story of King Lear is a history of art. Far back of Geoffrey of Monmouth's *Historia regum Britanniae*, in which Lear's story makes its first appearance in literature, is a folk tale of a daughter who angers her father by telling him that she loves him as much as salt,[1] but this story already has shape, although the shape of art in embryo. It is a narrative riddle, depending upon the double meaning of a word, and when the real meaning is recognized by the father, through some device such as serving him a feast without salt, both the anger of the father and the story dissolve. That the story appears in many variants indicates the universality of its appeal, but the emotions it aroused must have been limited largely to common curiosity in verbal puzzles and the pleasure, not confined to children, of discovering that children are more subtle than their parents. A narrative riddle, then, such as might be added to the collections of the Grimm brothers is the prototype of the story that Shakespeare transformed into a tragedy. That the history of the Lear story concludes in a consummation of art is testified to by another kind of history—the history of men's literary affections: tragedy, on the whole, has proved to be the most moving of literary forms, and to most critics *King Lear*, although not the most flawless, is the most tragic of Shakespeare's tragedies.

The problem of artistic consummation, being the problem of magnitude in the highest degree, is imperiled by its own scope, but fortunately there is a part of *King Lear* that by assent is its most tragic region, the region where suffering takes on such dimension that even Shakespeare could find no better word than "madness" to contain it. Furthermore, since the madness of Lear is almost entirely Shakespeare's invention[2] and is crucial in the transformation of the many

---

1. Wilfrid Perrett, *The Story of King Lear from Geoffrey of Monmouth to Shakespeare* (Berlin, 1904), pp. 9 ff.

2. "Lear's madness has no place in the old story; it is Shakespeare's own invention" (George Lyman Kittredge, *The Complete Works of Shakespeare* [Boston, 1936], p. 1196). According to Perrett, certain versions of the story contain suggestions of madness (*op. cit.*, pp. 225–26), but these suggestions, as Perrett says, are remote and are limited to phrases (such as "crazed thoughts") and, moreover, they are probably stereotypes not intended to suggest actual madness, just as we speak only in figurative cliché when we say, "He was mad with rage."

stories of King Lear into the only *Tragedie of King Lear*, it brings us face to face with both the tragic art and the tragic artist. Now, to speak of a consummate poetic accomplishment is to imply that the kind of criticism which views all a writer's problems as unique has overlooked a part of the whole of truth. For, to speak of an artistic attainment as possessing magnitude in the highest degree is to imply the existence of attainments somewhat analogous and in this and that common respect somewhat inferior; it implies either this or the existence of a critic who has some a priori conception of a poem more wonderful than any yet written, in which case the critic should change to a more wonderful profession and contribute its culminating splendor. For us at least, it is certainly easier and wiser to say that every writer in each particular act of composing faces problems that have various levels of universality, and, if this were not so, we could not recognize any uniqueness in his achievement; the chances are we could not even recognize what he had written. In only certain senses, then, does Shakespeare forever elude us and refuse to "abide our question," for, if there are general problems confronting every writer, we should be able to ask questions that Shakespeare of all men made no attempt to elude.

At a high level of universality, to write anything well, whether it be intellectual or imaginative, is to assume at least two obligations: to be *intelligible* and to be *interesting*. Intelligibility, too, has its levels of obligation, on the lowest of individual statements, and even on this level the obligation is never easy to fulfil and perhaps even to genius could be a nightmare if what the genius sought to represent was "madness." Only to a limited degree, however, can individual statements be intelligible—and in many instances and for a variety of reasons the individual statements are meant to be obscure, as in "mad" speeches. Since full intelligibility depends upon the relations of individual statement to individual statement, the concept of intelligibility, fully expanded, includes *order* and *completeness;* for a fully intelligible exposition or poem having relations has parts, and all the parts ought to be there and add up to a whole. The second major obligation, that of being "interesting," includes *unexpectedness* and *suspense,* for expository as well as imaginative writing should not be merely what the reader expected it would be—or why should it be written or read?—and the unexpected should not be immediately and totally announced (in other words, expository and imaginative writing should have suspense), for, if the whole is immediately known, why should the writer or reader proceed farther?

But the accomplished writer gives his selected material more than shape—he gives it proper *size*. For a piece of writing to have its proper size is an excellent thing, or otherwise it would be lacking in intelligibility or interest or both. Thus, if Lear's anger had been transformed into madness in a single scene, all the odds are that such a transformation would seem beyond belief, and it is just as certain that the play would have died in the memory of men for want of suspense. On the other hand, the madness of Lear could have been drawn at such length that the spectator, like Kent, could not continue to view the suffering or, worse still, until the spectator began to suspect an author was manipulating suffering for suspense—and in either case the spectator would feel that he had seen too much. Moreover, the size of any literary particle ·is not a matter of quantity only. Every art has ways of making a thing seem bigger or smaller than the space it occupies, as Cordelia is more wonderful by far than the number of lines she utters and is even tragically present when she is tragically absent, and as Lear becomes more gigantic when he can utter only a few lines or broken lines or none at all.

We have come close to the special realm of imaginative or poetic writing, with its special obligations, two of which we shall refer to as *vividness* and *probability*. As poetic writing is the representing or "making" of human experience, so the poet is the writer who possesses the powers and devices that transfer "life" from flesh to words. These possessions of a poet are not merely a knowledge of "life"; Machiavelli knew much about successful and unsuccessful rulers and wrote *The Prince*, and analysts know much about madness and come no closer to *King Lear* than case reports. Shakespeare "made" many rulers, successful and otherwise, and one he "made" mad. In so far, then, as a poem possesses "life," it has *vividness*. A poem, however, makes not "life" only but a "world." Hence any of its parts, when related to the others, must seem *probable*. Not any living being may enter *Lear*, and the few who may are severely limited in freedom of thought, speech, and action. What may happen in a poem must be compatible with the general conditions of "existence" as postulated by the poem; and what actually does happen and the order in which it happens must appear as adequately caused by the constitution of the individual characters and by the circumstances in which they are placed. The same legendary figure may enter two worlds and in the early Elizabethan play may spell his name "Leir" and survive his misfortunes, but, having ventured upon the thick rotundity of Shakespeare's world, he cannot be saved, and certainly not by the alteration of any neoclassical poet.

In certain ultimate senses the world that is each poem is bound together so that it binds the hearts of those who look upon it, of whom the poet is one. To look upon a poem, then, as distinct from looking upon much of the succession of life, is to be moved, and moved by emotions that, on the whole, attract us to it and are psychologically compatible. All of us, therefore, seem to be asking for less than we expect when we ask that poems have *emotional unity;* but this is so commonly the language of the request that we shall assume it means what we expect it does—that the emotions aroused by any good poem should be psychologically compatible and also of a kind out of which attachments are formed. We may ask for many other things from poems—biographical information, or political or theological wisdom—but, in making any of these further requests, we should recognize that we are asking for what only certain good poems give, and then generally not so well as something else. What is here taken as ultimate in poetry is what is true of all good poems : they give a high order of distinctive pleasures, and it may be said summarily of high and distinctive pleasures that no man seems in danger of exceeding his allotment.

In a way a poet is untroubled about all this—about writing or writing poetry, for these are abstractions that cannot be engaged in, and he is trying to find the first or next word, and after "thick rotundity" he listens to "of"and is troubled, and then hears "o' " and so moves on to other troubles, leaving behind him "the thick rotundity o' th' world." In a way, then, even in a long life a poet never writes poetry—just a few poems; and in this sense a poet's problems do not begin until he closes in upon a piece of paper with something less abstract in mind than writing or writing poetry. He may wish, as many lyric poets have wished, to write a drama or a novel, but the story is so distinct from the lyric that few poets, despite a tendency of poets to be expansive in their ambitions, have been eminent in both poetic arts. Shelley and Keats had a maximum of aspiration but hardly a minimum of gift for plot and character, and even Browning, with his surpassing delineation of men and women in dramatic monologue, could not make anything happen in a drama. Coming closer to the paper on which *King Lear* was written, we also know that to have the characters tell their own story on a stage raises problems very distinct from those required for putting the story between the covers of a novel. It may seem that the distinction between manners of presenting a story is largely classificatory; yet stories are so locked artistically to those selected to tell them that great novels seldom remain great when they are strutted upon the stage, and vice versa. Particular manners of presentation are particular artistic problems, and particular artistic gifts are needed to solve these problems, and, if not, who are those who are both great novelists and great dramatists? And, more particular still, who among dramatists wrote both great comedies and great tragedies, although tragedy is only drama that moves certain emotions in us? Yet these two dramatic arts are so distinctive that Shakespeare is the single answer to the question of what dramatist eminently possessed both the tragic power and the power of moving to laughter. Even more specialized, personal, and unique are the problems to be focused on in this study—what confronted Shakespeare and Lear, who stood outside when a storm arose and a daughter ordered a door shut. Mind you, before this particular moment Lear had been a successful king and Shakespeare had written great tragedies, but neither had ventured far into madness.

This was a lonely moment in art; yet the moment that is the poet's moment is not his alone, and his problems that seem highly unique would not even occur if he were not concerned, however secretly and for whatever reasons, in loading each particular vein with what can generally be recognized as ore. It is true that he would have no poetic problems at all if each particular moment of art did not have to enter the general world of art, for unattended self-expression is another occupation, altogether lonely.

We propose to follow Lear and Shakespeare across the heath to the fields of Dover on what for both was a unique experience, and then to be even more particular, considering the individual scenes leading to this meeting of Lear and Gloucester when in opposite senses neither could see. And, for smaller particulars, we shall consider an incident from one of these scenes, a speech from this incident, and, finally, a single word. In this declension of particulars, our problems will be some of those that were Shakespeare's because he was attending Lear and at the same time was on his way toward a consummation in the art of tragic writing.

II

At the end of Act II night has come, an external storm threatens, and an external door is shut; in Act IV, scene 6, Lear, "fantastically dressed with weeds," meets Gloucester and Edgar upon the tranquil fields of Dover, the tempest now a tempest of the mind and at its worst. To view this large expanse of suffering as a single dramatic unit is also to see that, in the form of organic life called a poem, "parts" are "parts" and in certain senses "wholes." By the end of Act II the major external causes of Lear's madness have occurred; by Act IV, scene 6, they have brought Lear to "the sulphurous pit" and unrestrained madness, from which, even in the next scene, he is somewhat "restored." For a variety of reasons we shall state the unity of this dramatic episode in terms of a change that it brings about in Lear's thoughts and beliefs concerning man, the universe, and the gods, a change in thought that is both a cause and a projection of his madness.

Prior to this episode (and presumably always before it), Lear believed in a universe controlled by divine authority, harmoniously ordered and subordinated in its parts, a harmony reflected in the affairs of men by the presence of political and legal institutions, and social and family bonds. Men were the most divinely empowered of divine creations, and the special power of kings was a sign of their special divinity. At the end of this episode (Act IV, scene 6), the world that Lear tells Gloucester he should be able to see even without eyes is one in which man is leveled to a beast and then raised to the most fearful of his kind: the source of man's power, as with the beast's, is sex and self, but above the girdle which the gods inherit is the special gift of reason; only it is a kind of sadistic ingenuity by which man sanctifies his own sins—the universally inevitable sins of sex and self—by declaring them anathema for others ("Thou rascal beadle, hold thy bloody hand! / Why dost thou lash that whore? Strip thine own back"). Therefore, as king, Lear dismisses the phantom of the adulterer arraigned before him, because, all offending, "none does offend, none—I say none!"

The moment we imagine Shakespeare's pen in our hand and Act III unwritten, we begin to sense the immensity of the problem that arises merely from the first general requirement of all good writing, intelligibility. For the problem is to make clear that the mind of Lear progressively loses its clarity and comes at last to a moment everyone will recognize as "the worst" and be willing to take as "madness." Analogically, what is needed are recognizable circles of the inferno descending to the pit and ways of knowing when the pit has been reached. To present a character becoming more and more disintegrated emotionally, therefore, is fundamental but not enough, since emotions under pressure lack outline and precision, with the result that the best of lyric poets know their task is to find "objective correlatives" for what otherwise would remain in prison or confusion. In the next section, dealing with the scenes leading to Lear's madness, we shall see how Shakespeare uses actions, which are more discernible than emotions, to mark the descent into the pit; here we are concerned with the fact that Shakespeare added "thought" to action and emotion, and "thought" in many ways is more precise than either of the other two. In solving this problem of intelligibility, then, Shakespeare was "abundant," utilizing the maximum of means, and one way we have of knowing at what circle Lear is stationed for the moment is to learn what Lear for the moment believes is the nature of men, beasts, and gods.

When intelligibility was first discussed, it was expanded to include the concepts of "order" and "completeness." Order, being a matter involving all the parts, is a matter for later consideration, but we may already observe that the change in Lear's thought during this large episode is a complete change. Lear does not have merely different thoughts about the nature of the universe and of those who crawl upon it; the beliefs he has about the universe at the end of Act II are philosophically opposite to those he expresses upon the fields of Dover, and a complete change is one that goes as far as it can. Thus, because the change in Lear's thought is so bitterly complete, we recognize the pit when Lear has reached it. Shakespeare also took care that we should know where Lear started. Lear's last speech in Act II is the first one he gives in which thought of a general nature is directly expressed; it is appropriate to his character and the accumulated situation that at this moment he should say man is not man without some gorgeous possessions not needed to keep his body warm, and the speech is also a location point before the heath by means of which we can more easily see what a falling-off there was.

Ultimately, however, it is only of secondary importance that Lear's thoughts clarify our understanding; they lack the power of poetry if they are not moving. Let us begin less intensely, and therefore with the second requirement of all good writing, to be interesting, for, if we are not interested, we surely will not go farther and be moved. Until his last speech in Act II, Lear's thoughts have all been particular and have been concentrated upon the individual natures of his daughters and their husbands. This is appropriate to the circumstances and Lear's character, which is driven rather than given to philosophical speculation; yet, partly as a result, Lear is a character, even by the end of Act II, with whom we have only slight bonds of identification; he is an old man over eighty years, who, so late as this, is in the process of discovering that two of his daughters are nonhuman and that the one who could say "nothing" was alone worthy of all his love. In contrast to *Hamlet* and *Othello*, *King Lear* is a tragedy in the course of which the protagonist becomes worthy of being a tragic hero, and one dimension that Lear takes on is the power of thought. Moreover, his thoughts upon the heath and upon the fields of Dover are of universal significance and therefore "interest" us, for the question of whether the universe is something like what Lear hoped it was or very close to what he feared it was, is still, tragically, the current question.

Earlier we said that material of general, human interest could be handled by an artist in such a way as to take on an added interest—the interest of the unexpected or surprising. It is surprising in life or in literature for a serious man to reverse his philosophical beliefs about the common human problems, but Lear's change in thought is dramatically as well as philosophically unexpected, for the beliefs that have become the protagonist's by Act IV, scene 6, are his antagonists'—Goneril's, Regan's, and Edmund's—who also hold that sex and self are the sole laws of life. Lear has indeed "veered around to the opposite"; it is as if the tortured came to have the same opinion of the rack as the inquisitors.

There is, finally, the contribution that this change makes to the special emotional effects produced by tragedy. Now the tragic writer is also upon the rack, pulled always two different ways, for the deep emotions he stirs he also alleviates. A certain alleviation of fear and pity is necessary to make the emotional effect of tragedy one that we are consumed rather than repelled by; and proper tragic alleviation excludes any supposed consolation that might come from the avoidance of disastrous consequences after we have been asked to suffer emotions such as are aroused by clear premonition of disaster.

By the time that we and Edgar are confronted with the "side-piercing sight" upon the field of Dover, the grounds are many for fearing that Lear and all that is admirable are condemned by some hopelessly formidable perversity of power ultimately beyond challenge. Othello's fate was his own—at least many of us could have escaped it; but Lear's tragedy comes to a point where it threatens what we should wish to be with inevitable inclusion. As a very minimum, we know suffering such as the sufferer can account for only by believing the worst that can be thought of everything, including himself. The minimum, therefore, has some kind of maximum of fear and pity—we are almost certain that such suffering will leave him without the power to better his fortune and without the mental resources needed to gain a clear picture of what is the truth, if this is not it. And, indeed, in the end Lear is deprived of Othello's modicum of consolation—that of seeing the situation as it was—for he is not even permitted to believe that he and Cordelia can be God's spies (pitiful, imprisoned spectators of a conspiratorial universe), since in the same scene the role of a nonparticipant in the universe proves to be nonexistent, Cordelia is murdered, and the mind and body of Lear are asked to suffer no further vexation.

We perhaps do not think sufficiently of the other task of the poet who makes intense emotions—the task of constantly taking away something from them lest they become intolerable or change to some other emotions not intended or desirable, just as the unrestrained grief of Laertes at the grave of Ophelia produced contempt and indignation and not compassion in the heart of Hamlet. Our fear and pity for Lear are both magnified and mitigated. These terrifying thoughts are held by him when he is mad, and their validity is further denied by all those in the play who are intelligent, loving, and somewhat disengaged—their complete validity is called into question by even the existence of people such as Kent, Edgar, and Albany. In addition, the action is arranged from beginning to end (that is, from the beginning of Act III to Act IV, scene 6) in such ways that fear does not become horror, or pity some kind of excruciating anguish. In the first scene in Act III, before we see Lear on the heath, we are given subdued assurance that friends are organizing to rescue him and the kingdom. This scene can be criticized for its execution, because it is a scene merely of talk between Kent and a Gentleman, whose talk is obviously directed to us as much as to themselves, but the intention to save us from horror is right. Moreover, throughout the scenes leading to Lear's madness there are continuing preparations to remove him to Cordelia, and, oppositely, the intervening actions of the antagonists do not make their complete success probable, for Cornwall is killed, Albany becomes disillusioned, and jealousy turns Goneril and Regan upon themselves. And, finally, although scene 6 is constructed to magnify our fear and pity by confronting us with both Gloucester and Lear and their combined anguish, it is also designed to alleviate our suffering and serves as a superlative example of the paradoxical task of the tragic artist. The thoughts to be expressed by Lear upon the fields were Gloucester's as he approached the cliffs of Dover ("As flies to wanton boys are we to th' gods. / They kill us for their sport"), but Gloucester has been purged of these thoughts just prior to Lear's expression of them, and, since Lear and Gloucester have been made parallel in so many ways, one might assume that Shakespeare had constructed this scene to assure the beholder that the beliefs he is about to hear from Lear are not the final beliefs of either. We must recognize, however, that a certain number of critics read *King Lear* in such a way that Gloucester's lines are taken as a condensation of Gloucester's and Lear's and Shakespeare's ultimate "philosophy," although this seems to me to be an interpretation of another book, possibly one written by Hardy. Surely, though, by the end of the scene, if our feelings and the creator do not deceive us, the world is such as to make a man a man of salt—but for purposes more magnificent than the laying of autumn's dust.

III

So far our view of *King Lear* has been both panoramic and confined. In looking upon the large expanse of lines from the end of Act II to Act IV, scene 6, we have confined ourselves to the reversal in Lear's thoughts and feelings that occurs therein and makes it a single, though large, tragic episode. Lear and Shakespeare had conceptions of the tragic that mark them as men who saw "feelingly," but, as a dramatist, Shakespeare had his own set of dismaying problems—the dramatic problems of objectifying tragic thoughts and feelings into commensurate actions and then of dividing and arranging these actions into parts which would be themselves little tragedies and yet stations on the way to some more ultimate suffering. In making these problems ours, we become more particular and yet, in certain ways, closer to the general qualities of great writing which, in order to have a name, must also have a local habitation.

Many a tragic drama has itself met a tragic ending for lack of drama, and the odds increase that this will be the case when the tragedy in some central way involves internal changes, changes in thoughts and states of mind. Byron, too, wished to depict a soul in torment, and he produced *Manfred*, but, despite the subtitle, "A Dramatic Poem," it is largely a series of soliloquies addressed to the Alps in inclement weather. Drama is movement, and, in the four scenes depicting the increasing tempest in Lear's mind, the stage is also in flux—the actors on it move naturally and interestingly, and other characters enter mysteriously and leave on secret missions. Moreover, these actions are designed not merely to keep the stage from becoming static while everything else is dynamic; they are in a higher sense dramatic actions, actions involving an *agon*, "objective correlatives" to the conflict in Lear's mind. Lear challenges the storm; he arraigns his daughters before a justice so perverted that it is represented by the Fool and Edgar disguised as a madman; he imagines impotently that he is raising an avenging army and is distracted by a mouse; and he assumes he is judging a culprit guilty of adultery and finds no sin because he finds the sin universal. Such are the inventions of a dramatic poet, and by them he makes the passage of Lear's tortured soul intelligible, probable, and tragically moving. Scholars are still in search of the exact meaning of certain speeches in each of Shakespeare's great tragedies—and we should like to assume that those who saw these plays for the first time did not have perfect understanding of all of the lines—but so great was Shakespeare's power to conceive of action from which thought and feeling can be readily inferred that all of us know Lear, Hamlet, and Macbeth more intimately than we know many men whose remarks we understand perfectly.

Yet a master of tragic drama would also sense that, in scenes depicting a great change in thought and state of mind, action should be kept to a certain minimum, lest too much outer clangor obscure the inner vibrations and tragedy pass over into melodrama. He would sense, too, that language suggesting madness, if sufficiently understood, would put tremendous demands upon our powers of concentration. Three scenes lead to the madness of Lear and are alternated with three leading to the blinding of Gloucester. Unlike the "internal" Lear scenes, the other three are action cut to the bone; and unlike the clogged language of Lear, the Fool, and Poor Tom, the speech of the conspiracy is lean, bare, and cruel. Removing us momentarily from Lear, these scenes relieve both our understandings and our feelings, but tragic "relief" quickly becomes tragic illusion, when the master-touch is upon it. We turn our eyes away from an old man seeking in suffering to discover the final cause of suffering, only to have it dawn on us that we have turned to a horrible replica of the action that was the immediate cause of this suffering, another old man tortured by his offspring and by Lear's as well. Suffering, then, as it works out its lonely and final course upon the heath, is combined with action such as initiated it. Moreover, in another way the two tragedies are one—Gloucester's attempts to rescue Lear from his suffering are the immediate cause of bringing on his own. Thus the interplay of these two tragedies gives to both more than either singly possesses of intelligibility, suspense, probability, and tragic concern.

But, although Gloucester's tragedy is also Lear's, our concentration is upon those scenes in which Lear goes mad and which collectively make intelligible the scene upon the fields of Dover, where his madness is complete. It is not enough, therefore, that action in these scenes is kept at a certain minimum and within this guarded minimum is maximal, or that the action also is dramatic, involving conflict. It has also to be action everywhere suggesting "madness," and, secondly, it has to be arranged in such a way as to lead Lear to "madness." Let us consider first the materials and then the order out of which such disorder is made.

Certainly, Shakespeare's choice was right in introducing no totally new material in these scenes that center in the depth of Lear's mind; they are made out of materials already in the play—Lear's Fool, Edgar who previously had decided to disguise himself as a madman, and the storm. Distraction that is great and is not the general confusion of a battle but centered and ultimately internal is rightly made out of a certain minimum of material that can be assimilated and out of material already somewhat assimilated. Moreover, such a reduction of material not only helps our understanding at a moment in literature when it stands most in need of help; actually, art attains the maximum of unexpectedness out of restricted sources (as a good mystery story limits the number of possible murderers) and out of material already introduced and about which we have expectations (as the best mystery stories are not solved by material that has been kept from us by the detective and the writer until the end). While on the heath, Lear might have been attacked by a gang of robbers and, in culminating suffering, have thought this some symbolic act, signifying that all men are beasts of prey; surely, it is much more surprising that it is the legitimate son of Gloucester, counterpart of Cordelia, who makes him think this.

Out of a proper economy of material, then, a maximum of madness is made, and everyone who has read *King Lear* has sensed that the heath scenes are composed of complex variations upon the theme of madness—a noble man going mad, accompanied by a character professionally not "normal," meeting a character whose life depends upon his appearing mad, amid a storm such as makes everyone believe that the universe and even the gods are not stable. We add that Kent, too, is present in these scenes and that a point constantly calm is useful in the art of making madness.

The musical analogy of a theme with variations must be used only up to a certain point and then dropped lest it stop us, as it has stopped some others, from going farther and seeing that these scenes are a part of a great poem and that in this part a noble man goes mad, which is something more than orchestration, although orchestration has its purposes. Ultimately, we are confronted with a poetical event; and the storm, the Fool, and Poor Tom are not only variations on madness but happenings on the way which collectively constitute the event. That is, the setting and two characters, all previously somewhat external to Lear, successively become objects of his thought, and then become himself transubstantiated. The storm becomes the tempest in his mind; the Fool becomes all wretches who can feel, of whom Lear is one, although before he had not recognized any such wide identity; and then a worse wretch appears, seemingly mad, protected against the universe by a blanket, scarred by his own wounds, and concentrating upon his own vermin. He is "the thing itself," a "forked animal," with whom Lear identifies his own substance by tearing off his clothes, which are now misleading. We know Lear, then, by Lear's other substances, which are dramatically visible.

There is another substance present with Lear, for the madness that comes upon him is more terrible than the madness that translates everything into the ego; in the mind of Lear, when his madness is complete, all substances—the universe, man, and Lear himself—have been translated into the substance of his daughters, and perhaps something like this is what is technically meant by a "fixation." Although actually never appearing, Lear's daughters are the central characters in the inverted and internal pilgrim's progress that occurs upon the heath, and ultimately we know the stage of Lear's progress by his daughters' presence. In the first appearance of Lear upon the heath (Act III, scene 2) the daughters are already identified with the storm and the underlying powers of the universe, and Lear dares to defy them and to confront the universe, even though he now sees what he began to see at the end of Act II, that the ultimate powers may be not moral but in alliance with his daughters. Either possibility, however, he can face with defiance: in his first great speech to the storm, he calls upon it, as he had called upon the universe before, to act as a moral agent to exterminate even the molds of ingratitude; his second speech is one of moral outrage ("O! O! 'tis foul!") against universal forces that may have joined "two pernicious daughters" in a conspiracy against his head. In the beginning of his next scene (scene 4), he has still the power of defiance, but it is only the storm as a storm that he can confront; he knows that he no longer dares to think of his daughters, for "that way madness lies." Almost at that moment Poor Tom emerges from the hovel, and with him in Lear's mind another substance ("Hast thou given all to thy two daughters, and art thou come to this?"). The shattering of the resolution not to think on this substance leads Lear down the predicted way, and first to a complete identification with a mad beggar; then his mind, rapidly disintegrating, leaves equality behind and, in deferential hallucination, transforms the mad beggar into a philosopher of whom he asks the ancient philosophical question, "What is the cause of thunder?" At the end of this scene, then, Lear's thoughts return to the storm, but it is no longer a storm that he might possibly endure. By many signs Lear's final scene in Act III is the final scene on Lear's way to madness. Poor Tom places Lear's mind in the underworld with his opening speech: "Frateretto calls me, and tells me Nero is an angler in the lake of darkness. Pray, innocent, and beware the foul fiend." With this speech, Lear's thoughts literally enter the pit, and here he finds the forbidden women. What he knew at the opening of the earlier scene that he must avoid now becomes his total occupation, and the mind now revels in what the mind once knew it could not endure. Elaborately and in elation Lear arraigns his daughters upon the shores of the lake of darkness,[3] and, just before drawing the curtain, he asks the final philosophical question, "Is there any cause in nature that makes these hard hearts?"

It is later, properly much later, when we see Lear again, since by then he has found in madness an answer to the questions that led him there. Then, looming upon his mind, is a universe the basic substance of which is female:

> Down from the waist they are Centaurs,
> Though women all above.
> But to the girdle do the gods inherit,
> Beneath is all the fiend's [Act IV, scene 6, ll. 126–29].[4]

In the opening of this section we promised to say something about these scenes as being tragic wholes as well as parts of a fearful and pitiful event, and already a good deal has been said indirectly about their separate natures. But their natures are not only separate; they are tragic, each one arousing and then to a degree purging the emotions of fear and pity. In the first of these scenes, our immediate fear and pity for Lear as we see him trying to outface the elements are intensified by his second address to the storm in which he realizes that the universe may be allied with his daughters "'gainst a head / So old and white as this!" But, shortly, Kent enters, and that makes things somewhat better; then Lear has an insight into the nature of his own sins, and although his sins are pitifully small by comparison, still self-awareness of sin is a good no matter the degree or the consequences—and it is a good to Lear, purging his feelings so that at the end of this little tragedy he turns to the Fool in new tenderness and in a new role, for the first time considering someone else's feelings before his own ("How dost, my boy? Art cold? / I am cold myself"). And such, in a general way, is the emotional movement of the other two scenes in which Lear appears in Act III—they begin with Lear alarmingly agitated; the agitation mounts (with the appearance of Poor Tom or with the prospect of arraigning his daughters in hell); but in the enactment of the enormous mo-

3. In the Folio Lear's arraignment of his daughters is omitted (ll. 18–59 in Kittredge). The Folio also omits Edgar's soliloquy concluding the scene. The Folio is far more accurate in editoral detail than the Quarto but is considerably shorter, most scholars surmising that it represents a version of the play that had been cut for acting purposes. As dramatic magnifications of states of mind and feelings already embodied in the play, both Lear's arraignment of his daughters and Edgar's soliloquy are made of material that is often cut if a cutting has to be made for stage purposes. Certainly, it is not difficult to understand the omission of the soliloquy, but the deletion of the trial upon the edge of hell removes from the scene a tremendous amount of its drama and tragedy.

4. All quotations from Shakespeare, unless otherwise specified, are from Kittredge's *The Complete Works of Shakespeare*.

ment he (and we) get some kind of emotional release for which undoubtedly there is some clinical term, not, however, known to me or to the Elizabethans or to most people who have felt that at the end of each of these scenes both they and Lear have been given mercifully an instant not untouched with serenity on the progress to chaos. "Draw the curtains. So, so, so."

There are many tragedies of considerable magnitude the effects of which, however, are almost solely macrocosmic. The greatest of tragic writers built his macrocosms out of tragedy upon tragedy upon tragedy.

IV

The third time that we shall consider Lear upon the heath will be the last, for the full art of tragedy has three dimensions, like anything with depth. The tragedy with depth is compounded out of a profound conception of what is tragic and out of action tragically bent, with characters commensurate to the concept and the act—and, finally, it is composed out of writing. The maximal statement of an art always makes it easier to see how many lesser artists there are and why; and thus the author of *The American Tragedy* could not write— a failing not uncommon among authors—and the author of *Manfred*, although a very great writer in many ways, was so concentrated upon his personal difficulties that he could form no clear and large conception of the tragic, and his tragic action is almost no action at all.

In addition to the remaining problem of writing, one of the general criteria introduced early in this essay has not yet been dealt with directly—vividness, or the powers and devices that make a literary moment "come to life." For a consideration of both, we need units smaller even than scenes, and so we turn to what may be regarded as a small "incident" in one of the scenes and, finally, to a speech from this incident and a single word from the speech. It is easy to understand why the moments of a drama usually singled out for discussion are those that are obviously important and splendid with a kind of splendor that gives them an existence separate from their dramatic context, like passages of Longinian sublimity; but this study is so committed to the tragic drama that it will forego the sublime—although few dramas offer more examples of it— and concentrate, instead, upon an incident and a speech, the importance and splendor of which appear largely as one sees a tragic drama unfold about them.

On a technical level, this incident is a unit because it is a piece of dramatic business—in these lines, Shakespeare is engaged in the business of introducing a character:

KENT: Good my lord, enter here.
LEAR: Prithee go in thyself; seek thine own ease.
         This tempest will not give me leave to ponder
         On things would hurt me more. But I'll go in.

[To the Fool]

In, boy; go first.—You houseless poverty—
Nay, get thee in. I'll pray, and then I'll sleep.

Exit [Fool]

Poor naked wretches, wheresoe'er you are,
That bide the pelting of this pitiless storm,
How shall your houseless heads and unfed sides,
Your loop'd and window'd raggedness, defend you
From seasons such as these? O, I have ta'en
Too little care of this! Take physic, pomp;
Expose thyself to feel what wretches feel,
That thou mayst shake the superflux to them
And show the heavens more just.

Edg.: *[within]*   Fathom and half, fathom and half! Poor Tom!

Enter Fool [from the hovel]

Fool: Come not in here, nuncle, here's a spirit. Help me, help me!
Kent: Give me thy hand. Who's there?
Fool: A spirit, a spirit! He says his name's poor Tom.
Kent: What art thou that dost grumble there i' th' straw? Come forth.

Enter Edgar [disguised as a madman]

Edg.:   Away! the foul fiend follows me! Through the sharp hawthorn blows the cold wind. Humh! go to thy cold bed, and warm thee.
Lear: Hast thou given all to thy two daughters, and art thou come to this?
Edg.:   Who gives anything to poor Tom? whom the foul fiend hath led through fire and through flame, through ford and whirlpool, o'er bog and quagmire; that hath laid knives under his pillow and halters in his pew, set ratsbane by his porridge, made him proud of heart, to ride on a bay trotting horse over four-inch'd bridges, to course his own shadow for a traitor. Bless thy five wits! Tom's acold. O, do de, do de, do de. Bless thee from whirlwinds, star-blasting, and taking! Do poor Tom some charity, whom the foul fiend vexes. There could I have him now—and there—and there again—and there!

[Storm still (Act III, scene 4, ll. 22–64)].

Now, the business of introducing a character can be transacted quickly in brackets—*[Enter Edgar, disguised as a madman]*—and when the character is some straggler in the play or not so much a character as some expository information, like a messenger, then the introduction properly can be cursory. But in the drama of Lear's madness, Poor Tom becomes "the thing itself," and the mere size of his introduction is a preparation for his importance. And artistic size, as we said earlier, has qualitative as well as quantitative aspects.

From the time Poor Tom first speaks until the end of this passage, his name is given five times, and it is given the first time he speaks. Yet a complete introduction does more than fasten on a name, especially if the person is distinctive and we should be warned about him. Three times before Poor Tom appears, he is said to be a "spirit," and after he appears he says three times that "the foul fiend" is pursuing him, so that, leaving out for the moment his confirmatory actions and speeches, we surely ought to be forewarned by his introduction that he is "mad." It is not always needful to be so elaborate and repetitive, even when introducing a character of importance, but when, in addition, the moment of introduction is tense emotionally and the character is abnormal, we are grateful, even in life, to have the name repeated. Or, if confirmation is sought from literature, we may turn to the opening of the first scene of *Hamlet* and note how many times in the excitement the names of Bernardo, Marcellus, and Horatio are called back and forth and how often the ghost is referred to before he appears. This introduction, then, has one of the qualities of all good writing, intelligibility, and in circumstances not favorable to understanding.

Moreover, this is an introduction achieving a maximum of unexpectedness and suspense, effects desirable in themselves as well as qualitative signs that the character being introduced is dramatically important. The king is about to escape from the storm into the hovel, but, before doing so, he turns to the heavens with a prayer in behalf of all "poor naked wretches." Not from above but from within the hovel a supernatural voice cries out, "Fathom and half!" If a lesser pen had turned Poor Tom loose upon the stage at this moment with no further identification, we would have been dismayed, and, furthermore, the suspense latent in the unexpected would not have been realized. When he does come forth, we have identified and awaited him, but unexpectedly and in consternation Lear identifies him—identifies him as himself. Then, surely, it is unexpected that the *alter* Lear goes into the singsong of a mad beggar whining for a handout.

As merely unexpected, the entry of Poor Tom is a diversion and serves a purpose, that of momentarily affording us much needed relief. The art of tragic relief is itself worth a study, although all its highest manifestations are governed by two conjoined principles—the moment of relief should be psychologically needed, but the moment of relief should be a momentary illusion which, as it is dispelled, only deepens the tragedy. Mere unexpectedness thus becomes consummate unexpectedness, with what seems to be a turning from tragedy an entry into darker recesses; and the entry of Poor Tom, viewed first as a piece of technical business, is the appearance of greater tragedy. Lear's prayer, among its many dramatic reasons for being, is preparation for the appearance of something worse. The audience, after it becomes confident in its author, quietly assumes that, when something big is said and something big immediately follows, there is a connection between the two, although not too obvious— as Shakespeare himself said earlier in *King Lear*, the entry should not be so pat as "the catastrophe of the old comedy" (Act I, scene 2, ll. 145–47). The prayer comes out of suffering which has identified Lear with the Fool and with a whole class whose feelings before were unknown to Lear, "poor naked wretches, wheresoe'er you are." And "wheresoe'er" might unexectedly be within the hovel at hand, which was to be a refuge from suffering, and the wretch who emerges, poorer and more naked than the Fool, might be fraught with greater suffering. "Fathom and half, fathom and half!" he has called from within, and this is certainly a mysterious cry and, in the circumstances, not a rational utterance, but it is also a sounding of depth. Of the two tragic emotions, it is fear that is aroused by this cry, and it is fear that sends the Fool running out of the hovel, and it is at least in alarm, a diminutive of fear, that Kent commands the "spirit" to come forth. Then Lear's tragic complement appears, and almost in the next moment the pity aroused by the sight of unprotected madness is transposed to the object about which all pity should be centered in a tragedy—the tragic protagonist, who in startled compassion asks the new thing if the two of them are not identical in substance. Poor Tom's answer to the tragic question on the surface and at first seems no answer at all, but what nevertheless might be expected of a mad beggar, a routine whine for alms, a routine that one of the most ancient professions has invariably divided into two parts—first a self-commiserating account of the beggar's own suffering and then a prayer that the possible giver be spared any such suffering, the prayer being, as it were, anticipatory repayment which, by implication, can be taken back and changed to a curse. Surely, the art of panhandling here comes to life, and literary moments that come to life have been called "vivid." But it is Shakespeare's art, referred to by so many as "abundant," to make two moments come to life in one, and, from a mad beggar's routine emerges an answer to Lear's question and hence a moment filled with tragedy and latent with tragedy to come. As Poor Tom's account of himself proceeds, it becomes apparent, although not to Edgar, that he is describing Lear and his own father. At first the multiple identification is scarcely noticeable, since it depends only upon similarity in immediate and outer circumstances—others besides Poor Tom are led through fire and flood. Then the similarity becomes both more inclusive and deeper as tragic flaws and tragic courses of action become parallel—Lear and Gloucester, in pride of heart, are also trotting over four-inched bridges and coursing their own shadows for traitors. And, since the prayer for the possible almsgivers that immediately follows ("Bless thy five wits! . . . Bless thee from whirlwinds, star-blasting, and taking!") approaches the tragic ultimate in vain request, perhaps enough has been said about the introduction of "such a fellow" as was to make both his father and Lear think "a man a worm."

V

Given the confines of this paper, the speech to be considered must be short, for the focus finally is upon the smallest unit of drama, a speech, and the smallest unit of speech, a single word. Moreover, given our other commitments, the speech should also be in essence dramatic and tragic. Let us take, then, the speech in which Lear first recognizes his identity with unprotected nakedness scarred with self-inflicted wounds:

Hast thou given all to thy two daughters, and art thou come to this?[5]

This is not one of those speeches, somewhat detachable as sententious utterances or lyric poems from which are collected *The Beauties of Shakespeare;* yet upon the heath it is one of the great moments. It is tragic drama contracted to its essences—fear and pity. The question is asked in consternation and commiseration; and it arouses in us, who are more aware of implications than Lear, fear and pity in some ways more enormous than his.

These two qualities of the speech—its shortness and its enormousness—at the outset may be considered as somewhat separate and paradoxical qualities. The speech is short not only in over-all measurement but in the individual words composing it, for all of them, with the exception of "given" and "daughters," are monosyllables, and all of them are short qualitatively, being ordinary, colorless words. Of conceivable adjectives that could be attached to the daughters who had brought Lear to this place, none could be more simple, neutral, or needless seemingly than the number "two." What, if anything, can be said of such a complete contraction of language? Well, as a simple beginning, it is easy to understand, and the moment demands understanding. Then, too, just as language, it is unexpected. In forty-odd lines called an "incident," there are the "superflux" of prayer, the eerie cry of Poor Tom, the scurrying prose of the Fool and Kent, the singsong and shivering rhythms of Poor Tom that rise into an actual line of song—and then this, to be answered by a long beggar's whine, colorful but seemingly confused, since the speaker, as announced, is from Bedlam. This is a great deal of dramatic dialogue for forty lines, and perhaps might be contrasted to certain modern schools of writers who have found the essence of drama and reality to be iteration and reiteration of monosyllables. But Shakespeare's contractions are not exhaustions of his language, which was almost limitless in its resources. Ultimately, the kind of verbal contraction here being considered is right because the immediate moment of tragic impact is a contraction—abdominal, in the throat, in the mind

5. The Folio reads: "Did's't thou give all to thy Daughters? And art thou come to this?" We shall analyze the speech as it is given in our text and as it appeared in the first Quarto. Although in several particulars the Folio has contracted the first half of the question, an analysis of either version of the speech would be substantially the same.

impaled upon a point. The vast tragic speeches of Shakespeare are anticipations of impending tragedy or assimilations of the event after its impact, like scar tissue after the wound. Thus every appearance of the ghost in the first act of *Hamlet*, being awaited, is immediately preceded by a long, imaginatively unbounded speech; but, when the ghost reveals his tragedy, his son, who makes many long speeches, can only exclaim, "O my prophetic soul! / My uncle?" Othello enters Desdemona's chamber with a culmination of tragic resolutions, and his opening speech ("It is the cause," etc.) has the magnitude of his fears and his resolutions; but he has no speech, not always even complete sentences, with which to answer the prayers of Desdemona; and her last prayer, that she be allowed to pray, he answers with the ultimate words, "It is too late." In Shakespeare, as in life, the instances are many that the enormous moment, precisely at its moment, contracts body, mind, and utterance.

From life, however, come only the suggestions for art's patterns, not art's final accomplishments. Specifically, life makes it right that Lear's speech at this moment is not a "speech"; yet art demands that no moment of such import call forth, as it often does in life, some truly little, inadequate response. It is the task of the artist to give the enormous its proper dimensions, even if, as in this instance, the illusion has to be preserved that only some little thing was said. Our task, therefore, is to look again at these few, short, ordinary words to see how they add up to what our feelings tell us is something very big. Here, as elsewhere, there can be but the suggestion of a complete analysis; and, in respect to words, the accomplished writer lifts this one and this one and this one and listens to both sound and significance.

Rhythmically and metrically, Lear has asked a tremendous question. Its return to iambic rhythm after seven lines of mad cries and scurrying conversation should in itself encourage the actor to add some dimension to its delivery, and metrically it is seven feet, for, although there is a pause after the fourth foot ("two daughers"), it is all inclosed within a question, and the second part ("and art thou come to this?") mounts above the first. A seven-foot mounting question is a big question. Moreover, the fact that the words, with two exceptions, are monosyllables gives them collectively a pounding effect, especially when they are blocked by so many dentals, only three of the fourteen words being without *d*, *t*, or *th*, and these ("given all" and "come") stand out as it were by their phonetic displacement, two of them being the verbs and "all" being probably more important than either. The fourth foot ("two daughters") has also properly been lengthened, "daughters" being terminal to the first half of the question and being, in addition, the largest word uttered. Rhythm, too, makes this foot speak out, for only a schoolboy would scan it as a foot with a feminine ending ("twŏ dáugh tĕrs"); although no one seemingly can be sure how "daughters" was pronounced at this time, anyone ought to be sure that in this place the second syllable of "daughters" gets as much emphasis as the first and the whole foot is as long roughly as this scansion ("twō daúgh térs").

Grammatical mode of utterance brings us closer to significance. Some dimension, some significance, goes out of the speech if it is not a question but a declaration: "Thou gavest all to thy two daughters, and now art come to this." Gone is some of the immediacy of the moment, too big at its occurrence to be believed and recorded as fact. To a degree, then, fear and pity are made out of grammar, and, if we say that each point so far discussed is a little matter and singly is no great accomplishment, then all we have said is that much of art is composed of little brush strokes and that this is especially true when what is being composed is "the seemingly simple."

Yet there is one big word within this speech—the one right word, the one word that is not a touching-up of another word which could itself have remained without the notice of aftertimes. The right word is also in the right place; it is the last word, "this." Perhaps we are accustomed to thinking of the *mot juste* as a word giving a definite, irreplaceable image, and certainly *the* right word should be irreplaceable and in some sense definite; only there are moments so tremendous that their exact size is without any definite boundary. There are moments, moreover, which have a size that is unmentionable, moments which cannot, at least at the instant, be fully faced or exactly spoken of by those who must endure them. Poetry may make a perfection out of what would be an error in exposition, and moments such as these may set at naught the rule of composition teachers that "such," "it," and "this" should not be used without a definite, grammatical antecedent. Likewise, what has been said about "this" has a relevance to "all" in the first part of the question that is for this moment the exact question:

> Hast thou given *all* to thy two daughters,
> And art thou come to *this*?

There is always a test that should be made of such matters—can we, after searching, find something at least as good? The test does not always lead to humiliation, and always it should lead to some improvement of ourselves, but the most rigorous test of Shakespeare is Shakespeare himself. Marcellus' first question to Bernardo, both of whom have twice seen the ghost, is the forced mention of the enormous and unmentionable: "What, has this *thing* appear'd again to-night?" The ghost of Hamlet's father, as it is awaited, is "this thing," "this dreaded sight," "this apparition," sometimes "it," more often "'t," but never the ghost of Hamlet's father. In the first soliloquy Hamlet's thoughts move past the canons of the Everlasting, past the general un-profitable uses of the world, until they come to the loathsome point focal to his whole universe: "*That it should come to this! /* But two months dead! Nay, not so much, not two." So a second time in Shakespeare we have "come to this." And at the end Hamlet comes to his own tragic moment which he believes can-not be avoided: "If it be now, 'tis not to come; if it be not to come, it will be now; if it be not now, yet it will come: the readiness is all." In themselves, "it," "to come," "be," "will," and "all" are some of the smallest, least precise and colorful words in our language; but words are so important that from the least of them can be made the uttermost in meaning and emotion—the suffering of man triumphed over by some slight touch of serenity. "Let be."

II

LITERARY CRITICISM AND THE CONCEPT OF IMITATION IN ANTIQUITY[1]

RICHARD McKEON

THE term "imitation" is not prominent in the vocabulary of criticism today. In such use as it still has, it serves to segregate the bad from the good in art rather more frequently than to set the boundaries of art. Yet as late as the eighteenth century imitation was the mark and differentia of the arts, or at least of some of them. To the critics of that century, literature and painting were imitative arts, and it was still important to debate whether or not music was an art of imitation.[2] The term had begun to slip into disrepute in writings on the philosophy of art even before critics of art found it cumbersome or inappropriate, and substitutes for it with more familiar philosophic justification have long since been found; if it does occasionally return to use, with the proper protection of a warning that it does not mean literal representation of its object, it is seldom extended to include music or literature.[3]

The defense, such as it is, of "imitation" as a term applicable to poetry or suited to apply to all of the arts, has in our times fallen largely into the hands of historians of aesthetics and criticism; and although the fortune varies in the

1. Reprinted, with minor alterations, from *Modern Philology*, August, 1936.

2. Thus James Harris, in the second of his *Three Treatises* (first published in 1744) entitled "A Discourse on Music, Painting, and Poetry," treats poetry, painting, and music as three types of imitation differing in their media and modes of imitation (2d. ed. [1765], pp. 55 ff.), although he goes on to say that poetry disposes of the charm of "numbers" as well as imitation (p. 92) and music possesses, besides the power of imitation, the power of raising affections (p. 99), "whereas Painting has pretence to no Charm, except that of Imitation" (p. 92). Thomas Twining, on the other hand, in the dissertation "On Poetry Considered as an Imitative Art," which he prefaced to his translation of Aristotle's *Poetics* (first published in 1789), distinguishes four senses of imitation as applied to poetry: imitation by the sounds of the words, by description, by fiction, and by dramatic imitation; and he argues (2d ed. [1812], I, 35) that, since the last is the proper sense of imitation, it is incorrect to say that all poetry is imitation; only dramatic poetry is properly imitative. Moreover, in the second dissertation prefaced to his translation, "On the Different Senses of the Word, Imitative, as Applied to Music by the Ancients, and by the Moderns," Twining concludes his argument by quoting with approbation from James Beattie's treatise *On Poetry and Music* the statement that music should be stricken off the list of the imitative arts (p. 91) and by maintaining further that painting, sculpture, and the arts of design in general are "the only arts that are obviously and essentially imitative" (p. 92).

3. Thus George Santayana, in *Reason in Art*, Vol. IV of *The Life of Reason* (New York, 1917), pp. 144 ff., discusses sculpture, acting, and painting as modes of imitation. Music, poetry, prose, and architecture had, however, been treated in earlier chapters before the concept of imitation was introduced.

debate, the discredit which the term has suffered in modern criticism tends to be found earlier and earlier. "That the 'Imitation' doctrine of the *Poetics* is in some respects disputable need not be denied," according to Saintsbury,[4] "and that it lent itself rather easily to serious misconstruction is certain. But let us remember also that it is an attempt—perhaps the first attempt, and one that has not been much bettered in all the improvements upon it—to adjust those proportions of nature and art which actually do exist in poetry." "It is natural," Bosanquet says,[5] "that the earliest formula adopted by reflection should be strained to the breaking point before it is abandoned." "Aristotle, as his manner was," according to Butcher,[6] "accepted the current phrase and interpreted it anew. True, he may sometimes have been misled by its guidance, and not infrequently his meaning is obscured by his adherence to the outworn formula." Atkins writes:

> Moreover the statement [i.e., Plato's statement of the relation of the arts to each other and to the universe in *Laws* 889B–D] helps to explain why "imitation" (and not "creation" or "expression") has been adopted as the process common to all the arts. To the Greeks before Plato, devoid of a mystical sense of an invisible order of realities, the plain and obvious fact was that the artist did not produce the objects of real life, but their appearances only; and it was therefore inevitable that the impression produced on their minds was rather that of imitative representation than of creation, interpretation, or the like.[7]

The practice of historians of literary criticism would be conclusive, even if their evidence from the writers of antiquity were not impressive, in establishing the variety of the meanings which the term "imitation" has assumed in the course of its history. Yet that diversity of meaning is seldom the direct object of critical attention: the term is vague, inadequate, primitive, and its use involves a play on words when it does not lead to self-contradiction. But when one returns to the ancient writers on which these historical labors are employed, it is difficult to retain a sense of the limitations and deficiencies with which scholarship has enriched the term. Instead, constant vigilance is required to discover the ineptitudes which should result from the use of so inept a word. For all the attempts that have been made to define "imitation" and for all the care that has been exercised in examining the statements in which it occurs, the philosophical contexts in which the word "imitation" is used and methodological questions as they apply to its use have received little scrutiny. Yet the meaning of a word will alter with a change in either context or peculiari-

4. George Saintsbury, *A History of Criticism and Literary Taste in Europe* (New York, 1900), I, 54.

5. Bernard Bosanquet, *A History of Aesthetics* (4th ed.; London, 1917), p. 13.

6. S. H. Butcher, *Aristotle's Theory of Poetry and Fine Art* (4th ed.; London, 1923), p. 122.

7. J. W. H. Atkins, *Literary Criticism in Antiquity* (Cambridge, 1934), I, 52.

ties of method, notwithstanding that the definition may be retained; and, if these remain unchanged, it is possible for the doctrine of imitation to persist in all essentials, even when the term has disappeared. If the critical views in which the word "imitation" appeared, no less than methodological devices peculiar to the systems in which the term was used, have survived the discredit of the term itself, the attempt to distinguish among the critical approaches of antiquity may not be without relevance to the modern analogues that have replaced them.

I

The word "imitation," as Plato uses it, is at no time established in a literal meaning or delimited to a specific subject matter. It is sometimes used to differentiate some human activities from others or some part of them from another part or some aspect of a single act from another; it is sometimes used in a broader sense to include all human activities; it is sometimes applied even more broadly to all processes—human, natural, cosmic, and divine. Like most of the terms that figure prominently in the dialogues, "imitation" as a term is left universal in scope and indeterminate in application. The dialectical method is used to determine its meaning in particular contexts, sometimes bringing out a meaning according to which any given statement in which it may occur is true, sometimes with equal force the meanings in which the statement is false; not infrequently both ends are accomplished in a single dialogue. Of existent objects, Plato says,[8] there are three things necessary for knowledge: the name (ὄνομα), the discourse or reason (λόγος), and the image (εἴδωλον); knowledge and the object itself are apart from these. Whether or not Plato wrote the epistle in which those distinctions are made, his practice seems to conform to it. "For as yet," the Stranger says at the beginning of the *Sophist*,[9] "we have in common concerning him only the name." He suggests that he and his interlocutor doubtless have the thing in mind as well; but they must come to an agreement concerning the thing by means of reason, not by the mere name without the reason. Somewhat later, in discussing angling, they arrive at agreement not only concerning the name but also concerning the reason or definition of the thing itself.[10] But when the search for the Sophist grows into an inquiry into being and non-being, pursued by way of word and reason, the Stranger remarks that in the case of being, as in that of every single thing which is supposed to be one, we call the single thing by many names and treat it as many.[11]

8. *Epist.* vii. 342A–B.

9. *Sophist* 218C.   10. *Ibid.* 221B.

11. *Ibid.* 251A–B. Consequent on this relation of names to things, Socrates frequently reproaches his respondents for finding many things where one is sought (as in *Meno* 72A or 77A), or again he is reproached by them for changing the meanings of his terms (as in

Not infrequently the speakers in the Platonic dialogues have reason to complain of the opposite difficulty, that many things are found to have the same name. It is probable that no small part of Plato's distrust of the written word is caused by the margin of independence which obtains between words, images, and reasons but which can be controlled in conversation by a skilled dialectician.

In any case, to require Plato to conform to an Aristotelian conception of definitions or terms, in which words are assigned univocal meanings, would be to distort his inquiry and make nonsense of much of his dialectic. It is invalid criticism to point out that a term like "imitation" has many meanings in Plato, and for the same reason it is questionable defense of the Platonic position to resolve the many meanings into one.[12] The word might be said to be defined in the course of the dialogues, but it receives no fixed meaning. The discussion proceeds by applying images and reasons to the elucidation of words, and in that process "imitation" and all like words suffer extensions and limitations. Unless the list is made indefinitely long to include infinite possible meanings, it is hardly accurate to say that the word has "several senses." From one point of view, "imitation" has only one meaning in Plato; from another, it has infinite meanings.

The methodological considerations which are so prominent in the use of words, and which control their meanings in what Plato would call a strange and wonderful fashion, may be stated in a way that has excellent Platonic precedent by setting forth the things to which Plato applied the word "imitation" and the other words which Plato applied to the same things—the many words which are applied to one thing, and the many things to which one word is applied. Without such considerations, on the other hand, inasmuch as they

---

Gorgias 483A); and, on the other hand, speakers are praised for reducing many or infinite things to one name and for finding appropriate names for each subdivision (as in *Theaetetus* 147C–148B).

12. J. Tate thus finds two kinds of imitation in the *Republic*: imitation in the literal sense, the mere copying of sensible objects, and imitation in an analogical sense, such that poetry in which imitation of this sort occurred could be considered nonimitative (" 'Imitation' in Plato's *Republic*," *Classical Quarterly*, XXII [1928], 23). In a later article ("Plato and 'Imitation,' " *ibid.*, XXVI [1932], 161–69), Tate refers to this as a distinction between a good and a bad sense of the term "imitation": poetry which is imitative in the bad sense is excluded from the ideal state, while poetry which is imitative in the good sense can be called nonimitative rather than imitative, depending on the sense in which the term "imitative" is used. In this second article Tate finds support in the remaining dialogues for his earlier interpretation of imitation in the *Republic*. W. C. Greene contrasts the "literal kind of imitation" implied in the tenth book of the *Republic* with the imitation in the second and third books of the *Republic*, which involves an attenuated form of the doctrine of ideas and which is criticized on ethical grounds in a not unfriendly spirit ("Plato's View of Poetry," in *Harvard Studies in Classical Philology*, XXIX [1918], 37–38). In Book x, according to Greene, Plato begs the question by assuming that the definition of imitation will cover the aim of poetry (p. 53). Imitation in its broadest sense was a metaphor to which Plato resorted, with evident dissatisfaction, to explain the relation of the world of sense to the world of ideas (p. 66).

underlie some of Plato's most esteemed devices for displaying the meanings of words, it is difficult to know how the Platonic doctrine of poetry (to mention only one application) can be stated, or how its relation to later theories can be estimated, or how the condemnations which Plato passed on poets can be judged. In one of its narrowest senses Plato used the word "imitation" to distinguish poetic styles into three kinds: pure narrative, in which the poet speaks in his own person without imitation, as in the dithyramb; narrative by means of imitation, in which the poet speaks in the person of his characters, as in comedy and tragedy; and mixed narrative, in which the poet speaks now in his own person and now by means of imitation.[13] In the *Republic* the preference among poets is for the unmixed imitator of the good, since the guardians of an ideal state should be educated to imitate only what is appropriate to them.[14] Even this discussion of style and the manner of imitation involves a distinction of objects of imitation into worthy and unworthy in terms of the scale of their perfection of being. Moreover, previous to the discussion of style, the examination of the tales themselves, limited to proper subjects among gods, heroes, and men, led to a distinction not between worthy and unworthy but between true and false. The truths of poetry are imitations of the good. Falsehoods in discourse are likewise imitations, but the objects of such imitations have no external existence. False tales are imitations ($\mu\iota\mu\eta\mu\alpha$) of a lie in the soul, an after-rising image ($\epsilon\tilde{\iota}\delta\omega\lambda\text{o}\nu$) of it. Poetry, even false, is not an unmixed falsehood, but requires the antecedent lie for its explanation.[15]

The terms alternative to "imitation" ($\mu\iota\mu\eta\sigma\iota\varsigma$) begin to make their appearance in the discussion of falsity. A lie occurs when one copies ($\epsilon\dot{\iota}\kappa\dot{\alpha}\zeta\epsilon\iota\nu$) the true nature of gods and heroes badly; it is comparable to a portrait which bears no resemblance ($\ddot{o}\mu\text{o}\iota\alpha$) to the painter's model.[16] The argument concerning imitation may, moreover, be applied to the form in which it is itself stated, for the lie of the poet is explained by the image and likeness of the painter. Even at this early stage "imitation" may be applied to poetry in several senses; according to one, dramatic poetry is imitative of the speech of the characters; according to another, false poetry is imitative of a lie in the soul; according to a third, true poetry is imitative of the good. The lawgiver will lay down laws and patterns ($\tau\dot{\upsilon}\pi\text{o}\varsigma$) to which the poet will be required to conform,[17] and as soon as the philosopher is given his function in the perfect state, he too enters into the imitative process. He imitates the things which truly are and assimilates ($\dot{\alpha}\phi\text{o}\mu\text{o}\iota\text{o}\tilde{\upsilon}\sigma\theta\alpha\iota$) himself to them. He should, moreover, be compelled to mold ($\pi\lambda\dot{\alpha}\tau\tau\epsilon\iota\nu$) human nature to his vision; no city is happy unless its

13. *Republic* iii. 392D–394C.

14. *Ibid.* iii. 397D.

15. *Ibid.* ii. 382B–C.

16. *Ibid.* 377E.

17. *Ibid.* 380C.

lineaments have been traced by artists who used the heavenly model (παρ-άδειγμα).[18] Through these varying applications the term "imitation" indicates a constant relation between something which is and something made like it: the likeness itself may be good or bad, real or apparent. When, consequently, poetry is examined again in the tenth book of the *Republic* and is found to be imitative, it is incorrect to suppose that the word "imitation" has been unduly extended or that it has been given a new literal sense. The imitator (μιμητής) is defined as a maker of images (εἰδώλου ποιητής) and is contrasted to the maker of realities; unlike the latter he has no knowledge of being but only of appearances.[19] Both varieties of maker, moreover, stand in contrast to an eternal reality. Like the painter who paints the picture of a couch, the imitator makes a product at three removes from nature, for he imitates not that which is but that which seems to be, not the truth but a phantasm.[20] Poetry, therefore, at that removal from truth, attains only a small part of the object, and the part it attains is not the object itself but an image (εἴδωλον) capable of deceiving. If the poet were able to produce the things he imitates instead of making only images, if he had knowledge of the truth, he would abandon imitation.[21] Truth and falsity, knowledge and opinion, reality and appearance delimit at each step the scope of "imitation"; but as its application has varied, it has marked consistently a contrast between the work of imitation and something else which is, in comparison with it, real.

Even when limited to poetry and analogous activities, then, the concept of imitation may expand and contract. It may embrace a part of poetry, or all poetry, or even philosophy as well. But it also extends to other human activities. All the arts are imitative. The painter is comparable to the poet in his imitative character;[22] a good picture is one which reproduces the colors and figures of its subject.[23] Music is an imitation (μίμησις), a representation (ἀπει-κασία), a copy (εἰκαστική); good music possesses a standard of rightness and is a likeness of the beautiful (ὁμοιότης τοῦ καλοῦ).[24] The entire art of dancing is the result of imitation of what is said in song or discourse.[25] Since values are determined either by the adequacy of the representation or the character of the object imitated, the standards in dance and song may be stated in moral terms: figures and melodies which are expressive of the virtues of body or soul, or of copies (εἰκών) of them, are good.[26] Or the term "imitation"

18. *Ibid.* vi. 500C–E.

19. *Ibid.* x. 601B–C.

20. *Ibid.* 597D–598B.

21. *Ibid.* 599A–B.

22. *Ibid.* 596E; *Sophist* 234B.

23. *Cratylus* 431C.

24. *Laws* ii. 668A–B; cf. vii. 798D–E; *Cratylus* 423D.

25. *Laws* vii. 816A.

26. *Ibid.* ii. 655B ff.; cf. vii. 812C.

may be expanded in another direction from poetry. All verbal accounts, including the dialogues themselves, are imitations. At the beginning of the dialogue which bears his name, Critias remarks that all discourse is imitation (μίμησις) and representation (ἀπεικασία); and he complains that his task is more difficult than the one that Timaeus performed, inasmuch as image-making (εἰδωλο-ποιία) is subjected to closer criticism when it represents well-known human subjects than when it represents divine things in which we are content with a small degree of likeness.[27] But in the *Timaeus* Socrates finds a difficulty in discourse almost the contrary to that of which Critias complained. To bring out the competence of the speakers in the succeeding dialogues, Socrates had been developing the contrast, in terms of the degree of their knowledge and the nature of their discourse, of philosophers and statesmen to the imitative tribe of poets and the wandering Sophists; the defects of his own presentation in the *Republic*, comparable to a defect he finds exemplified by the poets, arise from the fact that familiar things are easy to imitate, but what is unfamiliar is difficult to imitate in action and even more difficult in words.[28] Moreover, the component parts of poems, discourses, and dialogues are imitations. Words imitate things in a fashion distinct from that of music or design,[29] and the letters of which words are composed are themselves means of imitation. From letters and syllables, the lawgiver forms a sign (σημεῖον) and a name (ὄνομα) for each thing; and from names he compounds all the rest by imitation.[30] When the nature of things is imitated by letters and syllables, the copy (εἰκών) is good if it gives all that is appropriate, bad if it omits a little.[31]

Not only arts, philosophy, and discourse are imitation. Human institutions must be added to the list. All governments are imitations of the true government;[32] and the laws themselves, source of the true government, are imitations of particulars of the truth which are written down, so far as that is possible, from the dictation of those who know[33] But the expansion of the word "imitation" passes beyond human products, actions, virtues, and institutions; it extends to things themselves. All things change, imitating and following what happens to the entire universe; and the imitation conforms to its model even in conception, generation, and nutrition.[34] It extends finally to the first principles of things. The universe is distinguishable into three fundamental forms: the model

27. *Critias* 107B–C.

28. *Timaeus* 19D–20B.

29. *Cratylus* 423C–424B.

30. *Ibid.* 426C–427C.

31. *Ibid.* 431D.

32. *Statesman* 293E; cf. *ibid.* 297C. It is significant, once more, that the nature of that imitation of the true government is explained by recourse to an image or figure (εἰκών, σχῆμα) in which the king is represented (ἀπεικάζειν) as pilot and physician.

33. *Ibid.* 300B–C.

34. *Ibid.* 274A.

form (παραδείγματος εἶδος), the imitation of the model (μίμημα παραδείγματος), and the Space or Receptacle in which Becoming takes place. Figures enter and depart in the Receptacle, as in a lump of gold which is curiously manipulated, in imitation of eternal figures, stamped (τυποῦν) from them in a marvelous fashion.[35]

In its expansion and contraction, the word "imitation" indicates the lesser term of the proportion of being to appearance: if God is, the universe is an imitation; if all things are, shadows and reflections are imitations; if the products of man's handicraft are, his representations of them are imitations. If imitation is to be avoided, it is because of the danger of imitating, through error, ignorance, or falsehood, that which is not or that which is less than it might be or is less than that which imitates it. As confined to the arts, therefore, imitation is not coextensive with the productive arts; rather, it is a part of them, for they are divided into those which produce things which are and those which produce images (εἴδωλον); the latter is the imitative art. Even when art is contrasted to nature and chance, the arts are divided into those arts which produce images (εἴδωλον), related to each other but bearing little relation to truth, like music and painting, and those arts which co-operate with nature, like medicine, husbandry, and gymnastic.[36] The divine art suffers a like division, for in addition to natural objects which are the result of God's art, there are visions (φάντασμα) seen in dreams and waking, shadows (σκιά), and reflections seen in polished surfaces.[37]

Man likewise makes things which are, and he makes images. His imitative or image-making art (εἰδωλοποιικὴ τέχνη) is divided into two parts, the copymaking art (εἰκαστική), which follows its original in length, breadth, depth, and color, and the fantastic art (φανταστική), in which truth is abandoned and the images are given, not their actual proportions, but such proportions as seem beautiful. The products of the second branch of the imitative art are appearances or phantasms (φάντασμα), and they are no longer even like things which are.[38] The proportion of being to appearance may be pursued to even greater refinements: that portion of that fantastic art in which the artist uses his own person as his instrument, making his figure and voice seem similar to another's, is called imitation (μίμησις);[39] and the return is complete to the sense of imitation by which dramatic poetry was distinguished from other kinds

35. *Timaeus* 48E–49B; 50A–C.   36. *Laws* x. 889A–D.

37. *Sophist* 266B.

38. *Ibid.* 235B–236C. Cf. *Rep.* x. 598B, where painting is said to be an imitation, not of that which is as it is, but of appearance as it appears; it is an imitation of a phantasm, not of truth.

39. *Ibid.* 267A.

in the third book of the *Republic*. The proportion of truth to falsity, and the proportion of knowledge to opinion, as might be expected, play as constant a role in the discussion of imitation as the proportion of being to appearance. The art of midwifery which Socrates practices on Theaetetus to bring forth his ideas is employed to distinguish the image from the real offspring,[40] and it is unsuccessful when it produces mere lies and images (ψευδῆ καὶ εἴδωλα).[41] If statesmen had no knowledge of what they were doing, they would imitate the truth but would imitate it badly; if they had knowledge, the imitation would be the truth itself and no longer an imitation.[42] If a man had genuine knowledge of the things he imitated, he would abandon the fashioning of images and devote himself to real things and actions rather than to imitating them.[43] Yet, on the other hand, by imitation of the unvarying revolutions of the God, we may stabilize the variable revolutions within ourselves;[44] and there is intellectual delight in the imitation of the divine harmony manifested in mortal motions.[45]

Even in a hasty adumbration of the infinite gradations of meaning and application which the term "imitation" undergoes in the Platonic dialogues, it is apparent that a great many similar terms undergo similar variations and approximate similar meanings in the succession of subjects on which imitation is brought to play. Several such terms have been necessary for the preceding exposition. Imitation is the making of images (εἴδωλον). The art of image-making may produce copies (εἰκών) or phantasms (φάντασμα), the difference between the two being that a copy is like its object, a phantasm is not. Yet a copy, to be correct, must not reproduce all the qualities of that which it copies. The painter makes a copy when he represents (ἀπεικάζειν) the color and form of his subject.[46] The control of poetic copies was to be the specific object of the supervision of poets and other artisans in the third book of the *Republic*. They were to be compelled to embody in their work copies of the good and to be prohibited from setting forth copies of the evil.[47] Similarly, the competent critic in any of the arts must know, first, what the copy is; second, how correctly it has been presented; third, how well it has been executed in words, melodies, and rhythms.[48] Even philosophic arguments are copies, for the solution of the question whether injustice is profitable to the completely unjust man, in the *Republic*, is arrived at by fashioning a copy of the soul in discourse[49] (εἰκόνα πλάσαντες τῆς ψυχῆς λόγῳ) in order to show the propounder of that

40. *Theaeietus* 150A.

41. *Ibid.* 150E.

42. *Statesman* 300D–E.

43. *Rep.* x. 599A.

44. *Timaeus* 47C.

45. *Ibid.* 80B.

46. *Cratylus* 432B.

47. *Rep.* iii. 401B.

48. *Laws* ii. 669A.

49. *Rep.* ix. 588B.

view precisely what he is saying. There are copies (εἰκών) and likenesses (ὁμοίωμα) of ideas in which few, unfortunately, can see the nature which they copy;[50] and finally the universe itself is a copy of the intelligible (εἰκὼν τοῦ νοητοῦ).[51]

As these fundamental terms are expanded, others are added to the list. An image (εἴδωλον) is defined as a thing made in the likeness (ἀφομοιοῦν) of the true thing, but only after a preliminary skirmish in which images in water and in mirrors are invoked to explain images.[52] Reflection in mirrors and in water is a constant device by which Plato clarifies his use of images and copies: the images and phantasms of men and other things are seen in water preliminary to examining men and things in their true natures;[53] one's eyes would be ruined if one looked at the sun directly instead of at its copy in water or in something else of that sort;[54] one should make one's thought clear by means of verbs and nouns, modeling (ἐκτυποῦν) opinion in the stream that flows through the lips as in a mirror or in water;[55] the versatility of the imitative artist which produces the appearance, though not the reality, of all things is explained by comparison to a mirror;[56] the liver is so fashioned that the power of thought, proceeding from the mind, moves in the liver as in a mirror which receives impressions (τύπος) and provides images (εἴδωλον) and the spleen is like a wiper for the mirror.[57]

Images and copies, however, as the metaphor would suggest, provide no satisfactory substitute for reality, though they are a necessary stage in the approach to reality. To understand the image we must know the reality; but to know the reality we must dispose of images. If there are copies (εἰκών) of letters in water or in mirrors, we shall never know them until we know the originals, and we shall never be true musicians until we know the forms of temperance, courage, liberality, and the rest.[58] He who studies things that are in arguments and reasons (λόγος) is as distinct from him who looks at them in copies (εἰκών) as he is from him who considers them in their operations and works (ἔργον).[59] There are many variants to the figure. The mirror may even appear in a text in which the mind is like a block of wax,[60] on which perceptions and thoughts are impressed (ἀποτυποῦσθαι) like the imprint of signet rings (δακτυλίων σημεῖα);[61] these persist as memorial imprints in the soul (μνη-

---

50. *Phaedrus* 250B.

51. *Timaeus* 92C; cf. *ibid*. 29B ff.

52. *Sophist* 239D–240A.

53. *Rep.* vii. 516A–B.

54. *Phaedo* 99D.

55. *Theaet.* 206D.

56. *Rep.* x. 596D–E.

57. *Timaeus* 71B; 72C.

58. *Rep.* iii. 402B–C.

59. *Phaedo* 100A.

60. *Theaet.* 193C.

61. *Ibid.* 191D.

μεῖον ἐν τῇ ψυχῇ), impressions (τύπος), seals (σφραγίς),⁶² imprints or signs (σημεῖον),⁶³ and even footprints (ἴχνος);⁶⁴ and we remember as long as the image (εἴδωλον) lasts.⁶⁵ The soul is likewise a book in which memory, perception, and feelings inscribe copies (εἰκών).⁶⁶ Analogies might be multiplied or the list of terms further extended; but in that development, even in an attenuated form, the discussion turns, as is inevitable if the thesis is correct, from the specific doctrine of imitation to embrace the entire philosophy of Plato and from the process of imitation to the devices of dialectic. Even the figure of the divided line is set forth in terms familiar to the doctrine of imitation, although the movement is from copies to reality rather than from reality to copies: all things are divided into the visible and the intelligible, and each of these parts in turn is divided into two classes. The first of the two classes of visible things is the class of copies (εἰκών), which includes shadows (σκιά) and reflections or phantasms in water (τὰ ἐν τοῖς ὕδασι φαντάσματα).⁶⁷ The second class of visible things is that of which the previous is a likeness or copy, that is, natural things, and the proportion between the likeness (ὁμοιωθέν) and that of which it is a likeness is the proportion between the objects of opinion and the objects of knowledge. But the soul, when it comes to investigate the first portion of the intelligible part of the line, must treat as copies the things which are imitated in the first part of the line; it is for that reason that the geometer draws squares and diagonals.⁶⁸ Once the discussion pursues this direction, it is only a step from "imitation" to the terms which guard the loftiest reaches of the Platonic dialectic, to recollection (ἀνάμνησις),⁶⁹ to presence in (παρουσία),⁷⁰ and participation (μέθεξις, κοινωνία).⁷¹

To elaborate the full significance of the term "imitation," consequently, more is required than the simple enumeration of the list of other words equivalent to it or used in its explication. Each of the terms of that lengthy list varies with the variation of "imitation." The set of significances employed in the dialogues may indeed be conceived as a huge matrix composed of all the words of a language, each possessed of an indefinite number of shades of meaning, the particular meaning of a word at any given time being determined by the meanings of other words drawn from that matrix in conjunction with which it is used. It is inevitable that the doctrine of imitation should invade the philosophic

62. *Ibid.* 192A.

63. *Ibid.* 192B.

64. *Ibid.* 193C.

65. *Ibid.* 191D.

66. *Philebus* 38E–39B.

67. *Rep.* vi. 509E–510A.

68. *Ibid.* 510B–511A.

69. *Phaedo* 72E, 92D; *Phaedrus* 249C; *Laws* v. 732B.

70. *Gorgias* 497E; *Phaedo* 100D.

71. *Sophist* 256A, 259A; *Parmenides* 132D.

enterprise and the dialectical method. All discourse is an imitation, and the interlocutors of the dialogues are constantly using, discussing, and complaining of images, likenesses, metaphors, and copies. " 'Your question,' I said, 'requires an answer expressed in an image [εἰκών].' 'And you,' he said, 'of course, are not accustomed to speak in images.' "[72] The image is frequently successful, frequently bad.[73] Even more important, the proportion of being to appearance, of truth to probability, obtains in discourse as in other things. It is proper to conceive all things as imitations; yet imitation should be avoided. All discourse deals in likenesses; yet one must be on one's guard against likenesses (ὁμοιότης).[74] Used with knowledge, however, there is no danger in imitation, whether the imitation be of lesser things or of greater; and so, too, dialectic may move in either direction, it may clarify the lesser by the greater, or the greater by the less.[75]

The criteria of good, true, and beautiful derive from the same proportion of being to appearance which operated throughout the doctrine of imitation. If the artificer of any object uses the uniform and eternal as his model, the object so executed must of necessity be beautiful; but if his model is a created object, his work so executed is not beautiful.[76] Discourse concerning the abiding and unshakable should be, as far as possible, irrefutable and invincible; but accounts of that which is copied after the likeness of the model are themselves copies and possess only likelihood, for as Being is to Becoming, Truth is to Belief.[77] In like manner and for like reason the Good gives truth to the objects of knowledge and the power of knowing, and is itself more beautiful even than they.[78]

The pursuit of beauty does not follow a different path from that which leads to truth and goodness. It is no accidental consequence, therefore, and it is no evidence of an inexplicable insensitivity to poetry in a great writer, that poetry should fall so low in Plato's analysis or that the poet should have no place in the perfect state. Criteria of truth and morality are applied as a natural course to the poet's work. He is permitted even in the ideal state to tell his tales, properly censored, as an incident of education and as a means of inculcating virtue. He may tell tales concerning the gods, to teach men "to honor the gods and their fathers and mothers, and not to hold their friendship with one another in

72. *Rep.* vi 487E. Cf. *Laws* 644C; *Gorgias* 517D; *Symposium* 215A, and *passim*.

73. *Phaedo* 99E.

74. *Sophist* 231A.

75. Thus, in the *Republic* ii. 369A, Socrates proposes first to treat of the state and then to seek the likeness (ὁμοιότης) of the greater in the lesser, whereas in the *Sophist* 218D the lesser is used as the model (παράδειγμα) of the greater. Cf. *ibid.* 221C, 226B.

76. *Timaeus* 28A–B.

77. *Ibid.* 29C.   78. *Rep.* vi. 508E.

light esteem";[79] he may tell tales concerning heroes to inspire the virtues of courage and self-control or temperance; but the discussion of the one remaining subject of his tales, men, is interrupted because justice would properly be inculcated by such tales, and, since the nature and value of justice has not yet been determined in the dialogue, instructions concerning the limitations of his poems are not yet ready for the poet.[80] Before that is possible the one remaining virtue, wisdom, which is left for expression to the scientist and the dialectician, since the poet can make no contribution to it, must be examined. If then one seeks tales about men, that is, tales by which men may learn justice, the *Republic* itself is such a tale, one long dialectical poem written for the elucidation of justice. In the *Laws*, where the concern is no longer with an ideal state but with one which is second best,[81] the function of the poet and the musician, still rigorously censored, is enlarged. In the *Republic* he found himself in competition with the dialectician, sadly handicapped by his lack of knowledge: in the *Laws* he is in competition with the lawgiver, for the whole state is an imitation of the best and noblest life, which is the very truth of poetry.[82] It is not its imitative character but its lack of truth and knowledge which brings poetry to its low estate. Homer and all the poetic tribe are imitators of images of virtue (μιμηταὶ εἰδώλων ἀρετῆς) and of other things, but they do not lay hold on truth.[83] Poetry is a kind of madness comparable to the art of divination or prophecy, or to the art of purification by mysteries, or to that higher madness which seizes the soul when it contemplates in true knowledge, like that of the gods, essence, formless, colorless, intangible. But we are told that when the soul falls from such contemplation, it passes first into a philosopher or a lover; second, into a king or warrior; third, into a householder or money-maker; fourth, into a gymnast; fifth, into a prophet or mystic; sixth, into a poet or imitator; and there are but nine stages in this progressive degradation of the soul.[84] The poet, like the interpreter of the poet, may be inspired by a divine gift;[85] but like the statesman, who is similarly inspired, he possesses at best only right opinion which is short of knowledge,[86] and like Ion, his interpreter, he is repeatedly given the rhapsode's final choice between inspiration and injustice.[87]

79. *Ibid.* iii. 386A.

80. *Ibid.* 392A–C.

81. *Laws* v. 739A; vii. 807B.

82. *Ibid.* vii. 817B: "You are poets and we are poets in the same things, your rivals as artists and actors in the fairest drama, which true law and that alone can carry out, as our hope is."

83. *Rep.* x. 600E.

84. *Phaedrus* 244A–245A; 248C–E.

85. *Ion* 533D–E.

86. *Meno* 99A–E.

87. *Ion* 542A.

II

In Aristotle's usage, not only does the term "imitation" have a different definition from that which it had for Plato but, much more important, Aristotle's method of defining terms and his manner of using them have nothing in common with the devices of the dialogues. There is a double consequence of these differences. Whereas for Plato the term "imitation" may undergo an infinite series of gradations of meaning, developed in a series of analogies, for Aristotle the term is restricted definitely to a single literal meaning. In the second place and as a consequence of the first difference, whereas for Plato an exposition of the word "imitation" involves an excursion through all the reaches of his philosophy, "imitation" for Aristotle is relevant only to one restricted portion of the domain of philosophy and never extends beyond it. For Plato dialectic is a device by which words, normally opaque, may be made translucent so that a truth and a beauty which are beyond words may shine through them. Though it is a device formulated in terms of words and conceived for the manipulation of words, it is the thing which is held constant; and it is the thing to which the attention of the mind is directed, while the word, on the other hand, varies and is to be discarded once it has served its function as a stage in the progress to truth. Things can be learned, Socrates says,[88] either through names or through themselves; but although one may learn from the name, which is a copy (εἰκών), both whether it is a good copy and the truth of which it is a copy, it is better to learn from the truth both the truth itself and whether the copy is properly made. The end of the dialectical process may in a sense be said to be the definition of words, but any word may have many definitions. For Aristotle, on the contrary, the definition of terms and the establishment of principles are the beginnings of the scientific enterprise. Words may have many meanings, and Aristotle frequently enumerates divergent senses of a given word. But in science they must be terms and must therefore be univocal. A term is a word plus a meaning. Consequently, although the Aristotelian sciences are distinguished according to their subject matters, it is the term which is held constant; and a given object, under different aspects isolated by different terms, may move from science to science. As mind, man would be a subject for psychology; as animal, a subject for biology; as natural thing, a subject for physics; as moral agent, a subject for ethics; as tragic actor, a subject for poetics. There results from these two differences a third difference in the fashion in which Plato and Aristotle use words, among others the word "imitation." Plato may ask concerning a given thing in different contexts whether or not it is an imitation, and may arrive in two places, without inconsistency, at

88. *Cratylus* 439A–B.

two answers, that it is an imitation and that it is not an imitation; for Aristotle, if a given thing is an imitation, it cannot *not* be an imitation.

The method of Aristotle, then, proceeds by the literal definition of terms and by the division of the domain of knowledge into a number of sciences: the theoretical sciences—metaphysics, mathematics, and physics; the practical sciences or the sciences of action—ethics and politics; the "poetic" sciences or the sciences of making; each with its proper principles and, in the case of subordinate sciences, principles derived from superior sciences. Imitation functions in that system as the differentia by which the arts, useful and fine, are distinguished from nature. Art imitates nature, Aristotle was fond of repeating,[89] and, at least in the case of the useful arts, the deficiencies of nature are supplemented in the process of that imitation by art following the same methods as nature would have employed. "Generally, art partly completes what nature cannot bring to a finish, and partly imitates her."[90] Thus, if a house were a natural product, it would pass through the same stages that it in fact passes through when it is produced by art; and if natural products could also be produced by art, they would move along the same lines that the natural process actually takes. The fine arts differ from the useful in their means of imitation, and consequently in the end of their imitation, for they have no end beyond the perfection of their product as determined by their object and the means they employ. Apart from such differences they are imitations of nature in the same sense as the useful arts. The term, therefore, does not have the scope of application which it possesses in Plato; and such accidental coincidences of verbal expression as occur are in a limited region of philosophy, particularly in the discussion of poetry and most striking in the discussion of dramatic poetry. For Aristotle imitation is not, at one extreme, the imitation of ideas, such as philosophers and the Demiurge indulge in according to Plato; nor is it, at the other extreme, the imitation of appearances themselves imitations, such as satisfies the Platonic poet. Imitation, being peculiar to the processes of art, is not found in the processes of nature or of knowledge. For the natural is that which has an internal principle of motion, whereas the change which is effected in artificial objects is from an external principle. Moreover, for Aristotle imitation is not an imitation of an idea in the mind of the artist; such a statement would be meaningless in the context of the Aristotelian system, though one might properly point out that the forms of the things which proceed from art are in the mind of the artist.[91] Rather, imitation is of particular things; the ob-

89. *Physics* ii. 2. 194^{a}21–22; *Meteorol.* iv. 3. 381^{b}6.

90. *Physics* ii. 8. 199^{a}15–17.

91. *Metaphysics* vii. 7. 1032^{a}31–^{b}1.

ject of imitation, according to the statement of the *Poetics*[92] which seems to be intended to apply to all the fine arts, is the actions of men.

Aristotle says relatively little concerning the process of imitation, and that little has been subject to great differences of interpretation; yet what he says of natural objects and their production and of artificial objects and their making affords sound basis for reconstruction of his theory of imitation. The natural object, composite of form and matter, acts according to the natural principle of its being; in imitation the artist separates some form from the matter with which it is joined in nature—not, however, the "substantial" form, but some form perceptible by sensation—and joins it anew to the matter of his art, the medium which he uses. The action which he imitates may be "natural" to the agent, but the artist must attempt to convey not that natural appropriateness and rightness, but rather a "necessity or probability" suitably conveyed by the materials of his art. It is for this reason that "a likely impossibility is always preferable to an unconvincing possibility."[93] The analysis might be illustrated from the various arts. The man who sits for his portrait assumes a posture which is determined by the laws of gravitation, by the anatomy of the human body, and by the peculiarities of his habits; the painter must justify the line he chooses not in terms of physics or anatomy, but in terms of the composition which appears in the colors and lines on his canvas. A man performs an action as a consequence of his character, his heritage, his fate, or his past actions; the poet represents that action as necessary in his medium, which is words, by developing the man's character, by expressing his thoughts and those of men about him, by narrating incidents. For Aristotle, consequently, imitation may be said to be, in the fine arts, the presentation of an aspect of things in a matter other than its natural matter, rendered inevitable by reasons other than its natural reasons; in the useful arts it is the realization of a function in another matter or under other circumstances than those which are natural. It is no contradiction, consequently, that the artist should imitate natural things, and that he should none the less imitate them "either as they were or are, or as they are said or thought to be or to have been, or as they ought to be."[94] Art imitates nature; the form joined to matter in the physical world is the same form that is expressed in the matter of the art. Art does not abstract universal forms as science does, but imitates the forms of individual things. Yet, just as the form of man differs from man to man, so the actions of the historical Orestes differ from the actions presented as probable or necessary for Orestes in the plot of a play; and if Orestes had no historical counterpart, the play would still, in this sense of imitation, be an imitation of the actions of men.

92. *Poetics* 2. 1448ᵃ1.

93. *Ibid.* 24. 1460ᵃ26–27.   94. *Ibid.* 25. 1460ᵇ7–11.

Whereas the word "imitation" and related words appear in almost every dialogue of Plato, the incidence of the term "imitation" in Aristotle is limited, except for references to poetic problems in other works, almost entirely to the *Poetics*. It is the imitative element in his work that makes the poet a poet.[95] The various arts and the various kinds of poetry may be distinguished as modes of imitation; and therefore, approaching the problem in his accustomed scientific orderliness, Aristotle considers the arts according to the differences in the means, the objects, and the manners of their imitations. In the *Poetics* he has occasion to treat only of the arts which use rhythm, language, and harmony as their means of imitation, though color and form are mentioned as other means.[96] Flute-playing and lyre-playing use a combination of harmony and rhythm. The dance, with only rhythms and attitudes, can represent men's characters as well as what they do and suffer. The mime and the dialogue imitate by language alone without harmony. Other arts, including the dithyramb, the nome, tragedy, and comedy, combine all three means—rhythm, melody, and verse—differing from each other, however, in their manner of employment of these means. The object of imitation is the actions of men. With the differences of agents, the actions themselves are differentiated; and painters, musicians, and dancers can be distinguished and described according to the characters they represent. In this respect tragedy differs from comedy in that it makes its characters better rather than worse than the run of men. Given the same means and object of imitation, finally, two poems may differ in manner of imitation. One poet may speak at one moment in his own person, at another in the person of his characters, as Homer did; another poet may speak in a single person without change throughout; or in the third place the imitators may represent the whole story dramatically, as though they were actually doing the things described.[97] The familiar classification of the kinds of poetry thus recurs much as it appeared in Plato, and on this most concrete of the levels of Plato's dialectic Aristotle seems to come closest to the statement of his master. Yet, important distinctions must be made between the two statements. For Plato it is a classification of three kinds of poetry: that which is effected by pure narrative, that which is effected by imitation, and the mixed kind which is effected by both. The preference is for the "unmixed imitator of the good."[98] Aristotle's distinction is among the manners of imitation in poems whose object and means of imitation are the same; to the other aspects of poetic imitation one further imitative characteristic is added. The question of

95. *Ibid*. 9. 1451ᵇ28–29; 1. 1447ᵇ15.

96. *Ibid*. 1. 1447ª18 ff.

97. *Ibid*. 3. 1448ª19–25.   98. *Rep*. iii. 397D.

preference among the various types is reserved for a later place,[99] and takes the form of the question whether the epic or the tragic is the higher form of imitation, the unmixed form not being considered. Moreover, the choice is made, not on moral but on literary grounds, because tragedy attains the poetic effect better than the epic. Aristotle is engaged in making literal distinctions, within the field of imitative art, of imitative devices and characteristics; dramatic imitation is one further imitative device to be added to other aspects of poetic imitation; his terms do not change their meanings, and his criteria are derived from a restricted field of discussion without reference beyond. Plato, on the other hand, applies the word "imitation" by means of the proportion of the real to appearance; relative to the narrative, drama is imitation; relative to the good, narrative too is imitation. No restricted field of literature with criteria peculiar to itself is indicated; rather, the proportions mark off at each application portions of the whole of things, real and apparent, and the criteria, envisaging the perfection of being which man might attain in that whole, are moral.

These primary distinctions serve a function in Aristotle's analysis comparable to that of the first principles of a science, although poetics is not a theoretic science and, like ethics and politics, it has no first principles in the sense in which theoretic sciences do. These, however, are fundamental distinctions derived from the subject matter with which the inquiry is concerned, and they supply the apparatus about which the analysis of poetry is organized. There are six "parts" of tragedy: three—plot, character, and thought—determined by the object of imitation; two—diction and melody—determined by the means of imitation; one—spectacle—determined by the manner of imitation. For Aristotle, as for Plato, the object of imitation is of primary importance; but that statement has a different significance in the context of Aristotle's analysis. In the dialogues it directed our attention from earthly things to eternal objects of imitation; in the *Poetics* it focuses discussion on the plot as an imitation of the actions of men. The plot is "the principle and, as it were, the soul of Tragedy."[100] The poet must be more the poet of his plots than of his verses, for he is a poet by virtue of the imitative element in his work, and it is actions that he imitates.[101] Character and thought follow in importance in the order named, and of the remaining three parts of the tragedy only diction is given extended discussion. The conditions of art, therefore, by which its representations are rendered necessary or probable are derived primarily from the object of imitation, and the discussion of tragedy in the *Poetics* is concerned largely with plot and character. Even the unity so essential to the work of art is not unrelated to

99. *Poet.* 26. 1461^{b}26 ff.

100. *Ibid.* 6. 1450^{a}38–39.   101. *Ibid.* 9. 1451^{b}27–29.

its object of imitation, since "one imitation is always of one thing."[102] Some of the conditions of art, as derived from the actions of men, pertain to the nature of art in general; some, derived from actions of a given kind, are specific to the art forms that are devoted to that kind; some conditions derived from the means of imitation, similarly, are generic to several kinds of art, as the devices of rhythm are used in poetry, music, and the dance; some are specific to particular arts, tone to music, words to poetry, color to painting.

In Plato it proved to be impossible to consider art without regard to its moral and political effects. Aristotle is no less aware of those effects and their implications; but in virtue of his method, whatever pertains to the subject of a particular science is reserved for treatment in that science. Tragedy may be used as a political instrumentality in the state or it may reflect political doctrines or motivations in its speeches: in either case, it does not function as a work of art but is properly treated among the problems of politics and rhetoric. Art in the state and thought in the drama are subjects which Aristotle apparently does not consider parts of the subject matter of the *Poetics*, for the first would need to be referred to the principles of political science, and the second, since thought is "the power of saying whatever is appropriate to the occasion,"[103] falls within the scope of rhetoric and is referred to the Art of Rhetoric for treatment. Aristotle adds dryly that the older poets make their characters discourse like statesmen, and the moderns like rhetoricians. In the *Politics*[104] he treats the arts as instruments of teaching virtue and forming character. His attention centers almost entirely on music in the portion of the discussion of education which survives in that book. Rhythm and melody supply likenesses ($\delta\mu o i\omega\mu a$) of anger, gentleness, courage, temperance, and other qualities of character as well as their contraries; and the feelings of pleasure and pain at mere representations are not far removed from the same feelings about realities. The objects of senses like taste or touch furnish no likenesses to the virtues. There are figures in visible objects which do have that characteristic, but only to a small degree; and all people do not share in the feeling they occasion, for they are signs ($\sigma\eta\mu\epsilon\hat{\iota}o\nu$) rather than likenesses of moral habits, indications which the body gives of states of feeling. The connection of painting or sculpture with morals is therefore slight. But even in simple melodies there are imitations ($\mu i\mu\eta\mu a$) of moral habits, and the same is true of rhythms. It is primarily music among the arts which has the power of forming character; and Aristotle urges, therefore, that it be introduced into the education of the young.

102. *Ibid.* 8. 1451a30–35.

103. *Ibid.* 6. 1450b4–8; cf. 19. 1456a34–36.

104. *Politics* viii. 5. 1339b42–1340b13.

If analogies are to be drawn between Plato's views on imitation and those of Aristotle and if the latter is to be assimilated to his master, as having effected either a distortion and retrogression or an advance and specification of the doctrines he learned in the Academy, the most fertile grounds for such comparison are found in the brief section in the *Politics*, for art is there discussed as a political force and politics is an architectonic science, limited by its practical character to the use of the analogical method. But even in the *Politics* the word and the method of its use falls short of the scope which it has in Plato's dialectic. Art, moreover, is there considered not as art but as a political device. To cite what is said concerning art in the *Politics* in refutation or in expansion of what is said on the same subject in the *Poetics*, without recognizing that the one is a political utterance, the other an aesthetic utterance, would be an error comparable to looking for evolution or refutation between the statements of the *Republic* and the *Laws*, without recognizing that the one has reference to a perfect state, the other to a state possible to men as they are. In the Aristotelian approach the aspects of things are distinguished from each other and treated independently; the major branches of the sciences are separated, and within each branch the major subdivisions; and since imitation is the differentia of art, and since the fine arts are further differentiated from the useful arts by their ends and their means, and since finally the fine arts are distinguished from each other by their respective means and the objects appropriate to those means, it follows not only that there is a branch of knowledge whose subject matter is the products of the arts, but also that each of the arts may be the subject properly for like investigation. The *Poetics* is such an examination of poetry in itself, not in its relation to education, morals, statesmanship, nature, or being. In Plato's analysis, on the other hand, poetry cannot be considered in isolation; it is one of the numerous strands of man's life and takes its importance and meaning from those strands; it bears analogies to all the other arts, to the phenomena of nature and the actions of the gods; distinctions in art parallel those of education, of science, of moral, social, and political life; in the dialectical examination of all these activities the same contraries are employed, the one and the many, being and becoming, the true and the false, knowledge and belief, the fair and the foul, and all of them involve imitation. Art is, therefore, never dissociated in the Platonic approach from the full context of life; and it is always subject to moral, political, educational, and scientific criticism, for there can be no other, no purely aesthetic, criticism of art.

The Platonic and the Aristotelian approaches to the consideration of art differ, therefore, not in the manner of two doctrines which contradict each other, but rather in the manner of two approaches to a subject which are mutually incommensurable. Even more, the differences of the two approaches and the peculiarities of the two methods indicate in themselves no superiority of the one over the other, nor are problems soluble by the one which are impervious to the analysis of the other. Although there is no place for distinct sciences, independent of each other, in Plato, there are none the less abundant devices by which to make distinctions; and likewise, although all problems are assigned to their proper scientific context in Aristotle and although each science has its proper domain, its proper scope, and frequently methodological devices peculiar to itself, knowledge is not hopelessly atomized, for there are devices by which to consider phenomena in the context of all the varieties of problems.

There are complementary dangers, moreover, in cross-references from one work of either of these philosophers to another. Plato never employs one dialectical strand alone: in the *Republic* and the *Laws* poetry is treated by means of analogies drawn successively from the numerous strands of political life; in the *Phaedrus* the analogies bind it to the other arts, particularly to the art of rhetoric; in the *Ion* it appears in connection with the divine gift of inspiration. Moreover, even between the *Republic* and the *Laws* the analogies have shifted— as indeed they shift from book to book within each of those works—for the context of one is the idea of a perfect state, the other the construction of a state short of perfection with specific social, economic, and political characteristics. What is said about poetry in one of these contexts cannot be taken to be literally the same or literally contradictory to what is said of poetry in any of the other contexts. Just as the meaning in each dialogue is brought out by a dialectical development, so the translation from dialogue to dialogue requires similar dialectical modification. The doctrine of Plato concerning poetry cannot be built up by collecting quotations in which the word "poetry" appears throughout his works; the result of such an enterprise indeed is no doctrine whatever but, as the history of criticism has abundantly illustrated, a collection of inconsistent statements. Contrariwise, whereas in Plato's treatment the concepts of art and imitation are generalized or particularized to various dialectical contexts, in Aristotle the treatment of art and imitation, considered in their own right and in their proper science, may be supplemented by a consideration of them as they impinge on the problems of other sciences, on grammar, rhetoric, logic, ethics, politics, physics, psychology, or metaphysics. But to collect from the works concerned with the various sciences quotations in which the words "imitation" or "poetry" or "art" appear, with the intention to place them one after the other and so find in them a coherent doctrine, results in an assemblage of statements as confused as the corresponding collections from the dialogues of Plato. As the statements of Plato require dialectical approximation to each other, the statements of Aristotle require the intrusion of proper principles from the appropriate sciences to permit transition from one to the other.

III

In Aristotle the term "imitation" is given a literal meaning and is limited in application to works of human art; in Plato the meaning is developed and contracted in analogies so that the word cannot be said to have determined application but is sometimes more general, sometimes more restricted, than any use in Aristotle. The word was used in still other senses by other writers in antiquity, but considerations of method are not so important in the fashions of their usage, and the systematic implications are not subtle. None of the writers on literature employed the dialectical method of Plato in any but a highly attenuated and faltering manner. Their definitions are literal like those of Aristotle, but in their writings the term "imitation" does not appear in a context of subject matters distributed in various scientific disciplines. Rather, the meanings in which they use the term are derived for the most part from one of the meanings which it assumed in Plato's dialogues, usually degraded and rendered static or, what amounts to the same thing, in a meaning which "imitation" might have had if Aristotle had used it in some other work than the *Poetics*, as, for example, the *Rhetoric*.

A third variant to the meanings of Plato and Aristotle may therefore be said to derive from the tradition of writers on rhetoric. In age, this view is at least contemporary with the other two, and it has perhaps an even longer and certainly less distorted history since the age of Plato. "For the rest," Isocrates says,[105] "he [the teacher] must in himself set such an example [παράδειγμα], that the students who are molded [ἐκτυποῦν] by him and are able to imitate [μιμήσασθαι] him will, from the outset, show in their speaking a degree of grace and charm greater than that of others." Though Aristotle wrote a *Rhetoric* (and, if Cicero and Quintilian are correct, justified himself in teaching rhetoric by turning a scathing epigram against Isocrates), he confines his attention to the analysis of the means of persuasion available to the orator and finds no place for aphorisms concerning the imitation of past orators. He does say that man is the most imitative of animals and learns at first by imitation;[106] he distinguishes repeatedly in his works between sciences, which are acquired by learning; virtues, which are acquired by habituation; and arts, which are acquired by practice (ἄσκησις). It would be easier to find analogies in Plato for Isocrates' use of the term; but for Plato it would have that meaning only as applied to early education, for in maturity one would imitate, not the poet but him who knows. Strictly even then imitation is of the virtues and the truth,

105. *Against the Sophists* 18.
106. *Poet.* 4. 1448^{b}5–9.

not of the wise man. Yet imitation in this rhetorical sense, imitation of other artists, continued to be used in the writings of rhetoricians and orators. Cicero frequently recommends the imitation of good models, and Dionysius of Halicarnassus composed a treatise *On imitation*, preserved unfortunately only in fragments, which he tells us consisted of three parts, the first on imitation in general, the second on the choice of writers for imitation (including poets, philosophers, historians, and orators), the third on the proper methods of imitation. The last subject, which was never completed by Dionysius, is one to which Quintilian returns,[107] for to his mind there are three essentials in the formation of the ideal orator—power of speech, imitation, and diligence of writing.[108] Imitation alone, to be sure, is not enough,[109] for invention must precede imitation, and the greatest qualities of the orator, including invention, are beyond imitation.[110] One should consider, Quintilian says, first whom to imitate, second what to imitate in the authors chosen.[111] Imitation, he reminds us, should not be confined merely to words; one should consider also the appropriateness with which orators handle circumstances and persons, their judgment and their powers of arrangement, their concentration of all parts of the speech to the end of victory. Yet his own treatment of imitation is confined almost wholly to the question of style. According to Dionysius of Halicarnassus, imitation is "a copying of models with the help of certain principles," but it involves a kind of psychological elevation as well: it is an "activity of the soul inspired by the spectacle of the seemingly beautiful."[112] Longinus regards zealous imitation of the great historians and poets of the past as one of the roads which leads to sublimity.[113]

We, too, then, when we are working at some passage which demands sublimity of thought and expression, should do well to form in our hearts the question, "How perchance would Homer have said this, how would Plato or Demosthenes have made it sublime, or Thucydides in his history?" Emulation will bring those great characters before our eyes, and like pillars of fire they will lead our thoughts to the ideal standards of perfection. Still more will this be so, if we give our minds the further hint, "How would Homer or Demosthenes, had either been present, have listened to this passage of mine? How would it have affected them?"[114]

---

107. *Institutio oratoria* x. 2. 1–28.

108. *Ibid.* x. 1. 3. Cf. *Rhetorica ad Herennium* i. 2. 3 (ed. Marx), in which three aids to proficiency in oratory are enumerated: art, imitation, and exercise. "Art" is preception which gives a certain way and reason of speaking. "Imitation" is that by which we are impelled with diligent reason to be similar to some model in speaking. "Exercise" is assiduous use and custom in speaking. Cf. Cicero, *De oratore* ii. 22–23.

109. *Institutio oratoria* x. 2. 4.

110. *Ibid.* 2. 12.

111. *Ibid.* 2. 14. 27.

112. *On Imitation* A. iii (28).

113. *On the Sublime* 13.

114. *Ibid.* 14.

Imitation of past authors, however, though it may be useful as a device for training orators or as a touchstone for sublime passages of prose and poetry, will not supply an object of imitation or a subject matter for poetry. To be sure, as an English poet was later to suggest, to imitate Homer was to imitate nature, but nature has become too generalized to supply the function exercised in the object of imitation as conceived in Plato or Aristotle. In the Platonic usage, the object of imitation is consistently that which is, or being, through all the variations of the meaning of the word. For Aristotle the object of imitation in poetry is the actions of men, though some of the arts may imitate character and passion as well. According to Aristotle the plot, the soul of the tragedy, gives unity to the work. Plot is seldom discussed by the later writers; but instead character, thought, or even natural things become the chief object of imitation. According to Dionysius, poets and prose writers must keep their eye on each object and frame words to picture them or borrow from other writers words which imitate things. Nature, however, is the great originator and teacher in these matters and prompts us in the imitation of things by words, as when we speak of the bellowing of bulls,[115] or in the arrangement of words, as when Homer reflects the effort of Sisphyus rolling his rock uphill in the verses in which he describes it.[116] Plutarch marks this transition to the imitation of natural objects most explicitly. Imitation, he says, is of actions or works (ἔργον) or things (πρᾶγμα),[117] and apparently these terms are equivalent in his usage. One of the problems to concern him most is that imitations of ugly or even disgusting objects should be pleasing, a subject on which Aristotle touched for an opposite purpose in treating the origin of poetry, for he argued that imitation is natural to man since he finds even the imitation of disgusting objects pleasing.[118] The young should be taught to praise the genius and the art which imitates such subjects, according to Plutarch, but to censure the subjects and actions themselves, for the excellence of a thing and the excellence of its imitation are not the same. For him, as for Dionysius, the grunting of a hog, the noise of pulleys, the whistling of the wind, and the roaring of seas are the instances from which a discussion of imitation takes its natural beginning. But while poetry is based on imitation, in this sense, and employs embellishment and richness of diction suited to the actions and characters, Plutarch adds the warning, somewhat Aristotelian in language but Platonic in the development he gives it, that it does not give up the likeness of truth, since the charm of imitation is probability.[119] Imitation has the same significance for Longinus when he is not using the term

115. *On Literary Composition* 16.

116. *Ibid.* 22.

117. *Essay on Poetry* 3.

118. *How a Young Man Should Study Poetry* 3.   119. *Ibid.* 7.

to recommend the imitation of great writers: just as people who are really angry or frightened or worried or carried away by jealousy or some other feeling speak incoherently, "so, too, the best prose writers by use of inversions imitate nature and achieve the same effect. For art is only perfect when it looks like nature and nature succeeds only by concealing art about her person."[120] Demetrius cautions against crude imitation of the poets.[121] The dictum of Aristotle, that art imitates nature, has suffered a like degradation with the transformation of the word "imitation."

Although nature still supplies the object of imitation, imitation is no longer the central concept, either in the sense of Plato or in that of Aristotle, about which the analysis of poetry is organized. Occasionally, one of the later writers, like Plutarch, will take up the question of the truth of poetry and puzzle over the intentional and unintentional falsification of the poets; but although the men who followed Plato learned from him to worry concerning lies about the gods, the Platonic proportions of truth to falsity, of being to appearance, do not play upon poetry again in antiquity. Truth, if it is discussed, is usually measured in these later times by asking whether or not the event took place, and whether the object was such as it is represented. On the other hand, what later writers learned from Aristotle applicable to literature, they derived from the *Rhetoric* rather than from the *Poetics*, as indeed might be surmised, since it was a period which held rhetoric in high esteem and most of the writers in the tradition were professed rhetoricians. Yet that change marks them as significantly different from Aristotle, since to confuse rhetoric and poetics would in his system be a Platonizing error. He, himself, distinguished the two disciplines sharply: only two of the six "parts" of tragedy—thought and diction—are properly treated in rhetoric; and only one of them—thought—receives the same treatment in Aristotle's *Rhetoric* and *Poetics*. Aristotle's concern with action therefore and the emphasis he puts on plot, the soul of the composition, with its beginning, middle, and end, are not repeated in later writers.[122] With the gradual disappearance of plot, the Aristotelian scheme of the parts of the poem breaks down and the most prominent of his critical principles become irrelevant. Principles and criteria must be supplied from the tradition of rhetoric, and imitation moves to a place of comparative unimportance in the analysis of poetry. Rhetoric, according to Aristotle, is the faculty by which in any subject we are able to win belief in the hearer. That belief is produced by means of invention, disposing of three means: the character and behavior of

---

120. *On the Sublime* 22.   121. *On Style* ii. 112.

122. Horace's brief treatment of plot, which includes the enjoinder that the middle harmonize with beginning and end, is typical of the few remnants of the treatment of that aspect of the poem (see *Art of Poetry* ll. 119–52).

the speaker, the character and passions of the hearer, and the proofs which are alleged in the words of the speaker. If some other effect in the hearer is substituted for belief, as Longinus substituted ecstasy, such an analysis might be suited to any branch of literature. The time might even come when invention might take the place of imitation, as indeed Quintilian had recognized its greater importance while protesting it was not a subject of art. The "parts" with which the analysis deals gravitate about thought and diction, or some variant of the elements of rhetoric. According to Dionysius, two things require attention in all forms of composition: ideas and words, subject matter and expression.[123] According to Longinus, there are five sources of the sublime: power of thought and emotion, which proceed from natural genius; and figures, diction, and arrangement, which proceed from art.[124] According to Demetrius, each of the four kinds of style consists of thought, diction, and arrangement.[125]

IV

The consequences of these changes for the analysis of literature would be too long to enumerate. Whereas Plato considered poetry in the context of the total activity of man or in the context of the eternal ideas, poetry came to be considered more and more in isolation. On the other hand, the Aristotelian mode of analysis was not followed, for the work of art was not considered, in itself, objectively. Rather, it was the poets who were the subject of consideration in an environment of other poets whom they imitated and of audiences whom they pleased. The Hellenistic and Roman literary critic was sometimes a Platonist whose universe was limited to the literary world, sometimes an Aristotelian engaged in the rhetoric of poetry and prose. Since the plot had lost the central importance it had for Aristotle, imitation is of persons, actions, and things. Where Plato could be led by his dialectic to moral indignation at the imitation of the roll of thunder, the squeak of pulleys, the bleat of sheep,[126] or Aristotle could limit imitation to the actions of men and invoke aesthetic principles for the comparative judgment of kinds of poetry differentiated by the characters of the men imitated, later critics found occasion only to insist on the difference between the imitation and the object imitated and to separate admiration of the technique by which the one was produced from approbation of the other. Moreover, as criticism ceases to turn largely on action and the plot, the work of art as a whole passes out of the purview of the critic and attention is concentrated on analyzing the characteristics and determining the effectiveness of individual passages.

123. *On Literary Composition* 1.

124. *On the Sublime* 8. 1.

125. *On Style* ii. 38, etc.

126. *Rep.* iii. 397A–B.

The kinds of poetry, moreover, which Aristotle was careful to distinguish in terms of the means and object of imitation, are treated without distinction; and citations are drawn not only from poets of different kinds but from historians, orators, and philosophers as well. But most important of such differences, containing them as consequence, is the fact that after Plato and Aristotle, who judged literature primarily by reference to its object of imitation, there grew up a generation of critics, of numerous and long-lived progeny, who judged literature by considering its effect on the audience. Not that Plato or Aristotle was averse to considering the pleasure afforded by an object of art, but they subordinated such consideration to that of the object of imitation; and while the good work of art will be pleasurable to the mind prepared to understand it, pleasure as such, without consideration of person and object, would furnish no criterion for art. But the natural center of gravity in rhetoric is the audience, and the fourth variation of the meaning of imitation is marked by the disappearance of the term from its central place in criticism. For while a poet may imitate that which is, or the actions of men, or other poets, he pleases rather than imitates audiences. "It is not enough for poems to have beauty," Horace says,[127] "they must also be pleasing and lead the listener's soul whither they will. . . . If the speaker's words are inconsistent with his fortunes, a Roman audience, high and low will roar with laughter." The nature and origin of poetry is to please the mind.[128] "Poets desire either so improve or to please, or to unite the agreeable with the profitable. . . . The centuries of the elders reject plays without a moral; the haughty knights dislike dull poems."[129] Horace's criticism is directed in the main to instruct the poet how to keep his audience in their seats until the end, how to induce cheers and applause, how to please a Roman audience, and, by the same token, how to please all audiences and win immortality. But although imitation does not supply or illuminate these ends, it does help further them. The well-informed imitator is advised to take his models from life and custom and to derive from them a language faithful to life.[130] He should also study the Greek models;[131] the Socratic dialogues will supply matter, and words will follow quickly, once the matter is seen;[132] but the imitator is cautioned not to translate too literally lest his own style suffer.[133]

127. *Art of Poetry*, ll. 99–112.

128. *Ibid.*, l. 377.

129. *Ibid.* ll. 333–43. Cf. Plutarch, *How a Young Man Should Study Poetry* 1, 2, 3, 7, and 14 for another view in which pleasure and improvement vie; but for a contrasting view of the place of audience and pleasure in the judgment of art see Plato's *Laws* ii. 658A–659C and 668A–669B, or *Gorgias* 501D–502D.

130. *Art of Poetry* ll. 317–18.   131. *Ibid.* ll. 268–69.   132. *Ibid.* ll. 310–11.

133. *Ibid.* ll. 133–35; cf. his disdain for the servile herd of imitators and his statement of the fashion in which he followed Archilochus, *numeros animosque secutus Archilochi, non*

Imitation has been reduced to the imitation of other artists or to reflecting actual conditions or customs.

A fifth meaning for the term "imitation" of the same quixotic sort, that is to say, a meaning which, like the proportion of poet to audience, made the term unnecessary or impossible, remains to be indicated. Words may imitate thoughts, as Horace suggests; and if the analysis of poetry in terms of pleasure is an outgrowth of the rhetorical tradition, the analysis of poetry in terms of thought and diction is in a sense the lessened form which the Aristotelian poetic analysis took for later ages. Writers like Dionysius of Halicarnassus and Demetrius, when they limit themselves to relevant questions of words and their arrangements in relation to the thoughts they express, have in common with Aristotle the ideal of discussing the work of art in its own terms without reference to the universe, to authors, or to audience. But the object of imitation has been cut down to thought, and the subtlety of analysis is expended almost entirely on diction. Moreover, literature is considered in short passages, rather than whole works, and prose and poetry are treated together more or less indiscriminately. The problem of literature turns on propriety and the need to find distinguished thoughts and distinguished expressions and to clothe thoughts in appropriate words. These are problems which the term "imitation" was apparently not suited to embrace, and the writers in that tradition continued to speak only of the imitation of poets by poets and of things by words.[134]

Notwithstanding our changed attitude toward imitation, it requires no great alteration of terminology to recognize the tendencies of modern criticism in some of these five ancient attitudes, and there is much that is perhaps clearer in their example which might be considered with profit in the discussion of the nature of literature or the canons, tenets, or principles of criticism. Literature may be considered as a part of the social structure, and we have critics who engage in such social criticism today. It may be considered in terms purely of style, or in terms of the great writers and great works of the past, or in terms of the character and demands of audiences of the present and of posterity. It seems apparent that each of these approaches and each of their variants is distinct from the others. If its full intention is stated clearly, it is difficult to understand how one of them could be consituted the contradiction of the other, except in the sense

---

res et agentia verba Lycamben, and tempered the versification of Archilochus with Sappho and Alcaeus; the imitation was limited to measures and structure of verse and did not extend to subjects or arrangement (*Ep.* i. 19. 19–29).

134. Cf. nn. 112, 115, 116, 121, above. Demetrius returns frequently to the problem of onomatopoeia and the imitation of actions by words. Cf. *On Style* ii. 72. 94; iii. 176; iv. 221. Sometimes, however, he uses imitation in the sense of dramatic imitation in connection with the style of dialogues (*ibid.* iv. 226, 298).

that a given critic might prefer one to all the rest. Much that passes for differences of taste in literature consists in reality of differences of taste in criticism, of differences in the preferred approach to literature. A critic is seldom satisfied to make his own approach without having shut off all other roads. Such jealousy of one's own truth is not difficult to explain, for what I say, when I consider it my critical function to tell my experiences before works of art, may be expressed in words related to those you will use when you tell of art's social function; and those words will probably be used as in contradiction. What is needed is more than a definition of terms, for the terms used in definitions also vary in the context of the larger method and system in which criticism functions; ultimately contradictions and confusions are resolved by the exploration of the full philosophic implications of the attitude which the critic finds himself justified in assuming. It is not, perhaps, excessive to remark that the philosophic sweep in recent criticism has not been broad, nor has the interplay of implication been subtle. There have been few writers in the whole history of thought able to manipulate the Platonic dialectic; and of them, few have turned their attention to literature. There are few studies of literature in terms of its medium, the forms which are suited for expression in that medium, and the manner of such expression. It is hardly profitable or pertinent to regret that there have been few Platos and few Aristotles; but it is appropriate to remark on the misfortune, since there are so few, that we should neglect so signally to profit by their examples of method, but should be content in our studies and histories to find imperfections which they seem to possess only when their sentences are read without the logical and dialectical devices they supply to guide interpretation.

CASTELVETRO'S THEORY OF POETICS

BERNARD WEINBERG

IN THE history of modern literary criticism Lodovico Castelvetro figures as the man who invented the three pseudo-Aristotelian unities of time, place, and action. Or at least he is credited with having given the first complete expression to the time-place-action complex and with having thus exerted an important influence on the development of the classical doctrine. This is perhaps a correct estimate of his contribution. But it does not emphasize as fully as it should his real position in the movement away from the text of Aristotle and toward the theory of the French classicists. That position is not so much a matter of the incidental question of the unities as it is of his total philosophical approach, of his general treatment of poetic matters, of his method of analysis. For Castelvetro, whose *Poetica d'Aristotele vulgarizzata et sposta* dates from 1570,[1] represents in a sense a culmination of the tendencies already manifest in the first commentary on Aristotle's *Poetics*, Robortello's *In librum Aristotelis De arte poetica explicationes* of 1548.[2] He incorporates in his discussion the accretion of the intervening years; and what he produces, since it is more extreme, is much farther away from the text of Aristotle and much closer to the point of view of French classicism.

The first notable difference between Robortello and Castelvetro is to be found in their attitude toward Aristotle himself. For Robortello, the text which he is expounding is a masterpiece of clarity and logic. He pauses frequently to point out the excellence of its construction, to defend it against those who hold that it is fragmentary, imperfect, or erroneous. His intention is to justify and accept integrally the text of Aristotle; if he comes up with an essentially un-Aristotelian analysis, it is because of his incapacity to understand the text and because of long-standing habits of textual exposition, and not through any intention to disagree. With Castelvetro, the point of departure is a basic scorn for the text of the *Poetics*. The *Poetics* is not a complete work, but "a collection of poetic materials from which an art might be written";[3] it includes remarks

---

1. Vienna: Stainhofer, 1570. A second edition, posthumous, emended and corrected, appeared in 1576 (Basel: Pietro de Sedabonis); my analysis is based on this edition, from which all quotations are taken. I give page and line reference for the beginning of each quotation.

2. See my "Robortello on the *Poetics*," in *Critics and Criticism* (original ed.), pp. 319–48.

3. "vn raccoglimento di materie poetiche da comporre l'arte" (82. 23).

146

which Aristotle meant later to refute or reject;[4] many passages are out of place;[5] and there are obvious contradictions.[6] But these are merely matters of organization; Castelvetro's contempt goes farther. He does not hesitate to characterize certain ideas of Aristotle's as false: "Aristotle here and elsewhere is of the opinion that the same pleasure is derived from tragedy through reading it as through seeing it and hearing it recited in action; which thing I esteem to be false";[7] "Now, according to Aristotle, poetry always imitates one of the three things indicated by him. . . . This does not seem true to me, simply speaking";[8] "Now Aristotle assumes as simply true a thing which is not so at all."[9] He rejects Aristotle's ideas when they seem inadequately supported: "I should wish this to be shown to me otherwise than on his authority, since he seems to say and repeat several times this same thing without adducing a single reason of any value."[10] He goes so far as to ask the question, given the uselessness of Aristotle's precepts to the art of history: "What will prevent us, following the strength of this argument, from being constrained to say that these precepts are neither proper nor useful to poetry itself?"[11]

Nothing is farther from Castelvetro's mind, then, than to attempt a justification of the Aristotelian text. He tries to explain it when he can, to point out what he thinks Aristotle meant. But generally he uses it as a point of departure for the development of his own theories. His favorite device is to take a given passage in the *Poetics*, show how and why the distinctions made are incomplete and incorrect, and then proceed to his own set of distinctions on the same subject. We may take as an example his treatment of *Poetics* 1460ª26, on the impossible probable:

> Now, if I am not mistaken, this question would have been better understood, and greater light would have been shed upon the things which need to be said, if three divisions had been made, in each one of which would be the virtue to be followed and the vice to be avoided. And the first would be that of possibility and impossibility, and the

4. 35. 1, 111. 24.

5. 91. 36, 174. 8, 218. 16, 234. 30, 294. 33, 341. 24, 386. 30.

6. 275. 30.

7. "Aristotele qui, & altroue è di questa opinione, che quello diletto si tragga della tragedia in leggendola, che si fa in vedendola, & in vdendola recitare in atto. la qual cosa io reputo falsa" (297. 30).

8. "Hora secondo Aristotele la poesia rassomiglia sempre l'vna delle tre cose proposte da lui.... Il che non ci pare vero, simplicemente parlando" (583. 1).

9. "Hora presuppone Aristotele per cosa simplicemente vera quella, che non è cosi" (691. 15; cf. 315. 38, 386. 24, 491. 13, 694. 6, 697. 6).

10. "vorrei, che mi fosse mostrato per altro, che per autorita di lui, che pare dire, & ridire piu volte questo medesimo senza addurre ragione di niuno valore" (280. 29).

11. "che ci vetera, che seguendo noi il vigore di questo argomento non siamo costretti a dire, che non sieno ne conueneuoli, ne gioueuoli alla stessa poesia?" (7. 1).

second would be that of credibility and incredibility; these two divisions have been discussed so far. And the third would be that of usefulness and of uselessness to the constitution of the plot.

From this point he proceeds to a development of the distinction, to a sub-division into eight possible combinations, to the statement that the first and second divisions belong "to nature, or to civil and human reason," whereas the third is the proper province of the poet.[12] There are a score or more of similar passages. Castelvetro's real aim seems, then, to be the substitution of his own ideas for Aristotle's and the development of a set of statements which may properly be called "Castelvetro's theory of poetics."

I

Among those tendencies which, already in Robortello, marked a departure from the spirit of the *Poetics*, the most significant methodologically is the re-moval of the principal emphasis from the poem to the audience. Such a trans-formation means that all aspects of poetry are considered not in terms of the artistic exigencies of the poem itself but in terms of the needs or demands of a specifically characterized audience. Now in Castelvetro this tendency is pushed to the extreme: the audience is very carefully delimited and restricted, and every phase of the poetic art is considered in relationship to this audience. In the first place, Castelvetro assumes that Aristotle treats only such genres as were susceptible of public performance and that hence his audience is the "common people": "poetry was invented for the pleasure of the ignorant multitude and of the common people, and not for the pleasure of the edu-cated";[13] "for purposes of the common people, and for the pleasure alone of the rough crowd, was invented the stage and the representative [or dramatic] manner."[14] Any audience of the elite is specifically excluded: "it is not true that in poetic imitations one must pay greater attention to the distaste of the intelligent spectators than to the joy of the ignorant spectators."[15] At times, special segments or special conditions of the audience will have to be taken into

12. "Hora, se io non m'inganno, questa materia si sarebbe intesa meglio, & sarebbe data maggiore luce alle cose, che s'hanno da dire, se si fossero fatti tre capi, in ciascuno de quali fosse la virtu, che si douesse seguire, e'l vitio, che si douesse fuggire. E'l primo fosse quello della possibilita, & della'mpossibilita e'l secondo fosse quello della credibilita & della'ncredi-bilita, de quali due capi in fino a qui s'è parlato. e'l terzo fosse quello del giouamento della constitutione della fauola, & del non giouamento" (564. 12).

13. "la poesia fu trouata per diletto della moltitudine ignorante, & del popolo commune, & non per diletto degli scientiati" (679. 35).

14. "per cagione del quale commune popolo, & per diletto solo della moltitudine rozza è stato trouato il palco, & la maniera rappresentatiua" (23. 1).

15. "non è vero, che nelle rassomiglianze poetiche si debba tenere piu conto della noia de veditori intendenti, che della gioia de veditori ignoranti" (679. 32; cf. 29. 38, 113. 26, 147. 16, 164. 11).

account: its political complexion will determine its reactions to given works,[16] and those members of the audience who are parents will have a peculiar attitude toward given plots.[17]

Since the elite and the educated are thus rigorously excluded, certain qualities of the mind will be denied the audience:

poetry [was] invented exclusively to delight and give recreation, I say to delight and give recreation to the minds of the rough crowd and of the common people, which does not understand the reasons, or the distinctions, or the arguments—subtle and distant from the usage of the ignorant—which philosophers use in investigating the truth of things and artists in establishing the rules of the arts; and, since it does not understand them, it must, when someone speaks of them, feel annoyance and displeasure.[18]

"They are not, and cannot be capable of understanding scientific and artistic disputes, but they are able only to understand the events of the world which depend upon chance."[19] The audience will be almost completely lacking in imagination and will believe only the evidence of its senses: "Nor is it possible to make them believe that several days and nights have passed when they know through their senses that only a few hours have passed, *since no deception can take place in them which the senses recognize as such.*"[20] In matters not reducible to the senses, it will be incapable of going beyond what historical fact it knows— "We cannot imagine a king who did not exist, nor attribute any action to him"[21] —or beyond certain opinions which it holds as true; e.g., "the common people, which believes that God rules the world and has a knowledge of all particular things and a special care of them, also has the opinion that he does all things justly, and directs all things to his glory, and to the utility of his believers."[22] The consequences of this complete lack of imagination will be seen later; but it

16. 223. 2; cf. 61. 7.

17. 248. 8.

18. "la poesia sia stata trouata solamente per dilettare, & per ricreare, io dico per dilettare & per ricreare gli animi della rozza moltitudine, & del commune popolo, il quale non intende le ragioni, ne le diuisioni, ne gli argomenti sottili, & lontani dall'vso degl'idioti, quali adoperano i philosophi in inuestigare la verita delle cose, & gli artisti in ordinare le arti, & non gli'ntendendo conuiene, quando altri ne fauella, che egli ne senta noia, & dispiacere" (29. 36; cf. 25. 30).

19. "non sono, ne possono essere capaci, & intendenti di dispute di scienze, ne d'arti, ma solamente sono atti a comprendere gli auenimenti fortunosi del mondo" (23. 6).

20. "Ne è possible a dargli ad intendere, che sieno passati piu di, & notti, quando essi sensibilmente sanno, che non sono passate senon poche hore, non potendo lo'nganno in loro hauere luogo, il quale è tuttauia riconosciuto dal senso" (109. 27; italics mine).

21. "non ci possiamo imaginare vn re, che non sia stato, ne attribuirgli alcuna attione" (188. 25).

22. "il commune popolo, il quale crede dio reggere il mondo, & intendere tutte le cose particolari, & hauerne spetiale cura, porta anchora opinione, che egli faccia ogni cosa giustamente, & dirizzi ogni cosa a gloria sua, & ad vtile de suoi diuoti" (277. 34; cf. 278. 34, 337. 12).

is immediately apparent that the poet who must take it into account will be seriously restricted in his creative activity. In a similar way this audience will have a memory of limited capacity, and such technical devices as the division of tragedy into five acts will exist "to help the memory of the spectators to keep in mind an action which is not at all brief."[23] Conversely, an action which is related too succinctly will not be understood, and hence such a plot should be expanded.[24]

In addition to these limitations, the physical comfort and the convenience of the audience will need to be considered. We are speaking of poems presented before an assembled crowd; we must not ask the crowd to assemble for a poem so short that it would not be worth its while,[25] nor must we expect it to remain beyond a certain limit of physical endurance. Strangely enough, that limit is broadly conceived as extending up to twelve hours:

the restricted time is that during which the spectators can comfortably remain seated in the theater, which, as far as I can see, cannot exceed the revolution of the sun, as Aristotle says, that is, twelve hours; for because of the necessities of the body, such as eating, drinking, excreting the superfluous burdens of the belly and the bladder, sleeping, and because of other necessities, the people cannot continue its stay in the theater beyond the aforementioned time.[26]

Finally, this audience has as one of its characteristics the capacity to be pleased by certain things and to be displeased by others. Castelvetro studies this capacity in detail and finds several bases for pleasure and displeasure. One is knowledge: the audience takes pleasure in learning, "especially those things which it thought could not come about"; contrariwise, it dislikes stories from which it cannot learn anything, those which present commonplace events and rapidly lead to satiety.[27] Second, its hopes (or *volontà*): the audience is pleased by events which happen in accordance with its wishes, displeased by those which do not.[28] Third, the audience will relate the events of a poem to the fortunes of its own life; it will enjoy seeing the good happy and the wicked unhappy, since the case of the former will lead it to expect happiness from its own goodness and the case of the latter will give it a sense of security and of justice. On the other hand, if the good are unhappy, it will experience fear and

23. "per aiutare la memoria de veditori a tenersi a mente vna attione non miga brieue" (88. 31).

24. 164. 3.   25. 53. 27.

26. "il tempo stretto è quello, che i veditori possono a suo agio dimorare sedendo in theatro, il quale io non veggo, che possa passare il giro del sole, si come dice Aristotele, cio è hore dodici. conciosia cosa che per le necessita del corpo, come è mangiare, bere, diporre i superflui pesi del ventre, & della vesica, dormire, & per altre necessita non possa il popolo continuare oltre il predetto termino cosi fatta dimora in theatro" (109. 21; cf. 57. 11).

27. 553. 9.   28. *Ibid.*

pity, and if the wicked are happy, it will feel envy and scorn; but these will be only temporary displeasures, since they will give way to feelings of self-righteousness and of justice, which will be ultimately pleasurable.[29] With pleasure and displeasure will also be associated certain sentiments of a moral nature which will make the audience blush at "dishonest" actions, and hence reject them.[30]

Such is the audience for which Castelvetro's poet must write—ignorant, unlettered, lacking in imagination and memory, attentive to its creature comforts, bound by certain selfish considerations which limit its possibilities of pleasure.

What is more, the poet is not to attempt to improve this audience in any sense; Castelvetro specifically rejects any profit or utility as the end of poetry. The sole end of poetry, as far as the audience is concerned, is to delight, to give pleasure and recreation. Castelvetro summarizes his position in the following passage:

if we were to concede that the materials of the sciences and the arts could be the subject of poetry, we should also concede that poetry either was not invented to give pleasure, or that it was not invented for the uncultured crowd, but rather to teach and for persons initiated into letters and disputations; all of which will be seen to be false by the proofs that I shall now give. Now, since poetry was invented, as I say, to delight and give recreation to the common people, it must have as its subject those things which can be understood by the common people and, once understood, can make it joyous.[31]

The position is reiterated on several occasions, notably in his discussion of purgation in tragedy; he finds Aristotle in agreement with him on the matter of pleasure and sees the utilitarian notion of purgation (as he interprets it) as a contradiction on Aristotle's part:

For if poetry was invented principally for pleasure, and not for utility, as he demonstrated in the passage where he spoke of the origin of poetry in general, why should he now insist that tragedy, which is a part of poetry, should seek utility above all else? Why should it not seek mainly pleasure without paying attention to utility?[32]

Again, the contention of Plato or of his followers that poetry must serve the purposes of the state is attacked; no such end exists for it:

29. 121. 34, 122. 21.   30. 550. 8.

31. "se concedessimo, che la materia delle scienze, & dell'arti potesse essere soggetto della poesia, concederemmo anchora, che la poesia o non fosse stata trouata per dilettare, o non fosse stata trouata per le genti grosse, ma per insegnare, & per le persone assottigliate nelle lettere, & nelle dispute. il che anchora si conoscera essere falso per quello, che si prouera procedendo oltre. Hora perche la poesia è stata trouata, come dico, per dilettare, & ricreare il popolo commune, dee hauere per soggetto quelle cose, che possono essere intese dal popolo commune, & intese il possono rendere lieto" (30. 1).

32. "Percioche, se la poesia è stata trouata principalmente per diletto, & non per vtilita, come egli ha mostrato la, doue parlò dell'origine della poesia in generale, perche vuole egli, che nella tragedia, la quale è vna parte di poesia, si cerchi principalmente l'vtilita? Perche non si cerca principalmente il diletto senza hauer cura dell'vtilita?" (275. 30).

Moreover, the end of the government of the city is different from the end of poetry. For the end of the government of the city concerns living harmoniously together for the greater comfort and utility of the body and of the spirit, and the end of poetry concerns the mere pleasure and recreation of the auditors.[33]

In connection with pleasure, the question of purgation seems a very knotty one to Castelvetro. He explains it as an answer on the part of Aristotle to Plato's banishment of the poets on moral grounds; here, insists Aristotle, is a moral use for poetry.[34] The utility lies in the diminution of the passions of pity and fear in the audience or their expulsion.[35] But if it is admitted as a utility, this is only incidental to the real end of pleasure:

Those who insist that poetry was invented mainly to profit, or to profit and delight together, let them beware lest they oppose the authority of Aristotle who here [*Poetics* 1459ª21] and elsewhere seems to assign nothing but pleasure to it; and if, indeed, he concedes some utility to it, he concedes it accidentally, as is the case with the purgation of fear and of pity by means of tragedy.[36]

As a matter of fact, Castelvetro believes that purgation itself may be considered as a source of pleasure; thus he affirms that "Aristotle meant by the word ἡδονὴν [1453ᵇ11] the purgation and the expulsion of fear and of pity from human souls," and he goes on to explain how it can be pleasurable:

it comes about when, feeling displeasure at the unhappiness of another unjustly suffered, we recognize that we ourselves are good, since unjust things displease us, which recognition—because of the natural love that we have for ourselves—is a source of great pleasure to us. To which pleasure is joined still another, not at all inconsiderable, that when we see the excessive tribulations which happen to others, and which could happen to us and to those like us, we learn in a quiet and hidden way how subject we are to many misfortunes, and how we should not put faith in the calm course of the events of this world; and this pleases us much more than if another, as a teacher and openly in words, should teach us the same thing.[37]

33. "Anchora il fine del reggimento della citta è diuerso dal fine della poetica. Percioche il fine del reggimento della citta riguarda al viuere concordeuole insieme per maggiore agio, & vtile del corpo, & dell'animo, e'l fine della poetica riguarda il diletto simplice, & la ricreatione degli ascoltanti" (592. 10). He does admit, however, that poetry is in a sense subordinate to politics, along with many other arts, and that it must not be allowed to violate the teachings of political expediency (592. 14). On pleasure as the end cf. also 35. 30, 158. 41, and 394. 13.

34. 9. 4, 116. 24, 272. 15, 697. 13.

35. 117. 16, 299. 12.

36. "Coloro, che vogliono, che la poesia sia trouata principalmente per giouare, o per giouare, & per dilettare insieme, veggano, che non s'oppongano all'autorita d'Aristotele, il quale qui, & altroue non par, che le assegni altro, che diletto. &, se pure le concede alcuno giouamento, gliele concede per accidente, come è la purgatione dello spauento, & della compassione per mezzo della tragedia" (505. 38).

37. "è quando noi, sentendo dispiacere della miseria altrui ingiustamente auenutagli, ci riconosciamo essere buoni, poi che le cose ingiuste ci dispiacciono, la quale riconoscenze per l'amore naturale, che noi portiamo a noi stessi ci è di piacere grandissimo. Al quale piacere s'aggiugne questo altro anchora, che non è miga picciolo, che, veggendo noi le tribolationi

Note that the pleasures involved fit into the pattern of the capacities of the audience for pleasure and displeasure: the act of learning, the sentiment of self-righteousness. The other sources of delight and sadness indicated for tragedy and comedy belong to the same categories; the "novelty of the case" contributes to knowledge,[38] and to the tendency to relate poetic actions to one's own life will belong such feelings as these: the joy, in tragedy, at the cessation of the danger of death and, in comedy, at the revenge for some insult; the sadness, in tragedy, at the coming of death and, in comedy, at the suffering of some such insult.[39] In each case the spectator will identify the hero with himself or with someone dear to him.

If the end of pleasure and its achievement are related to certain characteristics of the audience, the means by which the end is to be achieved are similarly related. Here the main consideration is the lack of imagination on the part of the audience. In sum, the argument runs as follows: the audience will derive pleasure only if it identifies itself with the characters and the events; this identification is possible only if the audience believes in their reality; its belief in their reality will depend upon the credibility—the verisimilitude—of the presentation. It is here that imagination enters. If the audience were endowed with great capacities of imagination, it would "believe" things far removed from the conditions of "real life"; since it is not, it will "believe" only what seems to it to be in the realm of its own experience, to be "true." Since the argument is complex and since the real crux of Castelvetro's poetic system resides here, I shall examine it in some detail.

For Castelvetro, all considerations of verisimilitude oscillate between two poles: the impossibility of pleasure, on one side, without credibility, and, on the other side, the inadequacy of credibility, by itself, to produce pleasure. Credibility is the *sine qua non*, but it is only a beginning. If the audience is to experience the pleasure to be derived from learning, what is merely credible must be supplemented by what is rare, extraordinary, marvelous—in a word, by the incredible. The precise point at which the "incredible" becomes "inverisimilar" is a matter of subtle and difficult determination by the poet. The demand for both credibility and the marvelous is insistently made by Castelvetro throughout the text. First, credibility:

all [the spectators] do not know whether the action or the names are true or invented, but those who do not know it believe that the action is true and that the royal names are

fuori di ragione auenute altrui, & possibili ad auenire a noi, & agli altri simili a noi, impariamo tacitamente, & di nascoso, come siamo soggetti a molte suenture, & come non è da porre fidanza nel tranquillo corso delle cose del mondo. il che ci diletta molto piu, che se altri come maestro, & apertamente con parole ci'nsegnasse questo medesimo" (299. 20).

38. 35. 30, 158. 41.

39. 221. 35.

true, and therefore these things give them pleasure; and if they knew that they were
invented, they would feel displeasure in the same way as one who, having received a
jewel and thinking it to be good, enjoys it, but, learning later that it is false, he becomes
sad, and especially if it was sold to him for genuine.[40]

Just as in painting, so in poetry:

a monstrous thing, and which has never been, or is not, accepted by the common opinion
of the people as possible to come about, or as probable—such a thing put into poetry
cannot delight us, as far as the pleasure to be derived from resemblance is concerned.[41]

Whether the action be a true one or not, then, the spectator or the reader must
believe it to be such, must see in it a resemblance to the reality which he
believes exists. Next, the marvelous, which seems to be contained in the very
definition of pleasure:

Now, since someone might ask for what reason the marvelous was required in
tragedy, and was required in proportionately greater quantity in the epic, I answer that
the end of poetry, as has been said, is pleasure and that the marvelous produces pleasure,
and thus the marvelous is properly required in tragedy and in the epic, in order that the
poem may achieve its own proper end in these types of poetry.[42]

The end of poetry, as has been said several times, is pleasure, and the marvelous
especially produces pleasure; therefore, the tragic poet should, as much as he can, seek
the marvelous, and the epic poet, because of the ease that he has in so doing, must produce it to a much greater extent.[43]

As a matter of fact, these two ingredients—the credible and the marvelous—
are not entirely distinct; for the marvelous itself must be credible if it is to
produce the proper pleasure:

And it is said [by Aristotle] that the invention of incredible things is permitted the
poet if these incredible things bring about the end more marvelously than credible things
would. And I myself say that incredible things cannot produce the marvelous. As, for
example, if I hold it to be incredible that Daedalus should fly, I cannot marvel at the

40. "tutti non sanno, se l'attione, o i nomi sieno veri, o imaginati, ma quelli, che no
sanno, credono, che l'attione sia vera, ei nomi reali veri, & percio loro porgono diletto, &,
se sapessono, che fossono imaginati, sentirebbono dispiacere non altramente, che alcuno,
hauendo vna gioia, & reputandola buona, gode, ma risapendo, che è falsa, si contrista, &
spetialmente, se gli è stata venduta per vera" (212. 34).

41. "cosa monstruosa, & non mai piu stata, o non riceuuta dal commune giudicio del
popolo per possibile ad auenire, o per verisimile posta in poesia non ci puo dilettare, quanto
è al diletto procedente dalla rassomiglianza" (73. 42).

42. "Poscia, perche altri poteua domandare, per qual cagione si richiedesse la marauiglia
nella tragedia, & per proportione si richiedesse maggiore nell'epopea, si risponde, che il fine
della poesia, secondo che è stato detto, è il diletto, & che la marauiglia opera diletto, adunque la marauiglia non senza ragione si richiede nella tragedia, & nell'epopea, accioche la
poesia ottenga il debito fine suo in queste maniere di poesia" (549. 6).

43. "Il fine della poesia, come è stato detto piu volte, è il diletto, & la marauiglia spetialmente opera il diletto, adunque il poeta tragico dee, il piu che puo, procacciare la marauiglia,
e'l poeta epopeico per l'agio, che n'ha, la dee procacciare molto maggiore" (552. 42).

fact that he is said to fly, since I do not believe that he does fly. . . . For it is absolutely necessary that we have credible things if the marvelous is to be produced.[44]

As a result, in various incidental definitions of poetry, both ingredients are included, directly or indirectly expressed: "the proper function of poetics consists in the imitation, through harmonious words, of a human action which could possibly happen, pleasurable through the novelty of the case"; plot is "a discovery of an action which has never yet happened, in whole or in part, but which could possibly happen and which is worthy of being remembered."[45]

If we would understand these distinctions of terms, we must examine Castelvetro's treatment of the general question of possibility. He divides the whole realm of possible actions according to the following schema:[46]

I. Possible actions, *which have actually happened*
   A. Natural
      1. According to the course of nature
      2. Contrary to the course of nature (i.e.,.monstrous or miraculous happenings)
   B. Accidental
      1. Resulting from chance or fortune
      2. Resulting from the will of men
II. Possible actions, *which have not yet happened*
   A. and B. as above

Now Category I, since it includes accomplished actions, is essentially the province of history; it corresponds to Aristole's τὰ γενόμενα and is limited to particular actions, performed by specific persons. Actions of this kind are essential in tragedy and epic, which, since they deal with royal persons, cannot dispense with a historical basis; we, the audience, are incapable of imagining kings who did not exist, etc. But no poem may be composed entirely of such actions, since then it would be a history and not a poem at all. Comedy, of course, needs no component of historical events, since its persons and their actions are private and obscure.

Category II, on the other hand, is coequal with Aristotle's τὰ δυνατά; it is the realm of the universal, since the actions are possible for many persons; it is thus the realm of poetry. All poems must possess some component of actions

44. "Et si dice, che si permette la fittione delle cose incredibili al poeta, se le cose incredibili operano il fine piu marauiglioso, che non fanno le credibili. Et io dico, che le cose incredibili non possono operare marauiglia. Come, per cagione d'essempio, se io ho per cosa incredibile, che Dedalo volasse, non mi posso marauigliare, che volasse, non credendo io, che volasse.... Perche fa mestiere di cose credibili, se la marauiglia dee nascere" (612. 6).

45. "la dirittura della poetica consiste in rassomigliare con parole harmonizzate vna attione humana, possibile ad auenire, diletteuole per la nouita dell'accidente" (592. 8); and "vn trouamento d'vna attione non mai piu auenuta ne in tutto, ne in parte, la quale sia possibile ad auenire, & degna, che sene faccia memoria" (150. 17).

46. For the full text see 184. 39 ff.

which have not actually happened. But whereas in the first category the question of credibility does not arise, in the second it is of primary importance. In order that credibility may be assured (and hence verisimilitude) and that the necessary ingredient of the marvelous may nevertheless be present, the following three requisites are established for possible actions:

a) They must be similar to those actions which have actually happened
b) They must be similar to those actions which had the least probability of happening, but which did actually happen
c) The parts or parcels of such actions must individually be similar to those parts of actions which happened in various cases to various people

The matter of verisimilitude is further clarified by a later distinction between possibility and credibility: possibility is a potential of the action itself, which contains no impediment that would prevent the action from coming to realization; credibility is a suitability (a *convenevolezza*) of the action to the expectations of the audience, "by which a person may be led to believe that that action was brought to realization."[47]

With respect to credibility, then, it may be assured by several means: first, by the use of a historical basis for the action in certain genres; second, by a close adherence, in invented actions, to the conditions of "real" or "true" actions. At this point, the expectations of the audience again impinge upon the poet in a very important way, for the audience is the touchstone of natural probability and it will believe whatever conforms to its conceptions of reality. The case is especially clear with the comic poet, who invents everything:

> But let nobody believe for this reason that the creator of the comic plot has liberty to invent either new cities imagined by himself, or rivers, or mountains, or kingdoms, or customs, or laws, or to change the course of the things of nature, making it snow in summer and having men reap in winter, and so forth; for it is necessary for him to follow history and truth.[48]

The whole story of Oedipus runs against this natural probability, "for a private citizen who kills the legitimate king should be most sharply punished and not rewarded, nor should the queen be given him to wed and the kingdom as a dowry."[49] In the same way, certain apparitions of the ancient gods are unacceptable to the modern audience's conceptions:

47. 562. 30 ff.

48. "Ma non si creda percio alcuno, che il formatore della fauola della comedia habbia licentia di trouare o citta nuoue, & imaginate da lui, o fiumi, o monti, o regni, o costumi, o leggi, o di tramutare il corso delle cose della natura, facendo neuigare di state, & mietere d'inuerno, & simili. percioche gli conuiene seguire l'historia, & la verita" (189. 26; cf. 212. 15).

49. "percioche il priuato huomo, che vccide il re leggittimo, dee essere punito asprissimamente, & non premiato, ne gli dee essere data la reina a moglie, e'l regno in dota" (235. 10).

For you must know that the common people believe that God in the present day rules the world in a different way from what he did in ancient times. For the opinion is that in our times he rules it silently without showing himself in person through inspirations, through signs, or through visions, through admonitions to his servants, and through other means not understood nor considered by the coarse crowd; just as, on the other hand, the opinion is that in the first ancient centuries, in the time of the demigods, God intervened directly in the affairs of the world, by appearing personally and speaking with men.[50]

The natural probabilities so considered became a function of a given audience in a given time, losing any universal quality.

In this way the second means of assuring credibility comes to be very close to the third, which is the observance of decorum. A norm of *convenevolezza* is proposed. Again, the case of the comic poet is the most instructive. He may invent names for his personages: "But in so doing the poet must nevertheless pay attention to the usage of the place and the time when and where the action is supposed to have taken place, so that the names will not be exceptional for the given place and time."[51]

So for the conception of character:

For we know that the poet must follow what is appropriate [*il conueneuole*] in representing not only the persons under the sway of passions but the other persons, also, and the actions; which appropriateness is derived by the poet not from that which is in himself or from that which has happened to himself but rather from what is commonly found in that type of person similar to the one who is being represented, full attention being paid to the place, and the time, and the other circumstances; and from what usually happens to such a person.[52]

Such a notion of appropriateness is applied not only to persons of a given character (where it is related at once to the ἁρμόττοντα of Aristotle and to the Horatian decorum) but also to certain kinds of actions. If you speak of prophecy, for example, it must be in the light of invariable conventions. Vergil, here, has erred:

50. "Perche è da sapere, che la commune gente crede, che dio al presente regga altramente lo mondo, che non reggeua anticamente. Percioche è opinione, che ne secoli presenti lo regga tacitamente senza dimostrarsi in persona con ispirationi, con segni, o con visioni, con ammonitioni de suoi serui, & con altri mezzi non intesi, ne considerati dalla gente grossa. si come dall'altra parte è opinione, che ne primi antichi secoli al tempo de semidei dio hauesse cura del mondo, apparendo personalmente, & ragionando con gli huomini" (337. 12).

51. "Ma dee non dimeno riguardare il poeta in far cio all'vsanza del luogo, & del tempo, doue, & quando finge l'attione essere auenuta, accioche i nomi non sieno fuori dell'vsanza del predetto luogo, & tempo" (192. 14; cf. 192. 41 for other genres).

52. "Percioche noi sappiamo, che il poeta dee seguire il conueneuole non pure nel rappresentare i passionati, ma l'altre persone anchora, & l'attioni. il quale conueneuole non si raccoglie dal poeta da quello, che è in lui, o da quello, che è auento a lui, ma da quello, che suole essere communemente in quella maniera di persone simile a quella, che noi rappresentiamo, hauendo rispetto al luogo, & al tempo, & all'altre circostanze, & da quello, che le suole auenire" (372. 9).

Vergil sins in the decorum of prophecy, which does not usually descend to the use of proper names, nor to things so clear and so particular; but, withholding names, it usually indicates the persons and their actions with somewhat obscure figures of speech, as we see observed in the prophecies of Holy Scripture and in the *Alexandra* of Lycophron.[53]

If restrictive conventions of this type are multiplied not only with respect to characters but also with respect to actions, the possibilities of "invention" on the part of the poet soon disappear; this is indeed the case with Castelvetro.

But the multiplication of these commonplaces and these conventions would also tend to make the poem completely uninteresting to the audience itself; the cause of credibility would be perfectly served, yet the resulting poem would be thoroughly dull. The antidote to this danger is the cultivation of the marvelous. Castelvetro, since he is unwilling to admit any improbability, conceives of the marvelous as a kind of infrequent probability:

There are two kinds of probabilities [*verisimili*], one of which represents the truths which most frequently occur according to the fixed course of nature, and the other of which represents the truths which occasionally depart from the usual course; as, for example, it is probable that a clever, wicked man should deceive and not be deceived, and that a powerful man should vanquish and not be vanquished, since truly we usually see things come to pass in this way. And it is, moreover, probable that a clever, wicked man, wishing to deceive, should on occasion be deceived, and that a powerful man, wishing to conquer, should at times be conquered. So that one of these probabilities concerns the "many times" of truth, and the other the "few times" of truth, and thus the one like the other is probable. But the second, because of its rarity, is more marvelous and is said to be probable outside of probability only because of its rarity and because it turns aside from the path of the first probability.[54]

On various occasions he points out that what happens more frequently is less marvelous, hence less desirable in poetry;[55] thus a recognition which could easily come about, through the will of the person recognized, is less to be sought than one which would be more difficult.[56] In a similar way, as regards

53. "peccando Virgilio nella conueneuolezza della profetia, la quale non suole condescendere a nomi propri, ne a cose tanto chiare, & particolari, ma, tacendo i nomi, suole manifestare le persone, & le loro attioni con figure di parlare alquanto oscure, si come si vede osseruare nelle profetie della scrittura sacra, & nell'Alessandra di Licophrone" (219. 37).

54. "Sono due maniere di verisimili, l'vna di quelli, che rappresentano le verita, le quali auengono per lo piu secondo certo corso, et l'altra di quelli, che rappresentano le verita, che alcuna volta trauiano dall'vsato corso. come, è verisimile, che vno astuto maluagio inganni, & non sia ingannato, & che vn possente vinca, & non sia vinto, percioche veramente noi veggiamo per lo piu auenire cosi. & è anchora verisimile, che vno astuto maluagio, volendo ingannare, sia ingannato alcuna volta, & che vn possente, volendo vincere, sia vinto alcuna volta. Si che l'vn verisimile riguarda l'assai volte della verita, & l'altro le poche volte della verita, & cosi l'vno, come l'altro è verisimile. ma il secondo per la rarita è piu marauiglioso, & è detto essere verisimile fuori del verisimile pure per la rarita, & perche si torce dalla strada del primo verisimile" (400. 17).

55. Cf. 248. 13.

56. Cf. 252. 13.

purgation, what happens less frequently is more pitiable and more horrible.[57] The admission of this kind of improbable probability makes way for the acceptance of certain brands of "impossibility" in poetry. Of the four varieties of impossibilities which he distinguishes,[58] two are forbidden the poet; these are actions impossible for God and for men and actions impossible for men alone. The other two may be used by the poets; they comprise actions not impossible to God, such as miracles, and actions which seem impossible to men because of their rarity. Both of these are recommended to the poet whenever he can find a justification for using them:

> And it is a sufficiently evident matter why poetic fiction can and should receive these two kinds of impossibilities used in this way and justified by reason, since the poet seeks to move the reader or the listener to admiration [*marauiglia*], which proceeds principally from miraculous doings and from those doings which happen only very rarely.[59]

I should insist at this point that all degrees of probability as Castelvetro conceives them are natural probability rather than aesthetic probability; that is, probability is established in a work not by reference to the conditions of the work itself or to preliminary statements within the work, but by reference outside of the work to the operations of nature. This is especially clear in the example he uses for distinguishing between necessity and verisimilitude. Actions of both kinds are possible, hence admissible into poetry. If a man is wounded on the head, it is "verisimilar" or probable that he will die; hence the poet may represent his death. If a man is wounded in the heart, it is "necessary" that he die; hence the poet may represent his death.[60] Similarly for actions springing from character, all of which are really matters of decorum: it is "necessary" that a mother who resolves to kill her innocent children (cf. Medea) do so only with great perturbation of her soul (this is presumably because of the eternal character of mothers as mothers); it is "probable" or verisimilar that a person who has been full of fear in the past will continue to be so (this is presumably a matter of consistency).[61]

In all such considerations of historical truth or natural probability or necessity and verisimilitude, the primary aim is not the imitation of nature for the

57. Cf. 305. 31, 306. 3.

58. 608. 1 ff.

59. "Et è cosa assai manifesta perche la fittione poetica possa, & debba riceuere queste due maniere d'impossibilita cosi fatte, & informate di ragione, cercando il poeta di commuouere il lettore, o l'ascoltatore a marauiglia, la quale procede massimamente dall'operationi miracolose, & da quelle operationi, che auengono radissime fiate" (608. 41).

60. 188. 1.

61. 330. 40.

sake of making the poem resemble nature but rather the resemblance to nature
for the sake of obtaining the credence of the audience. Credibility remains the
ultimate touchstone.

II

A poetics which in this way seeks to give pleasure to an audience of limited
imaginative capacities presents a very special and a very difficult problem to the
poet. The problem is not to produce a beautiful work of art through the
ordering of all the parts to an artistically perfect structure. Questions of beauty
rarely concern Castelvetro. Rather, it is the task of the poet to find some way
of entertaining the audience while he keeps it convinced that what it sees (or
reads) is true, that is, of striking a proper balance between the probable and the
marvelous. "The greatest praise of a poet is that he makes the uncertain seem
certain through every means of which he is capable."[62]

The first means to the achievement of this end is the proper selection and
assorting of materials. In the tragic and epic genres this necessitates the choice
of a historical subject, to assure credibility, and the addition to that subject of
episodes or variations or developments that will make of it a new and interesting plot. This latter is the difficult part; for it is only in so far as he expands
or embroiders upon his historical *données* that a poet is an inventor, hence a
poet. "Invention is the most difficult thing that the poet has to do, and the
thing from which it seems that he derives his name, that is $\pi o\iota\eta\tau\grave{\eta}s$."[63] It is in
connection with this demand for invention that Castelvetro introduces a cri-
terion of originality:

> For a poet cannot compose a plot already composed by another poet, for this would
> either be history or a plagiarism. For example, if one should wish to arrange in a plot
> the events by which Orestes killed his mother, it would not be proper to follow any
> story of a son who killed his mother in the way in which she was killed in the plot
> composed on the subject by Aeschylus, or by Euripides, or by Sophocles. But it would
> be necessary that, setting aside all historical and poetical resemblances, he should give
> himself over to subtle searching and with his own wit to finding how that event might
> be made to come about in another way, which had not yet been narrated or written by
> anybody, just as those other poets had done.[64]

62. "al poeta, la cui sua maggiore lode è, che faccia la'ncertitudine parere certitudine
per tutte quelle vie, che puo" (210. 35).

63. "la quale inuentione à la piu difficile cosa, che habbia il poeta da fare, & dalla qual
parte pare, che egli prenda il nome, cio è $\pi o\iota\eta\tau\grave{\eta}s$" (78. 2).

64. "Conciosia cosa che il poeta non possa comporre vna fauola composta da alcun
poeta, percioche o sarebbe historia, o furto, come, se altri volesse ordinare in vna fauola,
come Oreste vccise la madre, non conuerrebbe seguire historia alcuna d'vn figliuolo, che
habbia vccisa la madre nella maniera d'vcciderla, ne la fauola composta di cio da Eschilo, o da
Euripide, o da Sophocle, ma conuiene, che lasciate da parte tutte le rassomiglianze o his-
toriche, o poetiche, si dea a sottigliare, & col suo ingegno a trouare, come possa essere
auenuto quel fatto in altra maniera, che non è anchora stato narrato, o scritto da alcuno, si
come fecero altresi que poeti" (67. 31).

Here, apparently, only the central action would be historical; the rest would be up to the poet. Put in another way,

> the plot of tragedy and of the epic can be constituted only of things which have actually happened and are known, the royal estate upon which it is founded making this necessary. These historical events must nevertheless be known only summarily, so that the poet may exercise and demonstrate his own genius and find the particular things and the means by which that action was brought to its conclusion.[65]

Either the historical subject itself or the decorations provided by the poet must, in part at least, partake of the nature of the marvelous.

A second means to convincing and amusing the audience is the disposition of these materials in accordance with the unities of time, place, and action. We have already seen, early in the discussion, how the physical comforts of the audience and its lack of imagination have to be taken into account by the poet; these two factors lead, respectively, to the unities of time and of place. With respect to time, the clearest statement is found in the comparison of tragedy and the epic:

> Now, just as the perceptible end of tragedy has found its proper compass within the revolution of the sun over the earth without going beyond this limit, in order to put an end to the discomfort of the audience and the expense of the actors, so the perceptible end of the epic has found its proper compass in being able to be extended over several days, since neither the discomfort of the listener nor harm or expense connected with the reciter took this possibility away from it.[66]

Essentially, then, the basic factor is that the audience can remain within the theater (for tragedy and comedy) only for a given time—maximum, twelve hours.[67] Besides, the action before its eyes will take place on a single spot, the stage. Hence two unities: "tragedy . . . must have as its subject an action accomplished in a small area of place and in a small space of time, that is, in that place and in that time where and when the actors remain engaged in acting, and not in any other place or in any other time."[68] For the imagination

---

65. "la fauola della tragedia, & dell'epopea non si puo constituire se non di cose auenute & conosciute, cosi richiedendo lo stato reale sopra il quale ella è fondata. Le quali cose auenute non dimeno non deono essere conosciute se non sommariamente, accioche il poeta possa essercitare, & far vedere il suo ingegno, & trouare le cose particolari, ei mezzi, per gli quali quella attione fu condotta al suo termine" (211. 18).

66. "Hora, si come il termine sensibile della tragedia ha trouata la sua misura d'vn giro del sole sopra la terra senza passare piu oltre, per cessare il disconcio de veditori, & la spesa de rappresentatori, cosi il termine sensibile dell'epopea ha trouata la sua misura di potere essere tirato in lungo per piu giornate, poi che ne disagio d'ascoltatore, ne danno, o spesa del recitatore non gliele toglieua" (534. 1).

67. 109. 23, 163. 26.

68. "la tragedia.... conuiene hauere per soggetto vn'attione auenuta in picciolo spatio di luogo, & in picciolo spatio di tempo, cio è in quel luogo, & in quel tempo, doue, & quando i rappresentatori dimorano occupati in operatione, & non altroue, ne in altro tempo" (109. 17).

of the audience, limited to the witness of its senses, will not permit it to believe that the action takes place in more than one locality—"restricted not only to a city, or a town, or a country place, or some such site, but even to that view which alone can present itself to the eyes of a person"[69]—or in a time in excess of that of the performance:

> But as for the magnitude of the plot, which is subjected to the senses and is taken in by sight and hearing together, I must say that it should be as long as would be an actual event, depending upon fortune and worthy of being written down in history that might come to pass, it being necessary that this imagined event of the plot should occupy as much time . . . as was occupied or would be occupied by a similar event if it really happened or were to happen.[70]

Ideally, then, the invented action should occupy no more time than a real action, and this time should not exceed the time of performance; the place should remain unchanged and be contained within the space visible to a person who himself did not move.

The extent to which the senses, especially sight, are a governing factor in this theory of the unities is indicated by the change in requirements when the epic is considered. For the events of the epic do not actually appear before the eyes of the spectator. Instead, they are narrated to him. Since he does not see them, he can admit broad variations of place and a discrepancy between time of performance and time of action. Castelvetro draws a distinction between perceptible time (*il sensibile*, that distinguished by the senses) and intellectual time (*lo'ntellettuale*, that conceived of by the mind). In tragedy, the two must be identical; in epic, there may be a wide divergency between them.[71]

As for the unity of action, which for Aristotle is the only important one and which for him is of the very essence of the work of art, Castelvetro's treatment of it is highly revelatory of his general attitude toward poetics. To begin with, he denies any necessity—in the nature of things—for limitation of a poem to a single action; as so frequently, he takes issue sharply with Aristotle here:

> For there is no doubt that, if in history one may relate in a single narrative several actions of a single person, . . . in poetry it will be possible in a single plot to narrate without being blamed for it several actions of a single person, just as similarly in poetry

69. "ristretto non solamente ad vna citta, o villa, o campagna, o simile sito, ma anchora a quella vista, che sola puo apparere a gli occhi d'vna persona" (535. 15).

70. "Ma della grandezza della fauola, che è sottoposta a sensi, & comprendesi con la vista, & con l'vdita insieme, è da dire, che sia tanta, quanta sarebbe quella d'vn caso fortunoso degno d'historia, che auenisse veramente, essendo di necessita, che corra tanto tempo in rappresentare questo caso della fauola imaginato.... quanto corse in simile caso, o correrebbe, mentre veramente auenne, o auenisse" (163. 13; cf. 381. 38, 533. 37).

71. 533. 23. The point of departure here is Aristotle's distinction (*Poetics* 1451ᵃ6) between τὴν αἴσθησιν and τὴν φύσιν.

one may relate without being blamed for it a single action of a whole people, for history does this with much praise. . . . And, indeed, in poetry not only a single action of a whole people may be narrated, but even several actions of a people. . . . And even if it were conceded to poetry to relate many actions of many persons or of many peoples, I do not see that any blame should come to it for this reason.[72]

Moreover, the presentation of a double or even a multiple plot would more readily serve the end of pleasure sought by the poet:

we should not marvel at all if several actions of one person or one action of a people or several actions of several persons delight us and make us attentive to listen, since such a plot carries with it, through the multitude of the actions, through the variety, through the new events, and through the multitude of persons and of the people, both pleasure and greatness and magnificence.[73]

Why, then, does Aristotle insist upon unity, and why does Castelvetro recommend it? The reason is different for the different genres. For tragedy and comedy, unity of action is a consequence of the unities of time and of place; it would not be possible to crowd, into a restricted space and into twelve hours, more than one action; indeed, sometimes one of these plays will contain only a part of an action.[74] For the epic, where this "necessity" does not exist, unity of action is sought for two other reasons: first, because such a unified plot is more "beautiful," less likely to satiate the spectator with an abundance of different things,[75] and, second, because such a plot demonstrates the ingenuity and the excellence of the poet:

In the narration of the single action of one person, which at first glance would not seem to have the capacity of keeping the minds of the auditors listening with delight, one discovers the judgment and the industry of the poet, who achieves that with one action of one person which others can hardly achieve with many actions and of many persons.[76]

72. "Perche non ha dubbio niuno, che, se nell'historia si narra sotto vn raccontamento piu attioni d'vna persona sola,... nella poesia si potra sotto vna fauola narrare senza biasimo piu attioni d'vna persona sola. si comme parimente nella poesia senza biasimo si potra narrare vna attione sola d'vna gente, percioche l'historia fa cio con molta lode.... Et non solamente pure nella poesia si potra narrare vna attione d'vna gente, ma anchora piu attioni d'vna gente.... Et, se le si concedera la narratione di molte attioni di molte persone, o di molte genti, non pero veggo, che biasimo alcuno le debba seguire" (178. 23). The argument rests upon an analogy between poetry and history which I shall indicate later.

73. "non sia punto da marauigliarsi se piu attioni d'vna persona, o vna attione d'vna gente, o piu attioni di piu persone ci dilettassono, & ci rendessono intenti ad ascoltarle, portando seco la fauola per la moltitudine dell'attioni, per la varieta, per gli nuoui auenimenti, & per la moltitudine delle persone, & della gente & piacere, & grandezza, & magnificenza" (179. 18; cf. 504. 36, 692. 31).

74. 179. 4; cf. 504. 19. Castelvetro thinks of the "action" as the whole of the traditional or historical story, not as the plot of the individual work of art.

75. 179. 16, 514, 29.

76. "in narrare vna attione sola d'vna persona, che in prima vista non pare hauer potere di ritenere gli animi ad ascoltare con diletto, si scopre il giudicio, & la'ndustria del poeta, operando quello con vna attione d'vna persona, che altri apena possono operare con molte attioni, & di molte persone" (179. 24; cf. 179. 16, 504. 23).

What is symptomatic about this position is its abandonment of any concern with the structural or formal beauties of the work and its insistence upon two such nonartistic considerations as the comfort and character of the audience and the glory of the poet.

A third means to the achievement of the ends with respect to the audience is what we might call, roughly, the total excellence of the work. This is in a way related to the unity of plot just discussed; a certain admiration, a certain sense of the marvelous, will result from the perfect execution of the poem. There might seem to be here an independent criterion of beauty, were it not for the fact that beauty is itself reduced to qualities already considered: "so that it [the plot] may turn out to be beautiful, that is, marvelous and probable."[77] Or, negatively, beauty is reduced to an absence of flaws from a form large enough to permit the perception of such flaws:

> For that thing is really beautiful in which no ugliness is discovered but in which, if there were any, it would be discovered; and that is really not beautiful which, being ugly, seems beautiful because for some reason its ugliness does not become apparent.[78]

The first consequence of this essentially negative criterion is that larger poems will be preferable to smaller; Dante is greater than Petrarch, since his poem is so "grande e magnifico" that, were there any errors in it, they would immediately be visible.[79] As far as the audience is concerned, such a poem shows the artifice of the poet and is a source of admiration. A second consequence is that magnitude of form will be accompanied by multiplicity of parts and by variety of developments, and that multiplicity and that variety, in turn, will be sources of pleasure.[80] These are major excellences of the poem, and they are to be sought in preference to such minor excellences as purity of diction, ornamentation through figures, and the sound of the verses. These latter may indeed supply pleasure, but it will be inferior to the pleasure derived from imitation.[81] Again with respect to total excellence, it should be noted that it is not an absolute quality but one discovered by comparison with other works: "for nothing reveals better the goodness or the badness of anything whatsoever than comparison."[82] The poet who would gain the admiration of his·audience must

77. "accioche riesca piu bella, cio è marauigliosa, & verisimile" (140. 39).

78. "Perche quella cosa è veramente bella, nella quale non si scopre bruttezza, ma, se vi fosse, vi si scoprirebbe. & quella veramente non è bella, che essendo brutta, per alcuna cagione non apparendo la bruttezza, par bella" (162. 28).

79. 164. 21; cf. 673. 19 ff. on the errors of tragedy.

80. Cf. 536. 32 and n. 73 above.

81. 74. 2.

82. "conciosia cosa che nulla scopra piu il bene, o il male di che che sia, che il paragone" (290. 31).

therefore keep in mind all the precepts and "apply them so excellently that his poem will surpass in all things the poems of past poets."[83]

III

These indications of the ways by which the art of poetry achieves its ends—ends with respect to the audience and ends with respect to the poet—may be taken as preliminary steps toward a definition of the art itself. If we would further approach such a definition, the best means is to examine the relationships that Castelvetro establishes between poetry and the other arts.

The art to which poetry is most closely akin is the art of history. Indeed, their kinship is so intimate that, if we possessed an adequate art of history, it would be unnecessary to write an art of poetry, "since poetry derives all its light from the light of history." Such an art of history would tell us

what things were memorable in greater and in lesser degree and worthy of having a place in history, and, on the other hand, which ones were not memorable and unworthy of being touched upon by the historian. And then it would tell us what things should be narrated briefly and summarily and which ones at length and in particular; and afterward what order and disposition should be followed in recounting the events. And, besides, it would not fail to tell us when and where should be intercalated digressions, and descriptions of a place or of a person or of other things. And then it would decide whether it is permissible to the author of the history to offer a judgment on things that he relates, blaming or praising them, and adapting them to the instruction and utility of the reader and to his conduct as a citizen. And similarly it would decide if it is proper and possible for the historian to present some matters by narration, others by dramatic representation, as the poet does, or whether, indeed, this is a prerogative of poetry alone. And, finally, it would tell us what kinds of words suit history in general and what kinds do not, and which particularly in certain places and which not.[84]

Precepts of this kind, were they properly presented in an art of history, would not have to be repeated in an art of poetry, being common to both arts. Now if we examine in detail these precepts, we discover that they do, in fact, cover the primary preoccupations of Castelvetro throughout his treatment of poetry:

83. "metterle in opera cosi eccellentemente, che la poesia sua trapassi in tutte le cose le poesie de poeti passati" (393. 31).

84. "quali fossero le cose memoreuoli piu, & meno per gradi, & degne d'hauer luogo nell'historia, & quali dall'altra parte non fossero memoreuoli, ne meriteuoli d'essere tocche dall'historico. Et poi ci sarebbe stato detto, quali cose si douessono narrare breuemente, & sommariamente, & quali distesamente, & particolarmente. & appresso, quale ordine, & dispositione fosse da seguire in raccontare le cose. Et anchora non ci sarebbe stato taciuto, quando, & doue si douessono intramettere digressioni, & discrittioni di luogo, o di persona, o d'altra cosa. Et poscia si sarebbe diterminato, se sia permesso all'autore dell'historia dar giudicio delle cose, che egli narra, biasimandole, o lodandole, & tirarle ad ammaestramento, & ad vtilita de lettori, & del viuer cittadinesco. Et parimente si sarebbe diterminato, se si conuenga, & se si possa per l'historico far palese alcuna materia per via di racconto, & di rappresentamento, come si fa per lo poeta, o se pur cio sia priuilegio della poesia sola. Et vltimamente ci sarebbe stato detto, quali maniere di parole si confacessero generalmente all'historia tutta, & quali no. & quali particolarmente a certi luoghi, & quali no" (5. 28).

choice of subject matter (sufficiently noteworthy to be marvelous); distinction between central plot and episodes; ordering of the plot, digressions, moral conclusions from the plot; use of the *récit* in tragedy and of dramatic scenes in the epic; and the general problem of diction. The two arts differ in two respects only: history presents events which actually happened, poetry those which have not occurred but which might occur, and poetry uses verse whereas history uses prose.[85] Otherwise they are so much alike that poetry may be defined as "a resemblance or imitation of history."[86]

Aristotle's likening of poetry to painting, thinks Castelvetro, is essentially erroneous; for there are more dissimilarities than similarities between the two arts. They are unlike, first, in the kinds of things which they represent. Painting (like history) depicts true things—the "cosa certa & conosciuta"— whereas poetry imitates probable things—the "cosa incerta & sconosciuta." Moreover, whereas poetry represents actions, painting at its best represents objects (historical painting is a definitely inferior genre). They are unlike, second, in the relationship to be expected between the imitation and the object; in painting, exact resemblance is to be demanded: "the slightest dissimilarity between the image and the man depicted can be blamed and condemned as bad art"; in poetry, the imitation is an expansion, an embellishment, an idealization of whatever real events may have been taken as a starting point. Third, the sources of pleasure in the two are unlike. Painting, appealing to the eye, delights precisely through this exact resemblance, which in poetry is displeasing; on the other hand, the imitation in poetry of an unknown, probable action "delights us beyond all measure." This is explained on the basis of the difficulty involved for the artist. For the painter, faithful rendering is the hardest procedure, shows the greatest talent, evokes the most unlimited admiration. For the poet, such rendering makes him a simple historian; it is the introduction of the "unreal," of the "invented," of the "marvelous," that constitutes his greatest glory. Castelvetro himself sees only one basis of comparison between the two arts, and that is on the score of the *convenevole*, which here means the representation of things as they should be; but I see no attempt on his part to reconcile this with the requirement, for painting, that things be represented as they are.[87]

In the light of the close affinity which other theorists, such as Robortello, saw between poetry and rhetoric, we are compelled to ask whether Castelvetro also treats the two arts as cognate. We discover immediately that he does not. He makes a number of references to Aristotle's *Rhetoric*, largely on matters of

---

85. On the necessity of verse cf. 115. 41, 190. 1.

86. "similitudine, o rassomiglianza d'historia" (28. 19).

87. For the main discussions see 586. 9, 72. 4, 41. 11, 342. 28.

diction, the passions, and thought, but does not proceed from them to the indication of a general similitude between poetic and rhetoric.[88] This is all the more remarkable, since, as we have seen, in its broadest lines Castelvetro's system is essentially rhetorical. Perhaps the explanation may be found in his insistence on declaring the close relationship between poetry and history, on treating poetic as if it were a branch of the historical art, and on eliminating—by denial or by silence—any other art which might be set up as a contender to history. In the last analysis, this wedding of poetry to history may constitute one of the most original features of Castelvetro's system.

As a result of this likening of poetry to history, some of the usual preoccupations of Renaissance arts of poetry disappear. The poet himself does not need to be divinely inspired, to write under the influence of the *furor poeticus*, to feel himself the passions which he incorporates in his characters; these are superstitions fostered by the poets to improve their credit with the ignorant masses.[89] Instead, he is a careful and deliberate artisan, who follows the precepts of the art so as to achieve, immediately, the pleasure of his audience and, ultimately, his own glory.[90] We have already seen how these precepts relate to the choice, the disposition, and the embellishment of his materials. Castelvetro treats the moot question of the relationship of the poem to nature only summarily and indirectly. The notion of imitation as introducing differences between an object in nature and that object as represented in a work of art is completely absent; indeed, in a work which is a commentary on Aristotle, none of the implications of the Aristotelian concept of imitation are present. So completely are these implications lost that imitation (*rassomiglianza*) is said not to be present when true or historical events are treated and to be present only in the details and embellishments "invented" by the poet—in accordance with probability, of course.[91] Still, in relationship to imitation, the distinction between πράξεως and δρώντων is wrested from its meaning in such a way that the thing represented becomes the action of the poem and the person representing becomes the poet (e.g., the *Aeneid* and Vergil).[92]

With the popular conception of the poet as divinely inspired now discarded, with all notions of the poem as an imitation of nature either distorted or abandoned, with the resemblance to painting specifically denied, Castelvetro's poetic system becomes a very special system for his times. Poetics turns out to be a branch of history, but with the special feature of a history that attempts to please its audience and bring glory to its author. Whatever in a poem relates to

---

88. Cf., for example, 257. 43 on the qualitative and quantitative parts in poetic and rhetoric.

89. 65. 12, 180. 7, 372. 30, 374. 15.

90. 68. 38, 374. 37, 394. 17.

91. Cf. pp. 583–85.

92. 114. 40.

the necessities of credibility derives its characteristics and its criteria from the science of history; whatever relates to the necessities of pleasing an audience whose character is very carefully delimited derives its characteristics and its criteria from the art of rhetoric. If there is any proper role for an art of poetry—and at times this is practically denied—it is in the combination of the precepts supplied by these two parent-arts, in the filling of gaps where, as in the case of the unities, the other arts do not afford specific recommendations. Or, to state the case more accurately, the poet considers himself as a kind of historian and relies openly on the teachings of history to guide him in his writing of poems; but there are places where these teachings are inadequate, and here the poet—even though he may not recognize the fact—has recourse to the fundamental relationships existing between a work using language and the audience to which it is directed. This second kind of activity leads him to formulate for himself—or to take over from the previous formulations of such theorists as Castelvetro—a set of special conventions or rules or practices which, taken together, compose an art of poetry. But that art is never an independent art, bearing always the traces of its origins in history and rhetoric. It has, therefore, very little to do with the "art" of Aristotle. Anyone who would adopt it, theorist or poet, would thus be committing himself to an essentially un-Aristotelian system of poetics, one which was even farther removed from the presuppositions of the original text than had been the theory contained in the commentary of Robortello.

THE THEORETICAL FOUNDATIONS OF
JOHNSON'S CRITICISM

W. R. KEAST

I

EVERY age, we are often told, rewrites Shakespeare in its own image. Perhaps each age performs the same service for other writers as well. At any rate Samuel Johnson, as he appears in modern discussions, seems often to reflect modern distinctions and modern preferences. Thus we find an American critic praising the English critic, F. R. Leavis, in these terms:

> Mr. Leavis is not a critic who works by elaborated theory. As between Coleridge, on the one hand, and Dr. Johnson and Matthew Arnold, on the other, he has declared his strong preference for the two latter—for the critic, that is, who requires no formulated first principles for his judgment but only the sensibility that is the whole response of his whole being.[1]

To distinguish so sharply between sensibility and principles as the guaranty of critical judgment is a modern habit, and it is common in our time, when this distinction is made, to prefer sensibility to principles. A somewhat similar view of Johnson appears in C. B. Tinker's essay, "Johnson as Monarch," but in terms of yet another distinction and preference. Despite the often outrageous injustice and inaccuracy of Johnson's critical statements, we rightly continue to read him, Tinker says, because he is a man "who can always be read with profit even when we dissent from the view set forth." "The explanation of this singular state of things lies, I think, in the fact that Johnson's criticism is not a *system*, every detail of which must be consistent with certain principles from which all casual expressions are supposed to derive." We read Johnson not to find out what to think about Milton or Pope, and not for any system, but "to enjoy the humor and the humors, the audacities and the prejudices of a man of genius"; in short, even when we concede that there are "frequently at work in his mind great fundamental convictions which are at the very heart and center of the man," it is "Johnson's tastes that we are eager to come at, his feelings about a given work of art and not that 'pomp of system and severity of science' (to use a phrase of his own) which he could bring to its praise or its destruction."[2] Here tastes and habits mirroring a distinctive personality are preferred

---

1. Lionel Trilling, "The Moral Tradition," *New Yorker*, September 24, 1949, p. 89.

2. Chauncey Brewster Tinker, *Essays in Retrospect: Collected Articles and Addresses* (New Haven, 1948), p. 28.

over principles and system. It is Johnson's practical criticism which it is now fashionable to praise, and his practice is customarily viewed as the product of sensibility or taste but seldom of reasoned views about the nature of art and criticism—save, in Tinker's phrase, as something Johnson could "bring to" a question after taste had made its determination. The common denominator of these modern estimates of Johnson's distinctive quality and value is the conviction evident in them that Johnson has or needs no principles, theory, or systematic view of literature and the belief that this absence of principles and theory from the conduct of practical criticism is a positive virtue.

But Johnson, we may recall, in his praise of Dryden as the father of English criticism spoke of him as the writer "who first taught us to determine upon principles the merit of composition"—and we may ask how this modern view of his own work as a critic would have struck Johnson. Or we may remember the definition of criticism he set forth as a preliminary to his *Rambler* papers on onomatopoeia:

> It is . . . the task of criticism to establish principles; to improve opinion into knowledge; and to distinguish those means of pleasing which depend upon known causes and rational deduction, from the nameless and inexplicable elegancies which appeal wholly to the fancy, from which we feel delight, but know not how they produce it, and which may well be termed the enchantresses of the soul. Criticism reduces those regions of literature under the dominion of science, which have hitherto known only the anarchy of ignorance, the caprices of fancy, and the tyranny of prescription.[3]

Johnson would have been outraged by the current notion that he had and needed no reasoned view of literature as a foundation for his critical practice and that he was fortunate in the freedom of sensibility so secured. Critics of this sort he once characterized pungently: "The ambition of superior sensibility and superior eloquence disposes the lovers of arts to receive rapture at one time, and communicate it at another; and each labours first to impose upon himself, and then to propagate the imposture."[4] But students of criticism are familiar with the wide gulf that often separates a critic's statements about what criticism ought to be from what in his practice it actually is. The modern view of Johnson may be correct in spite of Johnson's repeated stress on the importance of principles and "rational deduction."

Several important characteristics of Johnson's criticism, indeed, give encouragement to this view. Certainly no other English critic of equal reputation has been known as little by his systematic thought, as contrasted to his particular judgments on books and writers. In his critical writings systematic in-

3. *Rambler*, No. 92, in *Works* (Oxford, 1825), II, 431–32. Subsequent references to Johnson's writings, except for the *Preface to Shakespeare* and the *Lives of the Poets*, will be to this edition.

4. *Idler*, No. 50 (*Works*, IV, 298).

quiry is rarely met with and, when present, is introduced sparingly into discussions prevailingly occupied with concrete questions of evaluation. Unlike many of his contemporaries—including several whose theoretical work he admired—Johnson composed no treatises. And this reluctance to engage in extended statements of theory reflects Johnson's profound suspicion of abstract speculation, a suspicion to which he gave repeated expression in his writings and which, as we shall presently see, is one of the cardinal tenets of his criticism.

But if Johnson, by nature and habit, distrusted systematic theorizing about literature, we shall nevertheless miss some of the most important characteristics of his criticism if we suppose him to have played entirely or even primarily by ear. The proportion between principle and sensibility involved in the production of critical judgment must always be difficult to settle, but the alternatives presented to us in attempting to understand Johnson's criticism are not so stark as this statement would imply or as the modern comments already quoted would suggest. Johnson, if he was not a systematic writer, had at any rate a systematic mind: the kinds of critical problems with which he deals, the particular doctrines and judgments he puts forward, the stands he takes on the leading critical issues of his day, and the methods of argument he habitually employs can all be traced in his criticism, early and late, to a coherent view of literature and a coherent body of assumptions concerning both its practice and its evaluation. That Johnson distrusted theory there can be no question, but such distrust can become, as we shall see it did for Johnson, in itself a theoretical commitment. If, after his fairly explicit early periodical essays, the exposition of the theory comes to be increasingly elliptical, discernible more in its effects on his practice than in extended statement, this is to be understood as a sign not of his emancipation from general views about literature and criticism but of his increasing maturity as a critic, of his habituation to the flexible employment of his dominant assumptions, and, above all, of the generality and adaptability of his principles.

The theoretical positions I have in mind lie somewhere between the "great fundamental convictions" to which Professor Tinker refers and the immediate premises of critical argument. Although this is a wide zone, Johnson, unlike some of his contemporaries, does not fill it with a regular scheme of analysis. He does not, indeed, fill this zone at all, for his basic assumptions about literature are relatively few—although they are not, for that reason, any less important—and they are in essential respects very similar to those which underlie his discussions of moral and political questions. Nor does he, given the more remote positions which shape his statement of critical problems and supply premises for their solution, operate in a predictable deductive fashion in deciding particular cases. Although one is seldom surprised by the general lines Johnson follows in any literary argument, the concrete substance of his remarks is often unexpected. This combination of predictable direction and unexpected event, so characteristic of Johnson's criticism, results from the relative generality of his principles, which permits the same general premise to be brought to bear on a wide variety of cases; from the important role he assigns to circumstantial accidents in critical judgment—an aspect of his theory about which I shall have more to say later on; and from an uncommonly rich assortment of subordinate terms and distinctions which he employs, in combination with general premises, to yield results that are always the same, yet always different.

To attempt a recovery and restatement of Johnson's theory of literature and criticism and of his critical method has more than a merely antiquarian interest. Isolated from the more remote principles from which they are derived, Johnson's verdicts on particular books and writers are exposed to those constant changes of regard with which the history of literary reputations is filled, and his criticism is likely to be praised or condemned on no more secure ground than that the authors he treats please or disgust the temporary fancy of the reading public. The decline of Johnson's reputation as a critic in the early nineteenth century illustrates this hazard. But there is a more important value in reconstructing his theory than the protection of his reputation from exposure to critical caprice. If we are to learn from the monuments of humanistic culture, we must understand them in such a way as to make them assimilable, in some degree at least, to modern use. It is very difficult to learn or to improve the art of criticism by a study of the particular judgments of past critics on authors and works. In the service of developing the art of criticism, the chief significance of such particular judgments is in helping us to ascertain the principles of more general import which underlie them and which may be instructive or useful in other contexts. What Johnson has to say about *Lycidas* tells us, of course, something about Johnson the man, something about the unconscious factors in reading poetry, as M. H. Abrams has shown, and perhaps something about eighteenth-century culture. But it does not, by itself, tell us much that would enable us to approach more justly T. S. Eliot's latest poem. But the strictures on *Lycidas* may have such a value if properly taken: they derive— with whatever superaddition of Tory prejudice—from positions capable of formulation, of confirmation or revision, and of application to works superficially very different from *Lycidas*.

II

With a writer whose theoretical statements are diffused through contexts predominantly practical, and so often determined by the requirements of the topic immediately at hand, perhaps the best strategy for examining the theoretical foundations of his work is to begin with his pronouncements on broad literary questions and to test the hypotheses thence derived against his practice in more restricted contexts. For Johnson, the papers on criticism and the rules of art in the *Rambler* (Nos. 37, 125, 156, and 158) and the discussions of tragicomedy and the unities in the *Preface to Shakespeare* offer an especially advantageous point of departure, for here not only does he address himself at some length and in considerable detail to large questions of critical theory, but he seems to be engaged in an attempt to summarize and evaluate an entire critical tradition and to define the alternative with which he would supplant it.

The substance of Johnson's attacks on the rules for pastoral poetry and comedy, on the prohibition of tragicomedy, and on the dramatic unities are familiar enough to need no restatement here. It is important to note that in each case Johnson seeks to subvert accepted critical dogmas and to deliver literature from the fetters of prescriptive criticism. The interest of these attacks for our present purpose is not so much in the content of Johnson's arguments as in the characterization of his own method that is afforded by his analysis of his opponents. The precepts he opposes are in general, he says,

the arbitrary edicts of legislators, authorized only by themselves, who, out of various means by which the same end may be attained, selected such as happened to occur to their own reflection, and then, by a law which idleness and timidity were too willing to obey, prohibited new experiments of wit, restrained fancy from the indulgence of her innate inclination to hazard and adventure, and condemned all future flights of genius to pursue the path of the Maeonian eagle.[5]

The established rules have a uniform characteristic: each specifies, for the genre to which it applies, a peculiar limitation of literary means—language, character, subject, manner of presentation, and the like—which alone can be regarded, in the opinion of the critics, as the proper or artistic way in which to achieve the effect aimed at. Comedy must deal with low characters, pastoral speakers must use rustic diction, tragedies must be divided into five acts, lyric poems may be disorderly, serious and comic actions must not be mingled in one composition, the time of a represented action must equal the time of the representation.

In each case Johnson contends that alternative means may equally well achieve the desired effects. Why does he find the limitation of means enforced by critical precepts to be arbitrary and partial? For three reasons, which form the bases on which, indifferently, Johnson rests his case against the critics. First, because the limitations proposed as universally valid have been derived from the practice of particular poets; second, because nature is the object of the

5. *Rambler*, No. 158 (*Works*, III, 248).

poet's activity; and, third, because literary works are designed to satisfy the general conditions of pleasure. We may examine each of these in turn.

Poets, exercising their essential faculty of choice, have selected such subjects, diction, modes of organization, and the like as fitted their peculiar interests, abilities, and circumstances; these choices, if made by early or honored poets, have been identified by critics with the art itself rather than with the special causes which produced them. Thus tragedy and comedy arose merely from the selection by the ancient poets, according to laws which "custom" had prescribed, of the crimes of men or their absurdities as subjects for drama; and the lack of methodical connection of thought which critics have erected into a principle of lyric poetry had its origin in the vehemence of imagination and the extensive knowledge of the first lyrists. But, when poetry is thus viewed in relation to the selective activity by which it is produced, it is apparent that the imagination—the faculty which predominates in the poet's selection—is limitless in its capacities and hence that other choices, determined by causes equally accidental or capricious, may be made. Precepts derived from the activity of poets are consequently partial and aribitrary.[6]

If the imaginative power distinguishing the poet is "licentious and vagrant, unsusceptible of limitations, and impatient of restraint,"[7] the subject matter over which the selective activity operates has an equivalent characteristic. The poetic imagination roves unconfined in the "boundless ocean of possibility"; nature, in Johnson's view, is limitless in the range of choices it presents to the artist. Critics who limit comedy to men of a certain social class run into absurdity because "the various methods of exhilarating their audience, not being limited by nature, cannot be comprised in precept."[8] Those who condemn the mingling of tragic and comic scenes in Shakespeare fail to realize that this mingling accurately reflects "the real state of sublunary nature,"

which partakes of good and evil, joy and sorrow, mingled with endless variety of proportion and innumerable modes of combination; and expressing the course of the world, in which the loss of one is the gain of another; in which, at the same time, the reveller is hasting to his wine, and the mourner burying his friend; in which the malignity of one is sometimes defeated by the frolick of another; and many mischiefs and many benefits are done and hindered without design.[9]

The real state of sublunary nature—"this chaos of mingled purposes and casualties"[10]—is the poet's object. That some poets, like the ancient writers

6. *Preface to Shakespeare*, in Sir Walter Raleigh (ed.), *Johnson on Shakespeare* (London, [1931]), p. 16; *Rambler*, No. 158 (*Works*, III, 249–50); cf. also Nos. 23 (*Works*, II, 116), 121 (*Works*, III, 76–77), 125 (*Works*, III, 93), and 156 (*Works*, III, 239).

7. *Rambler*, No. 125 (*Works*, III, 93).

8. *Ibid.*, p. 94.

9. *Preface to Shakespeare* (Raleigh, *op. cit.*, pp. 15–16).   10. *Ibid.*, p. 16.

of comedy and tragedy, have elected to restrict themselves to a part of the diversified whole cannot warrant the critic in imposing a similar restriction on others. Critical rules, Johnson says, have too often been derived from precedents rather than from reason, and hence "practice has introduced rules, rather than rules have directed practice."[11]

When he considers the readers of literature, Johnson finds that the critics have made an analogous error. They have assumed or argued that the demands of readers are for specific pleasures arising from specifically distinct types of works. Johnson, having examined the tastes of the common reader with some care, is convinced that this is not so, that, instead, readers demand the more general pleasures of recognition and novelty. Is it asserted that Shakespeare's plays fail to move because the intermingling of tragic and comic scenes interrupts the passions in their progress? Speculative principles do not serve the critic so well as perception, for what do we find when we submit the case to the test of experience?

The interchanges of mingled scenes seldom fail to produce the intended vicissitudes of passion. Fiction cannot move so much, but that the attention may be easily transferred; and though it must be allowed that pleasing melancholy be sometimes interrupted by unwelcome levity, yet let it be considered likewise, that melancholy is often not pleasing, and that the disturbance of one man may be the relief of another; that different auditors have different habitudes; and that, upon the whole, all pleasure consists in variety.[12]

Whichever of these three bases Johnson uses to ground his case against earlier critics—whether the activity of poets, the real state of nature, or the general conditions of pleasure—he is endeavoring to replace what he considers narrow principles with principles more commodious. And this endeavor regularly leads him to forsake the view of art as manifesting itself in distinct species, a view presented in great detail in the treatises of his predecessors, for the ampler domain of nature, in which, as he conceives of it, distinctions and definitions hitherto thought inviolable and "natural" can be shown to be rigidities, arbitrary constrictions, or, at best, ideal manifestoes. One of the chief distinctions of Johnson from his predecessors in criticism is in this careful reduction of the realm of art, and this habit of regarding literature as a natural process, set in the context of other natural processes such as social behavior, and thus amenable to treatment in relation to its psychological causes and effects, its natural materials, and its circumstantial determinants. Literary works, for Johnson, must be thought of not as specifically identifiable objects, instances of fixed classes of works, and embodying more or less perfectly

11. *Rambler*, No. 158 (*Works*, III, 248).
12. *Preface to Shakespeare* (Raleigh, *op. cit.*, p. 17).

an ideal form but as human acts to be judged in relation to the agency of their production and appreciation. They are, consequently, "things modified by human understandings, subject to varieties of complication, and changeable as experience advances knowledge, or accident influences caprice."[13] Literature, like morals, having life as its object, is not "prescribed and limited": "since life itself is uncertain, nothing which has life for its basis can boast much stability."[14] The "performances of art," in consequence of their implication with human action and natural models, are "too inconstant and uncertain, to be reduced to any determinate idea"; a poem is an object "so mutable that it is always changing under our eye, and has already lost its form while we are labouring to conceive it."

> There is therefore scarcely any species of writing, of which we can tell what is its essence, and what are its constituents; every new genius produces some innovation, which, when invented and approved, subverts the rule which the practice of foregoing authors had established.[15]

It is important to notice an underlying paradox in Johnson's attack on earlier critics. He convicts them of fanciful prescription because they take an unwarrantably "scientific" view of literature; Johnson himself, intent as he says upon reducing under the dominion of "science" those regions of literature which have hitherto been under the influence of caprice, emphasizes the unpredictable, nonrational qualities in the process, materials, and effects of art. The importance of this point is not merely in the irony, of which Johnson was doubtless well aware, but in the fact that many of the characteristic features of his criticism grow out of his effort to find a secure ground for rational determination with regard to objects peculiarly unsuited to precise rational treatment. Johnson is known as a great rationalist, and in a sense he was: he sought to ground his statements on reason rather than on fancy or intuition, and he was convinced that such grounds could be discovered. But he was not a rationalist in the sense that he supposed all modes of existence to be equally amenable to rational treatment, or the human mind capable of arriving at certainty in all forms of discourse. In particular, he drew a sharp distinction between the operations of the mind in science and in the affairs and activities of men, including literature. The terms of this distinction help us to define the problems of the critic as Johnson saw them.

Johnson begins the *Preface to Shakespeare* with the observation that it has been charged, with some justice, that praises are without reason lavished on the

13. *Rambler*, No. 125 (*Works*, III, 93); cf. No. 23 (*Works*, II, 115) and *Lives of the Poets*, ed. G. B. Hill (Oxford, 1905), I, 18.

14. *Rambler*, No. 184 (*Works*, III, 361).

15. *Rambler*, No. 125 (*Works*, III, 93).

dead and that the honors due only to excellence are paid to antiquity. But the critic, Johnson points out, seeking to replace prejudice and caprice by reason, cannot disregard the opinion of mankind, liable though it is to error. He has no other criterion to use, for he deals not with objects having determinate natures, such as the objects of science, but with works of a different sort altogether:

> To works . . . of which the excellence is not absolute and definite, but gradual and comparative; to works not raised upon principles demonstrative and scientific, but appealing wholly to observation and experience, no other test can be applied than length of duration and continuance of esteem. . . . As among the works of nature no man can properly call a river deep, or a mountain high, without the knowledge of many mountains, and many rivers; so in the productions of genius, nothing can be stiled excellent till it has been compared with other works of the same kind.

"Demonstration," the work of the scientist, Johnson goes on to say, "immediately displays its power, and has nothing to hope or fear from the flux of years."[16] Science, he tells us elsewhere, pursues truth simply; and, since scientific statements bear a fixed and necessary relation to nature, their force is immediately evident to the rational mind.[17] But "works tentative and experimental," he continues, "must be estimated by their proportion to the general and collective ability of man, as it is discovered in a long succession of endeavours":

> Of the first building that was raised, it might be with certainty determined that it was round or square; but whether it was spacious or lofty must have been referred to time. The Pythagorean scale of numbers was at once discovered to be perfect; but the poems of *Homer* we yet know not to transcend the common limits of human intelligence, but by remarking, that nation after nation, and century after century, has been able to do little more than transpose his incidents, new-name his characters, and paraphrase his sentiments.[18]

Here again we see Johnson's conception of literature as a mode of activity, as one of the things men can do, and we observe the consequences of this conception: the limits of human ability cannot be specified; the relation of works of art to nature is not immediate but relative to the powers of poets and to the natural desires of readers; the excellence of literature is therefore "tentative," "gradual," and "comparative," and probability rather than demonstration is the utmost attainable by the critic.[19]

16. *Preface to Shakespeare* (Raleigh, *op. cit.*, pp. 9–10).

17. *Rambler*, Nos. 121 (*Works*, III, 76) and 184 (*Works*, III, 358–59); cf. Preface to John Payne's *New Tables of Interest* (1758), in *Samuel Johnson's Prefaces & Dedications*, ed. A. T. Hazen (New Haven, 1937), p. 144.

18. *Preface to Shakespeare* (Raleigh, *op. cit.*, p. 10).

19. *Rambler*, Nos. 92 (*Works*, II, 431), 93 (*Works*, II, 438–39), and 156 (*Works*, III, 239); *Adventurer*, No. 115 (*Works*, IV, 113); *Lives*, I, 14, 340, and II, 47.

The opposition between Johnson and the critics he attacks in the *Rambler* and the *Preface to Shakespeare* may be seen in terms of this distinction. The earlier critics, in his view of them, assumed for literary works a fixed relation to nature like that found in science; they therefore supposed it possible to deduce, from the objects represented or the effects proposed in works of different kinds, a determinate set of specifications for each literary genre. But Johnson, while not at all abandoning his effort to introduce into criticism as much certainty as the subject will permit, or his conviction that human nature and external nature possess certain common features which, when discovered or revealed by the passage of time, will provide the basis for reasoned statement, nevertheless abandons the pretense to certainty made by his predecessors and casts aside the principles and distinctions they have formulated.

The locus of principles for the evaluation of literature Johnson therefore transfers from art to nature. Given the relativity of art, which is a consequence of the view that it is a mode of activity rather than the perfection of objects having determinate characteristics, art itself cannot supply the principles for its own judgment, for, as we have seen, principles derived from the practice of poets or the traits of works are commonly arbitrary and accidental. The critic's recourse must be to nature. But here, too, difficulties arise. For Johnson, nature is infinitely complex and varied, and the human mind is incapable of encompassing it completely or of predicting its course in detail.[20] Hence Johnson's distrust of abstract speculation and the prominence, in his scheme, of time as a guaranty of opinion. But regardless of the difficulties involved in seeking natural principles which will permit the critic to give an account of literary excellence, the enterprise is sustained by the conviction that the common and general properties of nature are discoverable. Men are in essential respects everywhere the same. Experience tells us that the general conditions of pleasure are simple and fixed: all men take pleasure in the recognition of truth—the consonance of what is done or said to "the general sense or experience of mankind"[21]—and in the surprise of novelty or variety. No prediction can be made of the means by which these conditions may be satisfied, for Johnson will not, "like many hasty philosophers, search after the cause till . . . certain of the effect";[22] but the stability of the grounds on which literary ef-

20. *Rambler*, Nos. 13 (*Works*, II, 62), 70 (*Works*, II, 331–32), 63 (*Works*, II, 301), and 122 (*Works*, III, 80–81); *Adventurer*, Nos. 107 (*Works*, IV, 99), 108 (*Works*, IV, 101–2) and 131 (*Works*, IV, 135); Sermon XXIII (*Works*, IX, 500). Of Johnson's skeptical and empirical habit of mind, and of its consequences in his writings, J. H. Hagstrum has given an excellent account in "The Nature of Dr. Johnson's Rationalism," *ELH*, XVII (1950), 191-205.

21. *Lives*, III, 345.

22. *Rambler*, No. 61 (*Works*, II, 295).

ects may be produced affords a principle from which the critic can reason to
heir causes and hence from which he can argue questions of literary merit.

III

On the basis of these assumptions concerning the nature of literature and
he task of criticism, Johnson develops the scheme of analysis which underlies
his discussions of technical problems, works and genres, and individual au-
hors. Of the four elements in the literary process—author, work, nature, and
audience—the first and last are primary, and the other two are defined in rela-
ion to them. Literature is an activity or process directed to the pleasure and
instruction of the common reader. Works succeed or fail—are excellent or
poor—to the extent that they satisfy the general conditions of pleasure, name-
y, truth and novelty. Nature, being both regular and inexhaustibly varied, provides subject matter for art and, being external, a measure for judging it. The
extent to which works embody truth and variety depends on the power of the
author to discover these in nature, to select or invent matter which will embody
hem, and to represent it in words. All the steps in the process are relative to
he last—the satisfaction of the general conditions of pleasure—not only because this is the aim of literature but because, as we have seen, these condi-
ions, discovered by experience and guaranteed by the essential identity of men,
provide the first principle of critical reasoning. But critical reasoning is with
respect to the causes of literary pleasure; the critic's task is "to distinguish
hose means of pleasing which depend upon known causes and rational deduction, from the nameless and inexplicable elegancies which appeal wholly
o the fancy." Among the causes of literary pleasure—and hence of literary
excellence—the author is primary, not only because his selective activity initi-
ates the process, but because the traits of works, the extent to which they
exhibit general nature, and hence their capacity to excite pleasure are all
grounded ultimately in the powers of the author. Works are treated by Johnson as "performances" manifesting the powers of the author, as compositions
of materials which resemble—in themselves and in their conjunction—the
raits of nature, and as the sources of recognition or surprise in the audience.
Works figure in Johnson's scheme, consequently, as relative to all three, and
he terms in which works are discussed are derived from a prior consideration
of authors, nature, and readers. Nature also occupies a relative, rather than an
independent, position in the scheme. Nature is the link between author and
reader—the common elements that guarantee truth and the accidental variations
hat produce variety being the basis for selection by the one and for comparison
and judgment by the other. For Johnson, nature is not an ontological, but a
psychological, concept: it is defined, that is, not in terms of properties inde-

pendent of the mind but in terms of its capacity to produce certain responses in men. General nature is thus what all men everywhere recognize as like themselves, and particular nature is what men in general recognize as present only at certain times, under certain conditions, or among certain men. Both truth and variety arise from the constant linkage between human passions and their effects: the regularity with which the same passions produce effects of the same kind permits recognition and hence truth; the infinite accidental modifications in the actual manner in which the passions do their uniform work afford novelty and variety.

The consequences of the general assumptions set out in the preceding section and of the theoretical scheme just described are everywhere apparent in Johnson's critical writings. Thus we see at once why Johnson's criticism is predominantly practical and why he developed no "art" of poetry nor engaged much in the literary theorizing so common in his day. His distrust of "inactive speculation" here co-operates with his conception of literature: an elaborated theory would necessarily involve, in Johnson's terms, an analysis or prescription of the possible or proper in art. But such an analysis or prescription must be arbitrary, for although the general conditions of pleasing may be specified, the aspects of nature and the traits of works which may conduce to this end cannot, since nature offers boundless possibilities to the poet and since there is no discoverable limit to human powers.

Not only does Johnson's theory of literature give his criticism its prevailingly practical cast, but his distribution of emphasis among the major terms of his scheme leads to the disappearance or revision of terms and distinctions that had received elaborate treatment at the hands of Johnson's predecessors and contemporaries. We have seen that in the literary process as he conceived of it the traits of works are relative to the effects they produce, the subject matter they represent, and the powers of the author from which they derive. The terms in which Johnson discusses works are consequently terms drawn from his analysis of these three; he has little use for traditional terms whose meanings seem to him to depend on an a priori analysis of art as a whole or of one of its species. The subordination of the work to the nexus of causes originating in the author and terminating in the audience may be seen in his treatment of the traditional literary genres. Early distinctions among the genres arise, in Johnson's view, as we have seen in his discussion of comedy, tragicomedy, and the unities, from attempts to discriminate effects peculiar to the different genres and to isolate, in relation to these, specific subject matters, styles, and manners appropriate to each. Johnson finds most such discriminations artificial: writers on pastoral, he says, "have entangled themselves with unnecessary difficulties by advancing principles, which, having no foundation in the nature of things, are to be wholly rejected from a species of composition, in which, above all others, mere nature is to be regarded." Thus critics, defining pastoral as a dialogue of men tending sheep, have required that the manners be those of the Golden Age, the diction rustic, and the persons uncouth and ignorant. Johnson's handling of the rules for pastoral is characteristic of his method of dealing with the other genres. Some of the rules—such as that requiring chaste sentiments—he retains, not on grounds specific to pastoral but in relation to the end of poetry in general. Others he refutes on the basis of a more generalized definition of the genre: pastoral is considered as "a representation of rural nature, and consequently as exhibiting the ideas and sentiments of those, whoever they are, to whom the country affords pleasure or employment." The specific properties of the form are consequently reduced: "pastoral being the representation of an action or passion, by its effects upon a country life, has nothing peculiar but its confinement to rural imagery, without which it ceases to be pastoral." Rural imagery he does not attempt to define, and, indeed, he broadens even this property of the form by insisting that rural imagery is compatible with dignity of sentiment and beauty of diction.[23] The effect of Johnson's operation upon the received analyses of pastoral is not to eliminate the concept of the genre, but to reduce its value and importance as a principle of criticism by stripping it of most of its peculiarities, and to throw the emphasis in criticism away from the analysis of the genre and toward the more general causes on which, in common with other forms of poetry, it depends.

The disappearance or reduction in importance of traditional distinctions based on peculiar traits of works and genres is paralleled in Johnson's criticism by a generalized method of dealing with poetic subjects. Poetry has a universal subject—nature and passion—but particular works have as their matter more or less specific subjects selected or dictated by choice, convention, or accident from the wide realm in which the imagination is free to rove. Such subjects always raise for Johnson the question of how far they approximate the universal subject of poetry, i.e., of the degree to which they are capable of satisfying the general conditions of pleasure—truth and novelty. This alone is the test applied to poetic subjects. Johnson does not classify or evaluate them in relation to more specific ends; for such ends could not, as we have seen, be inferred with any certainty from common human nature. Nor does he differentiate them in relation to the poetic powers to which they are adapted; for poetic power, as we shall see, is generalized rather than subdivided, and all the faculties are adapted to all sorts of subjects. Thus, although comments on the values of different subjects occur repeatedly in Johnson's criticism, subjects of the most diverse sorts are submitted to a common test. Religion and mythology are both

23. *Rambler*, No. 37 (*Works*, II, 182–84).

poor subjects for poetry; they differ, of course, in many respects, but the reason for their inadequacy is the same—neither is "level with common life," neither offers anything on which the imagination can rest while the mind compares the life represented with the life it knows.[24] Religious, pastoral, didactic, and descriptive subjects are defective in that they offer little, if any, opportunity for novelty and variety.[25] On the other hand, the excellence of the subjects of biographies and of works so diverse as the *Odyssey*, Gray's *Elegy*, and Rowe's *Fair Penitent* rests on a common principle—the presentation to the reader of "parallel circumstances and kindred images," which have the power of "gratifying every mind, by recalling its conceptions."[26] Subjects, like genres, are treated in terms not of their specific differences but of their common qualities, and these common qualities are, in turn, described not in terms of the substantial properties of nature but in terms of their capacity to evoke responses of a certain kind in the readers.

The audience to which the entire literary process is directed is the common reader. The importance of the reader in Johnson's scheme—and the reason, consequently, for his regular appeal from critics and authorities to "the common voice of the multitude"[27]—lies not merely in the fact that literature has a pleasurable end, for such an end has been stated by critics in whose work the reader plays a relatively unimportant role, but in the fact that Johnson is seeking a stable basis in nature on which to rest critical inquiry and judgment: the audience is the only fixed element in the process; for while nature has invariable features, they can be identified only through general recognition, and while poets may excel in the power to discover and represent nature, we become aware of this capacity only through its effect upon us. Johnson's reader is defined merely in human terms, and works of art are discussed in relation to his demands. This procedure is the reverse of that employed by Dryden, for whom the proper judge of literature is the man capable of understanding and appreciating the best works, his detailed qualifications emerging from an examination of such works. Thus the audience, for Dryden, though it establishes the final cause of art, is subordinated to the art over which it presides.[28]

24. *Lives*, I, 51, 147, 181, 182, 295; II, 16, 284, 311; III, 228, 438, 439.

25. On religious poetry see *Lives*, I, 182, 291; II, 263–64; III, 310; on pastoral, *Rambler*, No. 36 (*Works*, II, 178), *Lives*, I, 163; on didactic, *Lives*, I, 437; II, 295; III, 242–44; on descriptive poetry, *Rambler*, No. 143 (*Works*, III, 179).

26. *Rambler*, Nos. 60 (*Works*, II, 286), 36 (*Works*, II, 178); Boswell, *Life of Johnson*, ed. Hill-Powell (Oxford, 1934), IV, 219; *Lives*, II, 67; III, 441–42; cf. also Raleigh, *op. cit.*, pp. 162, 165; *Lives*, I, 245, 302, 360–61, 363; II, 69; III, 397.

27. *Rambler*, No. 52 (*Works*, II, 250); cf. also No. 23 (*Works*, II, 116), and *Adventurer*, No. 138 (*Works*, IV, 147).

28. Cf., e.g., Preface to *All for Love* and *Dedication of the Aeneis* (*Essays of John Dryden* ed. Ker [Oxford, 1926], I, 195–97; II, 223–26).

For Johnson, readers are antecedent to art, in the sense that the properties involved in his definition of the proper reader are derived from an examination of human nature and not from an examination of literature. The demands which readers make of literature are not confined to literature but are, indeed, the general causes of pleasure, operative in the affairs of life as well. The proper reader is the common reader, the reasonable man, no other traits being involved than rationality and common experience of the world. Johnson excludes from his description of the audience of art all traits merely variable, for these would introduce an element of uncertainty into the deductions made from the effects of literature. Hence he does not follow some earlier critics in differentiating readers by the times or places in which they live, by their nationalities or tempers, by their education or acquired knowledge. He does not appeal to the best readers, to the most experienced, or to an aristocracy of taste.[29] He looks rather to "the common voice of the multitude, uninstructed by precept, and unprejudiced by authority."[30] "Of things that terminate in human life," he says in the *Life of Pope*, "the world is the proper judge: to despise its sentence, if it were possible, is not just; and if it were just is not possible."[31] And the highest attainments of art are defined in relation to this broad conception of the proper audience. West's *Imitations of Spenser*, successful as they are with respect to meter, language, and fiction,

are not to be reckoned among the great achievements of intellect, because their effect is local and temporary; they appeal not to reason and passion, but to memory, and presuppose an accidental or artificial state of mind. . . .Works of this kind may deserve praise, as proofs of great industry and great nicety of observation; but the highest praise, the praise of genius, they cannot claim. The noblest beauties of art are those of which the effect is coextended with rational nature, or at least with the whole circle of polished life; what is less than this can be only pretty, the plaything of fashion and the amusement of a day.[32]

Although the audience supplies in Johnson's scheme the basis for critical inference, it is not about the effects of literature that the critic reasons but about the causes of those effects. The task of criticism is "to distinguish those means of pleasing which depend upon *known causes* and rational deduction, from the nameless and inexplicable elegancies which appeal wholly to the fancy, from

29. Except when, as in defending Pope's *Homer*, he argues that a writer's first obligation is to please his immediate audience. This is a prerequisite to a broader and more permanent effect—Johnson would not have thought well of writers who addressed themselves directly to the ages—but it is not equivalent to such an effect, and the greatest works rise above this minimum level of achievement.

30. *Rambler*, No. 52 (*Works*, II, 250); cf. *Lives*, III, 441.

31. *Lives*, III, 210; cf. also *ibid.*, I, 175, II, 16, 132; Boswell, *op. cit.*, I, 200.

32. *Lives*, III, 332–33.

which we feel delight, but know not *how they produce it*."[33] In his search for causes explanatory of the effects of literary works and hence permitting judgments of praise or blame, the critic addresses himself primarily to the author. The crucial position of the poet, for Johnson, arises from the fact that it is the poet's activity which imparts to literature its peculiarly tentative and experimental character and from the fact that the power of the author is the ultimate ground on which rests the capacity of works to evoke pleasure. Johnson's treatment of the poet reflects the fundamental orientation of his theory to the natural conditions of artistic activity, and it displays the tendency we have noticed in his treatment of works, subjects, and readers to avoid derivation of his basic terms from an analysis of the peculiar traits of art. To conceive of literature as a mode of activity essentially like activity of any other sort removes, for Johnson, the basis on which many earlier critics had isolated the faculties characteristic of the poet, assigned them to particular genres, and distinguished poets from other men. Johnson's reduction of art to nature has consequences here in two directions: it dissolves the basis for a separation between poets and men in general, and it collapses essential distinctions among kinds of poetic effects and materials. A definition of genius which made it distinctive of one class of men, adapted to one sort of material, or productive of one sort of effect would have to be founded on a classification or hierarchy of mental faculties, natural objects, literary genres, varieties of effects, or classes of readers; but we have seen why Johnson believes such classification to be untrustworthy. In any case such distinctions would assign but a part of literature or nature to genius, and this would constitute a limitation on the concept. Johnson therefore views the mental powers of the poet as determined to their objects accidentally, not essentially. Repeatedly we encounter his ridicule of the notion that genius is "a particular designation of mind and propensity for some certain science or employment."[34] The "true Genius," he observes in the *Life of Cowley*, "is a mind of large general powers, accidentally determined to some particular direction."[35] Genius is merely the sum of all the powers of the mind operating with maximum effect; the separate ingredients of reason, imagination, fancy, judgment, are less important than their combination; and the separate work or materials of each counts for less than the total vigor of mind which can discover and represent "the whole system of life" in both its regularity and variety, which can join novelty and credibility by penetrating

33. *Rambler*, No. 92 (*Works*, II, 431–32); my italics.

34. *Lives*, I, 2.

35. *Ibid*. Cf. *Rambler*, Nos. 25 (*Works*, II, 124–25), 43 (*Works*, II, 208–9), and 117 (*Works*, III, 54–60); *Idler*, No. 61 (*Works*, IV, 332); *Letters*, ed. G. B. Hill (Oxford, 1892), II, 184; *Miscellanies*, ed. G. B. Hill (New York, 1897), I, 314, II, 287; Boswell, *op. cit.*, V, 34–35; D'Arblay, *Diaries & Letters*, ed. Austin Dobson (London, 1904), II, 271–72.

far enough into the recesses of nature to uncover the causes of human passion from which life derives both its unvarying order and its manifold combinations.[36]

The measurement of genius thus defined is for Johnson an essential part of the critic's task, for "the enquiry, how far man may extend his designs, or how high he may rate his native force, is of far greater dignity than in what rank we shall place any particular performance."[37] The "silent reference of human works to human abilities" occasioned by Johnson's theory of literature as activity, together with the absence from his theory of any definition of genius which would permit a fixed standard of measurement, accounts for the care he displays in establishing an alternative measure. "All human excellence," he points out in *Rambler*, No. 127, "is comparative . . . no man performs much but in proportion to what others accomplish, or to the time and opportunities which have been allowed him."[38] The comparative criterion for the measurement of genius or power Johnson finds in his concept of the "general and collective ability of man."[39] The most notable property of this standard of excellence, by which he avoids both the absolutism of a fixed definition of genius and the relativism of judging each man's performances merely by his own abilities, is that it is itself not absolute and final but relative and alterable. The general level at which men may operate cannot be determined precisely and finally because a new genius may always appear to break through the levels previously established and force a revision of our conception of what human nature may accomplish.[40] Johnson's conception of the general and collective ability of man is accordingly a concept of the limit of human capacity, not deduced from a consideration of the ends or objects or forms of poetry, but derived empirically, "discovered in a long succession of endeavours." If the succession is long enough and inclusive enough, it will guarantee in an empirical way that the limit derived is stable; and in practice we see that the conception of the limit of human power provided by the work of Homer has never been revised, so that we can say that his poems "transcend the common limits of human intelligence."[41] But it is important for our judgment of Johnson's criti-

36. On comprehensiveness as the mark of genius see *Lives*, I, 48, 55, 56–57, 183, 212–13, 234–35, 245, 294, 320, 413, 417, 457; II, 54, 120–21, 207; III, 298–99, 324, 333, 337–38, 359, 416–17, 427, 432; on the difficulties of defining and distinguishing the mental faculties see *Lives*, I, 235, Boswell, *op. cit.*, V, 34; on genius as force or vigor of mind, see *Rambler*, No. 168 (*Works*, III, 293), *Lives*, I, 170, 185; II, 64, 177, 204; III, 222, 223.

37. *Preface to Shakespeare* (Raleigh, *op. cit.*, p. 31).

38. *Works*, III, 106.

39. *Preface to Shakespeare* (Raleigh, *op. cit.*, p. 10).

40. *Rambler*, No. 92 (*Works*, II, 431).

41. *Preface to Shakespeare* (Raleigh, *op. cit.*, pp. 9–10).

186 *W. R. Keast*

cism to observe that it provides for such revision by basing its inferences on an induction from past performances rather than on an absolute scheme of values.

A further consequence of Johnson's treatment of literature as a mode of activity—a consequence which accounts in a large measure for his most characteristic form of critical utterance—is the introduction into the process of poetry and hence into the purview of the critic of a variety of factors which influence the poet's work in one way or another. Johnson's aim is always to make as accurate a determination as possible of the native power of the artist, apart from all external assistance or obstruction; but, since power is displayed in activity and since every activity has a circumstantial setting which determines, in important respects, its form and outcome, these circumstances must be isolated and evaluated in order to arrive at a firm estimate of the poet's power. The native ability of the artist is only one of the causes of a work of art; it is modified by intention, diligence, time and opportunity, chance and good luck, the availability of suitable materials, education, criticism, models, and a wide range of other forces over which the poet has no control.[42] By viewing poetry in the setting of its production, therefore, Johnson has greatly complicated the problems of the critic and, at the same time, has greatly refined his analysis. When the critic looks at the poem as a sign of a writer's ability, he must be aware of the complex array of causal factors which mingled in its production, and he must avoid the easy but false expedient of inferring ability or excellence directly from the traits of the work. The process of disentanglement by which the critic sorts out the circumstances of a work, distinguishing those traits genuinely attributable to the poet's native power from those dependent on some external or accidental factor, is essential to criticism as Johnson conceived and practiced it. The circumstantial method, of which history and biography are the basic tools, is forecast in the *Miscellaneous Observations on the Tragedy of Macbeth* (1745): "In order to make a true estimate of the abilities and merit of a writer, it is always necessary to examine the genius of his age, and the opinions of his contemporaries";[43] it is a major element in the organization of the *Preface to Shakespeare*, one long section of which is justified on the ground that "every man's preformances, to be rightly estimated, must be compared with the state of the age in which he lived, and with his own particular opportunities";[44] and it provides the formal principle for Johnson's

42. See, e.g., *Lives*, I, 19, 21, 35, 413, 415–18, 423–24, 443, 447, 458–59, 464–65; II, 145–47, 228; III, 217–20, 337–38, 268.

43. *Works*, V, 55.

44. Raleigh, *op. cit.*, p. 30; cf. *Proposals* (Raleigh, *op. cit.*, pp. 1–8 *passim*, esp. 3, 4, and 8); Preface to Thomas Maurice, *Poems and Miscellaneous Pieces* ([1779]; Hazen, *op. cit.*, p. 142); *Lives*, I, 318, 411; II, 145–47, 338–39, 433; III, 238–40.

greatest critical work, the *Lives of the Poets*, in which his characteristic linkage of biography and criticism is brought to perfection. The threefold division of the fully developed *Lives*, in which external circumstances, the intellectual character of the writer, and the qualities of his works are successively treated (a mode of organization also used, though in a different sequence, in the *Preface to Shakespeare*), is the counterpart in practice of the theory traced above.

Johnson's shift of the emphasis in criticism from art to nature and his persistent substitution of a more generalized formulation of artistic genius, literary genres, and related questions for the more particularized definitions of his predecessors may be regarded as a blurring of useful distinctions, as a relinquishment of ground gained in the development of criticism during the preceding century. So to view it, however, is to neglect the abuses and rigidities of critical theory between Dryden and Johnson and to undervalue the reconstructive service performed by Johnson in focusing attention once again on the dominant obligation of art to please its readers and the duty of critics to ground their judgments on real distinctions. Johnson's work, on the other hand, owing to his effort to dispense with encumbrances of traditional theory which he finds unjustified by empirical test, may appear to involve a total abrogation of principle, leaving only sensibility or force of personal preference and statement as the armor of the critic. To view his work in this light, however, is to separate his effort to re-establish criticism from the essential theoretical foundations on which it is based and to obscure features of his critical practice whose value was by no means exhausted in the solution of the problems for which they were originally formulated.[45]

45. I have discussed some aspects of Johnson's critical practice in relation to its theoretical bases in "Johnson's Criticism of the Metaphysical Poets," *ELH*, XVII (1950), 59–70.

III

THE PHILOSOPHIC BASES OF ART
AND CRITICISM[1]

RICHARD McKEON

REFERENCE back to philosophic principles to expose erroneous assumptions and to establish common grounds for judgments of fact or value could not be justified easily by the record of its success in producing agreement. Philosophers have frequently expressed the expectation that philosophic disagreements would be resolved by applying scientific principles to a subject matter for the first time or that doctrinal disagreements in particular fields of inquiry or action would be removed by discovering and expounding philosophic principles. Yet doctrinal differences seem to have persisted, after each such effort at resolution, translated into more inclusive and more obstinate philosophic oppositions, and the differences of philosophers have disappeared because they have been forgotten more frequently than because they have been resolved. Long before the formulation of such convictions in present-day varieties of pragmatisms and positivisms, the practical man, the artist, the scientist, and the theologian expressed impatience with philosophic considerations because they were impertinent to operations considered urgent, or incompatible with attitudes defended as realistic, or inadequate for ends assumed to be ultimate. The pragmatic impatience with theory and the positivistic exposure of "unreal" problems, however, even in their abbreviated expressions, are philosophies; and the dialectical consequences of principles are particularly apparent, though unexamined, in those minimal philosophies which are expressions of conviction concerning the subject of an inquiry or concerning the method by which the inquiry must be pursued. For general principles, which may seem arbitrary or indefinite in theoretic formulation, have precise significances and consequences in particular applications; while particular things, which may be assumed to have an obvious and simple guise in the beliefs unchallenged in habitual practical operations, possess, without trace of inconsistency, other specifications and characteristics in scientific theory. The significances of all philosophies, even those which are satirized as remote from reality and indifferent to experience, are tested in application to particular subjects; but convictions concerning the nature of things, even those of unwilling philosophers who acknowledge only one dogma of reality, are tested by the

1. Reprinted from *Modern Philology*, November, 1943, and February, 1944.

persistent differences which are the outstanding fact of intellectual history. Whether or not certainty is thought to be possible in human and natural investigations, it is no less true that the nature of things, in so far as it is known, is determined by philosophic principles than that philosophic principles are determined, in so far as they are verified, by the nature of things.

Any general discussion expounds at once the principles of philosophy which it employs and the subject with which it is concerned; but, of all discussions in which philosophy finds an application, the criticism of art is influenced in a peculiarly nice balance by commitment to principle, determination by subject, and use of method. As viewed in its application to the practices or objects of art, the problems of criticism seem to be determined in any one theory by concrete and empirically ascertainable facts and to depend on principles which are determined by the same facts. As viewed in the statements of critics and philosophers, however, the problems of criticism seem to have been determined by a vast diversity of principles used in almost countless approaches, each applied to phenomena irrelevant to other critical precepts and criteria. There is as much disagreement concerning the nature of art or concerning what a poem is— whether it is what is seen on the page or what is heard, whether it is what is imagined by the poet or felt by his reader, or what is judged by the competent or what lies behind or above the expression of any poet[2]—as there is concerning the nature of being or concerning what may be said to be—whether only things in time and space exist, or whether existence can be attributed only to operations and relations, or whether to be is to be perceived, or whether true being is Ideal or God alone truly is; nor is there any more disagreement concerning beauty, form, imagination, or judgment than concerning truth, virtue, knowledge, or law, and much the same indeterminacy is found in the terms and principles chosen as appropriate in any of these discussions. Yet examination of discussions in the philosophy of art affords clearer insight into the nature of philosophic problems and principles than would other applications of philosophy, since its subject matter no less than its history renders improbable the supposition that the resolution of philosophic differences depends on preliminary agreement concerning the character or even the identity of objects treated in rival theories. For agreement concerning an object usually conceals principles, both those employed to arrive at agreement and those ignored lest they forestall it; and the multiplicity and subtle shadings of theories of art adumbrate the general patterns which reappear in philosophic discussions with less distortion than speculations in those branches of philosophy in which dog-

2. Cf. S. C. Pepper, "The Esthetic Object," *Journal of Philosophy*, XL (1943), 477–82; R. Wellek, "The Mode of Existence of a Literary Work of Art," *Southern Review*, VII (1942), 735–54.

matism is more plausible concerning the things which terms point to or designate. The subject matter of the philosophy of art is, whatever its technical definition, a human process and production, and it is therefore influenced by theory as is the subject matter of no other branch of philosophy. Natural philosophers may suggest operations according to the laws they discover, but the "nature" of things is not directly affected by physics, and even moral philosophers must find means by which to make their intellectual analyses indirectly effective by habituation or will, apathy or passions. Notwithstanding the tendency of idealists to argue that all things are thoughts, or of materialists to reduce thought to the motion of matter, or of dialecticians to repeat some form of Socrates' identification of virtue with knowledge, there is no real danger of confusing the other branches of philosophy with their subject matters, whereas the discussion of art is itself an art, and is, in many analyses, possessed of the same characteristics and directed to the same end as the arts it treats.

What men have said about art may be examined and interpreted for philosophic purposes to elucidate the operation of philosophic discussions in general; but such a use of statements will achieve its philosophic purpose only in the measure that the analysis clarifies the interpretation of theories of art, their oppositions, and their histories. Things and principles are not independent, since principles are employed in any statement of things and things are involved in any statement of principles. Consequently, the examination of theories that have been stated or employed, if it introduces order into the principles applied to things, will also indicate the nature of things which determine principles. Three kinds of data may be differentiated in approaching the problems of art by way of what has been said as a preliminary or as a check to treating ascertainable facts or to following the implications of defensible theories; for facts, principles, and judgments are not always separate in the statement of a critical judgment or even the formulation of a philosophic argument, but they are readily separated in the oppositions and controversies of philosophers. The philosophic principles and the methods of criticism are usually treated indirectly by arguing in detail, after the relevant objects of discussion have been chosen without argument, concerning the "real" nature of those objects. The nature of art, the appropriate methods of criticism, and the true principles of aesthetics are all in a sense determined by the facts and the phenomena; but we are dependent on the testimony of critics, sophisticated or naïve, for the report of phenomena and on the principles of philosophers, deliberate or haphazard, for the criteria of their choice and evaluation. The facts may therefore vary or be approached in different ways; the evaluation of the facts may depend on different principles or on principles differently interpreted; the statements of the critics and the principles of the philosophers, finally, become in their expression themselves "things" subject to evaluation and explanation, and they are not exempt from the relativity of art objects and evaluations.

The consequences of these variabilities in art and philosophy, as well as in criticism, are apparent in the difficulties which impede efforts to achieve common designation, mutual intelligibility, and objective evaluation. Since there is little relation between the subjects, the terms, or the principles of the various analyses of art, it is seldom easy to translate the statement of one analysis into an equivalent statement in another; or, if the translation is possible, to relate the two theories to the same subject; or, if they do bear on the same kind of data, to derive comparable evaluations of any given object. In the consequent relativity of criteria of truth and relevance, any thing may be identified as a work of art and any characteristic may make it good or bad of its kind; any judgment may seem as valid or as true as any other; and any theory may be set forth plausibly as the unique and absolute truth or, at least, as more probable than other theories. These difficulties are not to be solved, if what has been said of the nature of the discussion of art is correct, by referring the problem to irreducible and stubborn facts or (what is the same thing) to indisputable and appropriate theories, but by examining the meanings of the various explanations and their relations to one another and by formulating criteria for the truth and utility possible to such theories. For such purposes consideration of the nature of art and of the philosophy of art may properly be focused in the statements of the critic and philosopher, since those statements can be treated, without prejudice to fact or principles, first, in their relations to the various subjects to which their principles make them relevant; second, in their relations to other forms of judgment, like science, history, philosophy in general, and art itself; and, third, in their relations to the various terms in which they are stated and which in turn derive varying significances from the ends and criteria proper to criticism in its various modes.

I

The subject matter and meaning of statements about art—what art is and what one discusses when one discusses art—are determined by the principles of discussion and the things discussed, for the choice of things and of aspects of things relevant to a question is a way of choosing and determining their scope and use. Both the things which are the subject matter and the principles which determine the discussion must be discovered from examination of the terms in which the theories are stated. The words of the statements are themselves ambiguous, and the things which they designate or to which they refer in different theories are too numerous and unorganized to reveal interrelations or system in meanings unless they are arranged according to principles, either principles employed in the statements or principles borrowed for their interpretation from theories concerning references of signs, forms of judgment, ways of being. The latter adjustment occurs constantly in philosophic discussion and critical evaluation, for any theory can be stated in terms of any other theory, usually at considerable expense to its sense and cogency, and every theoretic statement involves, in so far as it is presented as true, as adequate, or simply as different, a judgment passed on other theories, usually removing the need for further consideration of them, since they turn out to be irrelevant to the facts, unscientific, an earlier stage in what has been a progressive march toward a truth which will never be absolute, impractical, or abstract. Yet for all the differences in their subject matters and in judgments about them, the principles which theoretic statements invoke seem to bear a simple relation to one another, at least definite enough to bring them into some contact with other theories and to make them echo or oppose statements of other philosophers. Principles which are independent or contradictory determine a meaning for the statements of opposed theories as definitely as the consistent and fruitful principles of a single system determine the meanings of statements within that system; and it should be possible, therefore, to elucidate controversies and oppositions, much as the meaning of any system is reconstructed and understood, by means of the principles involved.

The words which are used to state the principles and to determine the subject matter of modern discussions of art emerge fairly clearly in the statements of their oppositions. The basic question among present-day oppositions is, perhaps, whether one discusses art adequately by discussing something else or by discussing art, for, in the former case, other oppositions turn on what precise subject other than art should be discussed and, in the latter case, on what art itself is. The theories which have been based on the assumption that the meaning of art is explained best, or solely, by means of other phenomena have recently, as in the past, borrowed the principles and terminology of aesthetics and criticism from some fashionable science, from semantics, psychoanalysis, or economics, from sociology, morals, or theology. The art object and the art experience are then nothing in themselves, since they are determined by circumstances[3] and require, like the circumstances which determine them, bio-

3. Cf. John Dewey, *Art as Experience* (New York, 1934), p. 4: "In order to understand the meaning of artistic products, we have to forget them for a time, to turn aside from them and have recourse to the ordinary forces and conditions of experience that we do not usually regard as esthetic." For Dewey the relevant phenomena are basically biological; cf. *ibid.*, p. 18: "In life that is truly life, everything overlaps and merges. . . . To grasp the sources of esthetic experience it is, therefore, necessary to have recourse to animal life below the human scale." The work of art is treated, finally, in terms of experience; cf. *ibid.*, p. 64: "The real work of art is the building up of an integral experience out of the interaction of organic and environmental conditions and energies." It is not to be identified, except potentially, with a physical object; cf. *ibid.*, p. 162: "It has been repeatedly intimated that there

logical, social, psychological, or historical principles of explanation.[4] The theories which have been based on the assumption that aesthetic phenomena should be analyzed separately, whatever the complexities of the relations in which the aesthetic object or experience is involved, have sought principles in the construction and unity of the art object viewed in terms of expression (in which experience and intention are matched to form), composition (in which details are organized in form), or communication (in which emotion is evoked by form). The art object may then be isolated by a variety of devices. It may

---

is a difference between the art product (statute, painting, or whatever), and the *work* of art. The first is physical and potential; the latter is active and experienced." A similar endeavor animated by similar purposes may lead to the eventual separation of art from experience; thus, e.g., T. C. Pollock states as his purpose (*The Nature of Literature* [Princeton, 1942], p. xiii) "to lay a theoretical basis for the investigation of literature as a social phenomenon in terms which are consonant both with our contemporary knowledge of language and with the development of modern science"; and in pursuit of that purpose he finds it necessary to differentiate "experience" from "literature" and to define literature in terms of uses of language (*ibid.*, pp. 55–56). This is no theoretic distinction, since Dewey's inquiry would give importance to the continuity of the aesthetic with other experiences and to the problem of conferring an aesthetic quality on all modes of production (*op. cit.*, pp. 80–81), while Pollock's problem is one of differentiating the use of language from other parts of human experience and the literary from other uses of language. Or, again, the consideration of other phenomena and other problems seems sometimes to lead to the conclusion that all aesthetic considerations are in comparison abstract and false; cf. M. Lifshitz, *The Philosophy of Art of Karl Marx*, trans. R. B. Winn (New York, 1938), p. 5: "Even the eighteenth century, the classic age of aesthetics, could not remain confined to abstractions such as 'the beautiful' and 'the sublime.' In the background of purely aesthetic discussions concerning the role of genius, the value of art, the imitation of nature, practical problems of the bourgeois-democratic movement intruded themselves with increasing insistence." Theories themselves, finally, are sometimes refuted by reference not to what they state but to the conditions under which they are stated. Dewey, thus (*op. cit.*, p. 10), disavows the intention of engaging in an economic interpretation of the history of art but states his purpose "to indicate that *theories* which isolate art and its appreciation by placing them in a realm of their own, disconnected from other modes of experiencing, are not inherent in the subject-matter but arise because of specifiable extraneous conditions." Cf. Dewey, *Reconstruction in Philosophy* (New York, 1920), p. 24: "It seems to me that this genetic method of approach is a more effective way of undermining this type of philosophic theorizing than any attempt at logical refutation could be." The variety of ways in which earlier or other theories have been discovered to be impertinent, inadequate, or false would supply a significant schematism for the history of thought. Modern philosophic disputes are usually tangential: positions are most frequently attacked because they are not scientific or fail to treat the facts; they are defended usually, not as scientific and factual, but as indicating work to be done, the progress of science, and the impossibility of certainty.

4. The explanation sometimes involves the reduction of art to the laws of some other science; cf. N. Bukharin, "Poetry, Poetics and the Problems of Poetry in the U.S.S.R.," *Problems of Soviet Literature*, ed. H. G. Scott (New York, n.d.), p. 195: "Poetic creation and its product—poetry—represent a definite form of social activity, and are governed in their development, regardless of the specific nature of poetic creation, by the laws of social development." The explanation sometimes involves the abandonment of older analytical techniques and the use of science in preparation for specifically aesthetic questions; cf. Y. Hirn, *The Origins of Art: A Psychological and Sociological Inquiry* (London, 1900), p. 5: "Modern aesthetic, therefore, has still its own ends, which, if not so ambitious as those of the former speculative science of beauty, are nevertheless of no small importance. These ends, however, can no longer be attained by the procedure of the old aesthetic systems. As the problems have

be isolated by making criticism itself an art, as Spingarn did when he prescribed as the only possible method of criticism the question, "What has the poet tried to express and how has he expressed it?"

All criticism tends to shift the interest from the work of art to something else. The other critics give us history, politics, biography, erudition, metaphysics. As for me, I re-dream the poet's dream, and if I seem to write lightly, it is because I have awakened, and smile to think I have mistaken a dream for reality. I at least strive to replace one work of art by another, and art can only find its *alter ego* in art.[5]

It may be isolated in relation to the artistic problem of creating art[6] or in relation to the aesthetic experience of perceiving art.[7] It may be isolated by the

---

changed with changing conditions, so too the methods must be brought into line with the general scientific development. Historical and psychological investigation must replace the dialectic treatment of the subject. Art can no longer be deduced from general philosophical and metaphysical principles; it must be studied—by the methods of inductive psychology—as a human activity. Beauty cannot be considered as a semi-transcendental reality; it must be interpreted as an object of human longing and a source of human enjoyment. In aesthetic proper, as well as in the philosophy of art, every research must start, not from theoretical assumptions, but from the psychological and sociological data of the aesthetic life." It is impossible to deal with concrete works of art or to explain artistic activity in relation to them. The tendency to engage in artistic production and artistic enjoyment for their own sake can be explained only by studying the psychology of artists and their public; and, in this study of the "art-impulse" and the "art-sense," the "art object" becomes an abstract and ideal datum. Yet such a study will be relevant to problems of aesthetics and criticism; cf. *ibid.*, p. 17: "Thus a theory of the psychological and sociological origins of art may furnish suggestions for those which have been considered as distinctive of aesthetic proper, such as the critical estimation of works of art, or the derivation of laws which govern artistic production." The explanation is sometimes distinct from the purely artistic concerns to which it is nonetheless pertinent; cf. H.Wölfflin, who finds that, of the three terms which he uses to analyze "style," one—"quality"—is artistically determined, while two—"expression" (which is the material element of style) and "mode of expression" (which is vision)—are historically determined (*Principles of Art History*, trans. M. D. Hottinger [New York, 1932], p. 11): "It is hardly necessary here to take up the cudgels for the art historian and defend his work before a dubious public. The artist quite naturally places the general canon of art in the foreground, but we must not carp at the historical observer with his interest in the variety of forms in which art appears, and it remains no mean problem to discover the conditions which, as material element—call it temperament, *zeitgeist*, or racial character—determine the style of individuals, periods, and peoples. Yet an analysis with quality and expression as its objects by no means exhausts the facts. There is a third factor—and here we arrive at the crux of this enquiry—the mode of representation as such. Every artist finds certain visual possibilities before him, to which he is bound. Not everything is possible at all times. Vision itself has its history, and the revelation of these visual strata must be regarded as the primary task of art history."

5. J. E. Spingarn, "The New Criticism," *Criticism in America: Its Function and Status* (New York, 1910), p. 14.

6. Cf. C. Bell, *Since Cézanne* (New York, 1922), p. 41: "In the pre-natal history of a work of art I seem to detect at any rate three factors—a state of peculiar and intense sensibility, the creative impulse, and the artistic problem." *Ibid.*, p. 43: "The artistic problem is the problem of making a match between an emotional experience and a form that has been conceived but not created."

7. Cf. the statement of Matisse quoted by H. Read (*Art Now* [London, 1933], pp. 72–73): "Expression for me is not to be found in the passion which blazes from a face or which is made

effort of the scientist to separate from extraneous considerations the form which determines the parts as well as the whole in a work of art.[8]

The echoes and apparent similarities which can be detected in modern discussions of art are due in part to the terms which emerge in them—"form" and "matter," "expression" and "content," or similar pairs of terms—differentiating principles of criticism bearing on organization or unity and materials organized or unified. Moreover, these principles of criticism are given content and precision by use of what seem to be comparable philosophic principles expressed in terms of "processes" and "relations," "symbols" and "effects." Yet, even within the broad modern orthodoxy in which problems are solved by operations and words, there are many warring sects who differ concerning the nature of operations and the analysis of symbols; and for each philosophic doctrine and substitute for metaphysics there is a variant interpretation of artistic form and aesthetic expression and of the material which is formed or expressed. The problem in each case is to locate the art object between artist and audience and in so doing to explain characteristics of the art object in terms suggested by that relation.

The opposition between those who examine the art object and those who examine the art object qua experience or act or symbol flows from two interpretations which can be put on those principles of criticism in view of opposed

---

evident by some violent gesture. It is in the whole disposition of my picture—the place occupied by the figures, the empty space around them, the proportions—everything plays its part. Composition is the art of arranging in a decorative manner the various elements which the painter uses to express his sentiments. In a picture every separate part will be visible and will take up that position, principal or secondary, which suits it best. Everything which has no utility in the picture is for that reason harmful. A work of art implies a harmony of everything together [*une harmonie d'ensemble*]: every superfluous detail will occupy, in the mind of the spectator, the place of some other detail which is essential."

8. Cf. K. Koffka, "Problems in the Psychology of Art," *Bryn Mawr Notes and Monographs*, IX (1940), 243–44: "We shall derive from this relationship a rule for the purity, or sincerity, of art. If, as we said, the artist wants to externalize a significant part of his own world with its particular ego-world relationship, then, if he is successful, the object which he creates will be such as to comply with the demanded relationship; and that means, looked at from the other side, that the way in which the Ego is drawn into the situation must be demanded by the art-object and not by any outside factors which, however they may be suggested by the art-object, are not part of it. And so we have arrived at what we call purity of art: demands on the Ego must not issue from sources that are extraneous to the art-object." Cf. also *ibid.*, pp. 246–47: "Thus what is 'extraneous' to a work of art, in the sense used in defining the purity of art, is determined by the subject and its self-limitation. We saw before that a work of art is a strongly coherent whole, a powerful *gestalt* and such self-limitation is a definite *gestalt*-property. But this determination of the term extraneous is still too narrow: a demand issuing from a part of an art object is extraneous and, therefore, an effect produced by it artistically impure, if it is not itself demanded by the total pattern of the work. For a *gestalt* not only makes its own boundaries, but also within its boundaries rules and determines its parts in a sort of hierarchy, giving this a central position, this the rôle of a mere decorative detail, that the function of contrast, and so forth."

philosophic principles, for the structure of the object of art may be found ι traits that it shares with the artist and his audience or in traits which distinguish the artist from the effects of his action and the audience from the stimulus to which it responds. The two interpretations of what seem similar or identical principles of criticism—"form" and "matter," "expression" and "content"— result from differences of analysis; they are not opposed in the sense that one is right and the other wrong (although either may be employed well or poorly by the critic), nor is the difference between them one that need be "resolved" or in which an appeal to the "facts" would embarrass either disputant. They are differences to be explained by the philosophic principles which underlie the use of the terms in criticism; and those philosophic principles, in turn, are expressed in similar terms of "process" and "symbol" interpreted either analogically in a dialectic of being and becoming[9] or literally in a logic of cause

9. Cf. K. Burke, *The Philosophy of Literary Form: Studies in Symbolic Action* (Baton Rouge, La., 1941), p. 124: "It is, then, my contention, that if we approach poetry from the standpoint of situations and strategies, we can make the most relevant observations about both the content and the form of poems. By starting from a concern with the various tactics and deployments involved in ritualistic acts of membership, purification, and opposition, we can most accurately discover 'what is going on' in poetry." *Ibid.*, pp. 89–90: "The general approach to the poem might be called 'pragmatic' in this sense: It assumes that a poem's structure is to be described most accurately by thinking always of the poem's function. It assumes that the poem is designed to 'do something' for the poet and his readers, and that we can make the most relevant observations about its design by considering the poem as the embodiment of this act. In the poet, we might say, the poetizing existed as a physiological function. The poem is its corresponding anatomic structure. And the reader, in participating in the poem, breathes into this anatomic structure a new physiological vitality that resembles, though with a difference, the act of its maker, the resemblance being in the overlap between writer's and reader's situation, the difference being in the fact that these two situations are far from identical." *Ibid.*, p. 102: "At every point, the content is functional—hence, statements about a poem's 'subject,' as we conceive it, will be also statements about the poem's 'form' " (cf. also *ibid.*, pp. 73–74). The dialectic of being and becoming is apparent in one of its most competent employments in Dewey's use of such terms as "form" and "expression" in the sense both of a process and of a product and in his treatment of "matter" in both connections. Cf. *Art as Experience*, p. 134: "Form as something that organizes material into the matter of art has been considered in the previous chapter. The definition that was given tells what form is when it is achieved, when it is there in a work of art. It does not tell how it comes to be, the conditions of its generation." *Ibid.*, p. 64: "An act of expression always employs natural material, though it may be natural in the sense of habitual as well as in that of primitive or native. It becomes a medium when it is employed in view of its place and rôle, in its relations, an[d] inclusive situation—as tones become music when ordered in a melody." *Ibid.*, p. 82: "Expression, like construction, signifies both an action and its result. The last chapter considered it as an act. We are now concerned with the product, the object that is expressive, that says something to us." Separation of these two meanings would in each instance be an error, and for this reason Dewey regrets the absence in English of a word that includes unambiguously what is signified by "artistic"—the act of production—and "aesthetic"—the act of perception and enjoyment (cf. *ibid.*, p. 46). Nor should artist and audience be separated, since "to perceive, a beholder must *create* his own experience" (*ibid.*, p. 54), nor matter from form, since "the truth of the matter is that what is form in one connection is matter in another and vice-versa" (*ibid.*, p. 128); and if one makes a conscious distinction of sense and thought, of matter and form, one does "not read or hear esthetically, for the esthetic value of the stanzas lies in the integration of the two" (*ibid.*, p. 132).

and effect.[10] This is a philosophic opposition, and the broad disputes concerning the possibility of conceiving or analyzing individual substances, natural or artificial, and concerning the reality of causes are only slightly transformed, in the discussion of artistic form and content, into disputes concerning the possibility or error of treating the form of the work of art independently of experience or strategies, the reality of the distinction of form and matter, and, most striking of all, the nature of matter—whether it is to be sought, on the one hand, in experience, tactics, emotions, temperament, *Zeitgeist*, racial characteristics or, on the other hand, in the "parts" of the work of art—and the nature of form appropriate to such matters.

When terms are defined by the method of analogy, the principles of the discussion are found in the fundamental metaphor or metaphors.[11] Poetry may be conceived as vision, contriving, or imitation, experience, imagination, or emotion, symbol, action, or relation. Any one of these may be generalized or specified to determine a sense in which all men, or the best of men, or the best of some peculiarly fortunate kind of men, are poets or poems,[12] since the traits of the poet or the structure or contents of the poem are universally those of mankind or even of the Deity and the universe or since the poem or its expression or the emotion it embodies is universally intelligible or universally moving or corresponds with and reflects aspects of the universe or since its effects are homogeneous with the common experience or aspirations of mankind. When terms are defined literally, the principles of the discussion are to be found in the causes by which an object is to be isolated in its essential nature. If poetry is to be treated as poetry, it must be differentiated by its qualities as a thing or by the nature of the judgment appropriate to it or by its effects. Such distinc-

10. Cf. Koffka, *op. cit.*, pp. 209–10: "Perhaps the reader is somewhat baffled as to the kind of object-characteristics we are speaking about. They are to be such as to affect the Selves directly, to play on their emotions; but where are such characteristics to be found in psychology? Indeed there was a time when psychology did not contain any place for such characteristics, when psychological data were reduced to sensations and their attributes, the secondary and some of the primary qualities of Locke. But psychology has changed a great deal since such a statement was true. Now it derives some of its most important explanatory concepts and principles from such perceptual qualities as round, angular, symmetrical, open; fast and slow, rough and smooth, graceful and clumsy; cheerful, glowering, radiant, gloomy —a list that could be continued through many pages. Let us add a few words about it. The examples in the first group, which the reader will be willing to accept at their face-value, show us a feature characteristic of all our samples: they are features that belong to extended wholes, not to atomic parts or points."

11. Burke (*op. cit.*, p. 26) recognizes in the synecdoche the " 'basic' figure of speech" for "both the structure of poetry and the structure of human relations outside poetry."

12. Cf. Coleridge, *Biographia literaria*, chap. xiv (*The Complete Works of Samuel Taylor Coleridge*, ed. Shedd [New York, 1853], III, 373): "My own conclusions on the nature of poetry, in the strictest use of the word, have been in part anticipated in some of the remarks on the Fancy and Imagination in the first part of this work. What is poetry?—is so nearly the same question with, what is a poet?—that the answer to the one is involved in the solution of the other" (cf. above, n. 9).

tions are possible only in the context of a philosophy, consciously or un-consciously employed, in which sciences are distinguished from one another by principles and subject matter and in which the same object, undefined but identified in time and space, is properly treated in the variety of subject matters relevant to its characteristics —physical, psychological, moral, political, and aesthetic. By the use of the analogical method a trait or some traits suggested by the poem, by the poet, or by the audience are used to explain all three— as life is explained by synecdoche, poems by actions, and poets by qualities in-tended to distinguish man from the brute and assimilate him to God—and all aspects of poetry are included in one analysis. By the use of the literal method the aesthetic analysis of poetry is concentrated on characteristics properly at-tributed to the poem, and other problems are treated in other sciences—the ideas and emotions which the poet sought to express or those which a given audience experienced are treated in psychology, if it is a question of the thought of the poet or the reaction of the audience, or in rhetoric, if it is a question of means and medium, while the moral and political consequences of the poem, if they are considered, require analysis in terms of virtues, actions, and institu-tions; and the poem as conceived in terms of its various causes and effects is distinct from the poem conceived in terms of structure and form. Properly executed and understood, a complete analysis by the one method should treat all characteristics considered by the other and should even result in comparable judgments: aesthetic, moral, psychological, and practical. But even in that happy coincidence, the statements of the two analyses would clash on every point. There is doubtless but one truth in aesthetics as in other disciplines, but many statements of it are found to be adequate, more are partially satisfactory, and even more have been defended.

Such differences in the philosophic principles which determine the force and application of principles of criticism indicate a second dimension of variation, for even the discussion of the meaning of "process," "relation," and "symbol" —whether they are to be interpreted analogically and organistically or literally and causally—involves the recognition, if only by gestures and asides to discredited and obsolete opponents, that other principles have sometimes been used. In the literal discussion of principles it is a problem of fundamental qualities, sequence of causes, and order of discrimination. The *poem* may be fundamental in the sense that poetic effects can be identified for examination and poets can be recognized for description only if the stimulus of the one and the product of the other possess a distinguishable poetic quality. The *poet* may be fundamental in the sense that poetic composition can be treated as a poem, and its proper poetic effects can be differentiated from the accidental associations of an uninitiated audience, only by appreciating the intent of the poet.[13] The *effects* may be fundamental in the sense that an unexperienced poem is no aesthetic object, whatever the virtues of its form and structure, and the poem variously understood is not one but many objects.

In the analogical discussion of principles the same shifts of emphasis may be detected in the fundamental metaphor which is derived originally from poet, poem, or audience and is then applied to all three (as when experience, symbolic act, or creation characterize all three)[14] or restricted to two (as when poet and poem are conceived on a different level of experience or imagination from those which characterize even the prepared reader)[15] or restricted to one (as

13. This process may apparently be carried through a series of steps if one is asked to consider the writer (say, of this paper) who considers the critic who considers the artist (who might conceivably consider, as Peacock did, the intellectual ancestors of the writer who considered the critic). Cf. D. A. Stauffer, Introduction, *The Intent of the Critic* (Princeton, 1941), p. 5: "His opinion is a safe guide, therefore, only if we know Coleridge the critic as well as we know *Hamlet*, the play criticized. Such examples of the necessity of rectifying a critical pronouncement by some inquiry into the critic's character and bias and intention might be multiplied. They show the question, 'What is the intent of the critic?' may be as important to the reading public as the prior question, 'What is the intent of the artist?' is to the critic himself."

14. Cf. above, n. 9, for Burke's differentiation of poet, poem, and reader in terms of physiology and anatomy. Poetry, so conceived, is part of our natures, and all men are poets. The symbol of this may be found in men's lives and their susceptibilities to the universal poetry of nature; cf. R. W. Emerson, "The Poet" (*Works* [Boston, 1929], II, 15–17): "Every man is so far a poet as to be susceptible of these enchantments of nature; for all men have the thoughts whereof the universe is the celebration. I find that the fascination resides in the symbol. Who loves nature? Who does not? Is it only poets, and men of leisure and cultivation, who live with her? No; but also hunters, farmers, grooms and butchers, though they express their affection in their choice of life and not in their choice of words. . . . The people fancy they hate poetry, and they are all poets and mystics!" Sometimes the poetry of nature may take narrow, or even geographic, boundaries in the special sensibilities of a people; cf. W. Whitman, *Leaves of Grass*, Preface to the original edition (1855) (London, 1881), pp. 1–2, 4–5: "The Americans of all nations at any time upon the earth, have probably the fullest poetical nature. The United States themselves are essentially the greatest poem. In the history of the earth hitherto the largest and most stirring appear tame and orderly to their ampler largeness and stir. Here at last is something in the doings of man that corresponds with the broadcast doings of the day and night. . . . Their manners, speech, dress, friendships —the freshness and candour of their physiognomy—the picturesque looseness of their carriage . . . —the terrible significance of their elections—the President's taking off his hat to them, not they to him—these, too, are unrhymed poetry." Or, again, the poetic nature, although essential to mankind, may be possessed in varying degrees; cf. W. C. Bryant, *Prose Writings*, ed. Parke Godwin (New York, 1884), I, 13–14: "In conclusion, I will observe that the elements of poetry make a part of our natures, and that every individual is more or less a poet. In this 'bank-note world,' as it has been happily denominated, we sometimes meet with individuals who declare that they have no taste for poetry. But by their leave I will assert they are mistaken; they have it, although they may have never cultivated it."

15. If all men are poets, it is then imperative either to introduce a distinction of degree, completeness, or kind to distinguish the poets from other men or to distinguish the poetic from the appreciative or critical processes. Emerson, following the first of these alternatives, makes the poet representative among partial men and finds half of man in his expression; cf. *op. cit.*, II, 5: "The breadth of the problem is great, for the poet is representative. He stands among partial men for the complete man, and apprises us not of his wealth, but of the common wealth. The young man reveres men of genius, because, to speak truly, they are more himself than he is. They receive of the soul as he also receives, but they more." Lowell distinguishes two lives, one of which the poet nourishes; cf. "The Function of the Poet,"

when poets are said to aspire to express a vision which cannot be stated adequately in any poem or be experienced fully by any audience).[16]

Literally or analogically conceived, therefore, the philosophic principles which lie behind the discussions of the critic select for him, by defining his terms, a subject matter and principles from the vast diversity which those terms

Century, XLVII (1894), 437: "Every man is conscious that he leads two lives, the one trivial and ordinary, the other sacred and recluse; the one which he carries to the dinner-table and to his daily work, which grows old with his body and dies with it, the other that which is made up of the few inspiring moments of his higher aspiration and attainment, and in which his youth survives for him, his dreams, his unquenchable longings for something nobler than success. It is this life which the poets nourish for him and sustain with their immortalizing nectar." Lowell emphasizes the likenesses which makes poets men intelligible to other men rather than the differences in the poet's observation which set him apart; cf. "The Life and Letters of James Gates Percival" (*Works* [Boston and New York, 1891], II, 156–57): "The theory that the poet is a being above the world and apart from it is true of him as an observer only who applies to the phenomena about him the test of a finer and more spiritual sense. That he is a creature divinely set apart from his fellow-men by a mental organization that makes them mutually unintelligible to each other is in flat contradiction with the lives of those poets universally acknowledged as greatest." The second of the two alternatives is involved in definitions of poetry which derive from the genius of the poet or the differentiation of the poem relative to creator and to critic. Coleridge thus relates his definition of poetry to genius; cf. *Shakespeare: With Introductory Matter on Poetry, the Drama, and the Stage* (*Works*, IV, 21–22): "To return, however, to the previous definition, this most general and distinctive character of a poem originates in the poetic genius itself; and though it comprises whatever can with any propriety be called a poem (unless that word be a mere lazy synonyme for a composition in metre), it yet becomes a just, and not merely discriminative, but full and adequate, definition of poetry in its highest and most peculiar sense, only so far as the distinction still results from the poetic genius, which sustains and modifies the emotions, thoughts, and vivid representations of the poem by the energy without effort of the poet's own mind,—by the spontaneous activity of his imagination and fancy, and by whatever else with these reveals itself in the balancing and reconciling of opposite or discordant qualities, sameness with difference, a sense of novelty and freshness with old or customary objects, a more than usual state of emotion with more than usual order, self-possession and judgment with enthusiasm and vehement feeling,—and which, while it blends and harmonizes the natural and the artificial, still subordinates art to nature, the manner to the matter, and our admiration of the poet to our sympathy with the images, passions, characters, and incidents of the poem. . . ." Samuel Johnson accounts for the changes of judgment and taste by distinguishing the poetry based on nature and truth from that of fanciful invention; cf. "Preface to Shakespeare," in *Johnson on Shakespeare*, ed. Raleigh (London, 1929), p. 11: "But because human judgment, though it be gradually gaining upon certainty, never becomes infallible; and approbation, though long continued, may yet be only the approbation of prejudice or fashion; it is proper to inquire, by what peculiarities of excellence *Shakespeare* has gained and kept the favour of his countrymen. Nothing can please many, and please long, but just representations of general nature. Particular manners can be known to few, and therefore few only can judge how nearly they are copied." According to Matthew Arnold, the critical power is of a lower rank than the creative; cf. "The Function of Criticism at the Present Time," *Essays in Criticism: First Series* (London, 1910), p. 4: "The critical power is of lower rank than the creative. True; but in assenting to this proposition one or two things are to be kept in mind. It is undeniable that the exercise of the creative power, that a free creative activity, is the highest function of man; it is proved to be so by man's finding in it his true happiness. But it is undeniable, also, that men may have the sense of exercising this free creative activity in other ways than in producing great works of literature or art; if it were not so, all but a very few men would be shut out from the true happiness of all men."

16. The content and aspiration of poetry are so lofty that in the fullest sense they may exceed not merely the appreciation of the audience but the powers of the poet, and therefore Emerson concludes that we have no poems, although we do have poets; cf. "Poetry and

might encompass. If the poet is the source of distinctions or analogies, the discussion may be of character, knowledge, or technique; or of imagination, taste, or genius; or of beauty, truth, or moral goodness. If the poem is fundamental, all problems may be translated into those of form and content; or of imitation and object; or of thought, imagination, and emotions; or of activity and effects. The effects finally, if they are fundamental, may be treated in terms of expression and communication; or of context and moral, social, economic, or semantic determination; or of influence and emotion.

The critic's discrimination of poet, poem, and effect, like the philosopher's preoccupation with process and relation, is only one part or possibility selected from a larger intellectual pattern which extends beyond, and is constantly intruded into, the more limited vocabularies of the conversations and disputes about art which are expressed in terms of operations and symbols. The principles of art have been sought in the nature of things and in the faculties of man as well as in the circumstances of artistic production or the effects of aesthetic contemplation. The "things" which have been considered have been various— the products of human activities or the materials from which they have been worked, the activities or the ideas and emotions from which they originated, and the poet or man himself. Philosophers who treat art in terms of things may seek poetic or dialectical principles, in the former case differentiating the artificial things which are made by man from the natural things which are the subject matter of physics, and in the latter case discovering the qualities of art in nature, which is a "poem" or a "book" or a "creation" or an "imitation." The "faculties" have been used as causes of the production of art objects or as means of their appreciation, and philosophers who seek epistemological or psychological principles in the human faculties either distinguish the visions, powers, and performances of artists from those of other men or treat scientists, moralists, politicians, and even mankind as essentially, though in varying de-

---

Imagination," *Letters and Social Aims* (Boston, 1883), p. 74: "Poems!—we have no poem. Whenever that angel shall be organized and appear on earth, the Iliad will be reckoned a poor ballad-grinding. I doubt never the riches of Nature, the gifts of the future, the immense wealth of the mind. O yes, poets we shall have, mythology, symbols, religion, of our own." Lowell, on the other hand, distinguishes two functions which are united in the poet—the function of the seer and that of the maker—and which facilitate the distinction between what he sees and what he expresses; cf. *op. cit.*, pp. 432–33: "And however far we go back, we shall find this also—that the poet and the priest were united originally in the same person; which means that the poet was he who was conscious of the world of spirit as well as that of sense, and was the ambassador of the gods to men. This was his highest function, and hence his name of 'seer.' . . . Gradually, however, the poet as the 'seer' became secondary to the 'maker.' His office became that of entertainer rather than teacher. But always something of the old tradition was kept alive. And if he has now come to be looked upon merely as the best expresser, the gift of seeing is implied as necessarily antecedent to that, and of seeing very deep too."

grees, poets. The "processes" have been the actions and operations, causes and effects, relations and wholes by which men have been prepared to produce objects or to be affected by them; and operational or semantic principles are sought either by distinguishing the symbols or effects of art from those of science, practical affairs, and nature or by stating all human concerns and all knowledge in terms of pragmatic and symbolic analyses. The discrimination of such principles and systems is to be found, not in differences in the gross scope of possible statement, but in what is taken as fundamental and in the precision or effectiveness with which details can be treated. A discussion which is primarily concerned with the effects of art will entail consequences which bear on the nature of works of art and on the nature or intention of the artist; and all schools of philosophers, whether they talk realistically about the work of art or idealistically about the imagination or the conditions of aesthetic judgment or pragmatically about the experience of art, will be able to state and defend metaphysical and psychological, moral, and aesthetic judgments appropriate to their principles and approaches.

The contemporary writers whose statements concerning art and criticism have been used to illustrate a pattern in modern discussions, therefore, exemplify the "philosophic temper of the present" in the sense that they talk in terms of operations and consequent relations, and the dogma is widespread among those who use this vocabulary—among philosophers as well as others who profess an interest in philosophic principles, among physicists who write on the freedom of the will and God, sociologists who write about ideologies and "stages" of knowledge, educators who reform curricula with a view to the "circumstances" of the world today or tomorrow—that there are no independent things or "substances" and that the "faculties" of the mind—and the mind itself—are fictions. Within that terminological agreement, however, all the old disputes concerning principles seem to have survived in methodological oppositions which have introduced splits between pragmatists who would choose significant questions by the criterion of operations and logicians who talk of operations but find it desirable to distinguish operations concerned with things from operations concerned with words or, further, to distinguish words which designate things from words which designate other words; and between linguists for whom things and words are sufficient to explain the phenomena of communication and proof and semanticists who require, in addition, some treatment of meanings or even emotions and motives. These differences of content in the principles signified by the same words are clarified in the broader discussion of principles signified by other words, for the ancient problems involved, though unrecognized, in the oppositions of contemporary doctrines, are only gradually uncovered in the progress of disputes; and verbally different statements of similar conceptions serve to set apart the different conceptions contained in statements that are verbally similar.

The subject matter of discussions of art is determined by three considerations which bear on things and which depend on principles: first, the determination of the kind of things appropriate to the discussion is stated in general philosophic principles; second, the determination of the mode of classifying such things depends on the methodological definition of principles; third, the determination of the characteristics relevant to the evaluation of such things is stated in the principles of criticism. The meaning and the subject of any critical judgment depend on all three considerations, although writers who use the same or similar terms may agree on one or more, while differing on other determinations of their meanings. Plato and Aristotle, thus, seek general philosophic principles in the nature of things, while Bacon and Kant seek them in the human understanding, and Horace and Tolstoy seek them in operations. Yet each of these pairs, although associated in the choice of philosophic principles, is divided both by the methodological determination and use of those principles and by the principles of criticism determined by them. For all the similarities of their statements, therefore, the six philosophers treat six distinct, though intricately related, subject matters in their analyses of art.

Plato and Aristotle both discuss the nature of art in terms of imitation. Plato, however, uses the distinction of poet (or maker), model (or object of imitation), and imitation (or construction) to state the principles of his physics as well as his aesthetics and so to account for all things,[17] while for Aristotle those principles are the means of differentiating artificial from natural things; but, although human nature, in the poet and in his audience, is used in his analysis to account for the natural causes and origin of poetry, the principles of Aristotle's aesthetics, as derived from imitation, are the object, the means, and the manner of imitation.[18] As a consequence, although Plato and Aristotle both talk about imitation and about things, they talk about different things. Plato's discussion of poetry is about men, or men and gods, those imitated in the poem, those influenced by the poem, the poets who write the poems and find themselves in competition with lawgivers, rhetoricians, and dialecticians—inferior to all who know the truth and sixth among the lovers of beauty—and

17. *Timaeus* 28C ff.; *Republic* x. 596A ff.; *Sophist* 234A–B. For a fuller discussion of the point treated in this paragraph, see above, pp. 149–68. These passages and the others from Plato, as well as those from Aristotle, Longinus, and Vico quoted in this essay, are translated by the author.

18. The arts are differentiated according to differences of their means, objects, and manners in the first three chapters of the *Poetics;* the natural causes and origin of poetry are then taken up in chapter 4. 1448[b]4 ff. Once the definition of tragedy has been given, the six parts of tragedy are discriminated as means, objects, and manner of imitation (cf. *Poet.* 6. 1450[a]7 ff.).

the universe which is also a living creature and an imitation; whereas Aristotle's discussion of poetry is about tragedy and epic poetry, their plots which are their end or their soul, and their parts.[19]

Kant and Bacon, similarly, both discuss the nature of art in terms of imagination. Kant, however, differentiates the faculties of understanding, reason, and judgment in order to treat the representations of imagination and the judgments of taste; like Aristotle, who distinguishes theoretic, practical, and poetic sciences, he differentiates theoretic and practical knowledge from aesthetic judgment; but, like Plato, whose analysis of art applies equally well to nature, he finds the principles of his analysis, not in the arts or their products, but in the judgment of beauty which applies to nature as well as to art and which has affinities with the judgment of the sublime as well as with the understanding of the purposiveness of nature.[20] Bacon, on the other hand, differentiates poesy from history and philosophy by relating them to the three parts of man's understanding—imagination, memory, and reason—respectively; like Aristotle, he treats poetry in particular rather than the conditions of art in general, he distinguishes it from history, and he divides it into kinds (narrative, representative, and allusive); but, like Plato, he merges aesthetic with moral judgments.[21]

19. The early treatment of music in the *Republic* is in terms of its subject matter, under which is considered the adequacy of tales to the gods, heroes, and men portrayed (*Rep.* ii. 376E—iii. 392C); its diction, under which is considered the effect of imitative speech on character (*ibid.* 392C–398B); and its manner, under which is considered the effect of modes and rhythms (*ibid.* 398C–403C). We shall be true musicians only when we recognize temperance, courage, liberality, high-mindedness, and the other virtues and their contraries in their various combinations and images (*ibid.* 402C; cf. also *ibid.* viii. 568A–B; x. 607A). Poets, rhetoricians, and lawgivers who write with knowledge of the truth are to be called "philosophers" (*Phaedrus* 278C–D; cf. also *Laws* vii. 811C–E); poets are in competition with lawgivers (*Rep.* iii. 398A–B; *Laws* vii. 817A–D; ix. 858D). For the low place of the poet in the hierarchy of lovers cf. *Phaedrus* 248C ff.; and for the universe as a creation of divine art cf. *Soph.* 265C ff. According to Aristotle, the plot is the principle and, as it were, the soul of tragedy (cf. *Poet.* 6. 1450ª38); it is the end and purpose of tragedy (*ibid.* 1450ª22); it is the first and most important thing in tragedy (*ibid.* 7. 1450ᵇ21). The analysis treats of tragedy in terms of the unity and the parts of tragedies.

20. Kant, *Critique of Judgement*, trans. J. H. Bernard (London, 1914), Introduction, pp. 7 ff.: Part I, Div. I, Book II, "Analytic of the Sublime," § 23, "Transition from the Faculty Which Judges of the Beautiful to That Which Judges of the Sublime," pp. 101 ff.; Part II, "Critique of the Teleological Judgement," pp. 259 ff. The nature and the analysis of the Beautiful is distinct from the nature and analysis of the moral, yet the Beautiful may be a symbol of the morally Good; cf. Part I, Div. I, Book I, § 42, pp. 176–77: "Thus it would seem that the feeling for the Beautiful is not only (as actually is the case) specifically different from the Moral feeling; but that the interest which can be bound up with it is hardly compatible with moral interest, and certainly has no inner affinity therewith"; and Div. II, § 59, pp. 250–51: "Now I say the Beautiful is the symbol of the morally Good, and that it is only in this respect (a reference which is natural to every man and which every man postulates in others as a duty) that it gives pleasure with a claim for the agreement of every one else" (cf. also *ibid.*, § 52, pp. 214–15).

21. *Of the Proficience and Advancement of Learning*, Book II (*The Works of Francis Bacon*, ed. Spedding, Ellis, and Heath, III [London, 1857], 329, 343 ff.); *De augmentis scientiarum*, Book II, chap. xiii (*Works*, IV [London, 1858], 314 ff.). Aristotle's distinction is that poetry

As a consequence, although Bacon and Kant both talk about the imagination and the human understanding, the "imagination" of Bacon is a cognitive faculty, whereas the "imagination" of Kant is a faculty of presentation. Bacon's discussion of poetry is, therefore, about a branch of learning considered as form and matter, whereas Kant's discussion of art is about a form of judgment which relates the presentations of imagination to the concepts of reason and understanding and which applies to natural and artistic beauty.[22]

Horace and Tolstoy, finally, both discuss the nature of art in terms of operations. Tolstoy, however, defines art as a human activity which serves as a means of bringing about a community among men and of furthering their welfare.

> *Art is a human activity consisting in this, that one man consciously, by means of certain external signs, hands on to others feelings he has lived through, and that others are infected by these feelings and also experience them.*

Art is not as the metaphysicians say, the manifestation of some mysterious Idea of beauty or God; it is not, as the esthetical physiologists say, a game in which man lets off his excess of stored-up energy; it is not the expression of man's emotions by external signs; it is not the production of pleasing objects; and, above all, it is not pleasure; but it is a means of union among men, joining them together in the same feelings and indispensable for the life and progress towards well-being of individuals and of humanity.[23]

---

is more philosophic and graver than history, since its statements are rather of the nature of universals, whereas those of history are singulars (*Poet.* 9. 1451ᵇ5). Bacon draws his distinction from the matter of poetry and therefore makes the difference between poetry and history more nearly analogous to Plato's distinction between knowledge and opinion than to Aristotle's formal distinction between kinds of probability; and, as a consequence, he excludes, as parts of philosophy and parts of speech, all forms of poetry (satires, elegies, epigrams, odes, and the like) except the three which are treated as forms of feigned history, and he derives the moral judgment of poetry from this difference between it and history; cf. *De augmentis scientiarum,* Book II, chap. xiii, pp. 315–16: "As for Narrative Poesy,—or Heroical, if you like so to call it (understanding it of the matter, not of the verse)—the foundation of it is truly noble, and has a special relation to the dignity of human nature. For as the sensible world is inferior in dignity to the rational soul, Poesy seems to bestow upon human nature those things which history denies to it; and to satisfy the mind with the shadows of things when the substance cannot be obtained. For if the matter be attentively considered, a sound argument may be drawn from Poesy, to show that there is agreeable to the spirit of man a more ample greatness, a more perfect order, and a more beautiful variety than it can anywhere (since the Fall) find in nature. And therefore, since the acts and events which are the subjects of real history are not of sufficient grandeur to satisfy the human mind, Poesy is at hand to feign acts more heroical; since the successes and issues of actions as related in true history are far from being agreeable to the merits of virtue and vice, Poesy corrects it, exhibiting events and fortunes according to merit and the laws of providence; since true history wearies the mind with satiety of ordinary events, one like another, Poetry refreshes it, by reciting things unexpected and various and full of vicissitudes. So that this Poesy conduces not only to delight but also to magnanimity and morality. Whence it may be fairly thought to partake somewhat of a divine nature; because it raises the mind and carries it aloft, accommodating the shows of things to the desires of the mind, not (like reason and history) buckling and bowing down the mind to the nature of things." Cf. also *Of the Proficience and Advancement of Learning,* p. 343.

22. Kant, *op. cit.,* Part I, Div. I, Book I, § 23, pp. 101 ff., and § 45, pp. 187 ff.

23. *What is Art?* trans. A. Maude, in *Tolstoy on Art* (Oxford, 1924), p. 173.

Tolstoy's judgment of art, like Plato's, is predominantly moral, and, like Kant, he would attribute to art an important function in uniting theoretical knowledge and practical precepts. Horace, on the other hand, is concerned with the effects of poetry, not as they might be manifested in a moral, social, and religious union of mankind, but as they might be formulated in an "art" of poetry as practical precepts to instruct poets in their function, resources, and ends,[24] and in view of those ends to set forth the means poets should employ if they wish to please Roman audiences and to attain lasting fame. Wisdom is the principle and fountain of good writing, in the sense that moral philosophy and the Socratic pages will furnish the poet material;[25] and poets aim to teach or to please or to profit and amuse at the same time, in the sense that they attract the applause of the elderly by utility, of the young by amusement, and of all if they can blend the two.[26] Like Aristotle, Horace treats of poetry and its kinds, of the parts and the essential unity of the poem; and his analysis of poetry, like Bacon's, consists in treating the various kinds of subjects and the words and meters in which they can be adorned. As a consequence, although Horace and Tolstoy both consider the processes by which a poet fashions a work and the work influences an audience, the processes are entirely different in their respective treatments. For Horace they are external and causal: the poet uses any appropriate materials, old or new, in appropriate verbal form to win the approval of a select, though heterogeneous, audience. For Tolstoy the processes are internal and organic to mankind as a whole: the artist finds his material in feelings, and he makes that material intelligible to all by the form of his statement, in which the feelings are made infectious and by which mankind is united and improved.

If critics and philosophers sometimes find their subject matter in "beauty" and the "sublime," or "taste" and the "imagination," or "action" and "experience," whereas other critics and philosophers treat of poetry, or even of tragedy, the epic, and the lyric, or painting, sculpture, and music, the choice is not arbitrary or without consequences, but follows the methodological devices by which they employ their principles. Aristotle, Bacon, and Horace make use of different philosophic principles, since Aristotle treats of poetry by considering the poem as an artificial object, Bacon by considering it as a branch of learning subject to imagination, and Horace by considering it as a product of the poetic processes of composition; yet they agree methodologically, since they all begin their analyses with, and seek their principles in, a specifically human product, faculty, or activity for the purpose of discovering what is peculiar, in their respective approaches, to poetry or to some kind of poetry. Plato, Kant, and Tolstoy likewise make use of different philosophic principles, since

24. *Ars poetica* 304–8.
25. *Ibid.* 309–11.   26. *Ibid.* 333–44.

Plato treats of beauty and art in terms of an eternal pattern for imitation, Kant in terms of the a priori conditions of judgment, and Tolstoy in terms of an achievable perfection in human relations; yet they agree methodologically, since they all begin their analyses with, and seek their principles in, something fundamental in the nature of things, or the human faculties, or the community of feelings, which conditions in varying degrees all things, all imaginations, or all actions. What is essential in the one approach is accidental in the other. The philosopher who begins with beauty seldom has difficulty in discriminating or treating various kinds of art or even various kinds of poetry, although, to be sure, he frequently finds nothing real in the arts to correspond to the distinctions of "genres"; and the philosopher who begins with kinds of art objects usually has something to say of beauty, if only to identify it with some aspect of structure, or perception, or pleasure. The evaluation of the facts, so defined by principles and methods appropriate to them, requires a third step—the choice of the principles of criticism. The judgment of art as art may be separated from the consideration of its effects in education, morals, politics, and all the other relations which art may have to human institutions and activities; and thus Aristotle, Kant, and Horace separate the moral from the specifically aesthetic problem, while making provision, each in his way, for the indirect relation of the two problems—Aristotle by treating the moral and social effects of art in the *Politics*, Kant by relating the beautiful and the good while separating judgment and practical reason, Horace by using the moral precepts among the material to be transformed by the poet. The same facts about the objects of art may be evaluated, on the other hand, in such fashion that there is no separation of the aesthetic from other aspects of human activities, social institutions, or natural processes, except possibly for a tendency in such organic judgments to develop a fundamentally moral, economic, sociological, or religious bias, and thus Plato, Bacon, and Tolstoy each makes use of a moral criterion appropriate to his approach to the criticism of poetry and art—Plato requiring a knowledge of the Good, Bacon requiring the imagination of acts and events more agreeable to the merits of virtue and vice, Tolstoy requiring the perfecting of mankind. Differences which seem inconsequential or insoluble—such as those involved in the long discussions concerning whether painting, music, and poetry are the same essentially but different in detail, or different essentially though similar in some respects, or concerning whether art should be considered in itself or in its contexts, or whether the good, the beautiful, and the true mutually condition one another or are mutually independent—become significant if the varying meanings which critical terms assume in the context of philosophic principles are permitted to determine the meaning of the statements and are related to the subject matter of the criticism.

The changes in the subject matter of criticism may be seen compactly in the different applications of relevant criteria which such terms as "matter" and "form," "content" and "expression," have had in different philosophic and critical orientations. Thus Plato, Kant, and Tolstoy treat of the conditions of art rather than of the products of art, but Plato's critical judgments are based primarily on the nature of the object imitated, and the "matter" of art is man or more generally living creatues; Kant's critical judgments are based primarily on the subjective form of judgment, and the object of the judgment of taste is either nature or art, which follows the rule of nature;[27] Tolstoy's critical judgments are based on the feelings expressed and communicated, and not only is the "matter" of art feelings, but the sign distinguishing real art, apart from consideration of its subject matter, is the infectiousness and the quality of the feelings it transmits.[28] The content of "matter" and the relative importance of "form" and "matter" have shifted in the systematic context of these three kinds of criticism; and yet there is a continuity in the relevant traits of the "object" of art, for in Plato's doctrine it is found in the virtues portrayed, in Kant's doctrine it is found in the purposiveness of the representation, and in Tolstoy's doctrine it is found in the moral and religious feelings transmitted. Or, to reverse the order of comparison, the social community which is to be effected by art, according to Tolstoy, is present in the recognition of the empirical interest in the beautiful by Kant[29] and in the strenuous measures taken against poets by Plato to safeguard the perfect community of the *Republic* and the second-best community of the *Laws* from the dangers consequent on poetry. In general, these three modes of criticism have in common an appeal to criteria exterior to the work of art by which a comparison of arts with one another results in the discrimination of true art from spurious art or better art from worse: in Plato it is the criterion of truth and the moral effects of falsity

27. On the superiority of natural to artificial beauty cf. Kant, *op. cit.*, Part I, Div. I, § 42, pp. 178 ff.; on the relation of art and nature, *ibid.*, § 43, pp. 183 ff.; on the relation of the characteristics of the object in the judgment of natural beauty and the judgment of a product of art, cf. *ibid.*, § 33, p. 158; § 46, p. 188; and § 48, p. 194. Of the subjectivity of the judgment of taste, cf. *ibid.*, § 1, pp. 45–46: "The judgement of taste is therefore not a judgement of cognition, and is consequently not logical but aesthetical, by which we understand that whose determining ground can be *no other than subjective*" (cf. also *ibid.*, § 25, p. 161). The critique of taste, however, is subjective only with respect to the representation through which an object is given to it; it may also be an act or a science of reducing to rules the reciprocal relation between the understanding and imagination (cf. *ibid.* § 34, p. 160).

28. Tolstoy, *op. cit.*, chaps. xv and xvi, pp. 274–96.

29. Kant, *op. cit.*, Part I, Div. I, § 41, p. 174: "Empirically the Beautiful interests only in *society*. If we admit the impulse to society as natural to man, and his fitness for it, and his propension towards it, *i.e. sociability*, as a requisite for man as a being destined for society, and so as a property belonging to *humanity*, we cannot escape from regarding taste as a faculty for judging everything in respect of which we can communicate our *feeling* to all other men, and so as a means of furthering that which every one's natural inclination desires."

which justifies the condemnation of poetry in opposition to the art of the statesman; in Kant it is the criterion of genius and the free play of imagination which places music in a place inferior to poetry;[30] in Tolstoy it is the criterion of religion and the infectiousness of feelings that brands modern art as spurious in contrast to true religious art. The fundamental differences between them go back to the differences to be found in philosophic principles of processes, faculties, and things. Tolstoy, emphasizing the process of communication, finds *art* supplementing theory by making science intelligible and accomplishing the ends of practice by removing the need of external political control.[31] Kant, emphasizing the judgment, finds *criticism* the indispensable preliminary, not only to the appreciation of art and nature, but to theoretic knowledge and moral decision. Plato, emphasizing the nature of being, finds *philosophy* the necessary source of criticism and the basis of art.

Aristotle, Bacon, and Horace, on the other hand, treat of poetry rather than of beauty or nature or feeling. Yet for Aristotle the plot is the soul of the tragedy and the source of its unity, and words are the means of imitation, while for Bacon words are the form, and the content of the words is the matter which constitutes poesy a branch of learning analogous to history.[32] Like

30. *Ibid.*, § 53, pp. 215–18. Contrast Aristotle *Poet.* 26. 1461b26, in which the comparison of tragedy and epic in terms of their respective audiences is refuted and a comparison in terms of the unities achieved by their respective imitations and the pleasure appropriate to them is substituted.

31. Tolstoy, *op. cit.*, chap. x, p. 225: "The business of art lies just in this: to make that understood and felt which in form of an argument might be incomprehensible and inaccessible." *Ibid.*, chap. xx, p. 322: "True science investigates and brings to human perception such truths and such knowledge as the people of a given time and society consider most important. Art transmits these truths from the region of perception to the region of emotion." *Ibid.*, p. 331: "Art is not a pleasure, a solace, or an amusement; art is a great matter. Art is an organ of human life transmitting man's reasonable perception into feeling. In our age the common religious perception of men is the consciousness of the brotherhood of man—we know that the well-being of man lies in union with his fellow-men. True science should indicate the various methods of applying this consciousness to life. Art should transform this perception into feeling. The task of art is enormous. Through the influence of real art, aided by science, guided by religion, that peaceful cooperation of man which is now maintained by external means,—by our law-courts, police, charitable institutions, factory inspection, and so forth,—should be obtained by man's free and joyous activity. Art should cause violence to be set aside."

32. When Aristotle argues (*Poet.* 9. 1451a36) that the work of Herodotus would still be history if written in verse, the argument proceeds on the principle that the poet is concerned with the probability and necessity essential to the plot, which is the "first and most important thing in Tragedy" (*ibid.*, 7. 1450b21, 1451a9 ff.; 8. 1451a22 ff.), and on the principle that the poet is not distinguished by his use of verse as a means. When Bacon argues for the same conclusion, the argument proceeds on the principle that the difference between verse and prose is a difference in form and on the principle that the difference between history and poesy is a difference in matter. Cf. *De augmentis scientiarum*, Book II, chap. xiii, p. 315: "Now Poesy (as I have already observed) is taken in two senses; in respect of words or matter. In the first sense it is but a character of speech; for verse is only a kind of style and a certain form of elocution, and has nothing to do with the matter; for both true history may be written in verse and feigned history in prose. But in the latter sense, I have set it

Bacon, Horace analyzes poetry by treating subject matter and expression; but, unlike either Aristotle or Bacon, he recommends, as a device of imitation, the use of life and customs as an exemplar from which to draw living words; he is convinced that, if the matter is given, the words will follow, and he thinks of the problem of pleasing an audience in terms of decorum of subject and style.[33] Once again the content of "matter" and the relative importance of "form" and "matter" have shifted in the systematic context of the three kinds of criticism, and yet there is again a continuity in the relevant trait of the object of art which is for these critics the poem, the statue, or some like concrete object which requires some mark or measure of unity. In Aristotle's doctrine, unity is found in the plot, which has a beginning, middle, and end, and the relevant verbal unity depends on the unity of subject;[34] in Bacon's doctrine poetry is restrained with respect to words but quite unrestrained by matter;[35] and in Horace's doctrine unity has become a matter of decorum which depends on consistency in the relations of the parts of the poem to one another and appropriateness of the language to the matter, but it is otherwise unrestricted except in view of the reactions of audiences.[36] Or, again, the order of the comparison may be reversed, and the instruction, utility, and delight which are prominent in Horace's analysis may all be found in their appropriate functions in Bacon and Aristotle: in Bacon service to magnanimity, morality, and delectation are the mark of all poesy, while the clarification, or concealment, of a point of reason to make it intelligible or mysterious is the special function of one kind, parabolical poetry;[37] whereas in Aristotle tragedy has its appropriate

---

down from the first as one of the principal branches of learning, and placed it by the side of history; being indeed nothing else but an imitation of history at pleasure." Cf. *ibid.*, Book VI, chap. i. p. 443: "The Measure of words has produced a vast body of art; namely Poesy, considered with reference not to the matter of it (of which I have spoken above) but to the style and form of words: that is to say metre or verse."

33. Horace *op. cit.* 317–18; 311; 1–23; 86–118; 153–78 and *passim.*

34. *Poet.* 7 and 8, 1450^{b}21 ff.; for the unity of the epic cf. *ibid.* 23. 1459^{a}17; for unity of diction cf. *ibid.* 20. 1457^{a}28.

35. *Of the Proficience and Advancement of Learning,* Book II, p. 343: "Poesy is a part of learning in measure of words for the most part restrained, but in all other points extremely licensed, and doth truly refer to the Imagination; which, being not tied to the laws of matter, may at pleasure join that which nature hath severed, and sever that which nature hath joined, and so make unlawful matches and divorces of things: *Pictoribus atque poetis,* etc."

36. Horace *op. cit.* 23: "Denique sit quod vis, simplex dumtaxat et unum." The difference between Horace and Bacon is indicated by the fact that Bacon's quotation *Pictoribus atque poetis*—"poets and painters have always had an equal power of hazarding anything"—is, in the context of Horace's poem (*ibid.* 9–10), an injected anonymous objection which Horace grants only with restrictions on the kind of things that may properly be combined.

37. *Of the Proficience and Advancement of Learning,* Book II, p. 343: "So as it appeareth that poesy serveth and conferreth to magnanimity, morality, and to delectation." In parabolical poetry, ideas which are objects of the intellect are represented in forms that are objects

pleasure, which is that of pity and fear, and the effectiveness of plot structure depends on an element of astonishment, but the moral effects of poetry are reserved for treatment in politics, and poets are quoted for their doctrine in the sciences.[38] In general, the three modes of criticism have in common a concern with characteristics that can be found in the poem: Aristotle seeks a unity in the plot which organizes the parts as material and has its appropriate effect in pleasure; Bacon is concerned with the distinctive matter of poesy, and therefore he does not raise the question of unity but does find effects in pleasure, edification, and parabolic instruction; Horace is concerned with effects, and he is therefore indifferent to matter as such but finds unity in the interrelations of parts with one another and their relations to the manner of their expression. This, again, is a fundamental difference which goes back to differences of philosophic principles, for the first is an organic unity appropriate to a thing; the second is the free organization of matter appropriate to the imagination; the third is a union of content and expression suited to achieve a specified result.

The intricate interrelations of consequences in statement and doctrine which can be traced to the interplay of philosophic principles and methods make it possible to detect similarities and differences in the various modes of criticism and to trace the transformations which a rule or generalization undergoes as it passes from one intellectual context to another. On the basis of such systematic interrelations the canons of criticism can be compared in terms of the criteria appropriate to each philosophic doctrine. Tolstoy, thus, states three criteria which bear, respectively, on the importance of the content of the work of art to its audience, on its beauty of form, and on the relation of its author to it.

The value of every poetical work depends on three qualities:

1) The content of the work: the more important the content, that is to say, the more important it is for the life of man, the greater is the work.

---

of the sense; cf. *ibid.*, p. 344: "And the cause was, for that it was then of necessity to express any point of reason which was more sharp or subtile than the vulgar in that manner; because men in those times wanted both variety of examples and subtilty of conceit; and as hieroglyphics were before letters, so parables were before arguments: and nevertheless now and at all times they do retain much life and vigour, because reason cannot be so sensible, nor examples so fit. But there remaineth another use of Poesy Parabolical, opposite to that which we last mentioned: for that tendeth to demonstrate and illustrate that which is taught or delivered, and this other to retire and obscure it: that is when the secrets and mysteries of religion, policy, or philosophy are involved in fables or parables."

38. The tragic pleasure is that of pity and fear (*Poet.* 14. 1453[b]11); it is peculiar to tragedy (*ibid.* 13. 1453[a]35; 23. 1459[a]17; 26. 1462[b]12); it depends on the unexpected, the marvelous, and the astounding (*ibid.* 9. 1452[a]2; 14. 1454[a]2; 16. 1455[a]16; 24. 1460[a]11; 25. 1460[b]24). For the consideration of the moral effects of art cf. *Politics* vii. 17. 1336[b]12 ff.; viii. 5–7. 1339[b]10–1342[b]34. For the use of poets for theoretic purposes cf. the quotation of Homer, Hesiod, and myths in *Metaphysics* i. 3. 983[b]27; 4. 984[b]23; 8. 989[a]10; ii. 4. 1000[a]9; iv. 5. 1009[b]28; xii. 8. 1074[a]38; 10. 1076[a]4; and *passim.*

2) The external beauty achieved by the technical methods proper to the particular kind of art. Thus in dramatic art the technical method will be: that the characters should have a true individuality of their own, a natural and at the same time a touching plot, a correct presentation on the stage of the manifestation and development of feelings, and a sense of proportion in all that is presented.

3) Sincerity, that is to say that the author should himself vividly feel what he expresses. Without this condition there can be no work of art, as the essence of art consists in the infection of the contemplator of a work by the author's feeling. If the author has not felt what he is expressing, the recipient cannot become infected by the author's feeling, and the production cannot be classified as a work of art.[39]

For Kant there are two problems in art which require critical criteria—the problem of the judgment of the beautiful in art and the problem of the production of beautiful objects of art. Criteria are supplied in both, not by the artificial object, but by the faculties of the mind in their mutual interrelations or as guided by nature. There is no objective principle of taste, but the product of beautiful art must resemble, and yet be distinguishable from, nature;[40] there is no rule to govern the production of art, but genius is an innate mental disposition through which nature gives the rule to art.[41] Plato considers the problem of criticism in terms which reflect the influence of the same three variables—audience, work of art, and artist; but in the orientation of his analysis to truth the criterion of effectiveness is found in the object of imitation instead of the audience; the quality of the art object in the correctness of the imitation; and the virtue of the artist in the excellence of the execution of the copy.

Then must not the judicious critic of any representation—whether in painting, music, or any other art—have these three qualifications? He must know, first, what the object reproduced is, next, how correctly it has been reproduced, and third, how well a given representation has been executed in language, melody, or rhythm.[42]

39. "Shakespeare and the Drama" (*Tolstoy on Art*, pp. 445–46). Cf. "On Art" (*ibid.*, p. 82): "Therefore, though a work of art must always include something new, yet the revelation of something new will not always be a work of art. That it should be a work of art, it is necessary: (1) That the new idea, the content of the work, should be of importance to mankind. (2) That this content should be expressed so clearly that people may understand it. (3) That what incites the author to work at his production should be an inner need and not an external inducement." *Ibid.*, p. 84: "A perfect work of art will be one in which the content is important and significant to all men, and therefore it will be *moral*. The expression will be quite clear, intelligible to all, and therefore *beautiful;* the author's relation to his work will be altogether sincere, and heartfelt, and therefore *true*."

40. Kant, *op. cit.*, Part I, Div. I, § 45, p. 187: "In a product of beautiful art we must become conscious that it is Art and not Nature; but yet the purposiveness of its form must seem to be as free from all constraint of arbitrary rules as if it were a product of mere nature. . . Nature is beautiful because it looks like Art; and Art can only be called beautiful if we are conscious of it as Art while yet it looks like Nature."

41. *Ibid.*, § 46, p. 189: "Therefore, beautiful art cannot itself devise the rule according to which it can bring about its product. But since at the same time a product can never be called Art without some precedent rule, Nature in the subject must (by the harmony of its faculties) give the rule to Art; i.e., beautiful Art is only possible as a product of Genius."

42. *Laws* ii. 669A–B.

Whereas Kant had considered questions which involved the same three variables in terms of two problems concerned with the faculties of the mind and nature, Plato's formulation of the questions leads to the reduction of them all to problems which can be solved only by reference to the nature of the object.

For Aristotle, on the other hand, critical questions bear fundamentally, not on something external to the work of art, but on the poem itself, and questions of fault no less than of excellence are determined in view of the end of poetry and the use of devices within the framework of the plot which is the end of poetry. Questions concerning the artist, the work of art, and the audience, therefore, appear in his criticism, as in Plato's, transformed so as to be related to an object; but for Aristotle, unlike Plato, the orientation is to an artificial, not an eternal or even a natural, object, and the faults, alleged by critics, based on external criteria may be justified by consideration of the work of art itself. Criticism of the poet's art takes the form of alleged impossibilities; criticism of the faithfulness of the work to fact depends on alleged improbabilities; criticism of expression or meaning depends on alleged contradictions and improprieties of language. The dialectic of criticism as developed by the philosophers who argue analogically is in terms which depend on the criteria relevant to poet-poem-audience, or making-judging, or object; but the same problems appear in the tradition of literal criticism in terms which bear on the criteria relevant to organization-content-language, or making-judging, or language. Aristotle holds that faults in respect to impossibility, improbability, and contradiction may be justified if they contribute to the end of art. Impossibilities are faults in the poet's art, but they may be justified by reference to the requirements of *art*, if they contribute to the plot by making it, or some portion of it, more astounding.[43] Improbabilities are errors in the representation of fact, but they may be justified by reference to the *better* or to *opinion*, for the artist should portray men better than they are or he should take account of circumstances, of what men are thought to be and of the probability of things happening against probability.[44] Inconsistencies or contradictions of language may be

43. *Poet.* 25. 1460b22: "First, with respect to critical problems relating to the poet's art itself, if he has set forth impossibilities he has committed an error; but the error may be justified, if the poet thereby achieves the end of poetry itself—for the end has already been stated—if, that is, he thus makes this or some other part of the poem more astounding. . . . Again, is the error with respect to something essential to the art or only accidental to it? For it is less of an error not to know that the hind has no horns than to make an unrecognizable picture of one." *Ibid.* 1461b9: "In general the 'impossible' must be justified relative to the *requirements of poetry*, or to the *better*, or to *opinion*. Relative to the *requirements of poetry* a convincing impossibility is preferable to an unconvincing possibility."

44. *Ibid.* 1060b32: "If the objection is that the poet's narration is not true, the answer should be that perhaps it ought to be, just as Sophocles said that he made men as they ought to be, while Euripides made them as they are. . . . Again, relative to the question whether what has been said or done by someone has been well or badly said or done, we must examine not only what has been done or said, inquiring concerning it whether it is noble or base,

solved by consideration of usage, metaphor, punctuation, and the like.[45] By holding to the conception and standard of the unity of the work, the critic is able to follow Aristotle's dialectic in playing the technique of the artist against the opinions of the audience and both against the probabilities of the matter. Bacon, on the other hand, approaches poetry in terms of the matter accessible to and organized by imagination, and therefore treats of two problems of criticism in his characteristic effort to advance human learning: the estimation of existing poetry—and in this, unlike other branches of learning, he finds no deficiency—and recommendations for improvement—for which he finds no means.[46] Bacon has no criterion of organic unity, and he has little patience with questions of poetic language; his criticism, therefore, is almost entirely in terms of matter as object or product of imagination. Horace, finally, since he approaches poetry in terms of the technique of the poet, uses the terms suggested by *poeta-poesis-poema;* and, since the audience is pleased by a familiar or a consistent matter well expressed, and since words are fitted to matter, the problems of criticism consist—even those which bear on the unity of the poem and the choice of content—largely in questions for which the relevant criteria are found in terms of words.[47]

In application and precept, therefore, modes of criticism thus differently oriented will select different points of excellence in the work of the artist and indicate different objectives to be urged on his attention. The same traits will

---

but also who did it or said it, to whom, when, by what means, and for what end—whether, for example, he does it to secure greater good, or to avoid a greater evil." *Ibid.* 1461ᵇ12: "Such men as Zeuxis painted may be impossible but may be justified by the *better*, for the model ought to improve on the actual. The improbable must be justified by *what is commonly said*, and also by showing that at times it is not improbable, for there is a probability also of things happening contrary to probability."

45. *Ibid.* 1461ᵃ9 and 1461ᵇ16.

46. *Of the Proficience and Advancement of Learning*, Book II, p. 343: "The use of this feigned History hath been to give some shadow of satisfaction to the mind of man in those points wherein the nature of things doth deny it; the world being in proportion inferior to the soul; by reason whereof there is agreeable to the spirit of man a more ample greatness, a more exact goodness, and a more absolute variety, than can be found in the nature of things." *Ibid.*, p. 346: "In this third part of learning, which is poesy, I can report no deficience. For being as a plant that cometh to the lust of the earth, without a formal seed, it hath sprung up and spread abroad more than any other kind." Cf. *De augmentis scientiarum*, Book VI, chap. i, pp. 443–44: "But for poesy (whether we speak of stories or metre) it is (as I said before) like a luxuriant plant, that comes of the lust of the earth, without any formal seed. Wherefore it spreads everywhere and is scattered far and wide,—so that it would be vain to take thought about the defects of it. With this therefore we need not trouble ourselves."

47. Horace *op. cit.* 408–53, esp. 445–40: "A good and prudent man will censure lifeless verses, he will find fault with harsh ones; if they are inelegant he will blot them out with a black line by drawing his pen across them; he will cut out pretentious ornaments; he will force you to turn light on things not sufficiently clear; he will argue against what has been said ambiguously; he will mark what should be changed; he will become an Aristarchus"; cf. also *Epistles* ii. 2. 106–25.

be given not merely a different importance but a different meaning and locus in the statements of different critics, and they will become in one view the points of highest excellence and in another faults. Tolstoy insists on the essential importance of novelty in a work of art—it cannot be a work of art without something new in it—and he seeks the novelty in the content. Horace is indifferent to a novelty of content—he recommends a tale newly invented if it is consistent, while urging the traditional subjects even more strongly, particularly the themes drawn from Homer—but he defends with vigor the right of the poet to invent new words or to put old words to new uses.[48] For Kant novelty is translated into the originality of genius and is reflected in the freedom of imagination essential to the judgment of beauty.[49] For Bacon, who is concerned, not with the forms of judgment, but with the parts of learning, novelty is found in the lush and uncontrolled growth of poetry which makes useless and unnecessary any plans for its advancement. If the operation of novelty as a criterion is sought in Aristotle, it is found to have shifted once again, from judgment and learning to the object of art as it had shifted from the processes of composition to the faculties of the mind, and to have become the novel and marvelous element which contributes to the structure of the plot, while in Plato it is criticized as the fickle changeableness which is incompatible with the contemplation and imitation of an eternal model of beauty.[50] The choice of principles may seem a matter of initial indifference or of basic dogma, and the development of statement and determination of method may seem, in the critic who fits what he says to the instances he adduces, to depend on the facts of nature or art or experience, but the judgments of the critic may have a double effect on the facts by influencing the purposes of the artist and the taste of the audience; and therefore it is no less true that the nature and purposes of art depend on what the critic, broadly conceived, thinks his function to be than that the function of criticism is to judge the products and achievements of art.

II

Philosophic principles determine the meaning and subject matter of statements about art, and, conversely, the explication and application of statements

48. Horace *Ars poetica* 46–72.

49. Kant, *op. cit.*, Part I, Div. I, § 47, pp. 192–93: "Now since the originality of the talent constitutes an essential (though not the only) element in the character of genius, shallow heads believe that they cannot better show themselves to be full-blown geniuses than by throwing off the constraint of all rules; they believe, in effect, that one could make a brave show on the back of a wild horse than on the back of a trained animal. Genius can only furnish rich *material* for products of beautiful art; its execution and its *form* require talent cultivated in the schools, in order to make such a use of this material as will stand examination by the Judgement."

50. *Rep.* iv. 424B–C.

determine principles, for a single statement—an identical combination of words —may express or follow from different philosophic principles as it is variously defined and applied to various subject matters. Moreover, statements which seem explicitly to express the same or comparable philosophic principles may, as a result of methodological determination in use, apply now to a broad, now to a limited, subject matter, and in so doing they may unite the objects of art with those of nature or separate them, and they may analogize the products of the different arts to each other or differentiate them. Such differences in the application of principles to subject matter—involving questions concerning whether the same principles apply to nature and art or to moral action and artistic production—reflect changes in meaning which can be set forth in terms of method as well as of subject matter, for they result from separating theoretic, practical, and poetic judgments or in turn from merging (in varying manners of identification and varying degrees of mixture) considerations of knowing, doing, and making. The same differences in the determination and use of principles may therefore be seen in the functions attributed to artist, critic, and philosopher and in their relations to each other, for when subject matters and methods are distinct, the critic is distinguished from the artist and the philosopher, but when they merge the poet is critic, the critic is poet, or both are philosophers or—in lieu of philosophy for those philosophers who hold philosophy in disrepute—historians, sociologists, psychologists, semanticists, or scientists.

To discuss the function of the critic, therefore, is to discuss the function of the poet and philosopher. Indeed, the varying conceptions of the critic are illustrated historically in a dispute, which has been continuous since it was first formulated by the Greek philosophers and rhetoricians, between artist, critic, and philosopher. In the course of that dispute, the function of the critic has sometimes been limited to tasks less constructive or imaginative than those of the artist and less theoretic or intellectual than those of the philosopher; it has sometimes been broadened to include the functions exercised by both, while each of the disputants has claimed the functions of the others and the three have been collapsed repeatedly and again separated. The function of the critic may be identical with the functions of the artist and the philosopher either because criticism is conceived to be creative or intellectual or because art and philosophy are conceived to depend fundamentally on critical judgment; and if the functions of artist, critic, and philosopher are distinguished, it is because the critic operates in accordance with some form of philosophy which will permit him to seek causes and effects in the materials and forms of the artist. The function of the critic is determined alike in the fundamental assumptions of the philosopher, the critic, and the artist. It is determined in the principles from which the philosopher derives not only his system but the criteria by which to judge it and the rules of art by which to develop it, and even short of the development of a philosophy, the function of the critic is determined in the philosophic principles assumed in the critical judgments and criteria which artists and critics, as well as philosophers, evolve and apply. It is determined, likewise, in the conception of art which is the critic's minimum philosophy as well as the grounds of his judgments of art. It is determined, finally, in the conception of artistic purpose which is the artist's minimum critical theory and philosophy as well as the implicit formulation of his processes of production. The different conceptions of the functions of criticism, and the consequent variability of critical judgments, flow from assumptions and involve consequences which extend beyond variations in the functions of the critic to variations in art and philosophy, and the examination of criticism may fruitfully proceed through the consideration of (1) variations in the conception of art and the artist, which reflect consequences of criticism, and (2) variations in the conception of philosophy and philosophic method, which involve the grounds of judgments of value, to (3) variations in the conceptions of criticism itself and its applications.

Artists are necessarily critics in the act of artistic construction or composition. They sometimes, in addition to this active and illustrative criticism, explain what they have tried to do and relate it to the productions of other artists or the statements of other critics. Poets in particular have entered not only into that competition with other poets which is involved in the production of new poetic effects but also into competition with critics in defense of a conception of art and criticism, and with philosophers in justification of a view of life consonant with such critical values. They have frequently written as critics, expressing in their verses judgments of other poets, as Aristophanes did, or of poets and critics too, as Byron did. They have developed theories of criticism and poetics, both in verse—as did Horace, Vida, Boileau, Pope, and Browning —and in prose—as did Sidney, Dryden, Wordsworth, Coleridge, Shelley, Emerson, Bryant, and Newman. All the functions which the philosopher and the rhetorician have assigned to the poet reappear in the theories of poets: he is maker, contriver, and imitator; he is engaged in pleasing, instructing, and edifying; his poetry is a source of, as it is derived from, inspiration, enchantment, and imagination. In addition, however, the poet is assigned all the functions which any philosopher has sought to contrast to poetry in a more limited conception of the domain of art, and poets as critics have made converts of other critics and other historians and have taught them to present the poet eloquently not only as maker, but as seer, prophet, scientist, philosopher, moralist, and legislator, and to trace the history of all human knowledge and accomplishment from poetic beginnings or to poetic fulfilments. What the poet is conceived to be—since it determines how poetry will be read, for scientific truth and moral precept, for imaginative construction and emotional stimulation, for enrichment of experience and impetus to action, for pleasure and edification—becomes in itself the statement of a history, a morality, a politics, and a philosophy.[51] All sciences are dominated and perfected by poetry;[52] man and human

51. George Puttenham, *The Arte of English Poesie*, ed. G. D. Willcock and A. Walker (Cambridge, 1936), Book I, chaps. iii and iv, pp. 6–9: "The profession and use of Poesie is most ancient from the beginning and not, as manie erroniously suppose, after, but before, any civil society among men. . . . Then forasmuch as they were the first that entended to the observation of nature and her works, and specially of the Celestiall courses, by reason of the continuall motion of the heavens, searching after the first mover, and from thence by degrees comming to know and consider of the substances separate and abstract, which we call the divine intelligences or good Angels (*Demones*) they were the first that instituted sacrifices of placation, with invocations and worship to them, as to Gods: and invented and stablished all the rest of the observances and ceremonies of religion, and so were the first Priests and ministers of the holy misteries. . . . So also were they the first Prophetes or seears, *Videntes*. . . . So as the Poets were also from the beginning the best perswaders and their eloquence the first Rethoricke of the world. Even so it became that the high mysteries of the gods should be revealed and taught, by a maner of utterance and language of extraordinarie phrase, and briefe and compendious, and above al others sweet and civill as the Metricall is . . . so as the Poet was also the first historiographer . . . they were the first Astronomers and Philosophists and Metaphisicks." The sum of all wisdom is frequently found in a single poet; cf. Sir Thomas Elyot, *The Gouernour*, ed. Henry Croft (London, 1880), I, 58–59: "I coulde reherce diuers other poetis whiche for mater and eloquence be very necessary, but I feare me to be to longe from noble Homere: from whom as from a fountaine proceded all eloquence and lernyng. For in his bokes be contained, and most perfectly expressed, nat only the documentes marciall and discipline of armes, but also incomparable wisedomes, and instructions for politike gouernaunce of people: with the worthy commendation and laude of noble princis: where with the reders shall be so all inflamed, that they most fervently shall desire and coveite, by the imitation of their vertues, to acquire semblable glorie." According to Sidney, *The Defence of Poesie* (*The Complete Works of Sir Philip Sidney*, ed. Feuillerat [Cambridge, 1923], III, 5), poetry is the origin of all learning and the passport by which philosophers and historiographers first "entered the gates of populer judgements"; cf. *ibid.*, pp. 4–5: "This did so notably shew it selfe, that the Philosophers of Greece durst not a long time appear to the world, but under the masks of poets. So Thales, Empedocles, and Parmenides, sang their naturall Philosophie in verses. So did Pithagoras and Phocillides, their morall Councels. So did Tirteus in warre matters, and Solon in matters of pollicie, or rather they being Poets, did exercise their delightfull vaine in those points of highest knowledge, which before them laie hidden to the world." Or, again, poetry may be made to embrace all the higher activities of man, including the other arts; cf. Shelley, *A Defence of Poetry* (*The Prose Works of P. B. Shelley*, ed. H. B. Forman [London, 1880], III, 104): "But poets, or those who imagine and express this indestructible order, are not only the authors of language and of music, of the dance, and architecture, and statuary, and painting; they are the institutors of laws and the founders of civil society, and the inventors of the arts of life, and the teachers, who draw into a certain propinquity with the beautiful and the true, that partial apprehension of the agencies of the invisible world which is called religion." Or similar convictions may be expressed in terms of an evolution in which poets gradually fell from a high estate; cf. Lowell, *op. cit.*, pp. 432–33: "And however far we go back, we shall find this also—that the poet and the priest were united originally in the same person; which means that the poet was he who was conscious of the world of spirit as well as that of sense, and was the ambassador of the gods to men. This was his highest function, and hence his name of 'seer.' . . . Gradually, however, the poet as the 'seer' became secondary to the 'maker.' His office became that of

life are by nature poetical;[53] the universe itself is the creation, or at least the re-creation of poetic art.[54]

entertainer rather than teacher. But always something of the old tradition was kept alive. And if he has now come to be looked upon merely as the best expresser, the gift of seeing is implied as necessarily antecedent to that, and of seeing very deep, too. . . . Now, under all these names—praiser, seer, soothsayer—we find the same idea lurking. The poet is he who can best see and best say what is ideal—what belongs to the world of soul and of beauty."

52. Sidney, *op. cit.*, p. 19: "Now therein of all Sciences (I speak still of humane and according to the humane conceit) is our Poet the Monarch. For hee doth not onely shew the way, but giveth so sweete a prospect into the way, as will entice anie man to enter into it." Wordsworth, "Preface to the *Lyrical Ballads*" (*The Prose Works of William Wordsworth*, ed. A. B. Grosart [London, 1876], II, 91): "Poetry is the breath and finer spirit of all knowledge; it is the impassioned expression which is in the countenance of all science. . . . Poetry is the first and last of all knowledge—it is as immortal as the heart of man." These contentions concerning the nature of poetry are made in the face of opposition; cf. Peacock, "The Four Ages of Poetry" (*The Works of Thomas Love Peacock*, ed. H. F. B. Brett-Smith and C. E. Jones [London, 1934], VIII, 21): "The highest inspirations of poetry are resolvable into three ingredients: the rant of unregulated passion, the whine of exaggerated feeling, and the cant of factitious sentiment; and can therefore serve only to ripen a splendid lunatic like Alexander, a puling driveller like Werter, or a morbid dreamer like Wordsworth. It can never make a philosopher, nor a statesman, nor in any class of life a useful or rational man." Even in this estimate of poetry the function of the poet is conceived to extend to philosophy, politics, and the practical problems of life, and Shelley's reply to Peacock's criticisms merely asserts what Peacock denies. Shelley includes among poets, not only the authors of language and music, but also the institutors of laws, the founders of civil society, the inventors of the arts of life, and the teachers of religion (*op. cit.*, p. 104), and he denies the distinction between poets and prose writers, philosophers and historians, holding, indeed, that all authors of revolutions in opinion are necessarily poets (*ibid.*, p. 107). "Poetry is indeed something divine. It is at once the centre and circumference of knowledge; it is that which comprehends all science, and that to which all science must be referred" (*ibid.*, p. 136). "Poets are the hierophants of an unapprehended inspiration; the mirrors of the gigantic shadows which futurity casts upon the present; the words which express what they understand not; the trumpets which sing to battle and feel not what they inspire; the influence which is moved not, but moves. Poets are the unacknowledged legislators of the world" (*ibid.*, p. 144).

53. Hazlitt, "On Poetry in General" (*The Complete Works of William Hazlitt*, ed. P. P. Howe [London, 1930], V, 2): "It is not a branch of authorship: it is 'the stuff of which our life is made.' The rest is 'mere oblivion,' a dead letter: for all that is worth remembering in life, is the poetry of it. Fear is poetry, hope is poetry, love is poetry, hatred is poetry; contempt, jealousy, remorse, admiration, wonder, pity, despair, or madness are all poetry. Poetry is that fine particle within us, that expands, rarefies, refines, raises our whole being: without it 'man's life is poor as beast's.' Man is a poetical animal; and those of us who do not study the principles of poetry, act upon them all our lives, like Molière's *Bourgeois Gentilhomme*, who had always spoken prose without knowing it." Or, again, the poetic nature of mankind is at the background of the poet's direction of man and poetry's dominance of the sciences; cf. Whitman, *op. cit.*, pp. iv, vii: "Of all nations the United States with veins full of poetical stuff most need poets and will doubtless have the greatest and use them the greatest. Their Presidents shall not be their common referee so much as their poets shall. Of all mankind the greatest poet is the equable man. Not in him but off from him things are grotesque or eccentric or fail of their sanity. Nothing out of its place is good and nothing in its place is bad. He bestows on every object or quality its fit proportions neither more nor less. He is the arbiter of the diverse and he is the key. . . . Exact science and its practical movements are no checks on the greatest poet but always his encouragement and support. . . . In the beauty of poems are the tuft and final applause of science."

54. Augustine *De civitate Dei* xi. 21: "What else indeed is to be understood by that which is said through all things: 'God saw that it was good,' but the approbation of work done

To determine the function of the poet is to mark the scope of the other arts, of criticism, and of philosophy; and whatever poetry is distinguished from or opposed to, in one account, may be viewed as essentially poetical in another: music, painting, and the rest of the arts may be instances of poetry; the true critic may be poetic and creative; and Plato may be made a poet by the same processes as made Homer and Shakespeare philosophers. Poetry is expanded and contracted both with respect to the arts conceived as poetic and with respect to the practices thought proper to them. The critic and philosopher—or the poet and amateur functioning as critic and philosopher—may affect the practices and the interrelations of the arts. It is only a recent instance of an old complaint that Lessing expresses when he reproves "modern critics" for having crudely misconceived the relation of painting and poetry, sometimes compressing poetry within the narrow limits of painting, sometimes making painting fill the whole wide sphere of poetry, and for having generated by their spurious criticism a mania for pictorial description in poetry and for allegorical style in painting.[55] As criticism, operating through the activity of

---

according to the art which is the wisdom of God." Shelley, *op. cit.*, p. 140: "It reproduces the common universe of which we are portions and percipients, and it purges from our inward sight the film of familiarity which obscures from us the wonder of our being. It compels us to feel that which we perceive, and to imagine that which we know. It creates anew the universe, after it has been annihilated in our minds by the recurrence of impressions blunted by reiteration. It justifies the bold and true word of Tasso: *Non merita nome di creatore, se non Iddio ed il Poeta* [None deserves the name of creator except God and the Poet]."

55. G. E. Lessing, *Laocoon*, Introd. (*Werke*, ed. J. Petersen [Leipzig, n.d.], IV, 292). The discussion of the relation of poetry and painting goes back to ancient beginnings, to Horace, Plutarch, and Pliny, and by way of them to Simonides' conception of painting as silent poetry and poetry as speaking painting. Cf. also John Dryden, *Parallel of Poetry and Painting* (1695); Abbé du Bos, *Réflexions critiques sur la poésie et sur la peinture* (1719); Charles Lamotte, *An Essay upon Painting and Poetry* (1730); James Harris, "Concerning Music, Painting, and Poetry," *Three Treatises* (1744); Joseph Spence, *Polymetis; or, an Inquiry concerning the Agreement between the Works of the Roman Poets and the Remains of the Ancient Artists, Being an Attempt To Illustrate Them Mutually from One Another* (1747); G. E. Lessing, *Laocoon* (1766); Daniel Webb, *Observations on the Correspondence between Poetry and Music* (1769). Poetry may be conceived as the essential nature or the definition of painting and music, or it may merely share with them some common characteristics or effect some common responses. Cf. S. T. Coleridge, *Shakespeare: With Introductory Matter on Poetry, the Drama, and the Stage* (*Works*, IV, 39): "In my last address I defined poetry to be the art, or whatever better term our language may afford, of representing external nature and human thoughts, both relatively to human affections, so as to cause the production of as great immediate pleasure in each part as is compatible with the largest possible sum of pleasure on the whole. Now this definition applies equally to painting and music as to poetry; and in truth the term poetry is alike applicable to all three." Cf. also John Stuart Mill, "Thoughts on Poetry and Its Varieties," *Dissertations and Discussions: Political, Philosophical, and Historical* (New York, 1882), I, 89: "That, however, the word 'poetry' imports something quite peculiar in its nature; something which may exist in what is called prose as well as in verse; something which does not even require the instrument of words, but can speak through the other audible symbols called musical sounds, and even through the visible ones which are the language of sculpture, painting, and architecture,—all this, we believe, is and must be felt, though perhaps indistinctly, by all upon whom poetry in any of its shapes produces any impression beyond that of tickling

224   *Richard McKeon*

artists, affects art, those immanent critical processes in turn affect criticism and the philosophic ideas it embodies; and criticism and philosophy undergo like changes with the variations in art. The discussion of the function of the poet is a philosophic discussion, and its progress through the ages reflects the differences between those philosophers who find poetry and philosophy essentially the same and therefore seek only to determine whether poetry is perfect or deficient philosophy and whether philosophy is supreme or partial poetry and those philosophers who distinguish artistic constructions from philosophic speculations and therefore make use of art or criticism or philosophy to prevent the confusion of disciplines.

There is a rivalry between poetry and philosophy in so far as they are pertinent to the same ends and in so far as the same standards may be applied to both. The quarrel was ancient in the time of Plato,[56] and it has continued to the present because the tradition of discussion sets poetry to be judged against a standard of truth and reason, and philosophy to be criticized for its ineffectiveness and uncouthness. Plato banished the poets from the perfect state, not despite but because of the charm he acknowledges in their art, for it endangers the highest ends of man and the most vital functions of the state. The danger of poetry lies precisely in the fact that the poet, with all his art, may speak well and badly according to the standard of philosophic truth; and in the dialectic of Plato the indeterminacy for which poetry is criticized is removed only when the poet writes with knowledge, and then the poet is rightly called "philosopher." The standard applied to the poet is the same as that of the lawgiver, and therefore in the perfect state the philosopher is poet as well as ruler. Even in the second-best state delineated in the *Laws*, the principles of art are inseparable from those of morals, legislation, and philosophy; and, when a model is sought in that dialogue to indicate what is wrong and what is right in poetry, it is found in the discourse itself, which the interlocutor finds is framed exactly like a poem.[57] Moreover, the poet is under suspicion in that state as well as in the perfect republic, and writers of tragedies are viewed as rivals of lawgivers who are not philosophers as well as of those who are.

Best of strangers, we will say to them, we ourselves are poets, to the best of our ability, of the fairest and best tragedy, for our whole state is composed as an imitation of the fairest and best life, which we assert to be in reality the truest tragedy. Thus you

---

the ear." The three seem to overlap, without being identified essentially, according to Leigh Hunt; cf. "An Answer to the Question What Is Poetry?" (*Critical Essays of the Early Nineteenth Century*, ed. R. M. Alden [New York, 1921], p. 378): "Poetry includes whatsoever of painting can be made visible to the mind's eye, and whatsoever of music can be conveyed by sound and proportion without singing or instrumentation."

56. *Rep.* 607B.
57. *Laws* vii. 811C–D.

are poets and we likewise are poets of the same poems, opposed to you as artists and actors in the fairest drama, which true law alone, as our hope is, is suited to perfect. Do not imagine therefore that we will easily permit you to erect your stage among us in the market place and to introduce your actors, endowed with fair voices and louder than our own, and allow you to harangue women and children and all the people, saying concerning the same questions, not the same things as we do, but commonly and on most things the very opposite.[58]

This is a tradition of discussion and opposition which the poets were to continue, reversing the dialectic to find poetry in Plato's works while puzzling over his antagonism to poetry, to criticize the cold insensitivity of philosophy while claiming for poetry high philosophic insight, and to seek a truth in poetry while revising according to its standard the canon of true poets. All of the terms shift their meanings in the dialectic of this discussion. Plato is sometimes a poet, although philosophy is distinct from poetry, since, as Sidney argues, "who so ever well considereth, shall finde that in the body of his worke, though the inside and strength were Philosophie, the skin as it were and beautie, depended most of Poetrie."[59] He is sometimes an instance of the highest kind of poetry,[60] and philosophy is indispensable to poetry, since "no man," as Coleridge presents the case, "was ever yet a great poet, without being at the same time a profound philosopher."[61] He is sometimes essentially a poet, and Shakespeare is a philosopher, despite differences, such as Shelley emphasizes, in literary forms.[62] He is sometimes a true poet; and, since, as Emerson formulates the nature of poetry, poets are scientists and logicians, inspirers and lawgivers, some reservations must be made concerning the poetic quality of Shakespeare.[63]

58. *Ibid.* 817B–C.   59. Sidney, *op. cit.*, p. 5.

60. Coleridge, *Biographia literaria* (*Works*, III, 373): "The writings of Plato and Jeremy Taylor, and Burnet's *Theory of the Earth*, furnish undeniable proofs that poetry of the highest kind may exist without metre, and even without the contradistinguishing objects of a poem."

61. *Ibid.*, p. 381. The statement is applied in a discussion of Shakespeare and Milton.

62. *Op. cit.*, pp. 107–8: "Plato was essentially a poet—the truth and splendour of his imagery, and the melody of his language, are the most intense that it is possible to conceive. He rejected the harmony of the epic, dramatic, and lyrical forms, because he sought to kindle a harmony in thoughts divested of shape and action, and he forbore to invent any regular plan of rhythm which would include, under determinate forms, the varied pauses of his style. Cicero sought to imitate the cadence of his periods, but with little success. Lord Bacon was a poet. . . . Nor are those supreme poets, who have employed traditional forms of rhythm on account of the form and action of their subjects, less capable of perceiving and teaching the truth of things, than those who have omitted that form. Shakespeare, Dante, and Milton (to confine ourselves to modern writers) are philosophers of the very loftiest power."

63. Emerson, "Poetry and Imagination," *Letters and Social Aims* (Boston, 1883), p. 42: "For poetry is science, and the poet a truer logician," from whence it follows (*ibid.*, pp. 66, 68): "The poet who shall use nature as his hieroglyphic must have an adequate message to convey thereby. Therefore, when we speak of the Poet in any high sense, we are driven to such examples as Zoroaster and Plato, St. John and Menu, with their moral burdens. The Muse shall be the counterpart of Nature, and equally rich. . . . But in current literature I do not find her. Literature warps away from life, though at first it seems to bind it. In the world of

This rivalry of poetry and philosophy seems to disappear in the tradition of discussion in which poetry is contrasted literally to philosophy on all the points which served for their analogical comparison. Yet in the mixture of the traditions of literal and analogical discussion which constitutes the greater part of the history of thought, the effect of such distinctions is to supply points to serve as bases for later analogizing. The Platonic analogy of poetry and philosophy, thus, is combated in Aristotle's philosophy by distinguishing the kind of knowledge required for poetic constructions from other kinds of knowledge by its purpose; for theoretic knowledge is pursued for its own sake and for truth, practical knowledge for the sake of conduct, and poetic knowledge for the sake of making something useful or beautiful. The distinction having been made, however, the analogizing technique may be applied to it, and philosophers since the time of Aristotle have stated their basic principles by determining whether philosophy is essentially theoretic, or practical, or poetic. The conception of philosophy, therefore, is affected, no less than that of poetry, each time it is decided that philosophy is or is not poetry and that poetry is or is not philosophy: so long as the principles of philosophy are sought in the nature of things, philosophy may pretend to be fundamentally theoretic and speculative for all its practical implications and consequences;[64] when principles are sought in the nature of the human faculties or the development of human knowledge, practical knowledge tends to assume ascendancy in the hierarchy of the sciences;[65] and, finally, when principles are sought in operations and in the relations of symbols and when we seek substitutes for cer-

---

letters how few commanding oracles! Homer did what he could; Pindar, Aeschylus, and the Greek Gnomic poets and the tragedians. Dante was faithful when not carried away by his fierce hatreds. But in so many alcoves of English poetry I can count only nine or ten authors who are still inspirers and lawgivers to their race. . . . We are a little civil, it must be owned, to Homer and Aeschylus, to Dante and Shakespeare, and give them the benefit of the largest interpretation." Cf., also, Montesquieu, *Pensées diverses* (*Œuvres complètes de Montesquieu* [Paris, 1866], p. 626): "Les quatres grands poètes, Platon, Malebranche, Shaftesbury, Montaigne!"

64. Plato *Statesman* 259E, 285E–286A; *Rep.* vii. 518B–519D. Aristotle *Metaph.* i. 1. 981^{b}25–982^{a}3.

65. Kant, *Critique of Pure Reason*, trans. F. M. Müller (2d ed.; New York, 1919), Part II, "Transcendental Doctrine of Method," chap. ii, "The Canon of Pure Reason," pp. 647–48: "Pure reason, therefore, contains, not indeed in its speculative, yet in its practical, or, more accurately, its moral employment, principles of the *possibility of experience*, namely, of such actions as *might* be met with in the *history* of man according to moral precepts. For as reason commands that such actions should take place, they must be possible, and a certain kind of systematical unity also, namely, the moral, must be possible; while it was impossible to prove the systematical unity *according to the speculative principles of reason*. For reason, no doubt, possesses causality with respect to freedom in general, but not with respect to the whole of nature, and moral principles of reason may indeed produce free actions, but not laws of nature. Consequently, the principles of pure reason possess objective reality in their practical and more particularly in their moral employment" (cf. "Introduction to the Second edition," pp. 695–96).

tainty in the precisions of measurement, philosophy becomes an art again, since art takes precedence over the practical and the theoretic and man ceases to be *homo sapiens* and finds his best characterization in the functions of *homo faber*.[66]

The Platonic analogy of poetry and philosophy based on their common ends is closely related to the analogy of art and nature as imitation and exemplar. Aristotle countered that analogy with the distinction of natural objects, in which the principle of motion is internal, and artificial objects, whose cause must be sought in the idea and intention of artist or artisan. Like the analogy of poetry and philosophy, the analogy of art and nature was continued either in its original terms as a likeness found in things or in terms (derived from Aristotle's literal distinctions) which connect art and nature in characteristics found in the judgments of man or in his actions. Hobbes, thus, like Plato, not only treats art as an imitation of nature but conceives nature as a kind of art:

> Nature, the art whereby God hath made and governs the world, is by the *art* of man, as in many other things, so in this also imitated, that it can make an artificial animal. For seeing life is but a motion of limbs, the beginning whereof is in some principal part within; why may we not say, that all *automata* (engines that move themselves by springs and wheels as doth a watch) have an artificial life? For what is the *heart*, but a *spring*; and the *nerves*, but so many *strings*; and the *joints*, but so many *wheels*, giving motion to the whole body, such as was intended by the artificer? *Art* goes yet further, imitating that rational and most excellent work of nature, *man*. For by art is created that great LEVIATHAN called a COMMONWEALTH, or STATE, in Latin CIVITAS, which is but an artificial man.[67]

That analogy of God's creation in nature to man's creations in art lent itself easily to the terminology of Christian theology and, during the Middle Ages,

66. H. Bergson, *L'Évolution créatrice* (34th ed.; Paris, 1929), p. 151: "Si nous pouvions nous dépouiller de tout orgueil, si, pour définir nôtre espèce, nous nous en tenions strictement à ce que l'histoire et la préhistoire nous présentent comme la caractéristique constante de l'homme et de l'intelligence, nous ne dirions peut-être pas *Homo sapiens*, mais *Homo faber*." Cf. Dewey, *Reconstruction in Philosophy*, p. 71. Kant's emphasis on the conditions of thought and on *possible experience* leads to a philosophy in which practical rather than theoretical reason occupies the central place; Dewey's emphasis on the conditions of action and on *experience* yields a philosophy in which theory and practice are both arts; cf. *Experience and Nature* (New York, 1929), pp. 357–58: "But if modern tendencies are justified in putting art and creation first, then the implications of this position should be avowed and carried through. It would then be seen that science is an art, that art is practice, and that the only distinction worth drawing is not between practice and theory, but between those modes of practice that are not intelligent, not inherently and immediately enjoyable, and those which are full of enjoyed meanings. When this perception dawns, it will be a commonplace that art—the mode of activity that is charged with the meanings capable of immediately enjoyed possession—is the complete culmination of nature, and that 'science' is properly a handmaiden that conducts natural events to this happy issue. Thus would disappear the separations that trouble present thinking: division of everything into nature *and* experience, of experience into practice *and* theory, art *and* science, of art into useful *and* fine, menial *and* free."

67. *Leviathan* (*The English Works of Thomas Hobbes*, ed. W. Molesworth [London, 1808], III, ix).

bent even the Aristotelian view of God as First Mover and First Cause to its services. When, however, a philosophic basis was sought for our judgments of things by examination of the nature of our knowledge, art was analogized to nature by means of the human faculties which bring together traits by which Aristotle had distinguished them, as judgment, for Kant, bears on the perception of purpose in nature and the perception of beauty in nature and art and so serves as link between the practical and the theoretical:

The concept formed by Judgement of a purposiveness of Nature belongs to natural concepts, but only as a regulative principle of the cognitive faculty; although the aesthetical judgement upon certain objects (of Nature or Art) which occasions it is, in respect of the feeling of pleasure or pain, a constitutive principle. The spontaneity in the play of the cognitive faculties, the harmony of which contains the ground of this pleasure, makes the above concept [of the purposiveness of nature] fit to be the mediating link between the realm of the natural concept and that of the concept of freedom in its effects; whilst at the same time it promotes the sensibility of the mind for moral feeling.[68]

When, finally, a philosophic basis for our concept of nature and our judgment of values was sought in the examination of experience, purposiveness disappeared from nature as such and value from things as such, and art was analogized to nature by bringing together traits by which Aristotle had distinguished them, as all objects, for Dewey—the objects of the sciences and the objects of the arts—are tools, and art is natural, since it originates in natural tendencies in man and employs natural means to further natural ends.

In experience, human relations, institutions, and traditions are as much a part of the nature in which and by which we live as is the physical world. Nature in this meaning is not "outside." It is in us and we are in and of it. But there are multitudes of ways of participating in it, and these ways are characteristic not only of various experiences of the same individual, but of attitudes of aspiration, need and achievement that belong to civilizations in their collective aspect. Works of art are means by which we enter, through imagination and the emotions they evoke, into other forms of relationship and participation than our own.[69]

68. Kant, *Critique of Judgement*, Introd., pp. 41–42. E. A. Poe makes similar, though more simple, use of the faculties of the mind to put Aristotelian distinctions to un-Aristotelian uses; cf. "The Poetic Principle" (*Works*, ed. Stedman and Woodberry [New York, 1914], VI, 11): "Dividing the world of mind into its three most obvious distinctions, we have the Pure Intellect, Taste, and the Moral Sense. I place Taste in the middle, because it is just this position which in the mind it occupies. It holds intimate relations with either extreme, but from the Moral Sense is separated by so faint a difference that Aristotle has not hesitated to place some of its operations among the virtues themselves. Nevertheless, we find the *offices* of the trio marked with a sufficient distinction. Just as the Intellect concerns itself with Truth, so Taste informs us of the Beautiful, while the Moral Sense is regardful of Duty."

69. *Art as Experience*, p. 333; cf. also p. 79: "In other words, art is not nature, but it is nature transformed by entering into new relationships where it evokes a new emotional response." Cf. also *Experience and Nature*, pp. 136, 150–51, and esp. 358: "Thus the issue involved in experience as art in its pregnant sense and in art as processes and materials of

Nature is art because the universe, like the objects of art, is created, or because the judgment of purpose in nature, like the judgment of beauty, involves the free interplay of our faculties, or because our experience of things permits no sharp separation of our use, our knowledge, and our enjoyment of them; and each of these reasonable analogies is also reduced to literal-minded statements and criticized because it involves fictitious suppositions of eternal patterns of things, universal principles of thought, or collective aspects of epochs and civilizations.

The form in which Plato expressed his philosophy is indistinguishable from other forms of communication in his philosophy; for the subject matters of philosophy, poetry, rhetoric, and history are analogous, and the ends of the various forms of human activity are ultimately the same. It is no dramatic accident that Socrates spent part of the last hours of his life experimenting by divine direction with a poetic form; and there is no sharp line, in Plato's employment, between dialectic, myth, and history. Aristotle could therefore commend his recording of the Socratic method as the discovery of the universal in science and philosophy, and could deprecate his separation of the universal from the particular.[70] Aristotle's favorite means of differentiating the arts from one another is, in his sense, formal; and he therefore separated philosophy from poetry in terms, not of metrical forms, but of comparative universality, illustrating the distinction by placing poetry between philosophy and history.[71] So long as the principles of philosophy are sought in the nature of things, science is of universals, since it must apply to more than the particular instance; but, when the principles of philosophy are based on a preliminary examination of the nature of thought, the virtue of science may be found either in its universality (since scientific laws must be shown to be necessary, while their objectivity may be assured by the laws of thought) or in its particularity (since scientific laws must be shown to be objective, while their universality may be assured by the uniformity of nature). Poetry may in this stage of the discussion

---

nature continued by direction into achieved and enjoyed meanings, sums up in itself all the issues which have been previously considered. Thought, intelligence, science is the intentional direction of natural events to meanings capable of immediate possession and enjoyment; this direction—which is operative art—is itself a natural event in which nature otherwise partial and incomplete comes fully to itself; so that objects of conscious experience when reflectively chosen, form the 'end' of nature."

70. *Metaph.* xiii. 1078^b27–32.

71. *Poet.* 1. 1447^a16–20: "Even if statements concerning medicine or natural philosophy be set forth in metrical form, it is customary to call the author a poet. Yet there is nothing in common between Homer and Empedocles except the meter, and therefore it is right to call the one poet, but the other physicist rather than poet." *Ibid.* 9. 1451^b5–7: "Wherefore poetry is more philosophic and more serious than history, for poetry is expressive more of universals, while history states singulars."

be analogized to philosophy or to history; and the poetic quality, since it is midway between the general and the particular, may combine the two, or indeed it may be the source of the generality of philosophy or the particularity of history. Sidney borrows Aristotle's example to discover Empedocles a poet[72] and to assign to poetry the performance of moral tasks at which philosophy and history fail.[73] According to Bacon, on the other hand, poetry is nothing else than an imitation of history for the giving of pleasure,[74] while Newman can quote Bacon to illustrate Aristotle's doctrine that poetry is more general than history and can follow Aristotle's judgment that Empedocles was no poet but a natural historian writing in verse in support of the doctrine that natural history and philosophy are proper materials for poetry.[75] Wordsworth, on the other hand, makes use of vague echoes of Aristotle to support the position that poetry is the most philosophical of all writing and to contrast poetry to matter of fact or science.[76] Like "philosophy," which may be taken either as identical

72. Sidney, *op. cit.*, p. 4.

73. *Ibid.*, pp. 13–14: "The Philosopher therefore, and the Historian, are they which would win the goale, the one by precept, the other by example: but both, not having both, doo both halt. For the Philosopher setting downe with thornie arguments, the bare rule, is so hard of utterance, and so mistie to be conceived, that one that hath no other guide but him, shall wade in him till he be old, before he shall find sufficient cause to be honest. For his knowledge standeth so upon the abstract and generall, that happie is that man who may understand him, and more happie, that can apply what he doth understand. On the other side, the Historian wanting the precept, is so tied, not to what should be, but to what is, to the particular truth of things, and not to the general reason of things, that his example draweth no necessarie consequence, and therefore a lesse fruitfull doctrine. Now doth the peerlesse Poet performe both, for whatsoever the Philosopher saith should be done, he gives a perfect picture of it by some one, by whom he presupposeth it was done, so as he coupleth the generall notion with the particuler example."

74. *De augmentis scientiarum*, Book II, chap. xiii (*Works*, IV, 315); *Of the Proficience and Advancement of Learning*, Book II (*Works*, III, 343). Cf. above, n. 21.

75. Newman, "Poetry, with Reference to Aristotle's 'Poetics,'" *Essays Critical and Historical* (London, 1890), I, 12: "Empedocles wrote his physics in verse, and Oppian his history of animals. Neither were poets—the one was an historian of nature, the other a sort of biographer of brutes. Yet a poet may make natural history or philosophy the material of his composition."

76. Wordsworth, *op. cit.*, p. 89: "Aristotle, I have been told, has said, that Poetry is the most philosophic of all writing: it is so: its object is truth, not individual and local, but general, and operative; not standing upon external testimony, but carried alive into the heart by passion; truth which is its own testimony, which gives competence and confidence to the tribunal to which it appeals, and receives them from the same tribunal. Poetry is the image of man and nature. The obstacles which stand in the way of the fidelity of the Biographer and Historian, and of their consequent utility, are incalculably greater than those which are to be encountered by the Poet who comprehends the dignity of his art." Cf. *ibid.*, p. 86 n.: "I here use the word 'Poetry' (though against my own judgment) as opposed to the word Prose, and synonymous with metrical composition. But much confusion has been introduced into criticism by this contradistinction of Poetry and Prose, instead of the more philosophical one of Poetry and Matter of Fact, or Science." Cf. J. R. Lowell, "Shakespeare Once More," *Literary Essays* (Boston, 1894), III, 70–71: "The aim of the artist is psychologic, not historic truth. It is comparatively easy for an author to *get up* any period with tolerable minuteness in externals, but readers and audiences find more difficulty in getting them down, though

with poetry or as an imperfect truth perfected by poetry, "history" takes on two senses in this Platonic opposition of a complete and partial truth. Shelley contrasts history to poetry:

A poem is the very image of life expressed in its eternal truth. There is this difference between a story and a poem, that a story is a catalogue of detached facts, which have no other connexion than time, place, circumstance, cause, and effect; the other is the creation of actions according to the unchangeable forms of human nature, as existing in the mind of the creator, which is itself the image of all other minds. The one is partial, and applies only to a definite period of time, and a certain combination of events which can never again recur; the other is universal, and contains within itself the germ of a relation to whatever motives or actions have place in the possible varieties of human nature.[77]

Froude, on the other hand, finds the universality in that which is better and genuine in man and contrasts prose and verse but identifies the highest history with the highest poetry:

The prose historian may give us facts and names; he may catalogue the successions, and tell us long stories of battles, and of factions, and of political intrigues; he may draw characters for us of the sort which figure commonly in such features of human affairs, men of the unheroic, unpoetic kind—the Cleons, the Sejanuses, the Tiberiuses, a Philip the Second or a Louis Quatorze, in whom the noble element died out into selfishness and vulgarity. But great men—all MEN properly so called (whatever is genuine and natural in them)—lie beyond prose, and can only be really represented by the poet.[78]

Finally, if the principles of our knowledge and the nature of things are sought in the processes of experience, history may assume dominance among sciences and things, either in the sense of accounting for the historical succession of poetry and philosophy as forms of wisdom and explanation—as Vico finds the "Aristotelian" aphorism that nothing is in understanding that was not prior in sense exemplified in the sequence after an age of poets, whose wisdom is of the sense, of an age of philosophers, whose wisdom is of the understanding[79]—or in the sense that all things are histories—as Dewey finds

---

oblivion swallows scores of them at a gulp. The saving truth in such matters is a truth to essential and permanent characteristics." Lowell, moreover, appreciated the fashion in which Wordsworth's doctrine that *poetry* is *philosophy* involved the further identification of philosophy with a kind of *history*, the history of the poet's mind; cf. "Wordsworth" (*Writings* [Boston, 1898], IV, 397–98): "He was theoretically determined not only to be a philosophic poet, but to be a *great* philosophic poet, and to this end he must produce an epic. Leaving aside the question whether the epic be obsolete or not, it may be doubted whether the history of a single man's mind is universal enough in its interest to furnish all the requirements of the epic machinery, and it may be more than doubted whether a poet's philosophy be ordinary metaphysics, divisible into chapter and section."

77. Shelley, *op. cit.*, p. 108.

78. "Homer," *Short Studies on Great Subjects*, 1st ser. (New York, 1873), p. 410; cf. also "The Science of History," *ibid.*, pp. 32–35.

79. G. B. Vico, *Principii di scienza nuova*, Book II (3d ed.; Naples, 1744), I, 129 and 376. The relation between poetry and philosophy is conceived in terms of particularity and gen-

history basic to all knowledge and histories more truly known than mathematical and physical objects.[80] Aristotle's distinction of philosophy, poetry, and history has been made the basis for assigning to poetry or history functions and characteristics which Aristotle conceived as philosophic, and, as a final irony, historians of philosophy have reproached him for mistaking poets for philosophers, misled in his humorless literal-mindedness by Plato's gentle irony.[81]

While poets dispute the authority of philosophers, supplementing scientific inquiries, rectifying metaphysical reflections, and expounding lofty and enigmatic visions, and philosophers in their turn borrow the devices of the poet to expound the nature, function, and place of the arts and use the arguments of the moralist or the economist to banish poets from their perfect states or to instruct them in their tasks as educators or propagandists, the critic sometimes conceives his function to be distinct from that of the artist and dialectician and

---

erality (cf. *ibid.*, Book I, pp. 90–91): "Axiom 53. Men first perceive without noticing; then they notice with perturbed and agitated soul; finally they reflect with a pure mind. This axiom is the principle of poetic judgments, which are formed by the perception of the passions and emotions, unlike philosophic judgments which are formed through reflection by reason. Wherefore the latter approximate more closely to truth the more they are raised to universality, and the former are more certain the more they descend to particularity." The poetic truth may be true metaphysically when the physical truth is false (*ibid.*, p. 88). The history of mankind is analogized to the life of a man, and the infancy of the race is an age of poetry, prior to the formation of philosophy; the relation of art to nature is therefore complex—men supplement nature by the attentive study of art, but in poetry no one succeeds by art who has not the advantages of nature, and therefore, if poetry founded pagan civilization, from which in turn followed all the arts, the first poets were by nature. The people of the infant world were poets, and the arts are imitations of nature, a kind of *real poetry* (*ibid.*, p. 90). From this poetic wisdom derive on one branch a poetic logic, a poetic morality, a poetic economics, and a poetic politics, and on the other branch a poetic physics, from which proceed a poetic cosmography, astronomy, chronology, and geography (*ibid.*, p. 132).

80. *Experience and Nature*, p. 163: "And yet if all natural existences *are* histories, divorce between history and the logical mathematical schemes which are the appropriate objects of pure science, terminates in the conclusion that of existences there is no science, no adequate knowledge. Aside from mathematics, all knowledge is historic; chemistry, geology, physiology, as well as anthropology and those human events to which, arrogantly, we usually restrict the title of history. Only as science is seen to be fulfilled and brought to itself in intelligent management of historical processes in their continuity can man be envisaged as within nature, and not as a supernatural extrapolation. Just because nature is what it is, history is capable of being more truly known—understood, intellectually realized—than are mathematical and physical objects."

81. J. Burnet (*Early Greek Philosophy* [3d ed.; London, 1920], p. 127) argues that Aristotle is mistaken in treating Xenophanes as the founder of the Eleatic school and that this mistake originated in his misinterpretation of Plato. "Just as he [Plato] called the Herakleiteans 'followers of Homer and still more ancient teachers,' so he attached the Eleatics to Xenophanes and still earlier authorities. We have seen before how these playful and ironical remarks of Plato were taken seriously by his successors, and we must not make too much of this fresh instance of Aristotle's literalness." Cf. *ibid.*, p. 32: "It is often forgotten that Aristotle derived much of his information from Plato, and we must specially observe that he more than once takes Plato's humorous remarks too literally."

sometimes enters into competition with both, assuming the role of poet among poets and dialectician among dialecticians. The functions assigned to criticism reflect all the analogies and distinctions found in the ends of poetry and philosophy, the objects of art and nature, and the forms of history, poetry, and philosophy. For criticism may be conceived as a technique applied only to works of art, if the literal distinctions are maintained; or it may be implied in any knowledge, involved in any activity, and applied to any object. The history of criticism can be traced and understood, therefore, in part by differentiating kinds of criticism applied to art, and in part by finding the manners in which criticism, conceived more broadly in a variety of ways, applies to art in particular. In the analogical tradition the effort is to avoid unreal distinctions between the emotional and the intellectual, the moral and the aesthetic, the artistic and the practical; and the development of the tradition is therefore the evolution of a single dialectic in which opposed devices for achieving critical universality jostle one another: criticism is sometimes the application of a theory in the judgment of objects and actions; it is sometimes the technique which determines both theories and arts; it is sometimes, like theory, itself an art. In the literal tradition the effort is to find a technique proper to each subject matter and therefore to separate, for the purposes of accuracy and clarity, considerations of moral, political, scientific, metaphysical, and aesthetic characteristics even in the judgment of a single object; and the development of the tradition is therefore a succession of analyses which achieve critical particularity in application to objects of art, canons of taste, or means of production and manners of social use. Echoes of the one effort emerge from the mingling of the two traditions as speculations concerning the Good, the True, and the Beautiful; and the other effort leaves its mark in discussions of the individual arts.

For Plato, "criticism" was a general term applied to all processes of judgment, those involved in the common distinctions made by the interlocutors in the dialogues as well as the technical distinctions of reason, but used particularly for the judgments pronounced in law-courts in application of the law; the judgment of art is usually treated by Plato in the context of broader political and judiciary functions. There are two intellectual arts or sciences—the science of commanding, which is the proper art of the statesman, and the art of judging, which, since it pronounces on what falls under or is disclosed by the art of commanding, is also part of the statesman's art.[82] Judgment is a decision between better and worse in all fields: between the unjust and the just man,[83]

82. *Statesman* 259E–260A, 292B, 305B.

83. *Rep.* ii. 360D.

between possible kinds of lives and pleasures,[84] between pleasure and wisdom,[85] between true and false.[86] The criteria by which judgment pronounces on its subject matter to determine the comparative value of things among gods and men, and the degree of their approximation to the eternal good, are three: experience, intelligence, and discussion (λόγος), the latter being the "instrument" of judgment; in all three the philosopher has the advantage over other men.[87] The lawgiver, therefore, combats an erroneous doctrine—such as the separation of the pleasant from the just—by habituation, commendation, and discussion; and in the opposition of two judgments the character of the judge is reflected in the soundness of the judgment, for the judgment of the better man is more authoritative.[88] One might even concede the opinion of the majority of men that pleasure is the proper criterion of music and poetry, not the pleasure of any chance person, but of that man or those men who excel in virtue and education, for the critic should be a teacher; and when poets adapt their works to the criterion of the pleasure of their judges (so that their audiences become the teachers of the poets), they corrupt themselves as well as their audiences, whose criteria of pleasure ought to be improved by the judgments of better men rather than degraded to the common level.[89] The charm which causes pleasure, however, is usually accompanied by correctness or utility; and consequently the arts which are imitative and produce likenesses are not to be judged by pleasure or untrue opinion but by the proportion and equality they possess: to judge a poem, one must know its essence, for one must know what its intention is and what original it represents, if one is to decide whether it succeeds or fails in achieving its intention.[90] The critic of music, poetry, and the other arts is therefore the philosopher in the perfect state, or, failing that, the lawgiver and the educator.[91]

There are numerous ingredients of later criticism in Plato's philosophy—the moral emphasis; the use of the criteria of experience, intelligence, and words or discussion (any one of which might assume a dominant position in derivative forms of criticism); the prominence of pleasure balanced by various forms of rightness or utility; and, finally, the background of an eternal beauty, which things imitate, which philosophers and poets seek in their manipulations of words, and which cannot itself be expressed without recourse to eternal standards of truth and goodness. The influence of Plato on later criticism is to be found for the most part in the emphasis given to one or another

84. *Ibid.* ix. 580B–C; *Philebus* 27C.

85. *Philebus* 65A.

86. *Theaetetus* 150B.

87. *Rep.* ix. 581E–583A.

88. *Laws* ii. 663A–C.

89. *Ibid.* 658E–659C.

90. *Ibid.* 667B–668B.

91. *Ibid.* viii. 829D; xii. 948E–949A; vi. 765B.

of these critical criteria or aesthetic traits rather than in the dialectical association of them and the interplay among them which are essential to Plato's conception of criticism. In particular, criticism is reduced to narrower limits and the dialectic of its discussion is restricted and frozen in either of two ways: by limiting its application to works of art or literature, or by assigning to criticism the role of applying theory to practice in specific subject matters. The first restriction was accomplished, probably under Stoic and Epicurean influences, in Hellenistic Greece. The word "critic" is used in counterdistinction to "grammarian" in the "Platonic" *Axiochos* (366E), which may show Epicurean influences; and Crates, the Stoic philosopher, is credited with having first distinguished "critic" and "grammarian," the former being learned in all the erudite sciences, the latter being equipped to interpret unusual words and to treat of accents and similar properties of words; the critic thus is related to the grammarian as the architect to the craftsman.[92] It is probable that this literal distinction of critic concerned with meanings from grammarian concerned with words reflects the influence of Aristotle's restriction of the word "grammarian" to the treatment of words as sounds and symbols apart from significances, while the second manner of restricting "criticism" was developed from a like analogizing and fitting of the meaning of the term "criticism" to his division of the sciences. Aristotle held that every theory and every method admitted of two kinds of proficiency: scientific knowledge of the thing and a kind of broad educational acquaintance with the science, so that it is the mark of a well-educated man to be able to criticize and judge with some probability whether a thing is well or badly expounded.[93] In later writers Aristotle's conception of the theoretic and practical is confused with Plato's conception of the intellectual and practical, and every science (contrary to Aristotle's supposition) is made to have a theory and an application between which criticism mediates. Clausewitz, thus, in his treatise *On War*, devotes a chapter to criticism so conceived:

The influence of theoretical truths upon practical life is always exerted more through criticism than through rules for practice. Criticism is the application to actual events of

92. Sextus Empiricus *Adversus grammaticos* i. 79. For the evolution of κριτικός, γραμματικός, and φιλόλογος cf. Gudeman's article κριτικός, Pauly-Wissowa-Kroll, *Real-Encyclopädie der classischen Altertumswissenschaft* (Stuttgart, 1921), XI, 1912–15. In the course of the discussion "grammarian" is analogized to, or made synonymous with, "critic," and the identification as well as the discrimination of meanings is continued even into modern discussion. This discussion of the relation of grammarian and critic is frequently associated with the second manner of fixing and restricting the meaning of "critic" by consideration of the boundaries of the sciences. Both processes are illustrated, for example, by Octavius Ferrarius (*Prolusiones et epistolae: accesserunt formulae ad petenda doctoris insignia* [Padua, 1650], p. 116): "Sed Criticos nostros sive Grammaticos duplici crimine arcessis, altero quod ineptias sectantur acerrimo, altero quod non contenti finibus suis, audent etiam vestros limites revellere, et in scientiarum campum audacter transcendere."

93. *De partibus animalium* i. 1. 639ª1–6.

theoretical truth, and so not only brings the latter nearer to life but also accustoms the intelligence more to these truths through the constant repetition of their applications.[94]

The "critical narration" which Clausewitz employs in his treatment of war consists of three parts, each of which has its special pertinence and history in the development of criticism: (1) the historical discovery and establishment of doubtful facts; (2) critical investigation proper, which consists in tracing the effect from its causes; and (3) criticism proper, which consists in testing the means employed. These two particularizations of Platonic criticism divide between them the text of the poet (which may be interpreted analogically to apply to any subject) and the truths or significances of the sciences (which may be brought analogically to apply to any text).

The Platonic criticism may, on the other hand, be used to resist such particularization, for it may be made to apply to the whole of philosophy to become a preliminary to or substitute for dialectic. Protagoras and the other Sophists are prominent in the philosophy of Plato because they are the dramatic representation of the consequences which follow from denying objective Truth and Beauty: philosophy then becomes critical; I am the judge of the existence of things that are to me and of the nonexistence of things that are not to me;[95] we all sit in judgment on the judgment of everyone else;[96] the criteria by which we judge things are internal, as, for example, the coincidence of thought and sensation;[97] and each is his own best judge concerning what is future.[98] Yet those same relativistic devices are used by philosophers to avoid relativism and skepticism, for the certainty of knowledge of things and the universality of moral standards may be based on judgment, either in the sense of making criticism of human faculties a preliminary to philosophy or of making judgment the basis of first principles in each of the branches of philosophy. "Our age," Kant said, "is, in every sense of the word, the age of criticism, and everything must submit to it."[99] Criticism becomes a necessary prelude to the task of philosophy:

It will now be seen how there can be a special science serving as a critique of pure reason. Reason is the faculty which supplies the principles of knowledge *a priori*. Pure reason therefore is that faculty which supplies the principles of knowing anything entirely *a priori*. An Organum of pure reason ought to comprehend all the principles by which pure knowledge *a priori* can be acquired and fully established. A complete application of such an Organum would give us a System of Pure Reason. But as that would be a difficult task, and as at present it is still doubtful whether and when such an expansion

94. *On War*, trans. O. J. M. Jolles (New York, 1943), Book II, chap. v, p. 92.

95. *Theaet.* 160C.

96. *Ibid.* 170D.　　　　98. *Ibid.* 187E.

97. *Ibid.* 178B.　　　　99. *Critique of Pure Reason*, p. xix, n. 1.

f our knowledge is here possible, we may look on a mere criticism of pure reason, its ources and limits, as a kind of preparation for a complete system of pure reason. It ould be called a critique, not a doctrine, of pure reason. Its usefulness would be negave only, serving for a purging rather than for an expansion of our reason, and, what fter all is a considerable gain, guarding reason against errors.[100]

esthetic judgment, which bears on beauty in art or in nature, requires no inferce, theoretic or practical, to external things, but depends wholly on the free terplay of imagination and understanding. Judgment may, on the other hand, e the basis of philosophy, because judgment and common sense are equally istributed among men, unlike apprehension or conception of the things we idge, and truth and falsity are qualities which belong only to judgment.[101] ince judgment may be either intuitive or grounded on argument, the chief roblems of philosophy center about the judgment of first principles, among thers the first principles of taste:

I think there are axioms, even in matters of *taste*. . . . The fundamental rules of poetry id music, and painting, and dramatic action and eloquence, have been always the same, id will be so to the end of the world. . . . I do not maintain that taste, so far as it is quired, or so far as it is merely animal, can be reduced to principles. But, as far as it is unded on judgment, it certainly may. The virtues, the graces, the muses, have a beauty at is intrinsic. It lies not in the feelings of the spectator, but in the real excellence of e object. If we do not perceive their beauty, it is owing to the defect or to the perrsion of our faculties.[102]

n either sense the critic discovers the fundamental rules of philosophy and art, f the perception of truth and the apprehension or construction of beauty. essing remarks that the first person who compared painting and poetry was man of taste, an amateur who observed that they both produced pleasure in im, and that the second person, who investigated the inner cause of this leasure and found that it flowed from the same source, was a philosopher; lese two could not easily make a wrong use of their feeling or their reason, ut the third person, the critic, who reflected on the value and distribution of lese rules, might misapply them and so affect art and taste.[103]

100. *Ibid.*, pp. 8–9.

101. Cf. Thomas Reid, *Essays on the Intellectual Powers of Man* (*The Works of Thomas eid, D.D.*, ed. Sir William Hamilton [8th ed.; Edinburgh, 1895], I, 366). Reid cites Desrtes in support of his position: "Nothing is so equally distributed among men as judgment. Vherefore, it seems reasonable to believe, that the power of distinguishing what is true from hat is false (which we properly call judgment or right reason) is by nature equal in all men; id therefore that the diversity of our opinions does not arise from one person being enowed with a greater power of reason than another, but only from this, that we do not lead ur thought in the same track, nor attend to the same things." He quotes Cicero to the same ffect: "It is wonderful when the learned and unlearned differ so much in art, how little ey differ in judgment. For art being derived from Nature, is good for nothing, unless it ove and delight Nature." Cf. also *ibid.*, p. 243.

102. *Ibid.*, p. 453.   103. Lessing, *op. cit.*, p. 292.

If, finally, the hope of examining the conditions of all possible experience by criticism or of arriving at common principles of taste by judgment is thought to be as illusory as the appeal to eternal ideas, then principles are sought in actual experience, and criticism, as well as philosophy itself, becomes an art. Viewed in terms of the activity of man, according to Spingarn, critical judgment and artistic creation are fundamentally the same:

> The identity of genius and taste is the final achievement of modern thought on the subject of art, and it means that fundamentally, in their most significant moments, the creative and the critical instincts are one and the same. From Goethe to Carlyle, from Carlyle to Arnold, from Arnold to Symons, there has been much talk of the "creative function" of Criticism. For each of these men the phrase held a different content; for Arnold it meant merely that Criticism creates the intellectual atmosphere of the age, social function of high importance, perhaps, yet wholly independent of aesthetic significance. But the ultimate truth toward which these men were tending was more radical than that, and plays havoc with all the old platitudes about the sterility of taste. Criticism at last can free itself of its age-long self-contempt, now that it may realize that aesthetic judgment and artistic creation are instinct with the same vital life.[104]

Or criticism may be conceived to be properly neither impressionistic nor judicial, but to consist, as Dewey holds, in reliving the processes the artist went through to the end of deepening the appreciation of others:

> For critical judgment not only grows out of the critic's experience of objective matter, and not only depends upon that for validity, but has for its office the deepening of just such experience in others. Scientific judgments not only end in increased control but for those who understand they add enlarged meanings to the things perceived and dealt with in daily contact with the world. The function of criticism is the reëducation of perception of works of art; it is an auxiliary in the process, a difficult process, of learning to see and hear. The conception that its business is to appraise, to judge in the legal and moral sense, arrests the perception of those who are influenced by the criticism that assumes this task. The moral office of criticism is performed indirectly. . . . We lay hold of the full import of a work of art only as we go through in our own vital processes the processes the artist went through in producing the work. It is the critic's privilege to share in the promotion of this active process. His condemnation is that he so often arrests it.[105]

Or, finally, criticism may be conceived, as it was by Tolstoy, as one of the conditions which lead to the production of counterfeit art in our society, since art criticism is impossible in societies in which art is undivided and appraised by the religious conception of life common to the whole people, but it grows on the art of the upper classes, who do not acknowledge the religious perception of their time.[106]

104. *Op. cit.*, pp. 42–43.   105. *Art as Experience*, pp. 324–25.

106. Tolstoy, *What Is Art?* pp. 241–43. The analogy of Dewey's basic principles to those of Tolstoy may be seen in his condemnation of the separation of art from the conditions of life consequent on the growth of capitalism and the *nouveaux riches* and his condemnation of

The literal separation of the arts and the sciences requires the differentiation
f subject matters and methods, for the difference between the analogical and
ne literal is not to be found in any difference in the ease with which arts may
e separated or compared by the two methods, but in the priority given to the
ifferences or the likenesses, so that either differences are worked dialectically
:om basic similarities or similarities are found among things whose differences
ave been stated. "Criticism" and the related terms (κρίνειν, κρίσις, κριτικός),
vhich for Plato are general terms, are restricted in Aristotle's usage to
ne of the three kinds of sciences; and some of the peculiarities of the history
f criticism are to be attributed to the fact that they belong properly not to the
neoretic, or the poetic, but to the practical sciences or to the practical treat-
nent of any science which is possible since politics is an architectonic science:
ney do not appear in the *Poetics* (except as part of the title of a tragedy), but
ney are used extensively in the *Nicomachean Ethics*, the *Politics*, and the
hetoric, and their other appearances in the works of Aristotle can be explained
y the primarily practical sense given to them there. There are two sources of
novement in man, appetite and mind,[107] imagination being a kind of thinking.
he moral problem consists in a sense in submitting the appetitive part of the
oul to the rational.[108] The problem of art, on the other hand, turns primarily
n the application of knowledge to the organization of external materials, and
nerefore, unlike the moral virtues, the arts consist in the possession of knowl-
dge, and their products are themselves capable of excellence or virtue.

Moreover, the case of the arts is not similar to that of the virtues, for works of art
ave their merit in themselves, so that it is sufficient if they are produced having a cer-
ain quality, but acts performed in accordance with the virtues are not done justly or
emperately if they have a certain quality, but only if the one who performs them has a
ertain quality when he performs them: first, he must act knowingly; second, he must
:t by choice and by choice of the act for its own sake; and third, he must act from a
rm and constant character. These are not numbered among the essentials for the pos-
:ssion of the arts, except only knowledge; but for the possession of the virtues knowl-
dge has little or no weight, whereas the other conditions have, not a little force, but all,

---

ne criticism which results from these conditions (*Art as Experience*, pp. 8–11). Conversely,
olstoy pleads the importance of the proper kind of criticism, modeled on Matthew Arnold's
new of the purpose of criticism to find among all that has been written that which is most
nportant and best and to direct attention to it—unlike the actual criticism of the time, which
:t itself the task of praising such works as have obtained notoriety, devising foggy philo-
ophic-aesthetic theories to justify them, or of ridiculing bad work or works of another camp
nore or less wittily, or of deducing the direction of the movement of our whole society from
rpes depicted by writers and, in general, expressing economic and political opinions under
ne guise of discussing literary productions ("Der Büttnerbauer," in *Tolstoy on Art*, pp.
32, 386–87).

107. *De anima* iii. 10. 433ᵃ9.

108. *Nicomachean Ethics* i. 13. 1102ᵇ28; iii. 12. 1119ᵇ11.

since it is the very nature of the virtues to be acquired from the repeated performan
of just and temperate acts.[109]

Art and the virtues are both related to knowledge, but in different and chara
teristic fashions. The arts, since they are external principles of change, a
productive (that is, poetic) powers which are rational or (which is the sam
thing) sciences which are productive; they are themselves intellectual virtues.[110]
The virtues, since they are habits of action, involve knowledge, but they a
distinct from prudence, which is the intellectual virtue concerned with action.[111]
The arts share with the sciences the peculiarity that they may deal with opp
site things and may have opposite effects, as medicine may produce eith
health or disease, while the virtue or habit which produces a certain result do
not also produce the contrary.[112] It is possible, therefore, to speak of a virtue
art; and, indeed, wisdom, the highest of the intellectual virtues, may be d
tected in the virtue or excellence of art, but there is no virtue of prudence;
art, moreover, voluntary error is preferable to involuntary, but in matters
prudence and the moral virtues the reverse is true.[113] An intellectual proce
which is not the same as opinion or any particular science is therefore involv
in the virtues: intelligence (σύνεσις) is either the use of *opinion* in *judgi*
(κρίνειν) of what is said about matters which fall under prudence or the u
of *science* in *learning* about matters proper to science, and consideration (γνώμ
is right judgment (κρίσις ὀρθή) of the equitable. Intelligence differs from pr
dence in that prudence determines what ought to be done or not to be don
that is, it commands, whereas the function of intelligence is limited to maki
judgments, that is, it is merely critical.[114] There are, in all, four faculti
which treat of ultimate and particular things: intuitive reason (νοῦς) perceiv
principles and the particulars which fall under them in the context of scienc
prudence (φρόνησις) is concerned with action in the context of the rig
principles; while intelliegence (ούνεσις) and consideration (γνώμη) are co
cerned with judgment (κρίσις) of contingent particulars.[115] In an importa

109. *Ibid.* ii. 4. 1105ᵃ26–1105ᵇ5.

110. *Ibid.* vi. 4. 1140ᵃ1–23; *Metaph.* ix. 2. 1046ᵃ36.

111. *Nic. Eth.* ii. 6. 1106ᵇ36 ff.; vi. 13. 1144ᵇ1–1145ᵃ2.

112. *Ibid.* v. 1. 1129ᵃ13; *Metaph.* ix. 2. 1046ᵃ36 and 5. 1048ᵃ8; *De interpretatione* 1
22ᵇ36.

113. *Nic. Eth.* vi. 5. 1140ᵇ21–25; 7. 1141ᵃ9–12.

114. *Ibid.* vi. 10–11. 1142ᵇ34–1143ᵃ17; esp. 1143ᵃ10, 14, 15, 20, 23, 30.

115. *Ibid.* 1143ᵃ25–1143ᵇ7. This differentiation is of the utmost importance, not only f
the discrimination of the sciences from one another, but for the separation of knowledge fro
virtue in Aristotle's philosophy and in the literal tradition in general. The modern rev
against what passed for Aristotelianism may be stated succinctly as the reduction of the
four processes or "habits" to judgment. When first principles are known by "judgment"
"common sense" or *bon sens*, and when that ability to judge the true and the false is attribut

ense, therefore, actions require *judgment*, while objects of art are *known*. Or, o state the conclusion paradoxically in the modern cognates of the terms Aristotle used: "criticism" is essential in ethics and politics, while art is unferstood and explained in its proper "science."

The arts and the sciences are therefore associated and distinguished from ctions and practical affairs in the manner in which they are subject to knowl-dge and criticism. We are in general good judges or critics of those matters vith which we are acquainted, of a particular subject if we are trained in that or universally if we have a general education. Therefore the scientist is a judge of any matter that falls under his science, but his judgment does not differ from ais scientific knowledge; and a well-educated man is a good judge of any matter pertinent to the scope of his interest, but his judgment is the application of the rts he has learned to the argument or the construction. In questions bearing on the moral virtues or political actions, however, the application of reason is ess direct, for it is not easy to determine such questions by reasoning or to tate the resolution in words, since judgment depends on the particular fact and s based on perception; this is the reason why the young are educated in the rts and the sciences but are improper auditors of lectures on politics.[116] On he other hand, judgment and criticism have a peculiar place in ethics, since the noral virtues are habits of choice, and choice involves judgments.[117] Pleasure attends both the operation of the contemplative faculty on intelligible, and that

n general to all mankind, the distinction between theoretic and practical, between moral riticism and artistic knowledge, disappears. The line that runs back from the modern *bon ens* to the Stoic tradition, which Gilson traces, is therefore mediated by the Aristotelian *ynesis* and *eusynesia;* and Gilson overemphasizes the exclusive importance of the one element vhen he says, "La traduction latine de *bon sens* n'est possible qu'au moyen du gallicisme *bona nens*" (René Descartes, *Discours de la méthode*, ed. É. Gilson [Paris, 1925], pp. 81–83). Cf. Thomas Aquinas, *In decem libros ethicorum Aristotelis ad Nicomachum expositio*, ed. A. M. Pirotta and M. S. Gillet (Turin, 1934), Lib. VI, lect. 9, par. 1240, p. 409: "Unde dicit quod prudentia est praeceptiva, inquantum scilicet est finis ipsius determinare quid oportet agere. Sed synesis est solum judicativa. Et pro eodem accipitur synesis et eusynesia, id est, bonus ensus, sicut et iidem dicuntur syneti et eusyneti, id est sensati et bene sensati, quorum est ene judicare." Cf., for *bonus sensus*, *Summa theologica* IIa, IIae, qu. 51, a. 4; *Commentary n the Sentences* Lib. III, dist. 33, qu. 3, a 1, qu. 2; for *synesis, Summa theologica* Ia, IIae, qu. 57, a.6. The instrumentalist consequences of this shift may be seen in the fact that "judg-nent" is by contraries, and is explicated by the analogy of the carpenter's rule, which is the test (κριτής) of the straight and the crooked (cf. *De anima* i. 5. 411ᵃ2–7).

116. *Nic. Eth.* i. 3. 1094ᵇ27–1095ᵃ2; ii. 9. 1109ᵇ20–23; iv. 5. 1126ᵇ2–4; *De part. anim.* . 1. 639ᵃ1–639ᵇ14. It should be noted that the general "criticism" is of method and has no earing on substantive truth or falsity. Cf. *Posterior Analytics* ii. 19. 99ᵇ35; and for the psycho-ogical bases of judgment in sensation cf. *De anima* ii. 11. 424ᵃ5–6; iii. 9. 432ᵃ15–16, 12. 434ᵇ3–4.

117. The good man judges well of good and noble things; cf. *Nic. Eth.* i. 9. 1109ᵃ22–24; ii. 4. 1113ᵃ29–31. It is difficult to judge pleasure impartially (cf. *ibid.* ii. 9. 1109ᵇ7–9). Judgment is the result of deliberation and is antecedent to choice (cf. *ibid.* iii. 3. 1113ᵃ2–14). Responsibility depends on the source of the power to judge (cf. *ibid.* 5. 1114ᵇ5–8).

of the critical faculty on sensible, objects,[118] and in practical matters judgmen of fact takes precedence over the opinions of the wise.[119] When one proceed from the sphere of ethics to that of politics, the function of criticism or judg ment increases, for the transition is by way of the virtue of justice, and lega justice is defined as the judgment of the just and the unjust.[120] Something of th Platonic distinction between ruling and judging appears in the political discus sion of judgment, for those who govern must command and judge, while thos who are governed must judge and distribute offices.[121] The citizen is therefor defined by his participation in the deliberative and judicial processes of th state.[122] Judgment applies not only to the decision of the law court,[123] and t the action of magistrates and assembly,[124] but also to the general determinatio of public interest and justice,[125] and is finally involved also in deliberation.[12] These considerations of the function of judgment or criticism in politics de termine its central place in rhetoric, since that art exists to affect judgments.[12]

To be a good judge in moral and political questions, then, one must have ha experience in the sense of having performed actions by which habits have bee formed, while one may be a good judge in most of the arts by means of knowl edge and a kind of science of how the thing is made. The teaching of the scienc of politics presents peculiar problems, because it is a *science* or *art* of *actions*, an the application of knowledge to actions is not direct. Aristotle elucidates th difficulty by the analogy of the arts. Unlike the other sciences and arts, politic is not taught by those who practice it, for politicians seem to rely more o experience than on abstract reason, while the Sophists profess to teach it but ar ignorant of the science and its subject, since they confuse it with rhetoric an imagine that constitutions can be framed by making collections of existing laws reputed to be good. The kind of teaching and learning that is possible i

118. *Ibid.* x. 4. 1174^{b}31–1175^{a}3.

119. *Ibid.* 8. 1179^{a}9–20.

120. *Ibid.* v. 6. 1134^{a}30–32; cf. also *ibid.* 9. 1136^{b}32 ff.

121. *Pol.* vii. 4. 1326^{b}12–20.

122. *Ibid.* iii. 1. 1275^{a}22–23; 1275^{b}11–21; 6. 1281^{b}31.

123. *Ibid.* v. 6. 1306^{a}36–38.

124. *Ibid.* iv. 15. 1298^{a}28–33, 1299^{a}25–28; ii. 8. 1273^{b}9–13.

125. *Ibid.* iii. 9. 1280^{a}14–16; vii. 9. 1328^{b}13–24.

126. *Ibid.* iii. 10. 1286^{a}21–35; this is particularly true in questions of equity (*ibid* 11. 1287^{b}14–18).

127. *Rhetoric* ii. 1. 1377^{b}21–29, 1378^{a}20–23, 18. 1391^{b}8–20. The kinds of listeners de termine the purposes of speeches and therefore the classification of kinds of oratory: th familiar distinction of contemplative from critical reappears among the kinds of hearers (cf *ibid.* i. 3. 1358^{a}2–4). Similarly, the commonplace concerning the prudent man is stated i terms of the credit to be given to his powers of judgment (cf. *ibid.* 7. 1164^{b}11–14).

subjects pertinent to political judgment and criticism is illustrated by music, which differs from the other arts in the knowledge and experience required for its understanding. Even selection among constitutions involves "intelligence" and the ability to "judge" correctly; and, as in music, those experienced in this art are alone able to judge rightly the works produced in it and understand how and by what means they are perfected and what harmonizes with what, while those inexperienced in the art must be content if they do not fail to discern, as they do in painting, that the work is well or badly made. The works of the art of politics are laws, and, though collections of laws may be useful to those who are able to "contemplate" and "judge" them, those who approach them without such trained habits cannot "judge" them correctly, except by chance, and it is only possible that their "intelligence" may be improved by the study of the laws.[128] Music differs from the other arts in that it alone imitates the passions and the virtues, for the objects of other senses than hearing can be signs but not imitations of virtues.[129] The one way to become a competent judge of music, since it is directly concerned with virtues and passions, is to become a performer, notwithstanding the contrary conviction of the Lacedaemonians that one could acquire the ability to judge or criticize music by only listening.[130] The other arts, particularly painting and poetry, are imitations, too, but of agents and actions, not of virtues and passions.[131] The object of art may therefore be treated in those arts as an entity in itself, an artificial object related both to the actions it represents and to the emotions it causes, but not itself a state of mind; in the strict sense, therefore, knowledge rather than criticism is pertinent to those arts, and the "poetic sciences" follow the analogy of the theoretic sciences, which are concerned with entities and actualities, more closely than they do that of the practical sciences, which are concerned with habits and institutions.

The investigation of the nature of tragedy in the *Poetics* proceeds through three stages. Aristotle first differentiates poetry from the other arts by three characteristics possessed by any imitation—its object, its means, and its manner—and uses these distinctions to account for the origin of poetry and its differentiation into kinds. The origin of poetry is traced to two natural causes: imitation is natural to man and it is also natural for man to delight in imitation.

128. *Nic. Eth.* x. 9. 1180^{b}28–1181^{b}12.

129. *Pol.* viii. 5. 1340^{a}12–1340^{b}19. Cf. Dewey's treatment of the emotional character of hearing as distinguished from sight (*Art as Experience*, pp. 237–38); Reynolds, on the other hand, maintains that music and architecture are not imitative arts because they apply directly to the imagination (*Discourses Delivered to the Students of the Royal Academy*, ed. with Introduction and notes by Roger Fry [New York, n.d.], "The Thirteenth Discourse," p. 365)

130. *Pol.* 1339^{a}42–1339^{b}4; 6. 1340^{b}20–39.

131. *Poet.* 2. 1448^{a}1 ff.; 6. 1449^{b}24–28; and esp. 1450^{a}15–38 and *passim*.

Both causes are discussed in terms of the process of learning, for man learns first by imitation and the pleasure he takes in art is due to the fact that he learns from it. "Learning," however, is one manifestation of "intelligence," distinct from "criticism" because it treats of particulars which fall under science rather than the particulars proper to prudence.[132] This investigation of the origin and history of poetry, therefore, supplies the distinguishing features of tragedy and comedy—among which one significant conclusion is that the person who "knows" (not "judges" or "criticizes") about tragedies, good and bad, knows also about epics, since their parts are the same[133]—and it lays the foundation for the treatment of tragedy as such. The isolation of tragedy is accomplished by comparing the various arts as imitations in their relations to the artist's use of means, manner, and object of imitation. Once isolated, tragedy may be considered as itself a kind of whole or object. The distinctions which had previously been made in terms of external agents and exemplars may be translated into traits discoverable in the poem, and the poem may be analyzed in terms of its unity and structure as part and whole (in which the plot, defined as the arrangement of incidents and as the imitation of action, is the principle or soul of tragedy) and in terms of the adaptation of means to ends (in which the plot is the most important part and the end of tragedy).[134] As a poetic science the results of such inquiry will serve equally for instruction of poets and amateurs, and they are stated, therefore, indifferently as what poets should do or what they have done. This second stage of analysis is knowledge or science as it is possible in and appropriate to the arts. It is supplemented, finally, by a consideration of tragedy in comparison with the closely related art of epic poetry, first, by analysis of both as parts and wholes, second, by analysis of them with respect to the means used to achieve their comparable ends and the success or failure of those means. Such comparative considerations yield "evaluation" or "censure" (ἐπιτίμημα), for in addition to the task which the poet faces in the construction of his play he faces "problems" which take the form of objections to "errors" (ἁμαρτία) he has committed. Since they are concerned with "errors," these problems are solved by inference from postulates or assumptions which the poet lays down concerning his art, such as would justify him in using as means to his end (which becomes at this third stage the proper pleasure caused by his work) devices that may be subject to some defect relative to a science or to morals but irrelevant to the considerations of his art. One of these assumptions is that the standard of rightness in poetry differs from that of politics and other arts, for two kinds of error are possible in poetry: failures

132. *Ibid.* 4. 1448ᵇ4–19; cf. above, p. 512.

133. *Poet.* 5. 1449ᵇ17–20.   134. *Ibid.* 6. 1450ª15–36.

of art when the poet intended to describe a thing correctly, and technical errors, proper to some other art or science, which might be justified for the purposes of the poetic art.[135] "Evaluation" or "censure" differs, therefore, from "judgment" or "criticism" as art and science differ from politics and morals: the former is the solution of a problem by demonstration that the end envisaged in the art is achieved by the means employed despite their possible deviation from other standards; the latter is the discrimination, by means of intelligence and in accordance with the command of prudence, of the contingent circumstances pertinent to actions determined by moral habits and political institutions.

The literal tradition treats of the objects of art or their production or appreciation as something apart from other objects, actions, or sciences. Three ways in which art may be isolated are suggested by Aristotle's cautious procedure and inquiry; and three kinds of treatment may be differentiated, each literal both in the sense that it is concerned only with art, or only with art of a given species or kind, and in the sense that it is sharply differentiated from other attempts to make criticism literal. It may be concerned with the work of art itself and attempt to make "scientific" generalizations or rules; it may be concerned with the work of art as illuminated by consideration of the poet's thought and attempt to make "critical," though poetic not moral, discriminations; it may be concerned with the work of art as effective of an end and attempt to make technical or artistic "evaluations." Poetic "science" differs from theoretic and practical sciences, for it is concerned neither with knowledge as such nor with action but with artificial objects and products; and if such objects are to be isolated for consideration in themselves, there must be some preliminary consideration of the conditions of their production and some supplementary consideration of the effects of their contemplation. "Criticism" is the consideration of the work of art primarily in its relation to the artist, and the problem of "making" may therefore be treated either in terms significative of thoughts and emotions (which had been reserved as the material of the practical sciences) in the discrimination and judgment of states of mind and their expression, or in terms significative of facts and knowledge (which had been used as the material of the theoretic sciences) for the resolution of problems involved in the circumstances of the poet or in the interpretation of his statements. "Evaluation" is the consideration of the work of art primarily in its relation to the audience, and the change of orientation from poet to audience involves a shift in the uses to which the basic terms are put, for the terms of thought and emotion, of imagination and fancy, are now used for the resolution of problems involved in the effectiveness of devices and the selection of con-

135. *Ibid.* 25. 1460[b]6–21; cf. above, n. 113. On the implications of "censure" and its kinds cf. I. Bywater, *Aristotle on the Art of Poetry* (2d ed.; Oxford, 1909), pp. 328 ff.

tent, while the terms of knowledge and fact are used for precepts to guide the combination of thought and expression and the adaptation of both to circumstances. Criticism and evaluation or censure may then be distinguished from poetic science as variant attempts to set forth the nature and achievements of the arts literally in terms of the objects produced by artists and appreciated by audiences, and all three may be distinguished from the treatment of art in the total context of nature, thought, and experience in which knowledge, criticism, and evaluation are achieved at once and by single analogies or reductions.

The devices of "criticism," like those of "poetic science," bear on the work of art itself, but they are limited to questions similar to those initial considerations of Aristotle's *Poetics* in which the work of art is treated in relation to the artist and the conditions of its production. Criticism may, therefore, consist either in appealing to the known artist or judge or critic of works to be judged or in reconstructing the sense of those works and judging their value by learned commentary. Longinus, in the first manner, undertakes to seek a knowledge (ἐπιστήμη) and critical appreciation (ἐπίκρισις) of the sublime, realizing that judgment (κρίσις) in literature is the result of ripe experience and hoping to express the critical appreciation he seeks in rules and precepts.[136] The basic terms of his discussion are "nature" and "art," but the nature he is concerned with is the natural genius of the artist which is perfected or curbed by art,[137] and his rules are stated for the most part in terms of the virtues or faults of artists, which may be discerned by the artist as critic, by the expert, or by all mankind. Natural genius is fundamental, and sublimity is the true ring of the noble mind,[138] but the achievements of great authors may be used as touchstones and for emulation.

Accordingly it would be well for us, too, when we labor at anything which requires sublimity of style and loftiness of thought, to formulate in our minds how Homer would perhaps have said the same thing, how Plato or Demosthenes or, in history, Thucydides would have expressed it with sublimity. For these illustrious personages, presenting themselves to us for emulation and being as it were preeminent, will elevate our souls in some manner to the standards which our souls conceive. It will however be much more efficacious if we present this also to our mind: how Homer, if he had been present, or Demosthenes would have listened to such or such thing which I say, or how they would have been affected by it. This is truly a great contest, to submit our own statements to such a tribunal and audience, and to make believe that we are submitting the censure [εὔθυνα] of our writings to such great heroes as judges [κριτής] and witnesses. It would be even more stimulating to add: How will all posterity after me hear these writings of mine?[139]

136. *On the Sublime* vi.

137. *Ibid.* ii. 1–3.

138. *Ibid.* ix. 1–2.

139. *Ibid.* xiv. 1–3.

Treatment of literature in terms of the "judgment" of great writers yields rules which constitute a kind of "science" as well as standards for "evaluation," for the prudential discriminations of judgment become the type of knowledge and the basis for the technical and experiential censures of evaluation. The truly sublime is so constituted in nature that it elevates our souls; moreover, any man of prudence and experience (ἔμφρων καὶ ἔμπειρος) will recognize it; and finally all doubt will be removed concerning both the beautiful and the sublime if all mankind agrees despite differences of circumstances in the judgment (κρίσις).[140] Criticism in this first sense bears on the high moments of any branch of literature—poetry, rhetoric, history, or philosophy—and the genius is envisaged as a man of insight and feeling; criticism in the second sense bears on the meanings of all kinds of writings in a literal sense, as well as on the recondite meanings that might be found in poetry and fables, and in both the author is envisaged only in terms of the knowledge or learning to which criticism is an aid. Bacon makes use both of criticism and of "interpretation," the former applicable to all books, the latter limited to a kind of poetry and to myths.

There remain two appendices touching the tradition of knowledge, the one Critical, the other Pedantical. For all knowledge is either delivered by teachers, or attained by men's proper endeavours: and therefore as the principal part of tradition of knowledge concerneth chiefly writing of books, so the relative part thereof concerneth reading of books. Whereunto appertain incidently these considerations. The first is concerning the true correction and edition of authors; wherein nevertheless rash diligence hath done great prejudice. For these critics have often presumed that that which they understand not is false set down: as the Priest that where he found it written of St. Paul, *Demissus*

---

140. *Ibid.* vii. 2–4. The presuppositions which underlie this transition from the judgment of the genius to that of posterity are well expressed by Ch. Labitte, *Études littéraires* (Paris, 1846), I, 181: "Pour moi, ce me semble, il n'est qu'une manière un peu précise de songer à la posterité quand on est homme de lettres, c'est de se reporter en idée aux anciens illustres, à ceux qu'on préfère, qu'on admire avec prédilection, et de se demander: 'Que diraient-ils de moi? à quel degré daigneraient-ils m'admettre? s'ils me connaissaient m'ouvriraient-ils leur cercle? me reconnaîtraient-ils comme un de leurs, comme le dernier des leurs, le plus humble?' Voilà ma vue rétrospective de postérité, et celle-là en vaut bien une autre." The same rhetorical criterion of insight and agreement may be applied to other subjects, as when the mark of philosophy is sought in the "common experience" of men as opposed to the "special experience" of the sciences. Gibbon's record of his reading of Longinus illustrates the operation of this mode of criticism. On September 14, 1762, he writes (*Gibbon's Journal to January 28th, 1763*, ed. D. M. Low [New York, 1929], p. 142): "As yet I read my author more as a man of Genius, than as a man of taste: I am pleased and astonished rather than instructed." On October 3 he writes (*ibid.*, pp. 155–56): "The 9th chapter, which treats of the first of these, (the elevation of the ideas,) is one of the finest monuments of Antiquity. Till now, I was acquainted only with two ways of criticizing a beautiful passage; The one, to shew, by an exact anatomy of it, the distinct beauties of it, and from whence they sprung; the other, an idle exclamation, or a general encomium, which leaves nothing behind it. Longinus has shewn me that there is a third. He tells me his own feelings upon reading it; and tells them with such energy, that he communicates them. I almost doubt which is most sublime, Homer's Battle of the Gods, or *Longinus's* apostrophe to *Terentianus* upon it."

est per sportam, [he was let down in a basket,] mended his book, and made it *Demissus est per portam*, [he was let out by the gate]; because *sporta* was an hard word, and out of his reading; and surely their errors, though they be not so palpable and ridiculous, are yet of the same kind. And therefore as it hath been wisely noted, the most corrected copies are commonly the least correct.

The second is concerning the exposition and explication of authors, which resteth in annotations and commentaries; wherein it is over usual to blanch the obscure places, and discourse upon the plain.

The third is concerning the times, which in many cases give great light to true interpretations.

The fourth is concerning some brief censure and judgment of the authors; that men thereby may make some election unto themselves what books to read.

The fifth is concerning the syntax and disposition of studies; that men may know in what order or pursuit to read.[141]

In the more restricted region of poetry, however, the one relevant deficiency which Bacon notes is in the philosophic interpretation of ancient parables which he illustrates by developing the legends of Pan, Perseus, and Dionysus into significances applicable, respectively, in natural, political, and moral speculation.[142] Criticism may be achieved, in general, by appeal to what is universal or best in men's minds, or to the reconstruction of what one man said, or to the interpretation of the allegory concealed in stories and histories; the censure that accompanies these criticisms is by standards determined by comparison with great geniuses, or with other books in the field, or with the principles of philosophers. Broadly conceived, criticism so practiced is concerned either with sublime and beautiful feelings and the means by which they are expressed

141. *Of the Proficience and Advancement of Learning*, Book II (*Works*, III, 413–14). Cf. *De augmentis scientiarum*, Book VI, chap. iv (*Works*, IV, 493–94), where Bacon emphasizes the place of judgment in the critical processes: "There belongs thirdly to the critical part (and from this indeed it derives its name) the insertion of some brief judgment concerning the authors edited, and comparison of them with other writers on the same subjects; that students may by such censure be both advised what books to read and better prepared when they come to read them. This last office is indeed, so to speak, the critic's chair; which has certainly in our age been ennobled by some great men,—men in my judgment above the stature of critics." Machiavelli made excellent use of both fable and history (cf. *ibid.*, Book VIII [*Works*, V, 56]; *Of the Proficience and Advancement of Learning*, Book II [*Works*, III, 345, 453]), yet the Stoic use of the allegorical interpretation of poets seemed to Bacon vain: "Nevertheless in many the like encounters, I do rather think that the fable was first, and the exposition devised, than that the moral was first, and thereupon the fable framed. For I find it was an ancient vanity in Chrysippus, that troubled himself with great contention to fasten the assertions of the Stoics upon the fictions of the poets. But yet that all the fables and fictions of the poets were but pleasure and not figure, I interpose no opinion. Surely of those poets which are now extant, even Homer himself, (notwithstanding he was made a kind of Scripture by the later schools of the Grecians,) yet I should without any difficulty pronounce that his fables had no such inwardness in his own meaning; but what they might have upon a more original tradition, is not easy to affirm; for he was not the inventor of many of them" (*ibid.*, III, 345).

142. *Ibid.*, pp. 318–35; cf. *On Principles and Origins According to the Fables of Cupid and Coelum* (*Works*, V, 461–500).

ɔr with the learned and critical interpretation of statements and the meanings
hey express.

The consideration of the work of art itself may be in terms of its effects
ather than in terms of its organization or its author, and then the processes of
"evaluation" will take precedence over those of "criticism" or "science." If
appeal is made directly to audiences, rather than to posterity or any other universal audience which will approve only of the greatest artists, audiences are
diversified and numerous; and if meanings are sought directly in words, rather
han in the comparison of works on the same subject, the effects to be achieved
ɔy words are relatively few. The basic terms of evaluation are words and
hings, style and content, and the subject of censure may be either the suitabil-
ty of the manner of statement to achieve effects on various audiences, or faults
and improprieties from bad combinations of diction, composition, and subject
n various styles. As the concern with the character of the poet and with his
reatment of subject matter suggested analogies to the first part of Aristotle's
analysis, so the concern with effects on an audience and with the relative effec-
iveness of various poetic genres may be viewed as a translation of the topics
reated in the third part of Aristotle's analysis to a place of central importance.
Horace's constant worry over the tastes of actual audiences yields emphases
ɔpposite to those which Longinus derives from his audience of heroes: popular
udgment is fickle;[143] the public is sometimes right, sometimes wrong, but its
ɔarticular error is to esteem the ancient poets and to censure other works, not
ɔecause they are coarse or inelegant in style, but because they are modern;[144]
he absence of a discerning critic of unmusical verses has an unfortunate effect
ɔn Roman poetry;[145] the recommendation to the poet, therefore, is to choose
ubjects suited to his own powers, and if Horace imitated Archilochus it was
n spirit and meter, not in words or in subjects, so that even the imitation was a
ιovel departure by which he was the first of the Romans to use those num-
ɔers:[146] the preferred critic is the good and prudent man who censures lifeless
ines.[147] Similarly, Horace's treatment of kinds of poetry yields the familiar

143. *Epistles* i. 19. 37; cf. also i. 1. 71–76, where he speaks of the public as a many-
ιeaded monster imposing its "judgments"; and *Satires* i. 10. 72–77, where he advises the poet
ιot to try to please the crowd but to be content with a few readers. The differentiation of
ιudiences and their preferences or faculties is never far removed from the moral considera-
ions from which this form of criticism takes its origin; cf. Reynolds, *op. cit.*, p. 354: "Such
ιen will always prefer imitation to that excellence which is addressed to another faculty that
hey do not possess; but these are not persons to whom a painter is to look, any more than
ι judge of morals and manners ought to refer controverted points upon those subjects to the
ɔpinions of people taken from the banks of the Ohio, or from New Holland."

144. *Ep.* ii. 1. 63–92.

145. *Ars poetica* 263–64; the term used is *iudex;* cf. *Sat.* i. 10. 38, where Horace thinks
ɔf his poems as competing before Tarpa as judge: *certantia iudice Tarpa.*

146. *Sat.* 38–40; *Ep.* i. 19. 21–34. 147. Cf. above, n. 47.

genres rather than the parts of learning which emerge from Bacon's treatment. The effect of literature on audiences, however, may also be sought in the differentiation of styles, for in the rhetorical tradition in which Aristotle undertook to classify kinds of rhetoric in terms of audiences Theophrastus studied the "virtues," not of authors or of audiences, but of styles, and Cicero, Quintilian, Dionysius, and Demetrius classified first three, then four, styles in terms of their respective qualities and faults. Unlike Bacon, who treated words as the form, the content of statements being the matter, Cicero thought of words and speech as the material from which verse and the styles of prose are formed, and the styles are fitted to our thought.[148] Demetrius' classification of the elevated, the elegant, the plain, and the forcible styles depends at once on organizing parts into wholes and at the same time on fitting words and compositions appropriately to thoughts, so that his analysis of style differs from Horace's as the respective ends which they both derive from audiences differ, while in the place of the kinds of poetic composition, as classified by Horace or by Bacon, Demetrius arrives at kinds of style because the parts and wholes defined by thought in his analysis are verbal: members, phrases, periods. Finally, unlike Longinus' analysis, which is fixed on the expressions of the loftiest genius, Demetrius' inquiry is concerned with ways of fitting words to a variety of thoughts and with the faults corresponding to each of the possible styles. Evaluation may be achieved, in general, by comparing the effects of what is written on actual or chosen audiences or by measuring it against the canons for statements of the "kind" to which it belongs; the judges are either men conceived by various standards to be good and prudent or men judged to be expert in rhetoric or some other appropriate science of expression. Broadly conceived, evaluation so practiced is concerned either with qualities of genres of literature and art or with the virtues of style and expression.

III

The words used in criticism are relative to their subject matter, but the subject matter changes with changes of philosophic principle. The vocabulary of criticism is therefore applied now to all things—natural or artificial—and again only to artificial things or even to the things made in one art; and so restricted it applies now to entities, now to states of mind, and again to activities or expressions. Moreover, the consequent ambiguity in critical terms is not readily removed by stating critical or philosophic principles—whether for purposes of elucidating relative meanings or laying down the law of the true meaning— since the critic sometimes employs philosophic principles for the interpretation of art, sometimes uses criticism to dictate the principles of both philosophy and

148. *De oratore* iii. 45. 177.

art, and sometimes operates as artist, justifying at most his suspicion of philosophic or critical principles; or, again, if he thinks of his function as in some sense scientific, he conceives his knowledge on the model sometimes of the theoretic sciences, sometimes of the moral or practical sciences, sometimes of the aesthetic or poetic sciences. Changes of subject matter and changes of principles or manner of use of principles are rarely indicated by the introduction of new terms, and, even when they are, coined words or words borrowed from other disciplines merely illustrate anew the fashion in which the meanings of words shift within a discipline or by passage from one discipline to another. The history of critical discussions could be written in terms of a small number of words, which with their cognates and synonyms have moved back and forth from obscurity to prominence in the aesthetic vocabulary, or from neighboring vocabularies to criticism, or from one significance to another in different modes of criticism. Yet such relativity does not mean that standards are impossible or insignificant in criticism. It means rather that significances must be sought in the sense and application which statements of critical doctrines have in their context and relative to their purpose. It means, secondly, that the evaluation of critical statements should consist in a determination of their adequacy to the end for which they were formulated and of the relevance of that end to the explication of art and objects of art. The differentiation of meanings according to the variety of systems and purposes is itself neither criticism nor philosophy but a device preliminary to both and a substitute for the easy acceptance or refutation of statements according to preferred meanings which the reader justifies because (whether or not they leave the writer who is being interpreted much sense or consistency) they are determined by the *real* nature of art, or the *actual* limits of criticism, or the *true* precepts of philosophy.

The shifts of meaning do not, of course, occur as gross phenomena discernible in an idle glance, describable by simple tags, or remediable by semantic precepts and prohibitions. A purely "analogical" or a wholly "literal" set of terms is as mythical as "climates of opinion" or "dialectics of history" or any of the sets of terms that have been used to give meaning to such devices of explanation and discrimination—like realism, nominalism, conceptualism, or dogmatism, skepticism, criticism, or idealism, materialism, naturalism, and so through the dreary list of tags by which significant explanations are reduced to props for one more explanation that will in turn be honored and dismissed with a technical name. In the mixed tradition of discussion, however, the two usages are distinguishable by two movements in the meanings of terms: the analogical, by a dialectical doubling in which a word takes on two differentiated meanings, one good and one bad, or by a dialectical reduction in which a word retains only the minimal and slightest of its dialectical meanings; the literal, by a shift of the terms from subject matter to subject matter with accompanying changes of meaning.

These two kinds of change are rendered possible, and in turn are obscured, by the fact—on which the peculiarities of refutation and inference depend— that any statement or theory of criticism may be read and interpreted by any method of criticism and according to the principles of any philosophy. In the long history of variant uses to which Aristotle's *Poetics* has been put, for example, it would not be difficult to illustrate the fashion in which statements have been interpreted and reinterpreted to assume almost any philosophic form and significance, and have in turn been criticized for failing to take into account some implication of every significance that has been attached to them. Thus, the term "imitation" undergoes a typical series of literal shifts of meaning from Aristotle's application of it to the work of art as an imitation of nature, to the Hellenistic and Renaissance application of it to the artist imitating artists,[149] to the modern application of it to the amateur imitating the work of art or the artist.[150] Yet none of these need be literal, since man's imitation of man may be taken as essentially the same as his imitation of objects or as the objects' imitation of models which are of a higher degree of reality than man or human arts: the term "imitation" undergoes a typical series of analogical doublings and reductions, which may in turn be given literal definitions, from Plato's use of it to

149. Cf. above, pp. 138–39. The doctrine that the arts, or at least some of them, are essentially imitative of external things is, of course, not limited to antiquity but has had advocates in all the later ages, including the modern; cf. T. B. Macaulay, "Moore's Life of Lord Byron" (*Miscellaneous Works of Lord Macaulay*, ed. Lady Trevelyan [New York, n.d.] I, 476): "Poetry is, as was said more than two thousand years ago, imitation. It is an art analogous in many respects to the art of painting, sculpture, and acting. . . . Thus the objects of the imitation of poetry are the whole external and the whole internal universe, the face of nature, the vicissitudes of fortune, man as he is in himself, man as he appears in society, all things which really exist, all things of which we can form an image in our minds by combining together parts of things which really exist. The domain of this imperial art is commensurate with the imaginative faculty." Cf. also I. Babbitt, *The New Laokoon* (New York, 1910), chap. i, "The Theory of Imitation," pp. 3–19.

150. Cf. Dewey, *Art as Experience*, p. 325: "We lay hold of the full import of a work of art only as we go through in our own vital processes the processes the artist went through in producing the work." In the doctrine of *Einfühlung* or empathy the relation is between spectator and object, but it is contemplative rather than practical, and it is individualized to each spectator; cf. V. Lee, *The Beautiful: An Introduction to Psychological Aesthetics* (Cambridge, 1913), chap. ii, "Contemplative Satisfaction," and pp. 74–75: "I am speaking once more of that phenomenon called *Inner Mimicry* which certain observers, themselves highly subject to it, have indeed considered as Empathy's explanation, rather than its result. In the light of all I have said about the latter, it becomes intelligible that when empathic imagination (itself varying from individual to individual) happens to be united to a high degree of (also individually very varying) muscular responsiveness, there may be set up reactions, actual or incipient, *e.g.* alterations of bodily attitude or muscular tension which (unless indeed they withdraw attention from the contemplated object to our own body) will necessarily add to the sum of activity emphatically attributed to the contemplated object."

apply to nature, science, and art (in which the imitation of art is condemned unless it is with knowledge of the true), to the application of it to art in two senses, one good and one bad,[151] to the use of it in a sense in which it is opposed to genius and the antithesis of art.[152]

151. Coleridge, *Biographia literaria*, chap. xviii (*Works*, III, 421): "This and the preceding arguments may be strengthened by the reflection, that the composition of a poem is among the imitative arts; and that imitation, as opposed to copying, consists either in the interfusion of the same throughout the radically different, or of the different throughout a base radically the same." Both terms may be given literal definitions, as in Bryant, *Lectures on Poetry*, Lecture IV, "On Originality and Imitation" (*Prose Writings*, I, 35): "I propose in this lecture to say a few words on the true use and value of imitation in poetry. I mean not what is technically called the imitation of nature, but the studying and copying of models of poetic composition. There is hardly any praise of which writers in the present age, particularly writers in verse, are more ambitious than that of originality. This ambition is a laudable one, for a captivating originality is everything in art. Whether it consists in presenting familiar things in a new and striking yet natural light, or in revealing secrets of emotion and thought which have lain undetected from the birth of literature, it is one of the most abundant and sure sources of poetic delight." Or, again, the two senses of imitation—good and bad—and the two kinds of imitation—of nature and of artists—may be combined dialectically in such fashion that each meaning is set off by the others, as in Reynolds, *Discourses*, where the initial distinction between genius or natural ability and the study of authentic models leads to insistence on the importance of teaching young students to draw correctly what they see ("The First Discourse," pp. 7–13) and is then developed into a distinction between mere copying or exact imitation and selective imitation of the masters ("The Second Discourse," pp. 24–30), and, finally, mere imitation of masters and of nature is contrasted to the contribution of imagination, poetical enthusiasm, the grandeur of ideas and an ideal beauty, superior to what is to be found in individual nature but discernible by diligent study of the works of our great predecessors and the works of nature; cf. "The Third Discourse," pp. 49–53: "The first endeavours of a young Painter, as I have remarked in a former discourse, must be employed in the attainment of mechanical dexterity, and confined to the mere imitation of the object before him. Those who have advanced beyond the rudiments, may, perhaps, find advantage in reflecting on the advice which I have likewise given them, when I recommended the diligent study of the works of our great predecessors; but I at the same time endeavour to guard them against an implicit submission to the authority of any one master, however excellent; or by a strict imitation of his manner, precluding themselves from the abundance and variety of Nature. I will now add, that Nature herself is not to be too closely copied. There are excellences in the art of Painting beyond what is commonly called the imitation of Nature; and these excellences I wish to point out. The Students who, having passed through the initiatory exercises, are more advanced in the Art, and who, sure of their hand, have leisure to exert their understanding, must now be told, that a mere copier of Nature can never produce anything great; can never raise and enlarge the conceptions, or warm the heart of the spectator. . . . Could we teach taste or genius by rules, they would be no longer taste and genius. But though there are neither are, nor can be, any precise invariable rules for the exercise or the acquisition of these great qualities, yet we may truly say, that they always operate in proportion to our attention in observing the works of Nature, to our skill in selecting, and to our care in digesting, methodising, and comparing our observations. There are many beauties in our Art that seem, at first, to lie without the reach of precept, and yet may easily be reduced to practical principles." Invention is the power of representing a mental picture on canvas, and the great end of the art, in turn, is to strike the imagination ("The Fourth Discourse," pp. 73, 74). But painting is intrinsically imitative, and therefore imitation "in its largest sense" must be contrasted to imitation in the sense of following other masters; even genius is the child of imitation, and we learn to invent by being conversant with the inventions of others, while even nature, which is the source of all excellences in art, may be known through the selections made by great minds of what is excellent in nature ("The Sixth Dis-

While the word "imitation" undergoes these changes, related terms g
through like or proportional alterations. When art is an imitation of nature
and tragedy an imitation of action, the analysis may be, as Aristotle's was, i
terms of parts of tragedies of which the plot, itself a combination (σύστασις
or a composition (σύνθεσις), is the most important. Plot is important in a
analysis of objects of art because it is a combination of things or incident
(σύστασις πραγμάτων),[153] and it may be viewed for analytic purposes as syr
thesis or composition (σύνθεσις) of things, while only diction is analyzed as
composition of words.[154] Moreover, since beauty requires size as well as orde
and arrangement, the beautiful object of art is comparable as a structur
(σύστημα) to beautiful organisms or animals.[155] Again, literature may b
viewed, as it was by Longinus, in terms of the constituents (σύστασις) whic
yield sublimity; and of the five constituents chosen, two are natural, bein

---

course," pp. 142–43, 145, 148, 152). If a more liberal style of imitation is distinguished fror
mere servile imitation of one master (*ibid.*, pp. 156–68), imitation is the one means by whic
an artist may perfect his art; cf. *ibid.*, p. 171: "Thus I have ventured to give my opinion «
what appears to me the true and only method by which an artist makes himself master «
his profession; which I hold ought to be one continued course of imitation, that is not to cea;
but with his life." The fact that art is an imitation of nature does not mean, however, that I
who imitates her with the greatest fidelity is the best artist, for nature is not constituted «
particularities ("The Seventh Discourse," pp. 193–94). The Platonic sources of this dialect
are apparent in the dependence of art as imitation on an eternal beauty; cf. "The Tenth Di
course," p. 270: "Imitation is the means, and not the end of art; it is employed by the sculpt«
as the language by which his ideas are presented to the mind of the spectator. Poetry ar
elocution of every sort make use of signs, but those signs are arbitrary and conventional. Th
sculptor employs the representation of the thing itself; but still as a means to a higher end-
as a gradual ascent always advancing towards faultless form and perfect beauty." Therefo
the art of seeing nature or, in other words, the art of using models is the point to which all a
studies are directed ("The Twelfth Discourse," p. 344). Yet, consistently with this doctrin
Reynolds could object to the treatment of painting as only an imitative art, attributing th
theory to Plato, and could differentiate the respects in which painting imitates nature fro
the respects in which it, and all the other arts, depart from nature for the purpose of inspiri
the imagination ("The Thirteenth Discourse," pp. 353–66).

152. Kant, *Critique of Judgement*, Part I, Div. I, §§ 46–47, pp. 188–90: "*Genius* is th
innate mental disposition (*ingenium*) *through which* Nature gives the rule to Art. . . . Ever
one is agreed that genius is entirely opposed to the *spirit of imitation*." Yet, even for Kar
imitation has its purposes and uses in separating genius from teaching, and to make that di
tinction Kant repeats Aristotle's separation of judgment and knowledge, but assigns jud
ment, not to moral questions, as Aristotle did, but to the determination of the beautiful; c
ibid., pp. 191–92: "If now it is a natural gift which must prescribe its rule to art (as beautif
art), of what kind is this rule? It cannot be reduced to a formula and serve as a precept, f«
then the judgment upon the beautiful would be determinable according to concepts; but th
rule must be abstracted from the fact, *i.e.* from the product, on which others may try the
own talent by using it as a model, not to be *copied* but to be *imitated*."

153. *Poet.* 6. 1450ᵃ15, 32, 1450ᵇ22; 14. 1453ᵇ2, 1454ᵃ14; 15. 1454ᵃ34.

154. *Ibid.* 6. 1450ᵃ5; cf. also 1449ᵇ35; 12. 1452ᵇ31, 1453ᵃ3, 19, 23. A riddle is a σύνθε«
τῶν ὀνομάτων (22. 1458ᵃ28).

155. *Ibid.* 7. 1450ᵇ36–1451ᵃ6. For the similar conditions of beauty in nature cf. *De pa*
anim. i. 5. 645ᵃ17–26 and 645ᵇ14–20, and *Metaph.* xiii. 3. 1078ᵃ31 ff.

concerned with thought and emotion, while three are the contribution of art, being concerned with words, and of these verbal constituents the last, composition (σύνθεσις), when it achieves dignity and elevation, embraces all the rest.[156] Composition becomes the mere arrangement of words,[157] and it may be analogized, when the concern is with grandeur, to the structure (σύστημα) of the animal organism.[158] Finally, the problems of literature may be conceived, as Demetrius conceived them, entirely in terms of composition (σύνθεσις), which becomes a verbal organization to be contrasted to the intellectual meaning and combination (δύναμις καὶ σύστασις) imposed by argumentation.[159] In addition to moving literally in this fashion from subject to subject, the concept of "composition" undergoes the dialectical doubling in which verbal composition is contrasted to a higher or freer or more natural composition of feelings or ideas, as well as a dialectical reduction in which it becomes an improper term for aesthetic discussion. According to Goethe, it is a "thoroughly contemptible word."

How can one say, Mozart has *composed* [*componirt*] Don Juan! Composition! As if it were a piece of cake or biscuit, which had been stirred together out of eggs, flour, and sugar! It is a spiritual creation, in which the details, as well as the whole, are pervaded by *one* spirit, and by the breath of *one* life; so that the producer did not make experiments, and patch together, and follow his own caprice, but was altogether in the power of the daemonic spirit of his genius, and acted according to his orders.[160]

The terms for imitation were applied to things before imitation became psychological or verbal, and the terms for composition have persisted in their verbal associations and connotations after they have ceased to be applied to thoughts in their relations to one another and to words and to things in their artificial combinations and organic structures. Between these two sets of terms, controlling them and controlled by them, an even larger set of psychological terms undergoes similar alterations.

Thought (διάνοια) may be conceived, as it was by Aristotle, as one of the proper parts of tragedy distinct from character and plot, but relative to the object of imitation, while diction is treated as the means of imitation.[161] Or

156. *On the Sublime* viii. 1.

157. *Ibid.* xxxix.

158. *Ibid.* xl.; cf. also xi.

159. *On Style* i. 30–31. For "synthesis" or composition in Demetrius, cf. *ibid.* 4, 8, 9, 11; ii. 38, 40, 43, 45, 48, 49, 58, 68, 74, 92, 117, 121; iii. 179, 180, 186, 189; iv. 204, 221, 237, 239; v. 241, 246, 248, 299, 301, 303.

160. *Conversations with Eckermann and Soret*, trans. J. Oxenford (London, 1913), Sunday, June 20, 1831, p. 556.

161. *Poet.* 6. 1450ª7–15, 1450ᵇ4–8.

thought and emotions may be contrasted as nature to words and expression as art, both thought and words being sources of the sublime, as Longinus held, since the ring of the sublime is due to thought (διάνοια) no less than to melody,[162] and the thought (νόησις) and diction of a statement may be mutually explanatory, beautiful words being the very light of thought.[163] Or thought (διάνοια) may be set forth in words, which, according to Demetrius, express in periods either whole thoughts or parts of whole thoughts.[164] In the analogical tradition thought may appear, not among the parts but among the criteria of art, as when Plato requires that the poet compose with knowledge of the truth, thereby satisfying both moral and theoretic criticism, since virtue is knowledge;[165] or thought may function neither as part nor criterion, practical or theoretic, and the region of art may be found in the interplay of understanding and imagination, as when Kant distinguishes judgment from both pure and practical reason;[166] or thought may be invoked in its practical guise, controlling or guiding the passions and emotions, as when modern critics, like Newman, Tolstoy, or D. H. Lawrence, argue that art is essentially moral.[167] When psychological functions are distinguished in aesthetic theory, reason is recon-

162. *On the Sublime* xxxix. 4.

163. *Ibid.* xxx. 1.

164. *On Style* i. 2–3; cf. 30–31; ii. 38, 115; iii. 187; iv. 236, 239. It is worthy of note that in actual discussion thought seems to be equated to subject matter (πρᾶγμα); cf. *ibid.* ii. 75–76, where poetry and painting are compared; iii. 132–36, 156–62; iv. 190; iv. 239; v. 240, 302, 304.

165. Cf. Sidney, who borrows from the Aristotelian terminology to argue that poetry is the architectonic science (*op. cit.*, pp. 11–12).

166. In Kant's division of philosophy into theoretical and practical, the phenomena of art fall in neither since the feeling of pleasure and pain is intermediate between the faculty of knowledge and the faculty of desire (*Critique of Judgement*, § i, pp. 7–8; § iii, pp. 14–17). Croce, dividing philosophy into theoretic and practical in terms of activities rather than faculties, finds art one of the two divisions of the *theoretic* and aesthetics a science of expression and general linguistics (*Estetica come scienza dell'espressione e linguistica generale* [6th ed.; Bari, 1928], chap. viii, pp. 68–69). Maritain, distinguishing in terms of virtues, finds art one of the two domains of the *practical* order (*Art et scolastique* [Paris, 1927], chap. iii, p. 8).

167. Newman, *op. cit.*, p. 21: "We do not hesitate to say, that poetry is ultimately founded on correct moral perception; that where there is no sound principle in exercise there will be no poetry; and that on the whole (originality being granted) in proportion to the standard of a writer's moral character will his compositions vary in poetical excellence." Tolstoy, *What Is Art?* p. 307: "So that were the question put: Would it be preferable for our Christian world to be deprived of *all* that is now esteemed to be art, and together with the false to lose *all* that is good in it? I think that every reasonable and moral man would again decide the question as Plato decided it for his *Republic*, and as all the early Church-Christian and Mohammedan teachers of mankind decided it, that is, would say, Rather let there be no art at all than continue the depraving art, or simulation of art, which now exists." D. H. Lawrence, *Studies in Classic American Literature* (New York, 1923), p. 254: "The essential function of art is moral. Not aesthetic, not decorative, not pastime and recreation. But moral. The essential function of art is moral."

ciled with or opposed to the passions[168] and imagination.[169] In the relations of reason, imagination, and the passions, again, the literal tradition sets up distinctions which are in turn the subject of fruitful comparison by use of the analogical method. In the literal tradition pleasure may be selected among the passions as the distinctive mark of beauty[170] or the end of poetry;[171] or a particular pleasure of pity and fear may be the mark of tragedy.[172] Or, in turn, the passions may be broadened analogically to embrace poetry, which may be defined as the spontaneous overflow of powerful feelings,[173] or the expression of any feelings[174] or of certain moral feelings;[175] or art may be

168. Hazlitt, *op. cit.*, p. 3: "Plato banished the poets from his Commonwealth, lest their descriptions of the natural man should spoil his mathematical man, who was to be without passions and affections, who was neither to laugh nor weep, to feel sorrow nor anger, to be cast down nor elated by any thing. This was a chimera, however, which never existed but in the brain of the inventor; and Homer's poetical world has outlived Plato's philosophical Republic." Cf. Plato *Rep.* x. 605A–607A.

169. Addison, *Spectator*, No. 421: "The Pleasures of the Imagination are not wholly confined to such particular Authors as are conversant in material Objects, but are often to be met with among the Polite Masters of Morality, Criticism, and other Speculations abstracted from Matter, who, tho' they do not directly treat of the visible Parts of Nature, often draw from them their Similitudes, Metaphors, and Allegories. By these Allusions a Truth in the Understanding is as it were reflected by the Imagination; we are able to see something like Colour and Shape in a Notion, and to discover a Scheme of Thoughts traced out upon Matter. And here the Mind receives a great deal of Satisfaction, and has two of its Faculties gratified at the same time, while the Fancy is busie in copying after the Understanding, and transcribing Ideas out of the Intellectual World into the Material." Cf. also Hobbes, *op. cit.*, 1. 8 (*Works*, III, 58): "In a good poem, whether it be *epic*, or *dramatic*; as also in *sonnets*, *epigrams*, and other pieces, both judgment and fancy are required: but the fancy must be more eminent; but ought not to displease by indiscretion." In Hobbes's table of the sciences, poetry figures as one of the sciences which treat of consequences from the qualities of men in special, since its subject is consequences from speech manifested in magnifying, villifying, etc. (*ibid.*, p. 73).

170. Hume, *A Treatise of Human Nature*, ed. L. A. Selby-Bigge (Oxford, 1896), Book II, Part I, sec. 8, p. 299: "Pleasure and pain, therefore, are not only necessary attendants of beauty and deformity, but constitute their very essence."

171. Dryden, "Defence of an *Essay of Dramatic Poesy*" (*Essays of John Dryden*, ed. W. P. Ker [Oxford, 1926], I, 113): "I am satisfied if it [verse] cause delight; for delight is the chief, if not the only, end of poesy: instruction can be admitted but in the second place, for poesy only instructs as it delights."

172. *Poet.* 14. 1453b8–14.

173. Wordsworth, *op. cit.*, pp. 82, 96.

174. Hazlitt, *op. cit.*, p. 2: "Fear is poetry, hope is poetry, love is poetry, hatred is poetry; contempt, jealousy, remorse, admiration, wonder, pity, despair, or madness, are all poetry." Or the circle may be rounded, and the passions may return to truth, beauty, and power by way of imagination and fancy; cf. Hunt, *op. cit.*, p. 377: "Poetry, strictly and artistically so called,—that is to say, considered not merely as poetic feeling, which is more or less shared by all the world, but as the operation of that feeling, such as we see it in the poet's book,—is the utterance of a passion for truth, beauty, and power, embodying and illustrating its conceptions by imagination and fancy, and modulating its language on the principle of variety in uniformity. Its means are whatever the universe contains; and its ends, pleasure and exultation."

175. Newman, *op. cit.*, p. 23: "According to the above theory, Revealed Religion should be especially poetical—and it is so in fact. . . . It may be added, that the virtues peculiarly Christian are especially poetical—meekness, gentleness, compassion, contentment, modesty,

concerned with emotions only if they are joined to materials,[176] or with pleasure only if joined to utility,[177] or, finally, the beautiful may be separated wholly from interest or pleasure.[178] Imagination, in turn, apart from its relation to or distinction from understanding and the passions may require causal differentiation into genius as a source and taste as a standard of beauty, or dialectical doubling into imagination and fancy.

Such shifts in the meanings of individual terms, of course, select different subject matters for the proper domain of criticism and are selected by principles which determine the interrelations and compendency of terms. But, in addition to their factual consequences and philosophic implications, terms and their meanings may be examined in their interplay in each of the modes of criticism in which they approximate systematic use in individual writers and particular traditions, and in the influence of modes of criticism on one another in the evolution and development of terms and meanings. If terms like "imitation," "imagination," and "communication" change their meanings as they move from context to context, it should be possible not only to trace the pattern of individual changes in such terms but also to sketch the analytic schemes which determine the various meanings and the stages of change.

The intermixture of analogical and literal elements in the discussion of art suggests a classification according to six modes as a means of ordering the many forms of aesthetic analysis that have been practiced and that still continue to contest the interpretation, criticism, and evaluation of art. The six modes are differentiated by the variables and constants that are appropriate to their sets of terms and by the means which are used to delimit or define them.

"Dialectical" criticism may be viewed as a single mode among these six, comprising a vast, sometimes amorphous, series of forms, which merge or move from one emphasis to another to take up in altering but appropriate terms the continuing opposition of dialectical criticism to each of the five remaining forms of "literal" criticism. It is a single mode, despite its diversity, since the full universality of subject matter and scope which it achieved in the

---

not to mention the devotional virtues; whereas the ruder and more ordinary feelings are the instruments of rhetoric more justly than of poetry—anger, indignation, emulation, martial spirit, and love of independence."

176. Dewey, *Art as Experience*, p. 69: "Yes, emotion must operate. But it works to effect continuity of movement, singleness of effect amid variety. It is selective of material and directive of its order and arrangement. But it is not *what* is expressed."

177. Plato *Rep.* x. 607D.

178. Kant, *Critique of Judgement*, Part I, Div. I, § 4, pp. 50–51: "In order to find anything good, I must always know what sort of thing the object ought to be, *i.e.* I must have a concept of it. But there is no need of this, to find a thing beautiful. . . . The satisfaction in the beautiful must depend on the reflection upon an object, leading to any conception (however indefinite); and it is thus distinguished from the pleasant which rests entirely upon sensation."

hands of Plato is possible in any of the forms which it has assumed since his time. Since it is a dialectical mode, however, that achievement must await, in each form, a great dialectician or poet, while in the hands of lesser critics the mode deteriorates to timid and common-sense apologies for what seems extravagant or sophistical in the moral judgment of art or to literal repetitions of those judgments in limited—and sometimes trivial, sometimes oppressive—applications. In any of its forms, the terms of dialectical criticism reflect the two moments or aspects of the method: the differentiation of terms in application to subjects and their reduction in the solution of problems. In the form which Plato employed, it is a dialectic of things; and his analysis of art and making in terms of imitation, therefore, requires the differentiation of object of imitation (which itself has a quality or value), the imitation (whose value depends on its correctness and the value of its object), and the execution of the imitation (which adds considerations of skill and medium to the previous two criteria). The reduction of these differentiations is achieved by Plato's distinction between being and becoming, knowledge and opinion, for the criterion of excellence is in each case—within art itself as in science, action, and being—found in the eternal pattern of ideas. When the dialectic shifts in the use of other writers to a dialectic of knowledge, it retains its scope in the dimension left free for the judgment of beauty or the practice of art within a rigid and literal distinction between theoretic and practical. This may be accomplished in either of two ways, depending on whether knowledge is conceived in terms of the human faculties or in terms of the branches of learning. Kant, in the first manner, differentiated the objects and laws of nature from those of freedom—thereby separating natural philosophy from moral philosophy, the metaphysics of nature from the metaphysics of ethics—and in the region between the theoretical and practical uses of reason he found the place of judgment and imagination in the free interplay of the human faculties, unlimited in the sense that they embrace art and nature, beauty, sublimity, and purpose. As a consequence, there is a doubling of both subject matters and problems, for the beautiful is distinguished from the sublime (which is certainly included in the concept of beauty developed in the *Symposium*), and the problems of appreciation are separated from those of production in the distinction of taste from genius (whereas the problems of the poet, the interpreter, and the amateur are inextricably involved in one another as treated in the *Ion*). Art is no longer imitation in this reduction to judgment; but the rules of the arts have become basic and unchanging, and the operation of taste might be made to yield the rules governing the individual objects proper to each of the arts, while the operation of genius might adumbrate the guiding rules of nature. Comte, in the second manner, divides all human activities into theoretic and practical, the latter being the application of the former by means of intermediary arts.[179] The result is again the doubling of subject matter and problems, for abstract laws are distinguished from concrete actions, and the objective method which leads to that distinction must be supplemented by a subjective method by which the supremacy of morals and sociology is established.[180] The logic of poetry is to be found midway between the logic of thought and the logic of feeling.[181] When the judgment of beauty is assigned to the free activity of imagination and taste, located midway between the pure and the practical reason, there is some danger that the rules regulating the beautiful in art will receive only such vague formulation as is customary in the delineation of taste or the designation of genius; when the operation of art is assigned to a logic of imagination, operating midway between a logic of thought and a logic of feelings, there is some danger that it will appear primarily in the guise, not of fine art, but of incidents pertinent to morals and sociology or explicable in psychology. The dialectic may undergo a third shift, however, to a dialectic of processes and relations, in which Plato's three basic differentiations appear in the altered form they assume in the realm of becoming: communication or expression takes the place of imitation (with sincerity in the artist taking the place of correctness in the

179. *Cours de philosophie positive*, ed. E. Littré (3d ed.; Paris, 1869), I, 50: "Tous les travaux humains sont, ou de spéculation, ou d'action. Ainsi, la division la plus générale de nos connaissances réelles consiste à les distinguer en théoriques et pratiques." *Ibid.*, p. 55: "On concevra d'autant mieux la difficulté de construire ces doctrines intermédiaires que je viens d'indiquer, si l'on considère que chaque art dépend non-seulement d'une certain science correspondante, mais à la fois de plusieurs, tellement que les arts les plus importants empruntent des secours directs à presque toutes les diverses sciences principales. C'est ainsi que la véritable théorie de l'agriculture, pour me borner au cas le plus essentiel, exige une intime combinaison de connaissances physiologiques, chimiques, physiques et même astronomiques et mathématiques: il en est de même des beaux-arts. On aperçoit aisément, d'après cette considération, pourquoi ces théories n'ont pu encore être formée, puisqu'elles supposent le développement préalable de toutes les différentes sciences fondamentales. Il en résulte également un nouveau motif de ne pas comprendre un tel ordre d'idées dans un cours de philosophie positive, puisque, loin de pouvoir contribuer à la formation systématique de cette philosophie, les théories générales propres aux différents arts principaux doivent, au contraire, comme nous le voyons, être vraisemblablement plus tard une des conséquences les plus utiles de sa construction."

180. *Système de politique positive* (Paris, 1851), I, 433–35 and 447–49; IV, 171–84, esp. 171: "Les lois abstraites constituent donc le domaine commun de la science et de l'art, qui les destinent respectivement à discipliner notre intelligence et régler notre activité."

181. *Ibid.*, I, 451–52; "Quelle que doive être l'aptitude naturelle du nouveau régime envers la logique rationelle, principalement destinée aux philosophes, il est donc encore plus indispensable pour construire et développer la logique morale, essentiellement propre aux femmes et aux prolétaires. Entre ces deux voies extrêmes, la logique des vrais poètes, qui procède surtout par images, vient placer un lien général qui complète la constitution, à la fois spontanée et systématique, de la méthode humaine. Jusqu'ici l'image ne fut guère employée que pour perfectionner la manifestation, soit du sentiment, soit de la pensée. Désormais elle secondera surtout leur élaboration respective, d'après leur réaction mutuelle, dont elle constitue l'agent naturel. Tantôt l'image, rappelée sous le signe, fortifiera la pensée par le réveil du sentiment; tantôt, au contraire, l'effusion suscitera l'image pour éclaircir la notion."

imitation as a criterion), the emotions subsume the relevant problems of execution (for emotion is selective of material or of the ordering of material), and content is determined, not by the nature of the objects imitated, but by the interests of audiences or the interest of artists (for it is justified by its importance to the one or its pertinence to the intention of the other) or its appropriateness to the medium of expression.[182] Three problems emerge, where Plato treats the one problem of imitation and Kant the two problems of the production and the appreciation of beauty, for the reduction now operates on the artist (who is conditioned by experience or by his times and circumstances), and the art object (which cannot be considered in isolation), and the audience (which should reproduce in itself the operations of the artist and the structure of the art object) either by means of such inclusive and universal concepts as "experience" or the "brotherhood of man," which reconcile oppositions, or by means of the universalism of symbols which communicate emotions by expressing them and relate objects by signifying them. The resolution remains that appropriate to a dialectic of process and becoming; and, although some philosophers who take their subject matter from events and relations have, like Whitehead, returned to a Platonic dialectic of eternal objects, no modern semanticist has yet recognized his heritage by enunciating the logos-doctrine that haunts his study.

The terminologies of the five literal modes of criticism bear a double relation to the terminologies of the various forms of the dialectical mode: the terms employed in any form of the dialectical mode are usually also subjected to a literal treatment, intended to define them in the respects to which they were vague and to relate them to clearly distinguished matters, and those literal distinctions are usually analogized, at the next stage of discussion, in a dialectical treatment designed either to broaden them in more sensitive application or more reasonable definition or to show that they correspond to nothing real or essential in art. Since these attempts at literal definition are concerned to establish sharp boundaries, there results from them, not a single variegated mode of criticism, but a series of literal modes more or less sharply and successfully separated from one another and from the dialectical mode.

The mode of criticism which balances Plato's form of dialectical criticism, Aristotle's "scientific" criticism, may therefore be taken as the second mode, instituted in terms closely related to those of Plato's dialectic. In spite of the similarity of terms, however, the "scientific" method of the *Poetics* is distinct from the dialectical criticism of Plato; and much as dialectic, which is the method of science and philosophy for Plato, became a second-best

---

182. For Tolstoy's use of these distinctions cf. above, pp. 208 and 214; for Dewey's use cf. *Art as Experience*, pp. 69, 18, and *passim*.

method, based on opinions rather than on knowledge of things, for Aristotle, so, too, the treatment of imitation—in terms of object of imitation, the imitation itself, and its execution, which was easily translated in the dialectical tradition to audience, art object, and artist—formed the structure of Aristotle's rhetoric rather than of his poetics. He made use of a scientific method, rather than dialectic or rhetoric, to place his analysis of tragedy, considered as an object, in the context of his philosophic inquiries, for the first five chapters of the *Poetics* treat of phases of the operation of the artist in terms of object, means, and manner of imitation prior to analyzing tragedy in terms of construction and parts, while the last four chapters compare tragedy to a related art form and formulate replies to censures which ignore the ends governing the construction of tragedy. The scientific analysis which is framed between these preliminary and supplementary treatments of tragedy in terms of its efficient causes and its end brings the formulation of the circumstances and purposes of tragedy to bear on the analysis of tragedy as a whole consisting of six parts—plot, character, and thought arising from the object, diction and melody arising from the means, and spectacle from the manner of imitation—by finding a prime importance in plot and by treating plot at once as a combination of incidents, or, more literally, of things, and as the organizing principle of the tragedy. A criterion of unity and structure is thereby rendered available, and on it the possibility of a poetic science depends, for otherwise the analysis of an object of art must reduce the diversity of concepts that might be included under Aristotle's six terms to two broad analytic elements—form and matter—and must go for its criteria directly to the intention of the artist, or the reaction of the audience, or the technical achievement of the structure.

Such a criterion of unity disappears when the terminology of criticism is taken, not from things (the tragedy as an artificial thing and the incidents or "things" that compose its action) but from thoughts and aspirations, conceived either as universal, shared by all mankind but given particular expression by the poet, or as peculiar to the poet, and in need of explanation by his life and circumstances to make them intelligible to other men. Following the former principle, Poe could argue plausibly that "the phrase, 'a long poem,' is simply a flat contradiction in terms," for the poetic principle is the human aspiration for supernal beauty and the elevating excitement it occasions cannot be of long duration;[183] following the latter principle, T.S. Eliot could be moved to maintain that it is impossible to understand Shakespeare from any one of his plays, since the relation between the plays taken in order must be studied for years before any slight interpretation may be ventured,[184] and that Shakespeare indeed sup-

183. Poe, *op. cit.*, pp. 3 ff.
184. Eliot, "Dante," *Selected Essays, 1917–1932* (New York, 1932), p. 207.

plies in this personal and individual way a unity, not merely to his work, but to his times.[185] The two modes of criticism which employ these two principles approximate the equivalent forms of "dialectical" criticism more closely than other modes of literal criticism do, for the mind assumes a synoptic universality embracing things known and actions contemplated whether they are included analogically within its nature or separated literally from its proper activity.

The third mode of criticism, "poetic" criticism, proceeds from the poet, or more broadly the author, conceived as universal in the sense of being possessed of lofty thoughts and inspired by vehement emotions intelligible or moving to all mankind, to the particular language of the author's expression. The "objects of imitation" have been translated into the ideas and feelings which are the matter or content of the author's statement, and his "composition" is examined in a part-whole analysis into "periods" and "figures." This mode of criticism is properly called "poetic" both in the sense that it proceeds from the conceptions and expressions of great authors and uses them as touchstones for other statements, and in the sense that the critic's own expression must arouse reactions like those caused by the poet if the criticism is to be effective as a guide. It differs (as practiced, for example, by Longinus) from the equivalent form of dialectical criticism (as developed, for example, by Kant) in that it is concerned not with the conditions of the judgment of beauty and sublimity in general, but exclusively with their sources in literature.

The fourth mode of criticism, "scholarly" criticism, reverses this procedure and attempts to reconstruct the peculiar character and significance of an author from the corpus and development of his work. It was in this mode that the *ars critica* developed to such massive importance in the seventeenth and eighteenth centuries,[186] laying the foundations of the higher biblical criticism, furnishing the example of classical, and later modern, philology, and in the process revolutionizing historical method. It is based on the truth, converse to the basic truth of "poetic" criticism that poets are universal—and quite as obvious as it—that poets are particular, that their words, their references, and their intentions must be understood, if their statements and inventions are to be appreciated; that their various works have relations to one another and to the works of other authors, as well as individual marks of unity and particular high points of

185. Eliot, "Shakespeare and the Stoicism of Seneca," *ibid.*, p. 119: "It has been said that Shakespeare lacks unity; it might, I think, be said equally well that it is Shakespeare chiefly that *is* the unity, that unifies so far as they could be unified all the tendencies of a time that certainly lacked unity."

186. For an excellent review of "critical" literature as it bears on theological and historical problems in the seventeenth century see S. von Dunin Borkowski, *Spinoza*, IV: *Aus den Tagen Spinozas* (Münster i.W., 1936), 136–308 and 523–50.

excitement; that even when most original they seldom originate, but what is novel in their accomplishment may be understood by knowing what they, in turn, experienced and esteemed; and that the patterns of their lives and works are more easily perceived when the elements of which their works are composed are known independently. It differs (as practiced, say, by F. A. Wolf or Dover Wilson) from the equivalent form of dialectical criticism (as practiced, say, by Fechner) in that it is concerned, not with the formulation of scientific aesthetic principles, derived from the natural or biological sciences, to be applied in criticism to specific objects, natural or artificial, but with the use of the devices of the historical sciences to explain the significances of objects of art. The principles of scholarly criticism are the same as those of poetic criticism— expression and thought or emotion; form and content—but, whereas the poetic critic goes to other great authors to test the universal achievement of a given expression, the scholarly critic goes to other sources of information and other statements to elucidate the particular meaning of a given statement. Whereas the poetic critic proceeds from the elevation of soul caused by a statement to the examination of the manner of expression, the scholarly critic proceeds from the recovery of the author's meaning to the discovery of its effectiveness and value. As one consequence of this difference the poetic critic is concerned only with mall bits which constitute the high achievement of the author, whereas the scholarly critic tends to treat the whole body and context of his work. The poetic critic will proceed from the consideration of principles like the "good sense," "fancy," and "imagination" analyzed by Coleridge to abstract by practical criticism the marks characteristic of original poetic genius.

In the application of these principles to purposes of practical criticism, as employed in the appraisement of works more or less imperfect, I have endeavored to discover what the qualities in a poem are, which may be deemed promises and specific symptoms of poetic power, as distinguished from general talent determined to poetic composition by accidental motives, by an act of the will, rather than by the inspiration of a genial and productive nature.[187]

The scholarly critic will examine all the data bearing on the establishment of the text and its interpretation before venturing an evaluation of the quality of any part of it or the sense or imagination of its author.

Such considerations of genius and the author's circumstances disappear, in turn, when the terminology of criticism is taken, not from thoughts and feel-

187. *Biographia literaria*, chap. xv (*Works*, III, 375). The characteristics of genius are found in language and thought: (1) in the sweetness of the versification and its adaptation to the subject, (2) in the choice of subjects remote from the private interests and circumstances of the writer, (3) in images modified by a predominant passion or by associated thoughts or images awakened by that passion, (4) in depth and energy of thought. It is in virtue of the last characteristic that Coleridge argues that "no man was ever yet a great poet, without being at the same time a profound philosopher" (p. 381).

ings, whether in their universality or particularity, but from consideration of the effects of their expression. Such a causal analysis may be conducted either by studying the relation of the work to the audience to determine the *effects* that are produced or ought to be produced, or by studying the relation of the content to the style to determine the *means* that are effective or ought to be effective.

The fifth mode of criticism, "technical" criticism, which is developed in "arts" of poetry, constructs its precepts about what pleases or instructs audiences in terms relevant to thought and expression in a manner similar to poetic criticism. Yet the terminology which these two modes largely share is put to different applications and assumes different significances. The concern of poetic criticism is with the sublime and elevated moments achieved by literature; the concern of technical criticism, as practiced by Horace, Vida, or Boileau, is with any device which achieves a pleasant or a profitable effect. Therefore, the criterion for thought and expression is not the loftiness of thought, of expression, or of both together, but the decorum which relates them to each other and to the audience; its application is not limited to isolated moments, since it may apply significantly to the structure and unity of a work; and its incidence falls less upon content than upon devices and style.

The sixth mode of criticism, "formal" criticism, reverses the procedure of technical criticism, beginning with the work and the effort to express rather than with the audience and the effect of the expression. Its terminology, like that of technical criticism, bears a close relation to the terms used in poetic criticism, but the analysis is not limited to elevated thought but runs through a variety of contents and yields, not a single analysis, but a classification of styles (as in the case of Demetrius) or of uses of language (as in the case of I. A. Richards and some of his various rival semanticists). The concern of formal criticism is with the analysis of compositions or communications into their constitutive parts to evaluate the effectiveness or appropriateness of devices to purposes: figures of speech relative to subject matters and effects in the older analysis, strategies and devices of evocation relative to objectives and attitudes in the newer; it proceeds by a part-whole analysis from words or phrases to the composition as a whole; and the controlling consideration is the characteristic or thought which determines the devices suited to it. Consequently, the consideration of audiences and circumstances in technical criticism yields canons and censures for composition, whereas the consideration of the devices of language in formal criticism, since it takes language (according to the phrase of Demetrius) as a lump of wax from which anything may be molded, yields differentiations in effects to be achieved.

The principles employed by these various modes of criticism and the subject matters to which they are relevant are in the case of most of them so distinct from those of the others that statements constructed of the same words often turn out on examination of their meanings to be unrelated when apparently contradictory or equivalent when apparently opposed. It is important to recognize these variations of meanings, however, not because terms are necessarily inexact and criteria vague in criticism, but rather because the varieties of meanings are determined by the purposes and methods of the modes. Even the most impressionistic and subjective critic writes with the conviction that the expression at least of a personal or skeptical opinion is intelligible and to that minimum extent effective as communication; and in varying manners and degrees the critic works on the assumption that the appreciation, judgment, and evaluation of art follow laws which may be stated in terms of the matter or the form of objects of art, or the imagination, feelings, or reason of man, or his experience, his conditions actual or projected, or his manner of expression. It is therefore true (if the statement be interpreted in the dialectical mode of criticism) that the philosopher, the critic, the artist, and the amateur express the same thing, when each is sensitive and successful, the philosopher by choosing, through his principles, pertinent and analyzable characteristics, the critic by treating such characteristics in the objects he judges, the artist by embodying them in his appropriate medium, and the amateur by reacting to them in his experience of the object of art. What the critic directs attention to is the result of the labor of the artist and an ingredient in the experience of the intelligent amateur, even though neither would have made the explicit statement of the critic, and it should find a place and explanation in the system even of philosophies antagonistic to the critical presuppositions on which it depends. There are three dimensions of variability in the discussion of art. The artist at work with the natural materials which constitute his media and with the ideas and emotions which he seeks to express has a latitude of choice in the construction of his work and the effecting of his purposes, for the media may be used in a variety of ways and the responses may be secured by new and old devices: among the influences which might bear on the solution of his problem are the devices of other artists, the statements of critics, and the assumptions of philosophers. The critic contemplating the finished work of art finds in it as great a latitude for his interpretations as the artist found in the artistic materials for his manipulations: the example of other artists, the refutation or application of what other critics or scientists have said, and the substantiation of a philosophy may be among the influences which determine his choice. A changed conception of the imagination, or the rise of the proletariat, or the unbelief of the upper classes may lead to the institution of new critical systems and applications even in a single mode of criticism; and yet the three modern forms of dialectical criticism which have resulted from such changes apply to emirical data which overlap little or not at all: the Humanist critics to cultural, he Marxist to economic, and the Tolstoyan to moral and religious data. The philosopher, finally, takes the phenomena of art, the judgments of criticism, and the formulations of other philosophies among his subject matters, resolving their oppositions and contradictions within the scope of his own principles, and his resolutions become in turn one of the matters which the next philosopher may be concerned to explain. Even though principles do not achieve finality and universal adherence in philosophy, they do serve to state the purposes of the artist and the criteria of the critic. The shifts of artistic styles, critical evaluations, and philosophic principles illustrate the importance of standards and principles, and the alternations of advocacy of a set of principles and attack upon them do not constitute evidence for those who think to avoid the discussion of principles as stultifying in art, futile in criticism, and fantastic in philosophy. For even the technical questions of art and criticism—questions of materials and production, taste and judgment, intention and interests—have philosophic bases which serve to clarify the solutions to those problems and their relations to other proposed solutions.

The purposes and relative effectiveness of the various forms of dialectical criticism may be stated and judged in the terms used in the development of those forms of criticism, for the dialectical process employed in the discussion of art also determines the transition from one form of the dialectic to another and the issues which emerge in the oppositions of forms. The terms of that continued dialectic—largely the same and different primarily by the addition of technical terms to attach new significances to the continuing terms—are determined in their use and the differentiation of their significances by the things to which they are applied in the reductive scheme of each form of the dialectic. When the reduction is to things, as in the criticism of Plato, the characteristics of art are found in objects: the object of imitation, the object of art itself, and its objective characteristics or style. When the reduction is to faculties of the mind or to thoughts, as in Kant's analytic and dialectic, the characteristics of art are found in the taste by which it is judged and the genius by which it is produced: the objects of art and their relations to nature may be envisaged from rules derived from taste and genius. When the reduction is to processes and events, as it is in Tolstoy's or Dewey's operational inquiries, the characteristics of art are found in the act of expression: the emotions of the artist, the sophistication of the audience's reaction, and even the object of art may be differentiated as moments in the "union of moral community" or the identity of process and product. There is no reason why the complete dialectical development should not be possible in any of these reductive schemes. The peculiar virtue of dialectical criticism, however, is **not** in the isolation of art from other phenomena or of the aesthetic aspects in art as peculiar phenomena, but rather in the return of both to a broader context in which each object is considered in terms of the good, the true, and the beautiful, or as subject to the operation of pure reason, practical reason, or judgment, or as incident to the living processes of experience.

There are, however, three dangers which the analysis of art encounters in the dialectical mode of criticism which arise from the successive domination of one of the dialectical triad: the good, the beautiful, and the true. The moral implications of Plato's criticism have attracted more attention in the later discussions of art than the role which beauty plays in his conception of the nature of things or in the motivations of human actions; and, although under his influence art takes on a metaphysical significance in the philosophy of Plotinus, the meanings of Platonism have been exploited chiefly by moral critics from the Christian Church Fathers to Tolstoy. Kant, on the other hand, supplied analytical and dialectical devices to isolate beauty and the sublime from the subject matters of science and morality, but he did not himself state the rules which determine the objects of art as fully as he explored those involved in the activities of the pure and practical reason; and his heritage has been exploited less by critics who treat the phenomena of art than by idealists who, like Schelling, make aesthetics the center of philosophy and who do not consider art as a particular phenomenon but, on the contrary, construe the universe itself in the form of art and philosophy as the science of the universe in the potency of art. Dewey, in turn, has found in concepts like "inquiry," "instruments," and "experience," the dialectical device by which to reduce and confute all the distinctions made by idealists and by other philosophers: beauty and utility, art and science, practice and theory, morals and science, mechanical arts and fine arts, experience and nature, inquiry and knowledge—these and all like separations introduce distinctions which are unreal and problems which are false according to the principles of his philosophy; but the therapeutic effect of Dewey's dialectic depends rather on the abundance of mistaken distinctions which he can reduce to experience, thereby giving the concept a kind of refutative richness, than on specific or positive characteristics isolated in art or on methods evolved for the elucidation of art. As in the analyses of Plato and Augustine, the treatment of art recommended by Dewey is in the context of a synoptic analysis, and the direction of his thought is most nearly analogous to the hope repeatedly expressed by writers on aesthetics that at last, if their respective suggestions are followed, the inquiry will become scientific and the object of art or the appreciation of art will become an instance of physiological, psychological, sociological, ethnological, economic, or psychopathic phenomena, to be explained, used, and, when the circumstances warrant and the techniques are adequate, even cured as such.

The five modes of literal criticism, on the other hand, treat art as art, in some sense, by techniques and according to criteria distinct from those of other disciplines and sciences. The sharpness of this difference, however, does not preclude the possibility that dialectical criticism, sensitively and intelligently employed, may lead to the same conclusions in application to a particular set of problems as those justified by the use of a mode of literal criticism, for the intermingled universal principles of dialectic may, of course, be brought to bear on particular instances, and the specific principles of a literally aesthetic analysis may be supplemented by the application to the same object or event of principles proper to politics, ethics, psychology, or physics. The hope of universality in philosophy, indeed, depends on the possibility of such equivalences among the results of intellectual labor painstakingly and accurately carried forward in different perspectives, and the dangers of error indicated by disagreements arise from the misapplications, the miscarriages, and the mistaken interpretations of any given method rather than from the oppositions of methods. The dangers in the dialectical method are to be found in the loss of balance consequent on a dogmatic freezing of the dialectic in defense of an unexamined faith, for as a result the consideration of art or of any other subject may be submerged in other concerns or become itself the ruling principle of other considerations. The dangers in literal criticism arise from pedantic concentration on a trait proper to a form of literal criticism and the treatment of it subtly and in detail in isolation from the causes from which it originated, the effects which it might explain, and the phenomena with which it is related. The five modes of literal criticism which have been enumerated are related to one another in their common concern with the object or phenomenon of art as such. They differ from one another in the qualities selected as essential to art and the methods proper to the analysis of art. They may therefore be in opposition to one another; they may supplement one another; and any one of them may be the subject of such exclusive devotion—as program of research or manifesto of art—as to make it the peculiar interest of a school rather than a technique for inquiry or elucidation. Any one of them, finally, may suggest the terminology and the distinctions for a recrudescence of dialectical criticism devoted to the attempt either to give generality and therefore vitality to the distinctions used in a restricted fashion in literal criticism or to reduce and therefore rectify its separations.

The respective purposes and subject matters of the five modes of literal criticism may be isolated by consideration of the use they make of the causal analysis—the causes which contribute to the construction of the work and the effects which may be traced back to the work—and of the analysis of form and content or whole and part. In "scientific" criticism, as practiced by Aristotle, the causes and effects—the peculiarities of poets, their media, and their subjects, the proper pleasures of art forms, their peculiar structures, and probable criticisms—are translated into terms which may be identified in the work of art itself, and therefore the probability and necessity by which incidents are knit together in the unity of the plot may be distinguished from the natural probability which is imitated in the manner appropriate to the medium; character and thought in tragedy may be subordinated to the needs and end of plot; and diction may be treated as the matter whose potentialities are exploited in the construction of forms. In "poetic" criticism, as practiced by Longinus, natural causes are not translated into artistic causes, but nature and art alike contribute to the production of the sublime, for the causal analysis is analogical, the prime element in all natural production and therefore in literary effectiveness is the exemplar, and the function of scientific method is to control the effects of natural genius, not to explain the product of art.[188] The sublime, therefore, is contrasted as an overwhelming excellence and distinction of language to the arrangement and economy of things,[189] and the ideas and content become the "matter" organized in the organic whole of the composition of a great genius.[190] Thought, metamorphosed from the function it has for Aristotle as expressive of character and subservient to plot, has become the thought of the author and matter for his composition, and the effect of the sublime is not dependent primarily on the form and arrangements of facts or things. In "technical" criticism, as practiced by Horace, the diversification of effects considered is derived from the character of audiences, and therefore his analysis, like that of Longinus, depends on the nature of the poet and proceeds by considering content and expression, but the exemplar is found in the life and custom to be portrayed rather than in the performance of genius, and words no longer achieve effects independent of the persuasiveness of matter but follow the matter that is given. Horace's analysis, like that of Aristotle, embraces larger units than the analysis of Longinus and supplies even a criterion of unity; but, where Aristotle thought the complex plot preferable, Horace's methods incline him to simplicity. All three modes of criticism treat of causes to account for literary forms: the scientific mode treats the formal cause of objects of art by

188. *On the Sublime* ii. 1–3.

189. *Ibid.* i. 3–4. Where the plot had been a combination of "things" for Aristotle, the composition becomes for Longinus the means of adumbrating slowly the arrangement and economy of things (τάξις καὶ οἰκονομία τῶν πραγμάτων). Cf. the treatment of arrangements of thought and words in the consideration of the figure Inversion (*ibid.* xxii. 1–2).

190. *Ibid.* x. 1; xiii. 4.

analyzing their structure; the poetic mode finds form in that union of thought and expression which is consequent on the causality of the poet; the technical mode finds form in the verbal structure which secures effects in audiences. The virtues of the scientific mode are to be found in the analytic technique it supplies; the virtues of the poetic mode are in its manuductive guidance for judgment among monuments of art; the virtues of the technical mode are in the devices for censure and evaluation which may be derived from technical or strategic rules of the artist's craft.

The perversions of the three modes are likewise characteristic: the scientific mode may be reduced to a routine and dialectical application of "classical" rules for the unity of action, time, and place, the genealogical nobility of characters, and the rigid elevation of thought; the poetic mode may be translated from a method of judgment to a random dialectical biography of the adventures of a soul and the dialectical justification by selective example of any preference; the technical mode may degenerate from the canonic reaction of a selected audience as a standard—the Roman audience of Horace, the prince's court during the Renaissance, the urban population of Reynolds, the plain men of Tolstoy, the proletariat of the Marxists, or even a vaguely envisaged posterity which will rectify the errors of contemporary evaluation—to a dialectical relativity in which standards may be treated either in a history of the themes, forms, and media that were successively esteemed or in a canon of methods to achieve any results thought to be effective on the audiences of the moment.

The excesses or perversions of these three literal modes are avoided or rectified by other devices of literal criticism and by other subject matters to which those devices are applied. The "scientific" analysis usually occurs in the context of other methods appropriate to other aspects of art phenomena, and therefore the consideration of the form, structure, and material of works of art may be balanced by the consideration, in other sciences, of its psychological origins, social effects, and historical developments, which return the art object to its context in nature and society. "Scholarly" criticism, in like fashion, re-turns the genius and his expression from a universal and sublime isolation to the conditions of his life, times, and interests, which determined the idiom and manner of his expression as well as the temporal and local peculiarities of his objects. "Formal" criticism marshals the verbal or other technical devices by which a medium may be made to achieve any of the effects of which it is capable and from which the artist may choose, or the amateur recognize, devices and means. All three modes of criticism treat of content and form to account for the peculiarities of literary and artistic objects: in literature the scientific mode treats words as matter and other scientific methods are designed to seek the other manners in which the forms—the actions and incidents, the necessities and probabilities—appropriately expressed in literature may exist; the scholarly mode seeks in the circumstances of the artist the matter to which he gave form; the formal mode analyzes the verbal forms in which the vast variety of matters may be presented effectively. The virtues of the scientific mode are in the distinctions it makes possible between natural and artistic forms by means of their respective matters, and in the analysis that is therefore possible of particular artistic forms; the virtues of the scholarly mode are in the concrete significance it may give to the forms of an artist by considering the matters assembled in his experience and life and in the poetic appreciation and critical understanding that are thereby rendered possible of particular works; the virtues of the formal mode are in the differentiation of means of presenting the varieties of matter appropriate to communication, and in the practical evaluation and comparison of particular devices that is therefore possible. The scientific mode is perverted when artistic form or cause is confused dialectically with natural thing or cause, and art is treated as the exclusive or peculiar subject of some other science than the poetic; the scholarly mode is perverted when the investigation of the circumstances of the artist is pushed into details irrelevant to the traits of the art objects he produced, and still further perverted when those irrelevant traits are dialectically converted into the only explanation of his art; the formal mode is perverted when the machinery and terminology of distinction are carried to such refinements in the dialectical ordering and discrimination of tropes and figures that differences of effects and of matter are obscured or lost.

Needless to say, a given critic may successively employ more than one of these modes of criticism and may even combine two or more of them, crudely or effectively, in a single theory or application of criticism. Purity in adherence to a single mode is not necessarily a virtue in criticism since the differentiation of modes is in terms of the purposes envisaged in the criticism, and the identification of the mode employed by a critic is only a step toward the evaluation of his achievement in so far as such identification may indicate the appropriate criterion and thereby contribute to both the understanding and the judgment of his statements.

The pertinence of an examination of philosophic and critical principles in relation to art and criticism may, therefore, be illustrated by applying the distinctions treated in this essay to the essay itself. It is an essay in the dialectical mode of criticism, using as its reductive device concepts derived from semantics. It does not, however, use those semantic concepts in the form of dialectic in which the controlling principles are processes or symbols (as I. A. Richards, for example, reduces all meanings to symbolic or emotive uses of language) but rather takes advantage of the possibility of achieving full dialectical scope in any form of the dialectical mode of criticism to return to a dialectic of things on the model of Plato's usage. The manner of adherence to that mode may be seen in the subjects of the three parts into which the essay is divided: they are concerned in turn with the objects of criticism, criticism itself, and the terms of criticism, which are an adaptation of what Plato said about the criticism of art to the criticism of criticism, whereas the semantic mode of dialectic would translate these three (as was pointed out above when the three forms of dialectical criticism were considered) into some such considerations as the intention of the critic, the form of his criticism, and its pertinence to or effects on the audience. The effect envisaged in the three-fold division of subjects employed in the essay is to prevent the reduction of the treatment of criticism to some partially literal dialectic frozen to some one conception of the nature of art, or of the domain of criticism, or of the principles of philosophy. The essay is not, however, concerned directly with the criticism of art but with the criticism of criticism. It might be made the propaedeutic to an essay in the criticism of art which would then, under the guidance of the criteria and subject matters distinguished in the six modes of criticism, pursue one mode in an appropriate manner and to a relevant conclusion with some grounds for the expectation that its meaning and purpose might be more clearly perceived. But, although it adumbrates no solution of the problems of art or beauty, it may pretend to adequacy in treating what has been said about art and beauty, for being a dialectic of what medieval philosophers used to call second, as distinct from first, intentions, it accounts for the literal modes, as well as for the dialectical mode in which it is couched, without distortion or prejudice, since in the positive operation of the dialectic the virtues of each mode may be isolated and the refutative elenchus may disclose indifferently the failures and perversions of each mode.

A SELECTED LIST OF OTHER WRITINGS BY
THE CONTRIBUTORS TO THIS VOLUME

R. S. Crane: "History versus Criticism in the University Study of Literature," *English Journal*, XXIV (1935), 645–67; "Interpretation of Texts and the History of Ideas," *College English*, II (1941), 755–65; "Two Essays in Practical Criticism: Prefatory Note," *University Review* (University of Kansas City), VIII (1942), 199–202; "Semantics and the Teaching of Prose Literature," *College English*, IV (1942), 12–19; "English Neoclassical Criticism: An Outline Sketch," *The Dictionary of World Literature*, ed. Joseph T. Shipley (1943), pp. 193–203, also *Critics and Criticism*, pp. 372–88; "The Critical Monism of Cleanth Brooks," *Modern Philology*, XLV (1948), 226–45, also *Critics and Criticism*, pp. 83–107; "I. A. Richards and the Art of Interpretation," *Ethics*, LIX (1949), 112–26, also *Critics and Criticism*, pp. 27–44; *Critics and Criticism* (1952), Introduction; "On Writing the History of English Criticism, 1650–1800," *University of Toronto Quarterly*, XXII (1953), 376–91; "The Idea of the Humanities," *Carleton College Bulletin*, XLIX (1953), 3–18; "The Varieties of Dramatic Criticism," *Carleton Drama Bulletin*, V (1953), 47–66, also *Carleton Drama Review*, I (1955–56), 22–38; *The Languages of Criticism and the Structure of Poetry* (1953); "Literature, Philosophy, and the History of Ideas," *Modern Philology*, LII (1954), 73–83; "Observations on a Story by Hemingway," *Introduction to Literature*, ed. Louis Locke, William M. Gibson, and George Arms (3d ed., 1957).

W. R. Keast: "The 'New Criticism' and *King Lear*," *Modern Philology*, XLVII (1949), 45–64, also *Critics and Criticism*, pp. 108–37; "Johnson's Criticism of the Metaphysical Poets," *ELH*, XVII (1950), 59–70; "Wallace Stevens' 'Thirteen Ways of Looking at a Blackbird,' " *Chicago Review*, VIII (1954), 46–63; "The Element of Art in Gibbon's *History*," *ELH*, XXIII (1956), 153–62; *Samuel Johnson: Critical Essays, Prefaces, and Notes* (to appear in 1957).

Richard McKeon: "Rhetoric in the Middle Ages," *Speculum*, XVII (1942), 1–32, also *Critics and Criticism*, pp. 260–96; "Aristotle's Conception of Language and the Arts of Language," *Classical Philology*, XLI (1946), 193–206, XLII (1947), 21–50, also *Critics and Criticism*, pp. 176–231; "Poetry and Philosophy in the Twelfth Century: The Renaissance of Rhetoric," *Modern Philology*, XLIII (1946), 217–34, also *Critics and Criticism*, pp. 297–318; "The Nature and Teaching of the Humanities," *Journal of General Education*, III (1949), 290–303; "Philosophy and Method," *Journal of Philosophy*, XLVIII (1951), 653–82; *Freedom and History: The Semantics of Philosophical Controversies and Ideological Conflicts* (1952); "Semantics, Science, and Poetry," *Modern Philology*, XLIX (1952), 145–59; "Symbols, Myths, and Arguments," *Symbols and Values: An Initial Study*, ed. Lyman Bryson and others (1954), pp. 13–38; *Thought, Action, and Passion* (1954).

Norman Maclean: "An Analysis of a Lyric Poem" (Wordsworth's "It is a beauteous evening"), *University Review* (University of Kansas City), VIII (1942), 202–9; "From Dictionary to Poem—'A Likeness' by Robert Browning," *Promoting Growth toward Maturity in Interpreting What Is Read*, ed. W. S. Gray (1951), pp. 12–18;

"From Action to Image: Theories of the Lyric in the Eighteenth Century," *Critics and Criticism* (1952), pp. 408–60; "Personification but Not Poetry," *ELH*, XXIII (1956), 163–70.

ELDER OLSON: "Rhetoric and the Appreciation of Pope," *Modern Philology*, XXXVII (1939), 13–35; " 'Sailing to Byzantium': Prolegomena to a Poetics of the Lyric," *University Review* (University of Kansas City), VIII (1942), 209–19; "The Argument of Longinus' *On the Sublime*," *Modern Philology*, XXXIX (1942), 225–58, also *Critics and Criticism*, pp. 232–59; "Recent Literary Criticism," *Modern Philology*, XL (1943), 275–83; [Longinus and Reynolds], *Longinus, "On the Sublime," and Sir Joshua Reynolds, "Discourses on Art"* ("University Classics," 1945), pp. vii–xxi; "A Symbolic Reading of the *Ancient Mariner*," *Modern Philology*, XLV (1948), 275–79, also *Critics and Criticism*, pp. 138–44; "A Dialogue on Symbolism," *Critics and Criticism* (1952), pp. 567–94; "The Poetic Method of Aristotle: Its Powers and Limitations," *English Institute Essays, 1951* (1952), pp. 70–94; "Criticism," *Encyclopaedia Britannica* (1952 copyright); "Verse," *Encyclopaedia Britannica* (copyright 1952); "Education and the Humanities," *Pedagogía*, I (1953), 85–95; "Díalogo sobre la fonçion del arte en la sociedad," *La Torre*, I (1953), 51–70; "The Poetry of Dylan Thomas," *Poetry*, LXXXIII (1954), 213–20; *The Poetry of Dylan Thomas* (1954); "Louise Bogan and Léonie Adams," *Chicago Review*, VIII (1954), 70–87; "The Poetry of Wallace Stevens," *English Journal*, XLIV (1955), 191–98.

BERNARD WEINBERG: "The Poetic Theories of Minturno," *Studies in Honor of Frederick W. Shipley* (1942), pp. 101–29; "Scaliger versus Aristotle on Poetics," *Modern Philology*, XXXIX (1942), 337–60; "An Interpretation of Valéry's *Le Cimetière Marin*," *Romanic Review*, XXXVIII (1947), 133–58; *Critical Prefaces of the French Renaissance* (1950), Introduction; "Robortello on the *Poetics*," *Critics and Criticism* (1952), pp. 319–48; "From Aristotle to Pseudo-Aristotle," *Comparative Literature*, V (1953), 97–104; "The Problem of Literary Aesthetics in Italy and France in the Renaissance," *Modern Language Quarterly*, XIV (1953), 448–56; *French Poetry of the Renaissance* (1954), Introduction; "La 'Méthode scientifique' et les insuffisances de la critique littéraire au dix-neuvième siècle," *Rivista di letterature moderne*, V (1954), 245–49; "*Le Bateau ivre*, or the Limits of Symbolism," to appear in *PMLA*, Vol. LXXII (1957); *A History of Literary Criticism in the Italian Renaissance* (forthcoming).

PHOENIX BOOKS
Literature and Language

PHOENIX BOOKS
in Art, Music, Poetry, and Drama

PHOENIX POETS